Renaissance Poetry

RENAISSANCE POETRY

Edited and Introduced by

CRISTINA MALCOLMSON

LONGMAN
London and New York

Addison Wesley Longman Limited
Edinburgh Gate
Harlow
Essex CM20 2JE
United Kingdom
and Associated Companies throughout the world

*Published in the United States of America
by Addison Wesley Longman Inc., New York*

© Addison Wesley Longman Limited 1998

First published 1998

ISBN   0–582–05093–6 (csd)
ISBN   0–582–05092–8 (ppr)

British Library Cataloguing-in-Publication Data

A catalogue record for this book is available from the British Library

Library of Congress Cataloging-in-Publication Data

Renaissance poetry / edited and introduced by Cristina Malcolmson.
       p.   cm. — (Longman critical readers)
    Includes bibliographical references and index.
    ISBN 0–582–05093–6 (csd). — ISBN 0–582–05092–8
    1. English poetry—Early modern, 1500–1700—History and criticism.
  2. Renaissance—England.   I. Malcolmson, Cristina.   II. Series.
  PR533.R46   1998
  821'.309—dc21   98–17501
                                                                        CIP

Set by 35 in 9/11.5pt Palatino
Produced by Addison Wesley Longman Singapore (Pte) Ltd,
Printed in Singapore

Contents

General Editors' Preface

The outlines of contemporary critical theory are now often taught as a standard feature of a degree in literary studies. The development of particular theories has seen a thorough transformation of literary criticism. For example, Marxist and Foucauldian theories have revolutionized Shakespeare studies, and 'deconstruction' has led to a complete reassessment of Romantic poetry. Feminist criticism has left scarcely any period of literature unaffected by its searching critiques. Teachers of literary studies can no longer fall back on a standardized, received, methodology.

Lecturers and teachers are now urgently looking for guidance in a rapidly changing critical environment. They need help in understanding the latest revisions in literary theory, and especially in grasping the practical effects of the new theories in the form of theoretically sensitized new readings. A number of volumes in the series anthologize important essays on particular theories. However, in order to grasp the full implications and possible uses of particular theories it is essential to see them put to work. This series provides substantial volumes of new readings, presented in an accessible form and with a significant amount of editorial guidance.

Each volume includes a substantial introduction which explores the theoretical issues and conflicts embodied in the essays selected and locates the areas of disagreement between positions. The pluralism of theories has to be put on the agenda of literary studies. We can no longer pretend that we all tacitly accept the same practices in literary studies. Neither is a *laissez-faire* attitude any longer tenable. Literature departments need to go beyond the mere toleration of theoretical differences: it is not enough merely to agree to differ; they need actually to 'stage' the differences openly. The volumes in this series all attempt to dramatize the differences, not necessarily with a view to resolving them but in order to foreground the choices presented by different theories or to argue for a particular route through the impasses the differences present.

The theory 'revolution' has had real effect. It has loosened the grip of traditional empiricist and romantic assumptions about language and literature. It is not always clear what is being proposed as the new agenda for literary studies, and indeed the very notion of 'literature' is questioned by the post-structuralist strain in theory. However, the uncertainties and obscurities of contemporary theories appear much less worrying when we see what the best critics have been able to do with them in practice. This series aims to disseminate the best of recent criticism and to show that it is possible to re-read the canonical texts of literature in new and challenging ways.

RAMAN SELDEN AND STAN SMITH

The Publishers and fellow Series Editor regret to record that Raman Selden died after a short illness in May 1991 at the age of fifty-three. Ray Selden was a fine scholar and a lovely man. All those he has worked with will remember him with much affection and respect.

Acknowledgements

We are grateful to the following for permission to reproduce copyright material:

Cambridge University Press and the author for 'Marvell's "Horation Ode" and the politics of genre' by David Norbrook in *LITERATURE AND THE ENGLISH CIVIL WAR* ed. Thomas Healy & Jonathan Sawday (CUP, 1990); University of Chicago Press and the authors for extracts from 'To Fashion a Gentleman: Spenser and the Bower of Bliss' by Stephen J. Greenblatt in *RENAISSANCE SELF-FASHIONING* (1980) pp. 157–92, 'Puritanism and Maenadism in *A Mask*' by Richard Halpern from *REWRITING THE RENAISSANCE*, 1986 pp. 88–105, 334–8, p. 320 and 'Diana Described: Scattered Women and Scattered Rhyme' by Nancy Vickers in *WRITING AND SEXUAL DIFFERENCE* (1982) pp. 96–109; William Andrews Clark Memorial Library, University of California and the author for 'Mode in Narrative Poetry' by Professor Paul Alpers in *TO TELL A STORY: NARRATIVE THEORY AND PRACTICE* (Los Angeles, 1973). © 1973 by the Regents of the University of California; Cornell University Press for 'A Room Not Their Own: Renaissance Women as Readers and Writers' by Margaret Ferguson In *THE COMPARATIVE PERSPECTIVE ON LITERATURE: APPROACHES TO THEORY AND PRACTICE*, ed. Clayton Koelb and Susan Noakes. Copyright © 1988 by Cornell University; the Editor, George Herbert Journal for 'George Herbert & Coterie Verse' by Cristina Malcolmson in *GEORGE HERBERT JOURNAL* vol XVIII (Fall 1994/Spring 1995); the author, Patricia Parker for her 'Suspended Instruments: Lyric and Power in the Bower of Bliss' from *LITERARY FAT LADIES: RHETORIC, GENDER, PROPERTY* – pubd. Methuen – London & New York © 1987 Patricia Parker; Rutgers University Press for 'Astrophil and Stella: All Selfnesse He Forbeares' by Richard McCoy in SIR PHILIP SIDNEY: REBELLION IN ARCADIA. Copyright © 1979 by Rutgers, The State University of New Jersey; Wayne State University Press for 'Mediation and Contestation: English Classicism from Sidney to Jonson' by Don E. Wayne in *CRITICISM* 25:3 (1983) pp. 211–37.

Introduction

The phrase 'English Renaissance' has traditionally referred to the period between 1509 and 1660, from the accession of Henry VIII to the Restoration of Charles II after the English Civil War. This period in England has been defined as similar to the earlier renaissance in Italy because of an analogous 'rebirth' of interest in classical languages and literature, and because the new humanism led to an increasing confidence in the power of the English vernacular to produce significant literary creation. According to this traditional view, the result was the remarkable poetry by Wyatt, Sidney, Shakespeare, Donne and Milton.

The essays in this collection are intended to clarify why this conventional image of the 'Renaissance' in England has lost its explanatory value for many scholars. The term itself, heralded by Burckhardt in *The Civilization of the Renaissance in Italy* in 1860, evokes a sense of rebirth and a brand of creativity that obscures from view groups of people and material conditions crucial to an accurate understanding of the purposes of poetry during this time. Alternative approaches to the literary history of the period consider not only the writers listed above, but also the role of poetry in nationalism, the changing associations of poetry and class status, and the emergence of women writers. The essays in this collection represent many of the methodologies which have contributed to this transformation of knowledge: new historicism, cultural materialism, feminism, and an historically informed psychoanalytic criticism. In most of these approaches, the subject matter is not just poetry, but early modern society, and literary analysis is meant to result in the interpretation of culture.[1] Critics associated with these modes of analysis use widely divergent methods, and they do not agree among themselves about how poetry is linked with social formations. Nevertheless, their work has made possible a more thorough consideration of the intersection of literature with the ideologies sustaining and challenging the early modern social order.[2]

1

Lyric and history

One important change instituted by recent historicist approaches is the development of alternative ways of reading the lyric poem. In the first half of the twentieth century, New Criticism was responsible for reviving interest in the seventeenth-century lyric, but it also included a formalist emphasis on close reading which detached literary language from its social context. New historicism, cultural materialism, and feminism have made possible a renewed attention to lyric and history as well as an analysis of the role played by the lyric in the production of early modern and modern versions of selfhood, or what is termed 'subjectivity'. New Criticism is in fact one episode in the history of modern subjectivity and its belief in autonomy, since New Criticism separated poetic creativity and literary language from their social origins.

T.S. Eliot initiated the school of New Criticism through a series of essays which criticized biographical interpretation, which, Eliot claimed, distracted attention from the evaluation of the quality of the verse. Eliot argued for an analysis that stressed the structure and technical details of poetry rather than the personality of the writer. The result was a mode of analysis which focused almost exclusively on the poem as a special kind of language, exempt from the influences of social discourse.[3] Although Eliot and the New Critics that followed him at times discussed the historical context, they approached literary language as timeless and universal, significant and powerful because of its technical effects: 'There is surely a sense in which anyone must agree that a poem has a life of its own, and a sense in which it provides in itself the only criterion by which what it says can be judged.'[4]

This approach was applied with remarkable success to the 'metaphysical' poets, especially John Donne. T.S. Eliot, F.R. Leavis, Cleanth Brooks, Murray Krieger, and others developed readings which stressed paradox, ambiguity, complexity, and unity.[5] New Critics looked for contradictory attitudes in a poem but also sought out an underlying coordinating structure. In 'The Language of Paradox', Brooks examined the surprising coordination of sexual and religious imagery throughout Donne's 'Canonization', from which Brooks took the first part of the title of his book, *The Well Wrought Urn: Studies in the Structure of Poetry*. This title itself emphasizes the ability of language to shape a self-contained aesthetic world. In another essay, Brooks considered Marvell's 'Horatian Ode' in terms of its radically differing attitudes toward Cromwell, but Brooks also claimed that these attitudes could be resolved into an organic whole:

> I have quoted earlier Margoliouth's characterization of the *Ode* as
> a poem 'where royalist principles and admiration for Cromwell the

Great Man exist side by side'. I think that they do exist side by side, but if so, how are they related? Do they exist in separate layers, or are they somehow unified? Unified, in some sense, they must be if the *Ode* is a poem and not a heap of fragments.[6]

This New Critical interest in the organic unity of a text reinforced the belief that literary language could free itself from the constraints of the political or social context, even on such a controversial subject as Oliver Cromwell. It is interesting that Douglas Bush, a traditional literary historicist, long ago called Brooks' conclusions into question by claiming that his account of Marvell's 'Horatian Ode' did not uncover a special form of literary irony, but was simply an anti-Cromwellian reading in disguise.[7]

Recent, historically informed interpretations of lyric refute the belief in the autonomy of literature in a number of ways. A somewhat traditional approach is used at times to illuminate the verse through reference to a particular historical context. Like Bush, David Norbrook counters New Critical notions of ambiguity by arguing for an explicitly republican, anti-monarchical perspective in 'Marvell's "Horatian Ode" and the Politics of Genre', printed here. Arthur Marotti demonstrates that John Donne's lyrics were produced within the context of socio-literary coteries, which largely determined the subject-matter and style of the poetry so individually analysed by New Critics.[8] In my essay included here, 'George Herbert and Coterie Verse', I place Herbert within this network of coteries, and demonstrate that his use of secular love poetry for religious purposes was a fully established convention within this milieu. Despite the traditional nature of these arguments, they counter the New Critical view that poetry originates in an individual creative genius, rather than in particular social and political circumstances.

Other recent interpretations emphasize the role of the lyric in the production of a subjectivity determined by cultural conditions. Stephen Greenblatt finds that Thomas Wyatt's religious submission to God in penitential psalms is modelled on his political submission to Henry VIII.[9] In '*Astrophil and Stella*: "All Selfnesse He Forbeares" ', printed here, Richard McCoy argues that Sidney's sonnet sequence depicts Astrophil as divided between a status-oriented sense of deference and a more politically modern form of autonomy. Patricia Fumerton develops quite a different claim, that Sidney's sonnets construct a distinction between public role and private experience which is socially rather than politically modern. A difference in approach operates in Herbert studies as well, since some critics, like Leah Marcus and Michael Schoenfeldt, primarily discover evidence of submission to authority in Herbert's lyrics, whereas Deborah Shuger and I argue that *The Temple* moves toward a modern sense of autonomy.[10]

None of these interpretations emphasize the special nature of literary language, as New Criticism would, nor the discovery of the individualistic self, as traditional historicism might. In much recent work, lyric is approached as an arena in which the 'voice' of the writer has to be assessed in terms of its relation to a dominant system of hierarchical authority or an emergent belief in autonomy.[11]

Recent historicist approaches and traditional scholarship

All historicist approaches, old and new, are largely engaged with the remarkable changes occurring during this period, changes which were religious, political, social and economic. To summarize briefly, these changes included the Protestant Reformation; the consolidation of monarchical power and the eventual development of representative government; the growth of London as an urban centre, rising social mobility and the crisis of confidence over status distinctions; and the transition from a feudal to a capitalist economic system. But new historicism and cultural materialism differ from traditional scholarship because change is defined as cultural, and literary works are approached as participating in larger cultural practices. Although new historicism and cultural materialism have important differences, defined in the next section, I will focus here on what they share.

For both groups and in most cases, new modes of analysis replace a more static coordination of text and context. In 'old' historicism, the text either passively reflects what is imagined as 'real', political events or historical persons, for example, or it is seen as an autonomous foreground in relation to a static background: the intellectual history of ideas, the literary history of genres, or a collective, stable world view. Spokespeople for recent methodologies abjure 'positivist' versions of history. For them, history is not a matter of knowable external reality, but rather a series of documents from which versions of history are constructed. Both literature and history are approached as equally open to interpretation. In addition, the historical context is not construed as a static series of events or set of beliefs. Rather, history is the story of the dynamic operation of power or ideology in the act of establishing itself, or a clash of differing ideologies, in contradiction with each other.[12]

Some who are particularly critical of new historicism have concluded that its differences with previous methods are not so stark or, even, do not exist at all. Howard Horowitz and Stanley Fish have claimed that no matter how 'textual' new historicists imagine history to be, they will still be making a truth-claim about historical events, and using the same methods of proof as earlier literary historicists in order to persuade their audience. This is probably true, but it also illuminates what is different about new and old uses of history – new historicists make truth-claims which are quite unlike those of more traditional literary scholars.[13] At issue is not who Spenser's Red Cross Knight represents in Queen Elizabeth's court, or whether or not Wyatt's verse expresses Burckhardtian 'individualism'. In both of these cases, history is imagined as a stable background which provides the 'key' to the literary work. New historicists argue instead that the cultural practices operating in the social realm appear in a significant way in the literary realm. Literature is not a mere reflection of society; literature has a relative autonomy which makes it open to but not determined by social influence. Nevertheless, what it is open to is not primarily a name, a fact, or even an ethos, but rather a cultural practice in need of establishing itself, in the act of overcoming that which challenges it, or perhaps yielding in some way to resistance. According to Stephen Greenblatt, when Spenser fashions a gentleman in *The Faerie Queene*, the historical significance is not a reference to a particular courtly figure, like Sir Walter Raleigh, but rather the ritual of fashioning, the social discipline and psychic reorientation, which makes people like Spenser and Raleigh become gentlemen in the eyes of their society. Such 'civility' requires the defeat of opposing forces: sensuality, idleness, Irish and Native American populations. This process occurs in the pages of *The Faerie Queene* as well as in the Elizabethan court and in the political agenda of the British nation. When Patricia Fumerton analyses the ritual of the exchange of miniatures in the court in association with the sonnet sequence, her point is not that this material reflects a new concern for inwardness, emerging in the late sixteenth century, but that the exchange of miniatures and the sonnet sequence were social practices which participated in the construction of a new division between public and private experience. Literature itself, then, intervenes in the social realm. Unlike traditional scholars, new historicists use history to make visible the 'cultural work' performed by literature.[14]

Shared by most new historicists and cultural materialists is a definition of culture as a set of material practices which largely sustain existing power relations. Culture is therefore not made up of abstract values, intellectual ideas, or creative achievements, but rituals, experiences and habits which structure daily life according to prevailing social norms. Such a definition of culture stems from four particularly significant thinkers: Clifford Geertz, Louis Althusser, Raymond Williams and Michel Foucault. The work of these theorists has influenced in some way nearly all the essays printed in this collection. The discussion that follows is intended to illuminate how these theories of culture have led to new accounts of the role of literature in early modern society.

The anthropologist Clifford Geertz has been useful to new historicists because of his definition of culture as a system of symbolic actions:

> Believing, with Max Weber, that man is an animal suspended in webs
> of significance he himself has spun, I take culture to be those webs,
> and the analysis of it to be therefore not an experimental science in
> search of law but an interpretive one in search of meaning.[15]

A web of significance of this sort is analogous to an aesthetic creation
– 'symbolic action . . . which, like phonation in speech, pigment in
painting, line in writing, or sonance in music, signifies' (p. 10). There
is an 'informal logic of actual life' which can be interpreted in order
to understand, in part, how groups of people 'impose meaning on
experience' (p. 17). This logic is 'social and public . . . its natural habitat
is the house yard, the marketplace, and the town square' (p. 45). Geertz
interprets Western winks, Javanese funerals, Navaho curing rites, Queen
Elizabeth's coronation, and Balinese cockfights to discover how these
actions signify and create meaning for their participants. In his famous
example of the cockfight, Geertz analyses the battle and the betting that
accompanies it as having little to do with economic motivation, but,
rather, as a symbolic expression of the status system that organizes the
community:

> And as prestige, the necessity to defend it, celebrate it, justify it,
> and just plain bask in it . . . is perhaps the driving force in the
> society, so also . . . is it of the cockfight . . . Balinese go to cockfights
> to find out what a man, usually composed, aloof, almost obsessively
> self-absorbed, a kind of moral autocosm, feels like when, attacked,
> tormented, challenged, insulted, and driven in result to the extremes
> of fury, he has totally triumphed or been brought totally low.
>
> (pp. 436, 450)

As a 'collectively sustained symbolic structure', the cockfight reflects and
reproduces the primacy of status within Balinese sensibility (p. 448).

As Marxists, Louis Althusser and Raymond Williams are far more
concerned than Geertz with economic and social inequities, but they
also focus on practices in their accounts of society. Both Althusser and
Williams are linked with 'cultural materialism' because their work
moves away from a deterministic Marxist model, in which the economic
base dictates the ideological superstructure, to a theory which grants
relative autonomy to cultural production. Althusser argues that ideology
is not a monolithic 'false consciousness' foisted on the oppressed by the
self-interested ruling classes, but the result of the practices of several
institutions – church, education, family, law, the arts, sports – which,
separately, and at times in contradiction with each other, create the
attitudes necessary for the reproduction of the economic system.
These attitudes, like the reverence for prestige in Balinese sensibility,
are constructed through material practices, like cockfights: 'a small

mass in a small church, a funeral, a minor match at a sport's club, a school day, a political party meeting, etc.' For Althusser, however, the cockfight would not primarily be a dramatic theatre of prestige, but a means by which the ruling class reinforced its dominance over the ruled. Ideological practices reproduce 'sensibility', but they also construct an imaginary version of the individual's actual relationship to the economic system. Althusser calls this economically oriented social construction of the self 'interpellation'.[16] He might study not so much the owners of the cocks and their largely 'symbolic' bets, but the relationship between these central figures and those outside this élite circle – the small-time bettors, or what Geertz calls 'the extremely poor, the socially despised, the personally idiosyncratic' engaged in 'mindless, sheer-chance-type gambling games' at the margins of the cockfight (p. 435). Such an analysis might show that the ritual of betting is more economic than Geertz admits, since it represents 'imaginatively' the economic relations between the people with prestige and those without.

The literary critic Raymond Williams adds to Althusser's emphasis on ideological practices a theory of social change. He defines the system of beliefs associated with the ruling class as extending into all parts of lived experience, but it is also a process, actively regenerating itself against forms of resistance, which nevertheless have transformational potential:

> [Hegemony] is a whole body of practices and expectations, over
> the whole of living: our senses and assignments of energy, our
> shaping perceptions of ourselves and our world. It is a lived system
> of meanings and values – constitutive, and constituting – which as
> they are experienced as practices appear as reciprocally confirming.
> It thus constitutes a sense of reality for most people in the society
> . . . [Yet] the reality of any hegemony, in the extended and cultural
> sense, is that, while by definition it is always dominant, it is neither
> total or exclusive . . . It would be wrong to overlook the importance
> of works and ideas which, while clearly affected by hegemonic limits
> and pressures, are at least in part significant breaks beyond them.[17]

Williams identifies these breaks as works and ideas, but also 'new meanings and values, new practices, new relationships', and categorizes them as 'the emergent', which struggles against 'the dominant'. A third category, 'the residual', refers to aspects of the past which may support the dominant or have an oppositional relation to it. These differing kinds of cultural practices and attitudes make possible a more historically specific analysis. If Williams considered the Balinese cockfight, he might point out, as Vincent Pecora does, that this violent theatre of prestige is less significant as an example of the dominant élite than the brutal massacre of Communists by Balinese and Indonesians supported by US interests in 1965.[18] Williams' method makes possible the historical specificity that Geertz leaves out and the attention to social change that Althusser does not consider.

Michel Foucault also focuses on cultural practices, but his approach can be read as an alternative to Marxist theories. He structures history in terms of 'epistemes', or eras in which discourse and power take very particular forms. He uses the idea of an episteme in large part to avoid the promise of historical progress implicit in the Marxist scenario, which traces out the transition from feudalism to capitalism, and, in the future, to a classless society. Therefore, Foucault would reject the claim that the Communist groups in Indonesia were necessarily 'emergent', kept in check by a 'dominant' class. He is less concerned with an economically determined origin of power, and more interested in versions of micro-power, domination exerted in local, particular ways. Power is not initiated by a person or a ruling class; both rich and poor are constructed through institutional practices which determine their sense of themselves and enforce their willingness to submit to the particular version of power operating at the time. Instead of the Marxist view that ideology obscures from individuals their actual relations to the means of production, Foucault sees power as producing the rules by which truth is determined; that is, there is no social situation in which 'true' consciousness could replace the false. Because of his materialist principles, he begins with the institutional treatment of the body, from which, he claims, consciousness develops. Foucault discusses the Renaissance period in terms of the law of the sovereign, and the ability of monarchs to discipline and punish subjects. In the subsequent modern period, a new practice of individuation develops, but this practice is neither a mode of freedom nor the ideology of liberal economics. Individuation is itself a practice of power which turns people into 'subjects', obedient to authority even without a political emphasis on the power of the monarch. This new kind of 'subjectivity' is not a step toward a future socialist emancipation, but simply the next manifestation of the changing but relentless operation of power.[19]

The result of the use of these theories by new historicists and cultural materialists has been versions of early modern literary history which are significantly different from previous approaches. First, the humanist and Protestant movements, associated with the schools and the source of most canonical early sixteenth-century writers, have traditionally been characterized as morally free and high-minded until tainted through complicity with a corrupt court.[20] In new historicism, however, humanism and Protestantism are often approached as cultural practices which reinforce the dominant order, or which are implicated in monarchical power and imperialism from the outset. Such an account can explain why the Catholic-humanist Thomas More and the Protestant-humanists

Thomas Wyatt, Philip Sidney and Edmund Spenser considered court office less an unfortunate necessity than a position from which to express their absolutist and nationalist views.

Second, the court is analysed as a ritualized cultural site, whose practices not only established its own power, but also constructed its participants according to the rules which substantiated that power. This included the development of gentility and civility as modes of behaviour which ensured both deference to the monarch and the élite's control over other status groups and the means of production.[21]

Third, in his 'old' historicist study, *The Elizabethan World Picture: A Study of the Idea of Order in the Age of Shakespeare, Donne, and Milton*, E.M.W. Tillyard argued that British society during this period had a deep investment in a stable hierarchical system. However, new historicists like Montrose and Frank Whigham approach status as a set of material practices, in which the 'dominant' élite operates to substantiate its privilege and exclude others through modes of behaviour, clothing, language and forms of literature. Conceiving of hierarchy as a system in constant need of reassertion allows Montrose and Whigham to claim that some outsiders could enter the élite through successful imitation of upper-class ritual. Approaching hierarchy as constituting 'a sense of reality for most people in the society' but not as 'total', Don Wayne argues that in Ben Jonson's poetry the hegemony of the system was broken by 'emergent' practices and attitudes associated with a future middle-class ideology.[22]

Fourth, the definition of the prevailing cultural ethos as opposed to what is emerging has significantly changed. Previously a stable hierarchy was seen as the dominant belief-system, associated with monarchy and deference to political and religious authority. In opposition to this structure, a move toward representative government started to develop, associated with a secularly ambitious or religiously inward form of individualism. Cultural approaches to history, however, define this kind of individualism as itself the product of social institutions. Being an autonomous being separate from family, church, the schools and the state was therefore not a discovery of a pre-existing self, as Burckhardt argued in *The Civilization of the Renaissance in Italy*, but the effect of ideology, or, as Foucault might say, of power. The clash between corporate identity, produced, for example, by the status system, and a sense of autonomy, produced, perhaps, by the Protestant belief in the priesthood of all believers, cannot therefore be defined as socialization versus self-knowledge, but as the struggle between dominant and emergent practices and beliefs. To signal this new account of historical change, cultural critics use the term subjectivity rather than individualism.

New historicism and cultural materialism

I believe that new historicism and cultural materialism share a great deal, and that many critics would associate themselves with both groups. There is some evidence that these groups are uniting under the rubric 'materialist'.[23] However, in this section, I will outline the differences of opinion that have developed between people whose literary methodologies are finally quite similar.[24]

The major difference between cultural materialists and new historicists lies in a preference for the work of Marxist theorists like Althusser and Williams rather than that of Foucault. As stated above, Foucault emphasizes the impersonal, but coordinated operation of power in local, particular cases, whereas Marxist theorists are interested in how the economic system is related to ideology and forms of power. All three men eschew original Marxist definitions of ideology as a 'false consciousness' deluding the subordinate classes, but Althusser and Williams contend that cultural values, literary works, and an individual's sense of self are nevertheless implicated in the economic system. Therefore cultural materialists often adopt a Marxist account of history, organized in terms of transitions between economic systems, whereas Foucault structures history according to changes in the nature of power.

Cultural materialists criticize Foucault because his concept of historical epistemes includes no explanation for social change and no theory of resistance or individual agency. Jonathan Dollimore compares the two approaches:

> According to Marx, men and women make their own history but not in conditions of their own choosing. Perhaps the most significant divergence within cultural analysis is that between those who concentrate on culture as this making of history, and those who concentrate on the unchosen conditions which constrain and inform that process of making. The former allows much to human agency, and tends to privilege human experience; the latter concentrates on the formative power of social and ideological structures which are prior to experience and in some sense determining of it.[25]

Whereas new historicists 'concentrate on the formative power of social and ideological structures', cultural materialists look for situations in society and literature which are subversive to the ruling ethos, and which introduce 'significant breaks' beyond it. Raymond Williams' theory of social change, with its categories of residual, dominant and emergent, underlies much cultural materialist analysis. Allied with the attention to social change, especially for British cultural materialists, is a call for action in the present day, both in political and educational matters. On the other hand, new historicists influenced by Foucault frequently stress the ways in which these subversive expressions, although voiced, are nevertheless 'contained' and made harmless within the prevailing orthodoxy.

For example, cultural critics present startlingly different interpretations of the evocation of carnival in early modern literature. In the Medieval and Renaissance periods, carnival holidays included explicit inversions of hierarchical structures, when boys dressed as bishops, commoners as kings, and women as men. Some historians have argued that these rituals made it possible to imagine new modes of social organization, whereas others have claimed that this release from everyday life actually reinforced the structures of hierarchy by 'letting off stream', by allowing a temporary and relatively peaceful period of dissent.[26] Cultural critics are similarly divided about the effect of alluding to carnival in literature. Women dress as men in Shakespearean comedies, and the misrule of the tavern world disrupts the order of the court in Shakespearean histories: do these inversions solidify into a significant form of resistance or are they 'contained' by the reassertion of the *status quo* by the end of the play?

Cultural materialists would perhaps argue that carnival, what Williams might term a 'residual' practice, is nevertheless used to question the equity of the dominant hierarchical order, and to suggest the 'emergent' values of egalitarianism. Such a use would be initiated by the writer, who, as an historical agent, is contributing to the process of social change through his cultural and aesthetic choices. New historicists influenced by Foucault might reject the Marxist account of history implicit in such formulations, an account determined by the transition from feudalism to capitalism, and choose instead to attend to the ways in which hierarchical power exerts itself in particular instances. These critics might argue that carnival inversions present themselves as oppositional only so that the orthodox hierarchy can spread itself more widely through righting inversions that come to seem 'unnatural'.[27]

The problem with the differences articulated by new historicists and cultural materialists is that both schools reduce the complexity of the other. First of all, it is incorrect to identify containment exclusively with Foucault, since the cultural materialist Raymond Williams made the same point:

> It can be persuasively argued that all or nearly all initiatives and contributions, even when they take on manifestly alternative or oppositional forms, are in practice tied to the hegemonic: that the dominant culture, so to speak, at once produces and limits its own forms of counter-culture. There is more evidence for this view . . . than we usually admit.[28]

11

Williams' own influential analysis of the opposition between country and city in early modern and modern pastoral literature stems from the view that the idealization of the rural in pastoral literature is produced by the dominant culture in such a way as to limit any real opposition.[29] This suggests that the question of whether or not a work can be oppositional or subversive has to be answered in each individual case, rather than determined by a particular methodology.

In addition, it is significant that Stephen Greenblatt, a Foucauldian new historicist, studied with Raymond Williams some years ago, and is in some ways still influenced by his work.[30] Greenblatt often considers the 'emergent', but not as a disruption of the dominant order. Also, it should be admitted that Foucault does advocate resistance and 'the revolutionary process', but only through opposition at particular points to local exercises of power, and in ways which will avoid the mistakes of the USSR.[31] On the subject of agency, cultural materialists often suggest, as Dollimore does, that they appreciate human experience and choice whereas Foucauldians do not, but they need to admit how constrained these choices are. Given Williams' theories, it amounts to a choice between residual, dominant and emergent, not a happy moment of free action.

The real problem with Foucault's work for early modern literature is that, although his versions of history avoid Marxist theories of progress, they are also geared exclusively toward an explanation of modernity.[32] Foucault focuses on the early modern period not in order to illuminate the cultural system or episteme in depth, but in order to explain how the practices and institutions in contemporary life developed out of the past, or how they differed under an earlier episteme. He makes no claim to be getting to the bottom of or into detail about the workings of early modern systems of power. The past is used for the purposes of the present. But when new historicists analyse the early modern period using Foucault's versions of history, they centralize what to Foucault is only preliminary: absolutist discipline, madhouses, confessions about sexuality and the body. Thus their accounts start from an anachronistic basis, and tend to ignore the multiplicity of historical detail which could illuminate in a more accurate way the operation of the cultural system.

For these reasons, the work of people who are neither new historicists nor cultural materialists is exceedingly important. Historicist analysis which is determined by neither a Marxist interest in the transition from feudalism to capitalism nor a Foucauldian focus on the genealogy of modern systems of power can make available information ignored by these remarkably productive but imperfect methodologies. For example, Lawrence Manley's *Literature and Culture in Early Modern London* provides this kind of alternate reading, as does analysis focused on explicitly political concerns, like that of David Norbrook and Ann Baynes Coiro.[33]

Feminism

Feminist modes of analysis have most significantly reconfigured the field of Renaissance studies. The work of feminist historians and literary critics have illuminated the male-centred bias in such fundamental categories as 'Renaissance', 'individualism', and 'self-fashioning'. Feminism makes visible the extent to which our versions of early modern literary history have been limited to a consideration of élite white men. Feminists themselves could be accused of focusing only on élite white women; nevertheless their method of de-centring the established canon of literary works, literary themes and historical explanations provides a model for a more thorough opening of the field to the interests and writing of previously marginalized groups.

In the crucial article, 'Did Women Have a Renaissance?' (1977), Joan Kelly challenged the principle of periodization by arguing that the social and economic position of women grew worse during this era.[34] She claimed that the medieval lady in the feudal social order had far more political, educational and sexual freedom than the early modern woman in the upper and middle classes, for whom domesticity and chastity were emerging as ideals, and education, if available at all, was received only through male cultural authority. If the new distinction between public and private experience brought to some upper- and middle-class men the potential for upward mobility and a new appreciation for 'interiority', then the legacy of 'privacy' for the women of these classes was an increasing confinement inside the home, accompanied by the ideology of sexual purity. Kelly's study demonstrated that women's history differs significantly from men's, and that the term 'Renaissance' could only apply to a very specialized group. Some feminists have countered Kelly's argument by claiming that women writers did benefit from the humanist programme in the universities, although they were not allowed to attend, and that they did experience their own renaissance.[35] Nevertheless, the new potential for upward mobility and the aesthetic flourishing going on in the schools made little difference for most people during this period.

Why should this situation influence our sense of Renaissance poetry? Because the phrase itself inevitably compels a focus on the verse of a specialized group of men, the themes and genres engaging them, and the material conditions that determined their experience.[36] Feminist critics have not only brought to light poetry by women previously excluded by the literary canon; they have also greatly expanded our knowledge of the lives and the material conditions of women, especially of the upper and middle classes. Finally, they have interpreted canonical works using approaches which acknowledge gender as a fundamental category in the workings of the early-modern cultural system.

For example, in his study of the relationship between the humanist poet Spenser and the Elizabethan monarchy, Stephen Greenblatt refutes the established view that humanists complied with the court only under duress, and reveals the extent to which *The Faerie Queene* advocates the English national agenda, especially in its imperialist aims in Ireland and the Americas. Patricia Parker, however, points out in her subsequent article that Spenser's tensions with a female queen were as important as his role as her agent. Parker does not dispute Greenblatt's claim that *The Faerie Queene* preached the virtues of colonialism; she simply demonstrates that Spenser saw Elizabeth and her femininity as an obstruction to state goals. This article as well as numerous others have brought into view how fully power in the early modern period was imagined as masculine.

In the official sermons of the state-sponsored Anglican church, gender is constructed according to a hierarchical system which defines authority as masculine and subordination as feminine: 'some are in high degree, some in low, some Kings and Princes, some inferiors and subjects, Priests and laymen, Maisters and servauntes, Fathers and children, Husbands and Wives'.[37] Feminists have noted that a cultural nexus which equates wives with servants and children, and parents with 'fathers' needs to be defined not simply as hierarchical but also as patriarchal. Power and rule are constructed as masculine, and masculinity is defined as hierarchical, in terms of superiority and control over others, including women. This system undergirt King James I's representation of himself as father and husband to his country, and ensured that Queen Elizabeth I would face difficulties in establishing her authority. The state-prescribed sermons taught the subordination of women; the question for cultural critics is, to what extent did Renaissance poetry do the same?

If this question is posed about the Petrarchan sonnet, one of the most popular genres in the sixteenth century, the answers are varied and complex. The form has often been considered by critics in coordination with a court in which Queen Elizabeth's absolutism was hidden behind 'Petrarchan politics', a veil of conventionalized amorous language and modes of behaviour which forced her courtiers to address her as the distant beloved of courtly love and obscured from view her ultimate power over them. Critics often propose that Sidney's Petrarchan sequence *Astrophil and Stella* is a literary means of exploring or expressing the ambition and frustration he felt in his dealings with Elizabeth. Such formulations imply that Petrarchan poetry, despite gender norms, elevates the lady into a position of supremacy above the male poet, who acknowledges his submission and dependence.[38]

The problem with these formulations is that, although they acknowledge that Queen Elizabeth's gender determined a particular 'Petrarchan' mode of address and behaviour, they also assume that behind the veil of gender relations stands the reality of power relations, and that the truth of the relationship between Elizabeth and her courtiers is the fact of despotism. The sermon quoted above, however, demonstrates that gender and power were constructed in a complex intersection with each other, and that, for this culture, there was a fundamental conflict between monarchy and femininity. The failure to acknowledge this conflict keeps hidden the strategies used by male courtiers to control Elizabeth, as well as the more subtle sexual politics of the sonnet sequence.[39]

Nancy Vickers makes this sexual politics visible in her interpretation of Petrarch's *Rime sparse*. She locates the struggle for power in the sequence in terms of voice and subjectivity. The blazon which divides Petrarch's beloved Laura into a poetic list of multiple body parts is seen as a means of scattering the presence of a threatening female force associated with the goddess Diana. A fully embodied, speaking woman would make her a subject, not an object, and disrupt the process by which the male poet constructs his own subjectivity. These sexual politics have consequences for women readers and writers: 'Silencing Diana is an emblematic gesture; it suppresses a voice, and it casts generations of would-be Lauras in a role predicated upon the muteness of its player.'

Critics who study women writers seek to measure the effect of these strategies of subordination by discovering what kinds of women did write, and what they wrote about. Many approach this subject in terms of the cultural strictures on female speech and how women writers internalized, manoeuvred around, or directly resisted such strictures. The phrase 'women writers' signals that we still consider authorship to be masculine; dominant views of women in the early modern period also included an image of the ideal female as 'chaste, silent, and obedient'. These terms were interrelated: to speak too much or to publish was to be promiscuous. In 'A Room Not Their Own: Renaissance Women as Readers and Writers', printed here, Margaret Ferguson considers two kinds of responses to the cultural linking of chastity and silence: an anxious justification of female self-expression that disobeyed male authority without challenging the ideal of female chastity, an option usually chosen by highly religious women in the upper classes; and an overt defying of social and literary conventions by celebrating erotic desire, a method practised generally by urban, non-aristocratic women. Mary Ellen Lamb considers how the cultural sexualization of women's speech limited the possibilities for authorship in women among the Sidney family, including Mary Sidney Herbert and Mary Wroth. Wendy Wall argues that the discourses surrounding the new medium of print publication gendered it male, but that some women were able to circumvent this prohibition by constructing alternate tropes of authorship. Ann Rosalind Jones considers the love lyrics, including Petrarchan sonnets, written by women, and argues that, although love conventions were discourses of power, women like Louise Labé used a process of 'negotiation' to appropriate lyric convention for their own purposes. Heather Dubrow claims that the muting of the lady in the Petrarchan sequence is not so complete as Vickers makes it seem, and that women writers like Mary Wroth were enabled by the instability of gender difference in the lyric.[40]

Other studies have focused on the work of largely upper-class women in political and literary families or coteries. These books demonstrate that although women often chose the less threatening position of translator, writer of religious works, or patron, they nevertheless actively sought to influence the politics of the time, and played an important role in the literary exchanges that made up the coteries. Margaret Hannay, Mary Ellen Lamb, Louise Schleiner and Gary Waller have considered these networks, especially in the Sidney and Herbert families. Related to this approach is the crucial archival work still very much going on, which recovers women writers who have disappeared from view.[41]

This work is changing our understanding of literary history. It has been discovered that Aemilia Lanyer, not Ben Jonson, published the first country-house poem. Elizabeth Cary and Mary Sidney Herbert may have influenced Shakespeare through their plays. Herbert's metrical innovations in her translation of the Psalms may have been imitated by George Herbert and John Donne. We have yet to consider the role of the poetry of Lady Mary Wroth on the circle of writers surrounding her lover, William Herbert, a circle that included Shakespeare, Edward Herbert, John Donne, George Herbert and Ben Jonson. A comparison of works by women writers with canonical male writers has become influential in critical essays and classroom technique. Ann Baynes Coiro uses this method in 'Writing in Service: Sexual Politics and Class Position in the Poetry of Aemilia Lanyer and Ben Jonson'.[42]

Feminist critics disagree about the usefulness of the concept of subjectivity, with its emphasis on the power of institutions to determine consciousness. Many do not use this term, but rather 'autonomy' in order to refer to resistance to gender codes, or 'interiority', positively linked with developments in the Renaissance and Reformation. It has been argued that the term 'subjectivity' undermines the project of feminism to analyse gendered authors and gendered texts, and takes from women what they have been most seeking: some form of self-determinism. On the other hand, liberal feminists have been criticized for attributing to early modern women what recent historicism has finally debunked about early modern men: the discovery of a pre-existing, individualistic self. Materialist feminists use the term 'subjectivity' to keep in view the extent to which a personal 'voice' can be the product of ideological structures. These critics therefore attend to ways in which class differences can determine the perspective of women writers.[43] A related and important development in this field are studies about the literacy of early modern women, especially in terms of class position and privilege. This work can provide information on women who did not write, or who wrote in ways hidden from view by the literary rubric 'women writers'.[44]

Psychoanalysis

Psychoanalytic theory continues to offer intriguing interpretations of Renaissance poetry, although it has met with powerful opposition from some cultural critics. These critics argue that the models of subjectivity used by psychoanalysis project backwards on to an earlier period what is only formed in the modern age: a belief in a secular, complexly ordered interior world and a structure of desire organized according to the nuclear family. Foucault, in fact, argues that psychoanalysis is a modern form of power/knowledge which produces obedient subjects and non-transgressive subjectivities.[45] Many feminists, however, have found that psychoanalysis gives them the terms by which they can explain the psychic anxieties about women which appear in the work of male writers and which reinforce oppressive social institutions. In addition, many psychoanalytic critics use modern explanations of the difficult period of identity-formation in childhood to illuminate the crisis provoked by changing models of selfhood in the early modern period.

According to Nancy Vickers, Petrarch's use of the Ovidian myth of Diana and Actaeon, in which the hunter's vision of the naked goddess is punished by dismemberment, expresses a male fear of castration, a fear warded off by Petrarch through the dismemberment of the female body into the poetic blazon, and the silencing of Laura. Patricia Parker identifies the defeat of the witch Acrasia in Spenser's Bower of Bliss as a similar 'male remastery' of the power of Queen Elizabeth, who was seen by male poets as interfering with the political purposes of lyric poetry. Parker considers Verdant, the young, overpowered lover of Acrasia, in terms of his 'warlike armes', which are 'suspended' useless in a tree. These 'instruments' are characterized as martial, poetic and sexual, here made impotent through Acrasia's influence. The nearly naked Acrasia, like Diana, poses the threat of castration, but this threat is overcome through the Palmer's 'phallic and Mozaic staff', and Guyon's destruction of the Bower.

The articles by Vickers and Parker extend to Renaissance poetry the insights of a famous essay by Laura Mulvey on modern cinema.[46] She argued that the woman on screen is primarily an eroticized spectacle, a passive object of the male gaze, rather than an actor in narrative. Woman-as-image, although rendered passive from the outset, is nevertheless a threat because, in psychoanalytic terms, she evokes the childhood pleasure in looking (scopophilia) as well as one disturbing result of this looking for the male child, according to Freud: anxiety at the sight of the female genitals, which, to the male child, signify castration. In psychoanalytic theory, the castration complex is an important rite of passage in childhood since it brings about the end of the Oedipal complex, by leading the male child to give up his mother as an object of desire, and to accept the authority of the father. Therefore this traumatic sight of the penis-less female body can be associated with an erotic vision of the mother, and the onset of fears that preclude the possibility of incest.[47] Mulvey, Parker and Vickers suggest that any woman presented as an erotically beautiful spectacle can elicit these fears in men. This can particularly occur when the woman is of superior social status, like Queen Elizabeth or the Petrarchan lady, because she will evoke unconscious memories of a powerful and dangerously erotic mother, and set off violent defences against the strength of the female image. In Mulvey's and Parker's essays, this violence is associated with epic narrative, which overthrows the visual power of the image, and restores the onward motion of masculine action.

An important essay by Joel Fineman, not actually included in this collection, entitled 'Shakespeare's "Perjur'd Eye"', has contributed to psychoanalytic criticism of the period and debates about early modern subjectivity. Although a summary of the essay is provided, readers are also encouraged to consult the essay itself.[48] Fineman bases his contrast between the sonnets to the young man and those to the dark lady on Jacques Lacan's account of the constitution of the subject in childhood. According to Lacan, the castration complex turns the child from knowing himself through the visual, including the mother's face and the 'mirror stage', to the entrance into language, the 'symbolic'.[49] With the acquisition of language, the child accepts his position in the nuclear family, which includes a recognition of his inability to possess the mother, and his subordination to the father. But to speak according to 'the law of the Father' is also to repress one's real desires, creating a split subject; to say 'I' is to lie, to some extent, because a socially acceptable subjectivity requires that powerful incestuous desires be lost to the conscious mind, desires which nevertheless continue to influence conscious thought and action.

Fineman applies Lacan's theory of childhood development to an historical period, and claims that Shakespeare moves the Petrarchan tradition from an emphasis on the image or the visual to an emphasis on the verbal. The result is the constitution of a poetic subjectivity new to the Western tradition. According to Fineman, the young man sonnets are marked by a poetics of likeness because they assume that language mirrors or reflects a trustworthy image of the beloved. In addition, the poet himself admires this beauty, and hopes to form himself in its image.

The poetics of likeness follows the neo-Platonic tradition of Dante and Petrarch for whom Beatrice and Laura represent divine happiness or the poetic accomplishment these poets wish to attain. The choice of a male rather than a female object of desire in the young man sonnets makes more apparent the poetics of likeness already present in the tradition, and emphasizes the visual identification of the poetic ego with its ego-ideal. The dark lady sonnets, however, emphasize difference rather than likeness. The sense of difference in the sonnets includes not only a shift from a homosexual to a heterosexual object, but a recognition, similar to that in post-structuralism, that the verbal signifier is not a reflection or mirror of its signified. The title of the essay is 'Shakespeare's "Perjur'd Eye"' because the poet comes to realize that his words are not adequate to what he sees, and that lying rather than truth characterizes language as well as subjectivity. The dark lady sonnets are filled with a sense of loss not only because the poet now loves what he doesn't admire (the poems are openly misogynistic), but because he finds that the poetics of likeness misrepresented the truth from the outset. The 'darkness' of the lady refers to her dark but beautiful complexion, to her beautiful looks and her foul character, and to the darkness of language that she reveals: the lack of correspondence between how things appear, how they are, and how they are described. Just as the lady is double and duplicitous, so language operates in paradoxes and perjures itself.

Fineman claims that the sense of depth or personal interiority produced in the dark lady sonnets and in Shakespeare's plays is generated by this recognition of the darkness of language, which 'justifies and warrants poetic introspection'. Fineman's thesis is compelling but problematic because it maps the Lacanian model of the constitution of the subject on to the historical model of Renaissance individualism. The thesis is compelling because it hints at a historicizing of psychoanalysis: perhaps Lacan has described not a universal human process, but a model of individuation that came into being with Shakespeare and his age, and that became the norm in the modern period. But this thesis is problematic because it uses a modern theory to find what is modern about Shakespeare, and therefore it risks projecting backwards in time our own versions of interiority. It is difficult to use psychoanalysis to discover the origins of modern subjectivity, since psychoanalysis assumes as given exactly what needs to be traced out historically.

Several critics have begun the difficult work of historicizing psychoanalysis for the early modern period. Janet Adelman and Heather Dubrow have argued that the differences between the early modern and the modern nuclear family do not undermine but require qualification of psychoanalytic theories of the construction of gender. Valerie Traub has claimed that an historicized psychoanalysis is necessary in order to analyse desire and sexuality during this period, and that the unconscious is the site of resistance to the dominant culture.[50] This work provides the hope but not the assurance that a psychoanalytic model can be combined with cultural analysis without imposing on the past a modern sense of internality and sexuality.

After I selected the essays that comprise this collection, certain methodologies emerged which promise a fuller revision of the field of early modern studies. I can only summarize a few of their tenets here, but I urge readers to seek out the texts named below, as well as other works listed in 'Further Reading'.

Race studies

Critics who consider race have called into question the omission of this category from much new historicist and white feminist criticism. They have illuminated the various and often interlocking attitudes of the English toward people of other cultures, including the Irish, Native Americans, Jews and Africans. This set of attitudes expanded and became more significant as world travel increased, colonization began and the English entered the slave trade.

However, critics in the field disagree widely about how the historically determined, socially constructed nature of the concept of race should influence their analysis. In the early modern period, the word was not used to refer to people of a particular culture, but rather to mankind as a whole or to descendants of a common ancestor. The term was not yet associated with a belief in biological differences, a claim that was only fully established by the nineteenth century, and has been almost fully demolished in the twentieth. Eighteenth- and nineteenth-century scientists and philosophers believed that a race was a biologically differentiated group, whose shared intellectual, moral and emotional characteristics distinguished that group as 'naturally' superior or inferior.[51] The establishment of this definition of race seems to have been the result of capitalism and colonialism, since it did not exist in the early modern period.[52] What did exist is a matter of controversy, and much analysis is directed toward formulating an answer, as well as the most effective approach to the issue.

In some early criticism, race is dismissed as an anachronistic term, and literary representations of the difference between European whites and people of other cultures are defined as primarily theological, mythical, or as a form of exoticism.[53] Many recent literary critics have adopted the use of quotation marks to remind readers that 'race' is not a biological essence, but an historically determined category whose significance is not inherent, but must be deciphered.[54] Anthropologists and historians who study this period from the point of view of American studies have fastened on savagery as the precursor to the concept of race, since the English associated savagery with the Irish, and, later, with other peoples.[55] But some critics argue that the attempt to recover what alternative concepts influenced the English at the time involves erasing the issue to such an extent that the culture is inaccurately approached as 'race-neutral'.[56] These critics contend that racialized discourse emerged in the early modern period, and that such discourse had material effects.

While the majority of these studies consider prose or drama, Kim F. Hall applies the principles of black feminist criticism to lyric poetry as well as travel narrative, drama, English women writers, and material culture in *Things of Darkness: Economies of Race and Gender in Early Modern England* (1995). In her discussion of lyric, Hall argues that the binaries of light/dark or fair/black in descriptions of the Petrarchan mistress become racially charged as England expands its trade, colonization and practice of slavery into the 'New World'. The 'dark lady' topos includes not just a difference associated with language and gender, as Fineman argues, but provides a discursive link between the feminine, blackness and foreign wealth. It is in opposition to these racialized differences that white upper-class English men construct their versions of subjectivity in the sonnet sequence. Hall also argues that English women writers, like Aemilia Lanier, Elizabeth Cary and Mary Wroth, focus on the 'darkness' of Cleopatra and non-European groups in ways which legitimize the writer's subject position as civilized and spiritually 'white'.

In *Women, 'Race', and Writing in the Early Modern Period* (1994), the editors Margo Hendricks and Patricia Parker in the introduction define 'race' as a socially constructed term with culturally significant definitions in different historical periods. In ' "The Getting of a Lawful Race": Racial discourse in early modern England and the unrepresentable black woman', Lynda E. Boose attempts to avoid modern definitions of race by acknowledging that the English attitude toward 'almost all forms of cultural difference was unabashedly contemptuous', and by speculating that the black Prince of Morocco in *The Merchant of Venice* may not have seemed any more foreign than the German or Spaniard. On the other hand, in 'Juggling the Categories of Race, Class, and Gender: Aphra Behn's *Oroonoko*', Margaret Ferguson argues that the category of race should not be dispensed with, but that it should be interrogated through comparison between early modern and modern versions in order to acknowledge systemic injustices in that period which are similar to our own. In 'Civility, Barbarism, and Aphra Behn's *Widow Ranter*', Margo Hendricks contends that the goal is not to attend to 'whiteness', since this reinforces 'the ideological binarism produced by racial categories', but rather to uncover the history of 'discursive and social practices' which led Englishmen and women to increasingly define themselves in terms of colour. The other essays in the collection also develop feminist approaches which acknowledge differences between women, analyse how European women contributed to imperialism and racism, and formulate how questions of gender and sexual difference are linked with questions of colonialism and post-coloniality. In 'The Tenth Muse: Gender, rationality, and the marketing of knowledge', Stephanie Jed argues that the poetic works of the British colonist Anne Bradstreet and the Mexican nun Sor Juana Inez de la Cruz were separately but simultaneously labelled 'The Tenth Muse' in order to turn the cultural anomaly of a woman poet into a marketable commodity and an institutionalized form of knowledge about the 'New World'.[57.]

Lesbian/gay studies

Critics in the developing field of lesbian/gay studies have called into question the normative heterosexism that underlies much literary analysis, and have increased our knowledge of early modern cultural attitudes and practices associated with same-sex love. In *Homosexuality in Renaissance England* (1982), Alan Bray argues against the claim made in the late nineteenth century that the Renaissance was a time of sexual freedom, and provides evidence of an intense cultural antipathy toward homosexuality, but an antipathy quite unlike that of our own age.[58] Sex between men was severely condemned as an example of debauchery, but it was also considered to be possible to any man rather than the practice of a particular group. Interestingly enough, sex between women never made it on to the cultural radar screen, perhaps because it did not disrupt the institution of marriage and the inheritance of property. Homosexual acts were not imagined as precluding marriage between men and women. Bray demonstrates that, despite strong cultural antagonism, same-sex love became possible because of a number of reasons: the acceptance of homosexuality in the Greek tradition, scepticism among some about Christianity and its values, or a simple lack of coordination between church teaching and individual acts.

Literary critics in the field bring to light homoerotic relationships evident in literature but ignored by previous critics. In a collection of essays *Queering the Renaissance* (1994), the editor Jonathan Goldberg argues that the purpose of gay studies of the early modern period is not to 'out' or identify gay writers, a form of essentialism, but to analyse how homosexuality is constructed in the period and particular works.[59]

In 'Into Other Arms: Amoret's Evasion', Dorothy Stephens claims for Spenser a remarkable sympathy for the homoerotic relation he depicts between Amoret and Britomart; in 'Pleasure and Devotion: The Body of Jesus and Seventeenth-Century Religious Lyric', Richard Rambuss argues for the homoerotics of Christian devotion, by exploring the depiction of the penetrable body of Christ and the desire for union with it expressed by Crashaw, Donne and Herbert.

In *Between Men: English Literature and Male Homosocial Desire*, Eve Sedgwick provides an illuminating model for analysing bonds between men in the patriarchal, patronage-determined élite of early-modern England. One chapter considers Shakespeare's sonnets in this light. Alan Bray and Jonathan Goldberg have applied this model to the period in subsequent essays.[60]

Organization of the volume

This collection is intended to clarify how recent methodologies have transformed traditional questions about literary history. It also allows readers to compare these approaches. The first part provides three significantly different readings of Spenser's Bower of Bliss (*The Faerie Queene* Book 2, canto 12), which nevertheless build on one another. They represent the development from reader-response criticism, one of the first breaks with New Criticism and yet still based on 'close reading', to the cultural analysis of new historicism and the interpretation of the role of gender within culture in feminist criticism. The second part considers the English lyric and sonnet not simply in terms of the Petrarchan tradition, but in terms of the development of early modern subjectivity, as formulated within feminism, psychoanalysis, new historicism and cultural materialism. Readers should note that the essay on Spenser by Patricia Parker in the first section refers to and is illuminated by the article by Nancy Vickers on Petrarchan lyric in the second section.

The third part brings together a variety of approaches to the poetry and history of the seventeenth century. My article considers the social, coterie origins of poetry, including the religious lyric. Richard Halpern analyses Milton's poetry in terms of the transition from feudalism to capitalism. David Norbrook argues that only an explicitly political reading can illuminate Marvell's 'Horatian Ode'. These essays should illustrate that, even though many recent critics share the belief that literature is implicated in social practices, they have interpreted history in quite different ways.

No effort has been made in the volume or the 'Further Reading' section to cover Milton. Readers should consult *John Milton* (1992) in this series.[61]

Notes

1. STEPHEN GREENBLATT, *Renaissance Self-Fashioning from More to Shakespeare* (Chicago: University of Chicago Press, 1980), pp. 4–5; 'Towards a Poetics of Culture' in *The New Historicism*, ed. Aram Veeser (New York: Routledge, 1989), pp. 1–14.
2. For a comparison of the terms 'renaissance' and 'early modern', see *Rewriting the Renaissance: The Discourses of Sexual Difference in Early Modern Europe*, eds Margaret W. Ferguson, Maureen Quilligan and Nancy Vickers (Chicago and London: Chicago University Press, 1986), pp. xv–xvii.
3. 'Tradition and the Individual Talent', in *Selected Essays* (New York: Harcourt, Brace & World, 1964), pp. 11, 8.
4. CLEANTH BROOKS, 'Marvell's *Horatian Ode*', in *Andrew Marvell*, ed. John Carey (Baltimore: Penguin Books, 1969), pp. 179–80.
5. ELIOT, *Selected Essays*, pp. 241–64; LEAVIS, *Revaluation* (London: Chatto & Windus, 1936); KRIEGER, *The New Apologists for Poetry* (Minneapolis: The University of Minnesota Press, 1956).
6. 'MARVELL's *Horatian Ode*', p. 183.
7. 'MARVELL's *Horatian Ode*', pp. 199–210.
8. *John Donne: Coterie Poet* (Madison, Wis.: University of Wisconsin Press, 1986).
9. *Renaissance Self-Fashioning*, pp. 115–56.
10. See 'New Historicism and Cultural Materialism' and 'Other Historicist Approaches' under 'Further Reading'.
11. MONTROSE, 'Renaissance Literary Studies and the Subject of History', and JEAN E. HOWARD, 'The New Historicism in Renaissance Studies', *ELR*, 16 (1986) pp. 3–43.
12. There is evidence of a renewed interest in the use of formalist methods in analysing poetry of this period. The 1997 Modern Language Association convention included a session called 'Toward a New Formalism in Renaissance Studies', with speakers Richard Strier, Paul Alpers, Heather Dubrow and Joseph Loewenstein.
13. HOROWITZ, ' "I Can't Remember": Skepticism, Synthetic Histories, Critical Action', *South Atlantic Quarterly*, 87, 1988, pp. 786–820; FISH, 'Commentary: The Young and the Restless', in *The New Historicism*, pp. 303–16. See also *The Historical Renaissance*, eds Heather Dubrow and Richard Strier (Chicago and London: University of Chicago Press, 1988), pp. 2–3.
14. RICHARD STRIER, *Resistant Structures: Particularity, Radicalism, and Renaissance Texts* (Berkeley and Los Angeles: University of California Press, 1995), p. 70; MONTROSE, 'Renaissance Literary Studies', pp. 8–9.
15. *The Interpretation of Cultures* (New York: Basic Books, 1973), p. 5. Page numbers will appear in the text for subsequent quotations from this work.
16. 'Ideology and Ideological State Apparatuses (Notes Toward an Investigation)' in *Lenin and Philosophy and Other Essays* (New York: Monthly Review Press, 1971), pp. 168, 170–7.
17. *Marxism and Literature* (Oxford: Oxford University Press, 1977), pp. 110, 113, 114. See also *Problems in Materialism and Culture* (London: Verso, 1980).
18. 'The Limits of Local Knowledge' in *The New Historicism*, ed. H. Aram Veeser (New York: Routledge, 1989), pp. 243–76.
19. HERBERT L. DREYFUS and PAUL RABINOW, *Michel Foucault: Beyond Structuralism and Hermeneutics* (Chicago: University of Chicago Press, 1982).

20. G. K. HUNTER, 'Humanism and Courtship' in *John Lyly* (London: Routledge & Kegan Paul, 1962), pp. 1–35.

21. FRANK WHIGHAM, *Ambition and Privilege: The Social Tropes of Elizabethan Courtesy Theory* (Berkeley: University of California Press, 1984); also see GREENBLATT, 'To Fashion a Gentleman', printed here.

22. *Elizabethan World Picture* (New York: Macmillan, 1944); MONTROSE, 'Of Gentlemen and Shepherds: The Politics of Elizabethan Pastoral Form' in *ELH* 50 (1983), pp. 415–59; WHIGHAM, *Ambition and Privilege*; WAYNE, *Penshurst: The Semiotics of Place and the Poetics of History* (Madison: The University of Wisconsin Press, 1984).

23. *Materialist Shakespeare: A History*, ed. Ivo Kamps (London: Verso, 1995).

24. Some would heartily disagree with me; see especially CAROLYN PORTER, 'Are We Being Historical Yet?', *South Atlantic Quarterly* 87 (1988), pp. 743–86.

25. *Political Shakespeare: New Essays in Cultural Materialism* (Ithaca and London: Cornell University Press, 1985), p. 3.

26. See NATALIE ZEMON DAVIS, *Society and Culture in Early Modern France* (Stanford: Stanford University Press, 1975), pp. 124–51.

27. For the containment thesis, see GREENBLATT, 'Invisible Bullets: Renaissance Authority and its Subversion, *Henry IV* and *Henry V*', in *Political Shakespeare*, pp. 18–47; repr., revised and expanded in GREENBLATT, *Shakespearean Negotiations* (Berkeley: University of California Press, 1987), pp. 21–65. For an emphasis on resistance, see WALTER COHEN, *Drama of a Nation: Public Theater in Renaissance England and Spain* (Ithaca: Cornell University Press, 1985).

28. *Marxism and Literature*, p. 114.

29. *The Country and the City* (New York: Oxford University Press, 1973).

30. *Learning to Curse: Essays in Early Modern Culture* (New York, London: Routledge, 1990), p. 2.

31. *Power/Knowledge: Selected Interviews and Other Writings 1972–1977*, ed. Colin Gordon (New York: Pantheon Books, 1980). WALTER COHEN argues that Foucault's theory allows for resistance, but his historical analyses never focus on it: 'Political Criticism of Shakespeare', in *Shakespeare Reproduced*, eds Jean E. Howard and Marion F. O'Connor (New York and London: Methuen, 1987), p. 35.

32. *Michel Foucault*, pp. 118–20.

33. See 'Other Historicist Approaches' under 'Further Reading'.

34. *Becoming Visible: Women in European History*, eds Renate Bridenthal and Claudia Koontz (Boston: Houghlin Mifflin, 1977), pp. 139–64. See also JUDITH M. BENNET, 'Response: Attending to Early Modern Women in an Interdisciplinary Way', in *Attending to Women in Early Modern England*, eds Betty S. Travitsky and Adele F. Seeff (Newark: University of Delaware Press, 1994), pp. 96–102.

35. ELAINE V. BEILIN, *Redeeming Eve* (Princeton: Princeton University Press, 1987), pp. xxiii, 290; *The Renaissance Englishwoman in Print*, eds Anne M. Haselkorn and Betty S. Travitsky (Amherst: University of Massachusetts Press, 1990), p. 7.

36. On 'material conditions', see JUDITH NEWTON, 'History as Usual? Feminism and the "New Historicism"', in *The New Historicism*, pp. 159–65.

37. 'An Exhortation concerning good order, and obedience to rulers and magistrates', in *Certaine Sermons or Homilies appointed by the Queenes Majestie* (London, 1595), p. 13.

38. GREENBLATT discusses 'Petrarchan politics' in 'To Fashion a Gentleman', printed here. For analyses of Sidney, see McCOY, ' "All Selfnesse He

Forbeares"', printed here; and ARTHUR MAROTTI, '"Love is not Love": Elizabethan Sonnet Sequences and the Social Order', *ELH* 49 (1982), pp. 396–428. PETER STALLYBRASS and ANN ROSALIND JONES avoid this problem in 'The Politics of *Astrophil and Stella'*, *SEL* 24 (1984), pp. 53–68.

39. SUSAN FRYE, *Elizabeth I: the Competition for Representation* (New York: Oxford University Press, 1993).

40. See 'Feminism' under 'Further Reading'.

41. See 'Feminism' under 'Further Reading'. The Perdita Project directed by Elizabeth Clarke and Martyn Bennett at Nottingham Trent University is engaged in recovering manuscripts compiled by women.

42. *Criticism* 35 (1993), pp. 357–76. On Lanier, see *The Poems of Aemilia Lanier*, ed. Suzanne Woods (New York, Oxford: Oxford University Press, 1993). On Cary, see ELIZABETH CARY, *The Tragedy of Mariam the Fair Queen of Jewry*, eds Barry Weller and Margaret W. Ferguson (Berkeley, Los Angeles, London: University of California Press, 1994), pp. 26–30, 41–3.

43. For the use of the term 'autonomy' and the implication of female 'individualism', see MARGARET W. FERGUSON, 'Moderation and its Discontents: Recent Work on Renaissance Women', *Feminist Studies* 20 (1994), pp. 349–66; on interiority, see *The Englishwoman in Print*, pp. 24–5. On the danger of the denial of individuality, see CAROL THOMAS NEELY, 'Constructing the Subject: Feminist Practice and the New Renaissance Discourses', *ELR* 18 (1988), pp. 5–18.

44. SUSAN DWYER AMUSSEN, 'Studying Early Modern Women', in *Forum: Studying Early Modern Women*, ed. Leeds Barroll, *Shakespeare Studies* 35 (1997), pp. 59–66; FRANCIS DOLAN, *Dangerous Familiars: Representations of Domestic Crime in England, 1550–1700* (Ithaca: Cornell University Press, 1994), and 'Reading, writing, and other crimes', in *Feminist Readings of Early Modern Culture*, eds Valerie Traub, M. Lindsay Kaplan, Dympna Callahan (Cambridge: Cambridge University Press, 1996), pp. 142–67; MARGARET FERGUSON, 'Renaissance concepts of the "woman writer"', in *Women and Literature in Britain 1500–1700*, ed. Helen Wilcox (Cambridge: Cambridge University Press, 1996), pp. 143–68.

45. GREENBLATT, 'Psychoanalysis and Renaissance Culture', in *Literary Theory/ Renaissance Texts*, eds Patricia Parker and David Quint (Baltimore: The Johns Hopkins University Press, 1986); FOUCAULT, *Power/Knowledge*, pp. 60–1; *The History of Sexuality*, vol. I, trans. Robert Hurley (New York: Vintage Books, 1980).

46. 'Visual Pleasure and Narrative Cinema', *Screen* 16 (1978), pp. 6–18.

47. SIGMUND FREUD, 'The dissolution of the Oedipus Complex', in *The Standard Edition of the Complete Psychological Works*, trans. James Strachey, vol. XIX (London: The Hogarth Press, 1953), pp. 173–9.

48. The essay was originally printed in *Representations* 7 (1984), pp. 59–86. It has been reprinted in *Representing the English Renaissance*, ed. Stephen Greenblatt (Berkeley: University of California Press, 1988), pp. 135–62; and *Lyric Poetry: Beyond New Criticism*, eds Chaviva Hosek and Patricia Parker (Ithaca: Cornell University Press, 1985), pp. 116–31. See also FINEMAN's book *Shakespeare's Perjured Eye: The Invention of Poetic Subjectivity in the Sonnets* (Berkeley: University of California Press, 1986).

49. 'The mirror-stage as formative of the function of the I as revealed in psychoanalytic experience', in *Ecrits: a Selection*, trans. Alan Sheridan (New York: Norton, 1977). See also ANIKA LEMAIRE, *Jacques Lacan*, trans. David Macey (London, Henley, and Boston: Routledge & Kegan Paul, 1977), pp. 67–92.

50. See 'Psychoanalysis' under 'Further Reading'.
51. ANTHONY APPIAH, 'The Uncompleted Argument: Du Bois and the Illusion of Race' in *'Race', Writing, and Difference*, ed. Henry Louis Gates, Jr (Chicago: University of Chicago Press, 1986), pp. 21–37; APPIAH, 'Race', in *Critical Terms for Literary Study*, eds Frank Lentricchia and Thomas McLaughlin (Chicago: University of Chicago Press, 1990), pp. 274–87.
52. PETER FRYER, *Staying Power: The History of Black People in Britain* (London: Pluto Press, 1984), pp. 133–90; FRYER, *Black People in the British Empire: An Introduction* (London: Pluto Press, 1988), pp. 61–79.
53. G. K. HUNTER, 'Elizabethans and Foreigners' and 'Othello and Colour Prejudice', in *Dramatic Identities and Cultural Traditions: Studies in Shakespeare and his Contemporaries* (New York: Barnes and Noble, 1978), pp. 3–30, 31–59; PETER MARK, *Africans in European Eyes: The Portrayal of Black Africans in Fourteenth and Fifteenth Century Europe* (Syracuse: Syracuse University Press, 1974) and 'European Perceptions of Black Africans in the Renaissance', in *Africa and the Renaissance: Art in Ivory*, eds Ezio Bassani and William B. Fagg (New York: Center for African Art, 1988), pp. 21–31; LESLIE A. FIEDLER, *The Stranger in Shakespeare* (New York: Stein and Day, 1972).
54. *Women, 'Race', and Writing in the Early Modern Period*, (eds) Margo Hendricks and Patricia Parker (London and New York: Routledge, 1994). See especially the introduction; LYNDA E. BOOSE, ' "The Getting of a Lawful Race": Racial discourse in early modern England and the unrepresentable black woman', and MARGO HENDRICKS, 'Civility, Barbarism, and Aphra Behn's *Widow Ranter*', pp. 1–14, 35–54, 225–39.
55. AUDREY SMEDLEY, *Race in North America: Origin and Evolution of a World View* (Boulder: Westview Press, 1993), pp. 41–71; RONALD TAKAKI, *In a Different Mirror: A History of Multicultural America* (Boston: Little, Brown, 1993), pp. 21–50.
56. KIM F. HALL makes this argument and uses this term in *Things of Darkness: Economies of Race and Gender in Early Modern England* (Ithaca and London: Cornell University Press, 1995), p. 261. See also the very useful essay by PETER ERICKSON, 'Representations of Blacks and Blackness in the Renaissance', *Criticism* 35 (1993), pp. 499–527; and MARGARET FERGUSON's essay on 'Juggling the Categories of Race, Class, and Gender: Aphra Behn's *Oroonoko*' in *Women, 'Race', and Writing*, pp. 209–24.
57. BOOSE, pp. 35, 37; FERGUSON, pp. 212–13; HENDRICKS, pp. 225–6; JED, pp. 195–208, in *Women, 'Race', and Writing*.
58. (New York: Columbia University Press, 1982; updated 1995).
59. (Durham and London: Duke University Press, 1994). GOLDBERG refers to a discussion of this issue by Jeffrey Masten, pp. 301–4.
60. *Between Men* (New York: Columbia University Press, 1985), pp. 28–48. For BRAY and GOLDBERG, see 'Further Reading' under 'Lesbian/Gay Studies'.
61. Ed. Annabel Patterson (London and New York: Longman, 1992).

Part One
The Bower of Bliss: Formalism, New Historicism, Feminism

1   Mode in Narrative Poetry*

PAUL J. ALPERS

Paul Alpers has been and continues to be a leading formalist critic. His book *The Poetry of the Faerie Queen* (1967) was an important example of reader-response criticism. This methodology broke with the exclusive textual emphasis of New Criticism by claiming that poetry was structured in order to influence the reader, not to achieve organic unity. Nevertheless, one of the central characteristics of New Criticism still remained: a close attention to poetic detail and pattern which marginalized biographical and historical issues. In this essay, Alpers develops an account of the term 'mode' in order to argue that literary works can be classified according to the kind of human abilities that the text attributes to its hero and its reader. The classic critical problem of the Bower of Bliss, in which the Knight of Temperance intemperately destroys the Bower, cannot be explained in terms of the Canto's internal coherence, but in terms of the reader's developing knowledge of the difficulties of exercising spiritual strength. Alpers' essay maps out a pattern of 'anticipating, enduring, and understanding a spiritual danger' which illuminates the organization of the Canto. In his recent book *What Is Pastoral?* (Chicago and London: University of Chicago Press, 1996), Alpers argues that formalism continues to offer a legitimate and valuable approach to literature.

I

In this paper, I want to analyze the meaning and argue for the importance of the critical term 'mode'. Critics resort to this term and use it in crucial places, because it uniquely fuses formal and thematic considerations. It is the term to use when we want to suggest that the ethos of a work informs its technique and that techniques imply an ethos. Hence one

---

* Reprinted from *To Tell a Story: Narrative Theory and Practice* (William Andrews Clark Memorial Library, University of California, Los Angeles, 1972), pp. 25–56.

31

critic writes an article on 'The Augustan Mode in English Poetry'[1] – not the Augustan style or ethos. Another writes on 'The Comic Mode of *Measure for Measure*'[2] – not the comic style or form or structure or vision. When Helen Vendler, in her fine study of Wallace Stevens, wants to point out the difference between the so-called thought of a poem and the poem itself, she says, 'Such a paraphrase of the poem does not reveal its mode.'[3] Robert Garis uses 'mode' when he wants a single word to indicate the basic subject of his *The Dickens Theatre* – a book which concerns not style or characterization or dramaturgy or symbolism taken by themselves, but the human implications and dimensions of all these as they exist in whole novels.[4]

Clearly 'mode' is felt to be a powerful and comprehensive term. Yet, with one notable exception, there has been no theoretical discussion of it, and of the many writers who use it, hardly one defines it. The word does not appear in the Preminger-Warnke *Dictionary of Poetry and Poetics*. You will not find a definition of 'mode' in Josephine Miles' *Eras and Modes in English Poetry* or in Angus Fletcher's *Allegory: The Theory of a Symbolic Mode* or in Earl Miner's two books on seventeenth-century poetry, *The Metaphysical Mode* and *The Cavalier Mode*. Indeed, what seems remarkable about the word is that it can be used reliably and with great resonance, even without prior definition. Hence the purpose of this paper is less to correct or modify the *ad hoc* uses of the term than to explain and justify them. As an epigraph in Richards' *Practical Criticism* has it, 'Let us get closer to the fire and see what we are saying.'

To begin, I want to put aside two uses of 'mode' that are related to, but not the same as, its use as a critical term. The first is the musical term 'mode', which in both Greek and Church music refers to a diatonic scale that is selected out of a larger set of possibilities. Each mode was supposed to have certain inherent characteristics which gave rise to certain predictable emotional effects in the listener: hence one writer defines 'mode' as an 'ethically informed musical pattern'.[5] This suggests interesting parallels with the critical term, but we must remember that they are simply parallels; no modern critic who uses 'mode' thinks of himself as adopting the musical term.

'Mode' as a critical term should also be distinguished from its very common use in such phrases as 'modes of being', 'modes of understanding', and 'modes of imitation'. In such usages, the word never stands alone: it always occurs in the formula 'mode of *x*'. Its grammar thus directly reflects its meaning: 'a particular form, manner, or variety (of some quality, process, or condition)' (*OED*). The quality, process, or condition of which the thing is a mode must always be specified.

By contrast, the critical term stands independently, and we must now ask what it means. Fortunately, the one treatment of the term is full of insight and suggestion. This is the first chapter of Northrop Frye's

Anatomy of Criticism, entitled 'Historical Criticism: Theory of Modes'.
Frye begins by saying:

> In literary fictions the plot consists of somebody doing something.
> The somebody, if an individual, is the hero, and the something he
> does or fails to do is what he can do, or could have done, on the level
> of the postulates made about him by the author and the consequent
> expectations of the audience. Fictions, therefore, may be classified, not
> morally, but by the hero's power of action, which may be greater than
> ours, less, or roughly the same.[6]

He then goes on to specify five modes – myth, romance, high mimetic
(epic and tragedy), low mimetic (comedy and the novel), and ironic
– according to the hero's stature in relation to other men and to the
environment of other men. Frye himself never tells us why he calls these
categories 'modes'. But we can find an explanation in Angus Fletcher's
wonderfully illuminating comment on Frye's term. 'The term "mode"
is appropriate because in each of the five the hero is a protagonist with
a given strength relative to his world, and as such each hero – whether
mythic, romantic, high mimetic, low mimetic, or ironic – is a *modulor*
for verbal architectonics; man is the measure, the *modus* of myth.'[7]

From Fletcher's remark, I want to develop a more adequate definition
of 'mode'. But first, what is inadequate about Frye's use of the term?
Exactly what is inadequate about all his criticism, brilliant and enlivening
though it is: he treats literature and literary works as closed systems. He
therefore does not account for what is of the essence in ordinary and
ad hoc uses of the term 'mode' – the sense of the way the mind grasps,
assesses, contemplates, and relates itself to all the human and natural
phenomena that the work in question presents. Frye of course recognizes
that a literary work is the manifestation of a single intelligence and
makes its appeal to another intelligence. 'There can hardly be a work of
literature,' he says, 'without some kind of relation implied or expressed,
between its creator and its auditors.'[8] But Frye's account of this relation is
very unsatisfactory. At one point he says, very suggestively, that 'certain
standards of normality common to author and reader are assumed.'[9] But
it turns out that he thinks this is true only in the low mimetic mode –
that is, when the hero and world of the work are exactly like us and our
world. In the other modes, he tends to give the poet the human stature of
the hero and leaves the reader sitting in his armchair, still *l'homme moyen
sensuel*.[10] We can fit Shakespeare writing for the groundlings into this
scheme of things, but not Milton writing for a 'fit audience'. Frye never
explores the sense in which *any* work implies its audience. It never
occurs to him that his phrase about 'certain standards of normality
common to author and reader' might be a general truth about mode.

'Mode' is so powerful and trustworthy a term because it suggests the presence of unifying attitudes and sensibility in and behind literary techniques and conventions. As a practical critic, Frye knows about this as well as anyone, but as a theoretician he cannot get it steadily in view. The weakness of his large theoretical structures is revealed by a single sentence: 'As soon as the poet's personality appears on the horizon, a relation with the reader is established which cuts across the story.'[11] Frye sets up an opposition between completely impersonal narrative and the appearance of the poet's personality. He leaves no room for the figure who is so rightly, if boringly, familiar to us – the narrator who is the 'I' who tells the story, but who is not identical with the author in real life. By the same token, Frye treats the relation with the reader as 'cutting across' the story, which therefore is assumed to have an independent existence of its own, as if it were a real concatenation of events. Frye of course goes on to say that no work of literature is pure fiction, but the fact is that the sharp and naïve dichotomy suggested by this sentence becomes the basis of his largest theoretical division – that between fictional and thematic modes. The latter category includes all works, like didactic epics and lyric poems, in which the writer impresses his own world view, mind, or voice on the reader.

In Frye's treatment of mode, plot and thought, Aristotle's *mythos* and *dianoia*, are regarded as separate, antithetical, and ultimate categories. Along with them go the following pairs of opposites: Aristotle vs Longinus, objective vs subjective, catharsis vs response. These antithetical pairs are of the very essence of Frye's writing and thinking. We do not stop to object as we read, because he is always moving from one to the other, playing them off against each other or intimating their harmonies. But his prose, for all its energy and subtlety, crystallizes out into fixed dichotomies. In this particular list of opposites, he has left a no-man's-land between the terms in each pair, an uncharted territory between distance and absorption, between objective and subjective, in which lies a great deal of what interests us as critics and readers. Poetic narrative lies almost wholly in this unmapped territory; using Frye's terms, we can only say that any poetic narrative will be some combination of fictional and thematic modes.[12] But if we transfer Frye's definition of mode to the poet's and reader's relation to a work, I think we shall have a concept that is direct and unforced in application and powerful in implication.

The definition I have in mind is this: mode is the literary manifestation, in a given work, of the writer's and the putative reader's assumptions about man's nature and situation. As a critical concept, this definition provides a question we should put to all works: what notions of man's strength, possibilities, pleasures, dilemmas, etc., are manifested in the emphases, the devices, the organization, the pleasures, etc., of this work? We can now rephrase Fletcher's remark in the following way: 'The term "mode" is appropriate because the poet or reader is conceived as having a given strength relative to his world and the world of the poem; hence he is a *modulor* for verbal architectonics; man is the measure, the *modus*, of myth.' However, it would be very misleading to scrutinize a work and arrange its details in order to get a neat answer to the question, 'What is the mode of this work?' Rather, I think it much truer to say that when you engage in normal interpretation you will find that you have implicitly been engaged with this question. This would explain why 'mode' so often appears as a powerful summarizing term, but is almost never defined analytically, as if to be applied. I therefore want to explore the significance of the term by showing its relevance to two classical problems of interpretation in Renaissance poetry – Guyon's destruction of the Bower of Bliss, in Book II of *The Faerie Queene*, and the internal monologue, in Book IX of *Paradise Lost*, in which Adam decides to join Eve in her fall.

II

Here is the stanza in which Guyon destroys the Bower of Bliss:

> But all those pleasant bowres and Pallace braue,
> *Guyon* broke downe, with rigour pittilesse;
> Ne ought their goodly workmanship might saue
> Them from the tempest of his wrathfulnesse,
> But that their blisse he turn'd to balefulnesse:
> Their groues he feld, their gardins did deface,
> Their arbers spoyle, their Cabinets suppresse,
> Their banket houses burne, their buildings race,
> And of the fairest late, now made the fowlest place.[13]

Why is the problem this stanza presents a problem of mode? First and most obviously, because qualities of writing and experience are at issue, and it is for these that critics tend to invoke the word 'mode'. The severity with which Spenser renders Guyon's action is in sharp contrast to the seductiveness of the Bower itself. Critics who feel something has gone wrong here do so because they feel a sudden shift in the quality of the writing, a shift which they find unjustifiable in terms of the canto itself and unacceptable in its implicit views of human nature. Conversely, Guyon's action could be justified by arguing, with C.S. Lewis, that the quality of experience in the Bower is consistently sterile and repugnant. Whatever view we take of the canto will be an argument about its mode – that is, to return to our definition, about the literary manifestations of the writer's and reader's assumptions about man's nature and situation. And we shall see, I hope, how useful it is to approach questions of mode by the specific notion – which underlies the connection between *modus* as manner and *modus* as measure – of man's strength relative to his world.

Not only Lewis but many of his opponents assume that in the Bower of Bliss Spenser could not have intended us to feel the tensions which most of us in fact do feel when we read this canto. Yet from the very beginning, Spenser makes it clear that such tensions are of the essence of human experience. In the opening episode, he establishes a pattern for all the subsequent renderings of the trials of temperance. In this episode, Guyon and the Palmer pass in their boat between the Gulf of Greediness and the Rock of Vile Reproach – moralized versions of Scylla and Charybdis, as the whole canto is a moralized version of the *Odyssey*. Before reaching these twin perils, the Boatman describes them to Guyon and the Palmer in two vivid stanzas (3–4). However, when the boat arrives on the spot, we are given four more stanzas (5–8) of even more powerful description of the gulf and the rock. Finally, when the boat has passed through, the Palmer gives a moral interpretation (st. 9), even though both the Boatman's forewarning and the poet's direct description have been full of moral significance. We have, then, a clear pattern of anticipating, enduring, and understanding a spiritual danger. We can see that Milton was interpreting his master truly, when he praised this canto for showing the dependence of moral knowledge on experience and trial.

The subsequent episodes of the canto can be seen as developing and complicating the simple pattern established by this first one. In the sea voyage that occupies the first half of the canto, the increasing complexity of this pattern of moral encounter is achieved by the following devices: surprises and other complications of the Boatman's warnings, as when the maiden calling for help turns out *not* to be the anticipated siren;[14] Guyon's innocent but dangerous impulses to help damsels in distress or listen to attractive melodies (st. 28, 33); and the transformation of the Palmer's moralizations from mere commentaries to direct acts of rejection or of keeping the boat on its course (st. 16, 26). Moral understanding now tends to take the form of moral choice, and after Guyon and the Palmer land in Acrasia's realm, the pattern of anticipation, full experience, and understanding becomes a pattern of externalized narration and action. The ivory gateway to Acrasia's realm, with its depiction of Jason and Medea's destructive love, is analogous to the foreknowledge the Boatman had provided. We then meet Genius, and Guyon, having absorbed the Palmer's severity, overturns his bowl of wine and breaks his magic staff. We next enter an idyllic landscape, and by comparison with the preceding episode – where we encountered an artifact, not nature – what is morally suspicious is more diffused through and merged with what is attractive and, it seems, humanly valuable. By the same token, the description of Excess and her bower, which immediately follows, is more powerfully engaging than the description of Genius. We indubitably see Excess for what she is, but the issue, as Milton knew, is how the whole spirit

confronts and endures her pressures. Hence, whereas Guyon overturned
Genius' bowl 'disdainfully', he breaks Excess' cup 'violently' (st. 49, 57).
From these summaries, you will see that Guyon's vehement destruction
of the Bower is not a unique action to which all has been tending, but
coming as it does after the most alluring descriptions in the canto, the
last instance of the pattern seen in these two earlier episodes – which
themselves are developments of the pattern of episodes in the sea
voyage.

I think it is clear that we have been discussing the mode of this canto.
For one thing, we have been talking about what we would call, in
conversation, the way the poem works, and 'mode' is a good written
equivalent for this perhaps too casual phrase. Moreover, we have been
talking about mode as we have technically defined it. Milton's praise in
Areopagitica makes it clear that the literary techniques of the canto are
based on a view of 'man's strength relative to his world'.

> Assuredly we bring not innocence into the world, we bring impurity
> much rather: that which purifies us is triall, and triall is by what
> is contrary. That vertue therefore which is but a youngling in the
> contemplation of evill, and knows not the utmost that vice promises
> to her followers, and rejects it, is but a blank vertue, not a pure;
> her whitenesse is but an excrementall whitenesse; Which was the
> reason why our sage and serious Poet *Spencer*, whom I dare be
> known to think a better teacher than *Scotus* or *Aquinas*, describing
> true temperance under the person of *Guion*, brings him in with his
> palmer through the cave of Mammon, and the bowr of earthly blisse
> that he might see and know, and yet abstain.[15]

Finally, the concept of mode brings into focus one further problem:
what is the status of the actions which conclude these episodes? The
orthodox interpretation of the canto takes Guyon's destruction of the
Bower to be a unique and definitive action; it resolves all moral issues,
and all moral values inhere in it. But it is precisely this view that creates
critical difficulties, because Spenser makes no bones of the fact that
Guyon's destruction is wrathful and pitiless. Yet two stanzas after he
wrecks the bower, Guyon is wonderfully generous to and pitying of
Acrasia's victims. Either Spenser is confused, or he does not think the
destruction itself sufficiently renders man's resolution of the spiritual
issues posed by Acrasia. The pattern we have described in the canto
shows that the latter is the case, because Spenser makes us see that no
single act of rejection is unique and defining; rather, our spiritual life is
a continual sequence of experiences and choices. This view explains
Spenser's rendering of the sea voyage, in which he calls attention on five

separate occasions to the unflagging energy with which the Boatman rows along.[16] Similarly, formulas like 'Forward they passe' occur some dozen times,[17] because Guyon and the Palmer pass the various tests of choice and endurance not in order to settle issues definitively, but to keep on their steady course. Hence the canto ends with the Palmer acknowledging the moral dilemmas posed by Grill and summoning Guyon once more to his journey: 'Let *Grill* be *Grill*, and haue his hoggish mind, / But let vs hence depart, whilest wether serues and wind.'

Having shown that Guyon's destruction of the Bower is consonant with the workings of the rest of the canto, we must return to the problem with which we began – the particular quality of the stanza which renders that action. It is here particularly that we must extend Frye's concept of mode to include the reader. What we have seen so far could have been discerned by applying Frye's notions of the internal workings of a fiction. But only by directly attending to the reader can we give a positive account, a critical justification, of the poetic severity of that stanza, the way it enforces the phrase 'rigour pittilesse'.

We can begin to justify the stanza by pointing out that, throughout Book II, man's spiritual strength involves the very energies and forces that he seeks to control. Thus Guyon's aroused anger gives him strength to fight Furor and Pyrochles;[18] he is courteous when he resists Phaedria's blandishments;[19] immediately after disdaining Mammon's treasures with 'bold mesprise', he meets the giant Disdain, who embodies this particular characteristic.[20] When Guyon smashes the cup of Excess, his violence is the heroic counterpart of Excess' reaction: 'Whereas *Excesse* exceedingly was wroth' (st. 57). The repetition of this motif in Book II is due to Spenser's steady contemplation of a truth of which the major emblems are Guyon's faint after enduring Mammon's trial and Arthur's wounded, exhausted condition after his battle with Maleger[21] – that man's moral strength, when conceived as heroic and autonomous, has inherent limits and inescapably takes its toll of the human spirit. The frank portrayal of Guyon's destructive energies makes this point once more, and it is clear that his rigor and wrath are reactions to what Acrasia threatens – dissipation in the fullest sense. But the narrative in this stanza is markedly externalized, an effect increased by the formulaic listing in the final lines. We therefore do not feel the emotional forces at work, in the way we do when Guyon is 'exceeding wroth' at a blow from Pyrochles or prepares to battle Disdain. To adapt Helen Vendler's remark about Stevens, we cannot fall back on paraphrase. If we are to stay in touch with the details of Spenser's rendering and the quality of our experience in reading – for the counterpart of 'How does it work?' is 'What is it like to read?' – we must talk about the way our minds engage, take in, apprehend the truths and phenomena presented.   ·

We have so far described the patterns of the Bower of Bliss canto as more or less direct renderings of psychological experience. Spenser is not a dramatic writer in the ordinary sense, but we have talked as if the effect of his verse is to make us experience in ourselves what the characters experience in the allegorical fiction. But this ignores an essential characteristic of this canto – the repeated externalizing of phenomena into static, morally significant descriptions, for which the best single term is 'emblematic'. The canto is of course filled with emblematic settings – like the Rock of Vile Reproach, the Quicksand of Unthriftyhead, and the fountain with its metal ivy – and emblematic characters, like Phaedria and Excess. But the emblematic tendency also affects the rendering of action. Thus the transition between the sea voyage and the entry into the Bower of Bliss is the Palmer's taming Acrasia's beasts with his magical staff, made of the same wood as Mercury's caduceus (st. 40–41).

Because of the emblematic tendency in the writing, moral mastery in this canto appears not solely as achieved conquest or endurance of trial, as it does in the Cave of Mammon, but also as the conscious knowledge that emerges from such experience. It sounds as if we should be speaking of 'distance' here, but that word can be misleading. The descriptions of the bathing girls, of Acrasia's music, and of Acrasia herself are as 'close' as anything in Spenser. Conversely, there is much moral argument and reflection in the Cave of Mammon. But between the two cantos there are important differences in Guyon's relation to his experience and our relation to Guyon. The Cave of Mammon begins with a debate in which Guyon is a conscious spokesman for all mankind, and in Mammon's realm he directly encounters every significant emblem. He is central and prominent up to the very end of the canto, when he rejects Tantalus' plea, takes a long look at the tormented Pilate, and resists the temptation to eat from Proserpina's tree. Spenser does not render everything by means of Guyon's experience, but at any given moment Guyon can be a surrogate for the reader. In canto xii, on the other hand, our self-knowledge lies less in the shared experience of the hero's encounters than in contemplated images and patterns of experience, of which the hero is only a part. Thus our image of man at the beginning of the canto is not the autonomous hero, but a trio of figures who are an emblem of the composite soul. Guyon cannot be our surrogate here, and as the canto proceeds the reader more and more becomes the human center of the episode.

By the end of the canto, when *our* minds are expanding to experience and include more and more, Guyon and the Palmer are increasingly reduced. Thus the last incident of moral anticipation in the canto does not occur to the characters at all, but only to the reader. As Guyon and the Palmer approach the Bower, they hear 'a most melodious sound, / Of all that mote delight a daintie eare' (st. 70). After two ravishing stanzas, Spenser says:

> There, whence that Musick seemed heard to bee,
> Was the faire Witch her selfe now solacing,
> With a new Louer.
>
> (72)

There follows a severe and disturbing description of Acrasia gazing on her sleeping lover (st. 73). At this point it is impossible to tell that Guyon and the Palmer have not reached Acrasia. We assume that they have and that they are present when Acrasia's courtiers go on to sing the rose song (st. 74–75). In fact they do not arrive until after the song is ended. Their arrival occasions another description of Acrasia and Verdant, but this time it is erotic, intoxicating, captivating (st. 77–79). Clearly Spenser has made the *reader* undergo the same pattern of anticipated knowledge and full experience that the characters underwent in earlier episodes. Spenser gives no indication of how Guyon and the Palmer react to Acrasia's alluring beauty; by the same token, the grave meditation on Verdant's fate is in the poet's own voice, directed to us (st. 79–80). Guyon and the Palmer are not our surrogates here: they are not represented as having any thoughts at all. We see them in a wider context than they see; we see them from the outside; we see them in action:

> The noble Elfe, and carefull Palmer drew
> So nigh them, minding nought, but lustfull game,
> That suddein forth they on them rusht, and threw
> A subtile net, which onely for the same
> The skilfull Palmer formally did frame.
>
> (81)

This is an emblematic action, and not simply because it is a version of Vulcan's capturing Venus and Mars in his net. It is an emblematic rendering of the point we have already discussed: Acrasia must be defeated by valid manifestations of the spiritual powers she corrupts. The Palmer's net is emphatically an artifact, and in calling it 'subtile', Spenser makes it literally a strong version of Acrasia's silk and silver veil, of which he says, four stanzas earlier, 'More subtile web *Arachne* cannot spin' (st. 77). Where we apprehended Spenser's point in the Cave of Mammon by a sense of sharing Guyon's endurance of his oppressive and nightmarish experience, the image of the Palmer's net makes a similar moral point much more strictly a matter of conscious knowledge.

These points about the rendering of action and our relation to it are equally true of Guyon's destruction of the Bower of Bliss, which immediately follows the description of the capturing of Acrasia. By externalizing and fixing Guyon's devastation of the Bower, Spenser gives the form of conscious knowledge to our awareness of the limitations of action, the costs of heroic autonomy, the severity with which spiritual opposites clash in human experience, and the power of the necessities that reign in the wars of the spirit. If this stanza ended the canto, as Guyon's faint ends canto vii, it might appear to be simply the recommended action that vulgar notions of didacticism assume it is. But Spenser beautifully places it in relation to man's whole nature and moral experience when he turns to the generous and steadfast freeing of Acrasia's victims, now 'comely men' but still feeling shame, even wrath and resentment. As we go beyond it in this way, Guyon's destruction of the Bower becomes a true piece of self-knowledge for us, as we understand, acknowledge, and endure its bitter severity.

There is no mystery about why the Cave of Mammon and the Bower of Bliss differ as they do. The reader's relation to the two cantos closely parallels the hero's role in each. All Spenser has done in the final episode of the Bower of Bliss is transfer to us the powers he gave his human triad in the first episode – of anticipating, experiencing and enduring, and interpreting a spiritually significant encounter. Why then do we not simply describe the internal workings of a poem – what Frye calls fictional modes – and extrapolate from them? Because this involves too strict a commitment to the notion of autonomous fictions, of works as closed systems. Too much is then excluded, so that as practical critics we find ourselves without a positive interpretation of Guyon's final action and as theoreticians we find ourselves in Frye's position of having to devise an entire separate structure of thematic modes. But if we do not think of the reader's mind as a *tabula rasa* for taking the impression of the fictional modes, if, on the contrary, we think of ourselves as being, along with the poet and hero, the measure of the myth in question, then the two elements that are artificially separated as fictional and thematic come together in a powerful unifying concept.

III

Adam's decision to join Eve in her fall is perhaps the most difficult interpretive problem in a poem full of such problems. Within the scope of this paper, I cannot hope to establish decisively the interpretation I offer. But I hope it will be clear that, whatever interpretation is offered, questions about mode will underlie it. The problem about Adam's internal monologue, as everyone knows, is that it is full of emotional power and human appeal, while at the same time it assents to bringing death into the world and all our woe. We feel immense sympathy with Adam, and yet know he is doing something wrong; Frye neatly describes this as a clash between the dramatic and the conceptual.[22] The orthodox view of this clash is that Adam should not have been victimized by it: he knew what he was about to do was wrong, he should have resisted his feelings, and trusted in God to work something out. But as this argument appears, for example, in Lewis' *Preface to 'Paradise Lost'*, it tends to diminish the power of Adam's monologue or simply ignore its literary character. This defect is repaired in the affective criticism of Stanley Fish, who argues that we are meant to feel the power of Adam's monologue, but nevertheless are to judge against him. Fish regards *Paradise Lost* as a series of tests of the reader, which he calls 'good temptations'; interpreting Adam's monologue is our supreme test, just as the decision itself is Adam's.[22] Clearly Fish has a strong sense of mode, though he does not use the term. His book is distinguished by its full and rigorous working out of the human implications of the way *Paradise Lost* works, stylistically and structurally. Hence, in supporting his readings, Fish continually and explicitly appeals to what he regards as the views of Milton and seventeenth-century Christianity on 'man's strength relative to his world'.

I want to argue that Fish and Lewis and many other critics are wrong to say that Adam should have decided not to eat the apple and join Eve – or rather are wrong in the way they say it, for criticism too has its modes. Let us begin with a traditional problem of mode, the relation of Book IX to tragic drama, the form in which many Renaissance writers (including Milton himself at one time) conceived the Fall of Man. When we look at seventeenth-century tragedies about the Fall, we find their treatment of Adam's fall is quite unlike Milton's.[24] In every one of these plays, Adam at first refuses to accept the apple from Eve; a full argument ensues, in which Adam explicitly says that obedience to God has first claim on him; Eve repeatedly appeals to and plays on his love and fear of loneliness, and finally half lures, half forces him to yield. In this mode, the conflict in Adam's loyalties is explicit, and his motive for eating the apple is clearly unworthy of him. There is no doubt in any of these plays that Adam and his descendents reading his tragedy should and *could* choose God over Woman and Nature. In the scene in *Paradise Lost*, by contrast, there is no debate, argument, or internal conflict. Adam's dismay on hearing of Eve's sin immediately produces the internal monologue in which he decides to join her. We hear nothing of his obligations to God, only of his resolution in this crisis. It will be argued that Milton's point is that Adam does ignore God, but the debate about this passage is precisely whether the dramaturgy and the verse enforce this awareness on our part. In other words, any interpretive argument has to make or imply, as Fish does, an argument about mode. At this crucial moment, are we made to feel that Adam's strength relative to his world and ours to ours are such that a different choice could and should have been made?

We can investigate Adam's strength relative to his world by asking what is the status of the impulse on which he acts at this moment. It is no derogation of him to say that he acts on impulse, for he is still in a state of innocence, and his feelings are still in harmony with nature. But what does this mean in that small stretch of time – which does not exist in the Biblical account – between Eve's fall and Adam's? When Eve eats the apple, Milton says

> Earth felt the wound, and nature from her seat
> Sighing through all her works gave signs of woe,
> That all was lost.[25]

The question of Adam's strength is precisely whether he is included in the works of nature which all feel this wound. He himself says, 'I feel the link of nature draw me' (9.914). Those who argue that he can reject Eve and that therefore all was *not* lost assume that his powers transcend nature and its bonds and imperatives. Let us see what Milton tells us when he returns to Adam, awaiting Eve's return:

> Great joy he promised to his thoughts, and new
> Solace in her return, so long delayed;
> Yet oft his heart, divine of something ill,
> Misgave him; he the faltering measure felt.
>
> (9.843–846)

The 'faltering measure' is the motions of Adam's heart. But the deictic force of 'the' and the syntactic parallel of the two noun phrases, 'something ill' and 'faltering measure', enforce the reference to an external event, the general wound felt by nature's works. By making 'he the faltering measure felt' a separate clause, with no explanatory conjunction, Milton poises it between internal feelings and the external events indicated by the preceding clause. He thus makes us apprehend, in the intimacy and fullness of our reading, that Adam's forebodings are completely in touch with reality. It is one of the most compelling moments in the poem, and Milton confirms its significance when Adam's dismay at Eve's sin produces the fading of the roses in the garland he made for Eve (9.888–893). In the face of this, how can we say that Adam is wrong to feel the imperatives that determine his decision?

> Some cursed fraud
> Of enemy hath beguiled thee, yet unknown
> *And me with thee hath ruined*, for with thee
> Certain my resolution is to die;
> How can I live without thee, how forgo
> Thy sweet converse and love so dearly joined,
> To live again in *these wild woods forlorn*?
>
> (9.904–910, my italics)

I spoke of the line about 'the faltering measure' as compelling, and surely this is the word the common reader would use about Adam's monologue. But its validity is purely aesthetic. As a matter of theology, Milton would have rejected the notion that Adam was in any sense compelled to eat the forbidden fruit. So we find ourselves back at the heart of the controversy, with critics like Waldock telling us that 'we should allow no one, *not even Milton*, to prise us loose' from the effect of Adam's words,[26] and orthodox Miltonists quoting *De Doctrina Christiana* and other theological texts. We find that it is not sufficient to consider Adam taken by himself. We must directly consider how our own minds apprehend this moment and its human meaning. In a poem on this subject, narrating this event, is it possible that we can read poetically and not theologically? I think that it is – that is, that Milton wrote in such a way that he could avoid, for example, the question, which necessarily concerned commentators on Genesis, of whether the fall occurred when Eve ate the apple or not until Adam did.[27] If we read the phrase 'all was lost' the way theologians read the Bible, it seems to commit Milton to the view that Eve's fall was Man's fall. But the parallel passage, when Adam eats the apple, shows that Milton means to beg this particular question:

> Nature gave a second groan,
> Sky loured and muttering thunder, some sad drops
> Wept at *completing of the mortal sin*
> Original.

(9.1001–04, my italics)

But we are still left with the question: if the phrase 'all was lost' does not entail a theological commitment of the ordinary sort, how can it have the poetic force that it does?

The answer lies, I think, in the relation Milton establishes between the reader and the events of this book of the poem. Throughout the poem, Milton assumes a fallen reader (how could he not?), and it is by now widely recognized that he continually exploits and appeals to the reader's condition. But this does not mean that the reader has a fixed relation to the events of the poem. Consider two interventions of the poet's voice, one from Book IV, the other from Book IX. At the end of the 'Hail wedded love' passage, Milton says:

> Sleep on
> Blest pair; and O yet happiest if ye seek
> No happier state, and know to know no more.

(4.773–775)

When Eve leaves Adam to garden alone and promises to return at noon, he says:

O much deceived, much failing, hapless Eve,
Of thy presumed return! Event perverse!
Thou never from that hour in Paradise
Found'st either sweet repast, or sound repose.

(9.404–407)

Both passages are full of pathos, because both appeal to our sense of the
fragility of the state of innocence. But in Book IV, Milton speaks as if
Adam and Eve can maintain themselves in their happy state; the lines in
Book IX are spoken in the full knowledge that they did not. This suggests
something about Adam's and Eve's strength relative to their world in
these two books, but does not settle the issue of ours. For example, a
conservative Miltonist might argue that Milton's words in Book IX
reproach Eve – rightly sensing that if we speak of pathos here, we
acknowledge the limitations of our own strength. I do not know that one
could settle the issue on the basis of these lines alone. But it is certainly
the case that in Book IX, in contrast with earlier books, Eve exists in an
atmosphere of pathos. It manifests itself in her speeches, as when she
says, 'Frail is our happiness, if this be so, / And Eden were no Eden
thus exposed' (340); in her actions, as when she naïvely follows Satan; in
the poet's comments, as when he calls her 'fairest unsupported flower,
/ From her best prop so far, and storm so nigh' (432); and even in the
reactions of Satan, who is momentarily 'with rapine sweet bereaved' of
his fierceness when he sees her (461).

The strain of pathos in Book IX is an implicit manifestation of
something we can establish in direct terms: that as compared with Book
IV, both poet and reader are represented as diminished in strength
relative to their world. Compare the poet himself in the opening lines
of each book. In Book IV, he speaks in urgent, prophetic tones, as if
caught up in the illusion that Adam and Eve might yet escape Satan:

O for that warning voice, which he who saw
The Apocalypse, heard cry in heaven aloud,
Then when the dragon, put to second rout,
Came furious down to be revenged on men,
Woe to the inhabitants on earth! that now,
While time was, our first parents had been warned
The coming of their secret foe, and scaped
Haply so scaped his mortal snare.

(4.1–8)

In Book IX, the tone is more down to earth, occasionally brusque, and the
poet speaks out of constraint:

No more of talk where God or angel guest
With man, as with his friend, familiar used

To sit indulgent, and with him partake
Rural repast, permitting him the while
Venial discourse unblamed: I now must change
Those notes to tragic.

(9.1–6)

By the same token, Milton's self-portrait in this opening passage is stripped of heroic aspects; his inspiration is less fully felt and rendered than elsewhere in the poem; his Muse is uniquely represented as having a quite external relation to him. He will succeed, he says,

unless an age too late, or cold
Climate, or years damp my intended wing
Depressed, and much they may, if all be mine,
Not hers who brings it nightly to my ear.

(9.44–47)

In the case of the reader, it is the heroic similes that most explicitly show his relation to the events of this book. Take the passage that follows the description of Eve among her roses:

Spot more delicious than those gardens feigned
Or of revived Adonis, or renowned
Alcinous, host of old Laertes' son,
Or that, not mystic, where the sapient king
Held dalliance with his fair Egyptian spouse.

(9.439–443)

These similes have a particular character that belongs to Book IX. In Book IV, Eden is compared to later gardens and landscapes in order that we may apprehend, from our present knowledge and powers, the original state of innocence. The rationale of this poetic effort is like the view that pagan myths were intimations of Christian truth, so that Hesperian fables are 'if true, here only'. The characteristic movement in Book IV is indicated by the description of Eden (4.235–68), which begins with poetic diffidence – 'but rather to tell how, if art could tell' – and ends with so strong a manifestation of creative powers that Milton brings into the Garden of Eden Pan and the Graces and Hours of classical mythology.[28] By the same token, the list of gardens which cannot be compared to Eden is done with such scholarly, mythical, sensory, and rhetorical energy and sweep that Milton can proceed without a pause from it to our first sight of Adam and Eve. He is so in command of his and our resources that he can place Satan in a subordinate clause that specifies his incapacity to feel the delights we do (4.285). But in these lines in Book IX, he is brief and restrained. The noblest human imaginings, the gardens of Adonis and Alcinous, are sharply characterized as 'feigned', while the real garden is that of Solomon, enacting a severely moral interpretation of the fall of man. To call Solomon 'the sapient king' increases the moral stringency, for it represents him at his noblest and employs a word that is notorious for having a harmonious double meaning before the fall and a problematic one after it. Both the rhetorical manner of these lines and the nature of the allusions have the effect of putting fallen man, the poet and the reader, on the other side of the gulf that is fixed between Eden and our present world. This rendering of our situation is confirmed as the passage continues:

> Much he the place admired, the person more.
> As one who long in populous city pent,
> Where houses thick and sewers annoy the air,
> Forth issuing on a summer's morn to breathe
> Among the pleasant villages and farms
> Adjoined, from each thing met conceives delight,
> The smell of grain, or tedded grass, or kine,
> Or dairy, each rural sight, each rural sound;
> If chance with nymph-like step fair virgin pass,
> What pleasing seemed, for her now pleases more,
> She most, and in her look sums all delight.

> > (9.444–454)

What is striking about this simile is not simply that it draws on the everyday world, but that it is confined to it. It lacks the aura or resonance – the capacity to extend our apprehensions to diabolical, divine, or unfallen realities – that characterize other similes, even ones (like the superstitious peasant at 1.780–88) that are based on more disturbing or more ambiguous phenomena. Milton here limits our enchantment with Eden and with Eve to what remains of their original nature in the world as we know it.

Much of what I am saying needs more detailed justification, and my argument as a whole needs a more thorough survey of the similes – and much else – in Book IX. But my purpose here, as I said, is to sketch an argument in order to show the issues that any interpretation must engage. Therefore let me now state the general significance of what I have suggested about our relation to events in Book IX. It seems to me that almost all the dilemmas readers and critics feel in Book IX come from assuming that we follow it in the manner of an ordinary narration of events. Poet, character, and reader are thought to exist at the same moment of time, so that questions like 'What next?' or 'Why did that happen?' occur to them in more or less the same way. Obviously we know that the fall is going to occur as Adam and Eve do not, but the usual way of interpreting this is as a foreshadowing – the observer's analogue to the foreboding that Adam feels. By the same token, the usual way of treating a simile like the one about Solomon is to call it proleptic – foreshadowing the fall and its consequences. It seems to me that Milton has done something very different from this, something much more mysterious and sublime. All the details we have examined show that we are not moving with the action of the poem – as we inherently would if this were a drama – but are rather contemplating it from a fixed position, on the other side of the events that are unfolding. We know what is going to happen, but we are powerless to affect it – hence the plangency of a phrase like 'all was lost' or the heartbreaking effect of describing Adam, weaving his garland for Eve, as if he were already in the fallen world:

> Adam the while
> Waiting desirous her return, had wove
> Of choicest flowers a garland to adorn
> Her tresses, and her rural labours crown,
> As reapers oft are wont their harvest queen.

> (9.838–842)

And hence, most importantly, the heroic grandeur of Adam's decision to join Eve in her fall. It is heroic because it recognizes, assents to, and embraces the necessity of things. Its candid, almost naïve, grandeur comes from the fact that the acceptance of our lot is represented not as fallen man's self-awareness and sense of limitations, but as innocent Adam's committing himself to the future and to his kind. The decision has such power because it occurs at a unique moment in human history – when man is suspended between a state of innocence and a fallen condition. The gap between Adam and the reader closes here, and we can sense potentialities working in two directions: Adam committing himself to become like us, 'bliss or woe', and ourselves enacting our acceptance of life's conditions in the mode of Adam's candid grandeur. Again let me stress that this is not theology. A theologian necessarily follows the Biblical story as an ordinary narrative, with God as plot-maker and Adam and Eve as responsible agents. In Book IX, Milton's extraordinary rhetorical tactics have freed him from these necessities and enabled him and us to contemplate the fall under the aspect of its meaning for Adam's descendants. Hence Adam and Eve's debate about gardening separately is not an oblique way of finding a cause for the fall or of saying Adam and Eve were really fallen already or of assigning responsibility or blame; it directly opens up problems of human freedom, responsibility, autonomy, and dependence. By the same token, Adam's heroic choice renders not simply the responsibility that theology says is his, but that frank and unflinching acceptance of our lot that is of the essence of the tradition in which Milton wrote and of his conception of man.

IV

I want to conclude with some remarks about the implications of what I have said and argued. In the first place, I have not meant to suggest, as some readers and auditors have thought, that critics who use 'mode' without defining it are being vague or careless. Quite the contrary, what has impressed me about my own and other critics' use of this term is that it can be used reliably and with great resonance without a clear formal definition. I would say that my analysis of the term and its use would prove to be true of the way in which other critics use the word – or alternatively would define boundaries beyond which the word *would* be vague and not useful. But the ordinary usage of the term, the way it usually appears in critical discourse, has an important lesson for us. I think questions of mode arise most fruitfully as ways of understanding issues that arise in the normal course of interpretation. This implies a view of literary theory very different from that represented by Frye and many other writers. It means that a definition is not to be applied to a work as if it were an experimental tool for classifying or analyzing an object, but should serve to extend and clarify our awareness of what our minds observe, take in, and understand. In defining mode as man's strength relative to his world (and so forth), we are not, then, specifying an attribute to be isolated and classified. Rather, we are providing questions that enable us to understand what we see and, in the words of Richards' great epigraph, to see what we are saying. This is not to substitute mere subjectivity for a falsely conceived objectivity. On the contrary, the point of conceiving theory this way is to maintain our grasp on the connections that exist between works of art and the human mind.

This raises questions that are well beyond the scope of this paper. But one specific consequence of this view of literary theory is already implicit in this paper and should certainly be examined. On the one hand, I have not specified the mode of the Bower of Bliss canto or of Book IX of *Paradise Lost* in the sense of providing a characterizing adjective to go with the noun. On the other hand, I have distinguished the modes of these two narrative units from those of other units within the same work. Such minute discriminations and such thorough absorption of theoretical questions into practical criticism might seem to lose touch entirely with the kind of large-scale classifying of literary works that Frye's work represents, and that is, I entirely agree, an essential part of our self-awareness and capacity as readers. However, I think that what the interpretations in this paper exemplify is perfectly consistent and continuous in our understanding with Frye's large categories and discriminations. First, just as a side remark, let me remind you that there is nothing surprising in saying that units within *The Faerie Queene* and *Paradise Lost* differ from each other: it is a commonplace to talk about the encyclopedic character of these poems and their accommodation of a wide range of genres, literary models, styles, and subjects. But this observation is mainly defensive. The important thing to say is that there is no difficulty at all in discriminating the Cave of Mammon from the Bower of Bliss, but in a broader view saying that they have a common mode in comparison with *Orlando Furioso* or with *Gerusalemme Liberata*. Expanding our view, we could go on to talk about what *The Faerie Queene* and *Orlando Furioso* have in common by comparison with *Don Juan* or *The Charterhouse of Parma* – or perhaps we would want to put *Orlando Furioso* in between *The Faerie Queene* and these later works. In making such comparisons and discriminations of mode, we should use generic and other common terms as much as we can. Thus the mode common to the Cave of Mammon and the Bower of Bliss is allegorical, and it seems just to call *Gerusalemme Liberata* epic in mode and *Orlando Furioso* romantic (or whatever the adjective of 'romance' is). Nevertheless, it is essential to recognize that we do not have to provide a categorical name or characterizing adjective for every discrimination of this sort. That way lies Polonius. Frye's work is both an example and a warning in this respect. His best writing encourages us not only to see the continuity of certain fundamental problems, but also, by its dexterity and flexibility, to be able to make fruitful comparisons whether our field of vision is narrow or wide. But at the same time, Frye feels a need to project his theoretical categories as if they were attributes of an order of literature objectively conceived and even of the world itself. In this mode he proliferates terms and categories, and his criticism and criticism influenced by him become like Donne's satiric description of astronomy:

> For of Meridians, and Parallels,
> Man hath weav'd out a net, and this net throwne
> Upon the Heavens, and now they are his owne.
>
> (*First Anniversary*, 278–80)

Finally, I want to make some remarks about what I have referred to as the connection between works of art and the human mind. Throughout this paper, I have spoken of the poet's and the reader's minds almost interchangeably. If what I have said is on the right track, then we must envisage a much greater degree of parity between writer and reader than we usually do. The tendency to deify the writer is very marked in modern criticism, as is its corollary, the tendency to make critics a priestly caste, interpreting sacred scriptures. Deification is no less decisive when the poet-god is hidden and we are invited to look on his creation, the work itself. Critics as different as Frye, Wimsatt, and R.S. Crane give us no sense of the bonds or likenesses that exist between the mind that created a work and the mind that reads it. (In this respect, American critics differ markedly from the great English critics of this century, like Leavis, Empson, or Lewis.) Hence even when these critics turn their attention to the relationship between work and reader, they see it working in only one direction. The reader is conceived so passively, so much as a mere object of manipulation and field of operation, that he tends to be absorbed into the work itself. Thus the essay on generic criticism in Frye's *Anatomy* is called 'rhetorical criticism' on the grounds that 'genre is determined by the conditions established between the poet and his public'.[29] But Frye simply absorbs this relationship into his objective description of the various genres. The effects of generic structures and devices are seen as inherent in them; hence there is, so to speak, no space to be traversed between work and reader and therefore no sense of a true relation between them – only the effect of a work *on* the reader. The same criticism applies to Wayne Booth's *The Rhetoric of Fiction*, which, despite its title, has been most influential as a tool for analyzing the structures of works and tells us almost nothing about the reader.

Similar liabilities beset what is called 'affective criticism', despite its attempt to give the reader his due. The work of Stanley Fish – by all odds the most brilliant and searching of its kind – seems to me simply to turn the assumptions of Frye and Booth upside down. Instead of the work as an object, we have the work as a self-consuming artifact, which exists *only* in the reader's developing responses. The word 'response' itself and Fish's insistence on the reader's bondage to a strict moment-by-moment sequential experience are other signs that he regards the reader as essentially passive, the plaything of the work and its author. Where other critics examine the work as the poet's creation, Fish examines the reader as his creature, but he nonetheless views the poet as God. This is explicit not only in his work on *Paradise Lost*, but in his argument that Herbert 'makes the experience of his poems the discovery of their true authorship' (that is, God),[30] and in such splendid remarks as 'Pater giveth and Pater taketh away'.[31] Fish's view of the reader is explicit in the conclusion of his most important theoretical essay:

> Becoming good at the method means asking the question 'What does that . . . do?' with more and more awareness of the probable (and hidden) complexity of the answer; that is with a mind more and more sensitized to the workings of language. In a peculiar and unsettling (to theorists) way, it is a method which processes its own user, who is also its only instrument. It is self-sharpening and what it sharpens is *you*. In short, it does not organize materials, but transforms minds.[32]

What is unsettling in these words is not the challenge to theorists, but their human implications. To adapt Whitehead's famous witticism, there is no God and the critic is His prophet. But it is a tricky business, extrapolating social or moral views from a critic's work. To find elitist or hieratic views implicit in Frye seems to me relevant to our current educational dilemmas because they have much to do with Frye's influence. But such extrapolations probably do a good deal of injustice to what Frye personally perceives and thinks. And if his view of literature, or Fish's or anyone else's, is wrong, it is not because it unsettles our feelings or disturbs our self-esteem, but because it is wrong, and the way to show this is in concrete analysis and debate about concrete literary issues.

So I want to conclude by suggesting that in such debates our views of poet and reader will be of the essence, and that we most truly honor a writer not by transfiguring him out of all proportion or likeness to ourselves, but by thinking of him as a man among men, confronting and imagining a common condition, and writing of it in some way, some mode – celebrating, observing, execrating, accepting, whatever. It is this view of writer and reader that underlies a notion of mode and that brings out what the critical term shares, at its deepest level of implication, with the other meanings of the word. The critical term, the musical term, the grammatical term 'mood', and the phrase 'mode of x' have in common a view of any human act as being a selection from or specific manifestation of a larger reality or set of possibilities that no single act can encompass. As critics we do well to remind ourselves that this is true of the acts of our own minds. Perhaps we should talk less about critical theory and method and more about modes of criticism.

Notes

1. RALPH COHEN, in *Eighteenth-Century Studies*, I (1967), 3–32.
2. ROGER SALE, in *Shakespeare Quarterly*, XIX (1968), 55–61.
3. *On Extended Wings* (Cambridge, Mass.: Harvard University Press, 1969), p. 130.
4. 'There is a Dickens problem because we ordinarily do not regard the theatrical mode as capable of "serious" artistic effects and meanings. There is then another mode which does seem capable of these high matters, a mode for which we have no name because it is the only mode which we take "seriously."' *The Dickens Theatre* (Oxford: Clarendon Press, 1965), p. 31.
5. JOHN HOLLANDER, *The Untuning of the Sky* (Princeton: University Press, 1961), p. 208.
6. *Anatomy of Criticism* (Princeton: University Press, 1957), p. 33.
7. 'Utopian History and the *Anatomy of Criticism*', in Murray Krieger ed., *Northrop Frye in Modern Criticism* ('English Institute Essays') (New York: Columbia University Press, 1966), pp. 34–35.
8. *Anatomy*, p. 53.
9. *Ibid.*, p. 49.
10. *Cf.* his definition of 'mode' in the Glossary at the end of the *Anatomy*: 'A conventional power of action assumed about the chief characters in fictional

literature, or the corresponding attitude assumed by the poet toward his audience in thematic literature' (p. 366).

11. *Anatomy*, p. 52.
12. 'Every work of literature has both a fictional and a thematic aspect, and the question of which is more important is often simply a matter of opinion or emphasis in interpretation' (*Anatomy*, p. 53).
13. II.xii.83. *The Faerie Queene*, ed. J.C. Smith (Oxford: Clarendon Press, 1909).
14. Stanzas 27–28; *cf.* st. 17 and 30. I first was made aware of the patterns of anticipation and arrival in this canto by a seminar paper by MARCIA McCLINTOCK FOLSOM.
15. *Complete Prose Works*, vol. 2, ed. Ernest Sirluck (New Haven: Yale University Press, 1959), pp. 515–16.
16. Stanzas 5, 10, 21, 29, 37.
17. Stanzas 3, 5, 6, 9, 10, 14, 15, 17, 18, 19, 20, 27, 29, 34, 37.
18. iv.9, v.7.
19. vi.21, 26, 36.
20. vii.39–40.
21. vii.66, xi.48–49.
22. *The Return of Eden* (Toronto: University Press, 1965), pp. 83–84.
23. *Surprised by Sin: The Reader in 'Paradise Lost'* (New York: St Martin's Press, 1967), p. 270.
24. These tragedies (and many other analogues to *Paradise Lost*) are collected in Watson Kirkconnell (ed.), *The Celestial Cycle* (Toronto: University Press, 1952). The scenes summarized in this paragraph come from the following plays (page numbers are those of the scene of Adam's fall): HUGO GROTIUS, *Adamus Exul* (1601), pp. 175–85; GIAMBATTISTA ANDREINI, *L'Adamo* (1613), pp. 251–57; SERAFINO DELLA SALANDRA, *Adamo Caduto* (1647), pp. 326–31; JOOST VAN DEN VONDEL, *Adam in Ballingschap* (1664), pp. 466–70.

   It is interesting that in neither of Milton's two outlines of a tragedy of the Fall (*c.* 1640, preserved in the Trinity College, Cambridge manuscript) does he provide for a scene or scenes depicting the fall of either Adam or Eve. Modernized transcriptions of these drafts can be found in *A Milton Handbook*, eds J.H. Hanford and J.G. Taafe (5th edn, New York: Appleton, 1970), pp. 150–53, and *The Poems of Milton*, eds J. Carey and A. Fowler (London: Longman, 1968), pp. 419–21.
25. 9.782–4. The text is that of ALASTAIR FOWLER (London, 1968) ('Longmans' Annotated English Poets').
26. A.J.A. WALDOCK, *'Paradise Lost' and Its Critics* (Cambridge: University Press, 1947), p. 47.
27. See ARNOLD WILLIAMS, *The Common Expositor* (Chapel Hill: University of North Carolina Press, 1948), p. 123.
28. For a full discussion of this passage, see my essay, 'The Milton Controversy', in *Twentieth-Century Literature in Retrospect*, ed. Reuben A. Brower (Cambridge, Mass., 1971; Harvard English Studies 2), pp. 271–78.
29. *Anatomy*, p. 247.
30. 'Letting Go: The Reader in Herbert's Poetry', *ELH*, XXXVII (1970), 478.
31. 'Literature in the Reader: Affective Stylistics', *New Literary History*, II (1970), 130.
32. *Ibid.*, 160–61.

2 To Fashion a Gentleman: Spenser and the Bower of Bliss*

STEPHEN J. GREENBLATT

Stephen Greenblatt's *Renaissance Self-Fashioning: From More to Shake-speare* (1980) was one of the first examples of the methodology which he later named new historicism. In this chapter, he considers Guyon's destruction of the Bower of Bliss, but, unlike Alpers' reader-response analysis, Greenblatt interprets the passage in terms of a number of historical parallels: 'the European response to native cultures of the New World, the English colonial struggle in Ireland, and the Reforma-tion attack on images'. The 'cultural poetics' of the essay, associated with the work of Clifford Geertz, places literature in 'the texture of a particular pattern of life, or collective experience that transcends and completes its meaning'. The episode in *The Faerie Queene* is seen as indicative of the violence inherent to the establishment of British sovereignty and the English national character. Greenblatt takes his cue from Foucault when he argues that Spenser, the monarchy and Protestantism are aligned in their impulse to reinforce absolutist power. The essay considers aspects of the early modern period linked to the beginnings of 'modern consciousness', but these aspects are approached as reinforcing rather than subverting the dominant culture. I reproduce here the essay without its opening remarks on earlier chapters.

[. . .]

Despite its age and its well-documented limitations, one of the best introductions to Renaissance self-fashioning remains Burckhardt's *Civilization of the Renaissance in Italy*.[1] Burckhardt's crucial perception was that the political upheavals in Italy in the later Middle Ages, the

---

* Reprinted from Stephen J. Greenblatt, *Renaissance Self-Fashioning* (Chicago: University of Chicago Press, 1980), pp. 161–92.

transition from feudalism to despotism, fostered a radical change in consciousness: the princes and *condottieri*, and their secretaries, ministers, poets, and followers, were cut off from established forms of identity and forced by their relation to power to fashion a new sense of themselves and their world: the self and the state as works of art. But his related assertion that, in the process, these men emerged at last as free individuals must be sharply qualified. While not only in Italy, but in France and England as well, the old feudal models gradually crumbled and fell into ruins, men created new models, precisely as a way of containing and channeling the energies which had been released.

The chief intellectual and linguistic tool in this creation was rhetoric, which held the central place in the humanist education to which most gentlemen were at least exposed.[2] Rhetoric was the common ground of poetry, history, and oratory; it could mediate both between the past and the present and between the imagination and the realm of public affairs. Encouraging men to think of all forms of human discourse as argument, it conceived of poetry as a performing art, literature as a storehouse of models. It offered men the power to shape their worlds, calculate the probabilities, and master the contingent, and it implied that human character itself could be similarly fashioned, with an eye to audience and effect. Rhetoric served to theatricalize culture, or rather it was the instrument of a society which was already deeply theatrical.[3]

Theatricality, in the sense of both disguise and histrionic self-presentation, arose from conditions common to almost all Renaissance courts: a group of men and women alienated from the customary roles and revolving uneasily around a center of power, a constant struggle for recognition and attention, and a virtually fetishistic emphasis upon manner.[4] The manuals of court behavior which became popular in the sixteenth century are essentially handbooks for actors, practical guides for a society whose members were nearly always on stage. These books are closely related to the rhetorical handbooks that were also in vogue – both essentially compilations of verbal strategies and both based upon the principle of imitation. The former simply expand the scope of the latter, offering an integrated rhetoric of the self, a model for the formation of an artificial identity.

The greatest and most familiar of these manuals of behavior, Castiglione's *Book of the Courtier*, portrays a world in which social frictions, sexual combat, and power are all carefully masked by the fiction of an elegant *otium*. Because of its mastery of its own precepts, Castiglione's work masks the tedious conning of lines and secret rehearsals which underlie the successful performance. For a sense of these, we must turn to the cruder manuals, such as *The Court of Civil Courtesy* (1577), a handbook designed to help its reader to thread his way successfully through the labyrinth of social distinctions, to win at the game of rank. For example, if a host of equal or lower social rank seats a gentleman below an inferior, the author suggests that the gentleman casually sit down two or three places *below* even his assigned place; then if his host tries to move him back, he should say nonchalantly, 'As long as I find good meat, I never use to study for my place.'[5] The point, of course, is that this is spoken by someone who has intensely studied for his place.

Dissimulation and feigning are an important part of the instruction given by almost every court manual, from this comedy of manners, to Guazzo's defense of the pretence necessary to achieve an agreeable social presence, to Castiglione's idea of the sugar-coated pill of political virtue.[6] One of the most penetrating Renaissance studies of this feigning and indeed of the whole mentality of the courtier is Philibert de Vienne's brilliant mock encomium, *The Philosopher of the Court* (1547). According to the speaker of this little-known work, translated by George North in 1575, 'Our new and moral *Philosophy* may thus be defined: A certain and sound judgment, how to live according to the good grace and fashion of the Court.'[7] Where old-fashioned philosophers used to struggle to probe below the appearance of things to their essence, modern moralists need only pay scrupulous attention to surfaces: 'the semblances and appearances of all things cunningly couched, are the principal supporters of our Philosophy: for such as we seem, such are we judged here' (56–57). Acts which have plausible 'coverings and pretty pretexts' (50) are to be condoned; acts without them are condemned as crimes. This is not presented as the voice of conscious cynicism; quite the contrary, the speaker considers himself highly moral. He talks of commutative and distributive justice, of prudence, temperance, and magnanimity. Above all, he prizes honor, in defense of which a man may lawfully fight and, if need be, kill. But such extreme measures are rare; as in *The Courtier*, a man wins honor less by the sword than by the possession of grace, a quality which may be acquired through careful study and practice.[8]

Philibert's target is not the craftiness of a confidence man but the idealism, the high moral tone, that serves at once to advance the courtier's career and to conceal his rapacity from himself. The philosopher of the court has no intention of forgoing the pleasures of an unspotted conscience; indeed that conscience is one of the choicest products of the humanistic education that his social world requires of its participants. But the problem is to maintain this conscience in the face of the violations of its tenets in the reality of behavior at court. If those violations are invisible for much of the time, there are nonetheless moments at which a life pervaded by dissimulation must confront a moral tradition that insists, in the teachings of Socrates for example, that dissimulation is immoral. Philibert's interest is the working of the court mind at such moments, the social accommodation of an ethical embarrassment: '*Socrates* forbids such masking and general disguising, because we should not appear to be others than we are: and we also allow the same . . . But *Socrates* letteth us not, that having no desire to show ourselves contrary to that we would be esteemed, notwithstanding we dissemble, and accommodate ourselves to the imperfections of everyone, when the same doth present us danger, and is prejudicial unto us . . . Himself doeth serve us for example, for although he was ever like unto himself . . . yet was he the greatest dissembler in the world' (97–98).

By virtue of several convenient distortions and the discreet omission of the circumstances of his death, Socrates is absorbed into the ethos of rhetorical self-fashioning that Plato, in *Theaetetus* and *Gorgias*, has him condemn. For the philosopher of the court, Socrates is no longer opposed to a sophistic view of the world – 'the virtue of man consisteth not in that which is only good of itself, following the opinion of Philosophy: but in that which seemeth to them good' (12) – but one of its supreme practitioners. The potentially disillusioning conflict between social ideals and social behavior has been averted, and Philibert's speaker can conclude with a celebration of Protean man: 'This facility of the Spirit is not therefore to be blamed which makes men according to the pleasure of others, to change and transform himself. For in so doing he shall be accounted wise, win honor, and be free of reprehension everywhere: which *Proteus* knew very well, to whom his diverse Metamorphosis and oft transfiguration was very commodious' (101).[9]

Philibert has seen deeply into the mind he satirizes and cunningly mimics its forms of thought and expression. Indeed, there is some evidence that *The Philosopher of the Court* may have been taken at face value in England as a manual of court behavior.[10] If so, it is a startling tribute to the accuracy of Philibert's perception of the pressure on the court mind to preserve its idealism by transforming disruptive criticism into histrionic celebration and confirmation. This pressure intensifies as one moves closer to the center of power; at the very center even hostility and frustration wear the face of pervervid worship. Thus Sir Walter Ralegh may have chafed at Elizabeth's Spanish policy, wishing it more militant, but he did so only in the context of the 'romance' which he carried on with his royal mistress. She was Cynthia and he was the Ocean, she was Diana and he an adoring follower, she was the heroine of a chivalric romance and he her devoted knight. When he had incurred the disfavor of his sixty-year-old mistress, the middle-aged lover declared himself heartsick with loneliness and grief: 'While she was yet near at hand, that I might hear of her once in two or three days, my sorrows were the less: but even now my heart is cast into the depth of all misery. I that am wont to behold her riding like *Alexander*, hunting like *Diana*, walking like *Venus*, the gentle wind blowing her fair hair about her pure cheeks, like a nymph [etc.].'[11]

To accompany such fine sentiments, Ralegh even staged a scene of violent passion, modeled on the twenty-third canto of *Orlando Furioso*. His kinsman, Sir Arthur Gorges – no doubt acting upon instructions – carefully described the 'strange Tragedy' in a letter to Cecil, concluding 'I fear Sir W. Ralegh will shortly grow to be Orlando Furioso, if the bright Angelica persevere against him a little longer.' The key to the performance is provided in a postscript: 'I could wish her Majesty knew.'[12]

Ralegh was more flamboyant than most, but the phenomenon as a whole is familiar. Sir Robert Carey has left a record of the way he was caught up in Elizabeth's theatricals. In 1597, smarting at not having been paid for his services as Warden of the East Marches, he rode to Theobalds uninvited and requested an audience with the queen. Both Cecil and Carey's brother (who was then Lord Chamberlain) advised him to leave at once without letting the queen know of his rash visit, for they assured him she would be furious. But a courtier friend, William Killigrew, devised a better plan: he told the queen that she was beholden to Carey, 'who not having seen her for a twelvemonth and more, could no longer endure to be deprived of so great a happiness; but took post with all speed to come up to see your Majesty, and to kiss your hand, and so to return instantly again.'[13] Carey was then granted an audience and was given the money due to him.

How are we to take a story like this? Carey implies in his account that the queen was taken in. Perhaps; and yet without denying her a jot of her enormous vanity, we may be virtually certain that Elizabeth was well aware that he had not ridden from the Scottish marches in order to kiss her hand. By insisting upon the romantic fiction, she determined the whole tone of their subsequent dealings: Carey was no longer a civil servant demanding his pay, but a lover at the feet of his mistress. He had been absorbed into Petrarchan politics.

Not surprisingly, one of the most acute contemporary observers of these tactics was Sir Francis Bacon. If the courting and professions of love which the queen encouraged are viewed indulgently, 'they are much like the accounts we find in romances of the Queen in the blessed islands, and her court and institutions, who allows of amorous admiration but prohibits desire. But if you take them seriously, they challenge admiration of another kind and of a very high order; for certain it is that these dalliances detracted but little from her fame and nothing at all from her majesty, and neither weakened her power nor sensibly hindered her business.'[14] Bacon perceives first, that the romantic atmosphere of the court had a distinctly literary cast, and second, that it did not interfere with royal control. The two were in fact intertwined: Elizabeth's exercise of power was closely bound up with her use of fictions.[15] A surviving holograph of one of her speeches, at the close of a difficult session, enables us to glimpse the queen's characteristic strategy: 'Let this my discipline stand you in stead of sorer strokes,' she writes, 'never to tempt too far a Prince's pow...' The last letters are crossed out, and in their place she writes 'patience'.[16]

In an intensification of that political mode described by More, everyone perceives that power has been made to mask as patience or that it has assumed romantic trappings, but the perception that a fiction is being imposed is rarely turned against Elizabeth as it will be turned against James and Charles. The reasons for the queen's relative success are many and complex; they may be summarized by observing that it did not seem in the interest of a substantial segment of the population to attempt to demystify the queen's power, and hence it was enormously difficult to do so.

The queen's power was linked with fictions in a more technical sense as well: her reign, according to Ernst Kantorowicz, witnessed the first major secular elaboration of the mystical legal fiction of 'the King's Two Bodies'. 'I am but one body, naturally considered,' Elizabeth declared in her accession speech, 'though by [God's] permission a Body Politic to govern.' When she ascended the throne, according to the crown lawyers, her very being was profoundly altered; in her mortal 'Body natural' was incarnated the immortal and infallible 'Body politic'. Her body of flesh would age and die, but the Body politic, as Plowden wrote, 'is not subject to Passions as the other is, nor to Death, for as to this Body the King never dies'. Her visible being was a hieroglyphic of the timeless corporate being with its absolute perfection, just as, in the words of Coke, 'a king's crown was a hieroglyphic of the laws'.[17] She was a living representation of the immutable within time, a fiction of permanence. Through her, society achieved symbolic immortality and acted out the myth of a perfectly stable world, a world which replaces the flux of history.

Even without this elaborate doctrine, of course, kingship always involves fictions, theatricalism, and the mystification of power. The notion of 'the King's Two Bodies' may, however, have heightened Elizabeth's conscious sense of her identity as at least in part a *persona ficta* and her world as a theater. She believed deeply – virtually to the point of religious conviction[18] – in display, ceremony, and decorum, the whole theatrical apparatus of royal power. 'We Princes,' she told a deputation of Lords and Commons in 1586, 'are set on stages, in the sight and view of all the world duly observed.'[19]

In the official spectacles and pageants, everything was calculated to enhance her transformation into an almost magical being, a creature of infinite beauty, wisdom and power. But even her ordinary public appearances were theatrically impressive. A contemporary, Bishop Goodman, recalled in later years having seen the queen emerge from council on a December evening in 1588: 'This wrought such an impression upon us, *for shows and pageants are ever best seen by torchlight*, that all the way long we did nothing but talk of what an admirable queen she was, and how we would adventure our lives to do her service.'[20] Goodman was anything but a cynic, but, in recollection at least, he could see the royal appearance as a performance calculated to arouse precisely the emotions that he felt. And a performance it was. The queen's words to the crowd on that occasion – 'You may well have a greater prince, but you shall never have a more loving prince' – were repeated with variations throughout her reign. They were part of a stock of such phrases upon which she was able to draw when need arose. Her famous 'Golden Speech' of 1601 was little more than a particularly felicitous combination of these refrains – there is scarcely a phrase in it which she had not used again and again.

The whole public character was formed very early, then to be played and replayed with few changes for the next forty years. Already in her formal procession through the City on the day before her coronation, the keynotes were sounded. 'If a man should say well,' wrote one observer, 'he could not better term the city of London that time, than a stage wherein was showed the wonderful spectacle, of a noble hearted princess toward her most loving people, and the people's exceeding comfort in beholding so worthy a sovereign.' Where her sister Mary had been silent and aloof at her accession, Elizabeth bestowed her gratitude and affection on all. 'I will be as good unto you,' she assured her well-wishers, 'as ever queen was to her people . . . And persuade yourselves, that for the safety and quietness of you all, I will not spare, if need be, to spend my blood.'[21]

Mutual love and royal self-sacrifice – in her first address to Parliament some weeks later, she reiterated these themes and added a third, perhaps the most important of all: 'And in the end, this shall be for me sufficient, that a marble stone shall declare that a Queen, having reigned such a time, lived and died a virgin' (Neale, 1:49). The secular cult of the virgin was born, and it was not long before the young Elizabeth was portraying herself as a Virgin Mother: 'And so I assure you all,' she told the Commons in 1563, 'that, though after my death you may have many stepdames, yet shall you never have a more natural mother than I mean to be unto you all' (Neale, 1:109).[22]

Through the years, courtiers, poets, ballad makers, and artists provided many other cult images: in Ralegh's partial list, 'Cynthia, Phoebe, Flora, Diana and Aurora', to which we may add Astraea, Zabeta, Deborah, Laura, Oriana, and, of course, Belphoebe and Gloriana.[23] The gorgeous rituals of praise channeled national and religious sentiments into the worship of the prince, masked over and thus temporarily deflected deep social, political, and theological divisions in late sixteenth-century England, transformed Elizabeth's potentially disastrous sexual disadvantage into a supreme political virtue and imposed a subtle discipline upon aggressive fortune seekers. The best contemporary description of the effects of the romanticizing of royal power is by the queen's godson, Sir John Harington:

> Her mind was oftime like the gentle air that cometh from the westerly point in a summer's morn; 'twas sweet and refreshing to all around her. Her speech did win all affections, and her subjects did try to show all love to her commands; for she would say, 'her state did require her to command what she knew her people would willingly do from their own love to her.' Herein did she show her wisdom fully: for who did choose to lose her confidence; or who would withhold a show of love and obedience, when their Sovereign said it was their choice, and not her compulsion? Surely she did play well her tables to gain obedience thus without constraint: again, she could put forth such alterations, when obedience was lacking, as left no doubtings whose daughter she was.[24]

Harington's cunning description will repay close attention. It begins with the conventional rhetoric of adoration, the familiar language of countless panegyrics. The next sentence opens in the same mode – we have simply turned from her mind to her speech – but there is a subtle shift in the second clause: 'her subjects did try to show all love to her commands.' From mind to speech to commands – we have moved from poetical virtue to power. That power, however, is masked by the queen's persuasive speech, which not only transforms obedience into love but, in the phrase 'her state did require her to command,' suggests that it is *she* who is obeying an order while her subjects are privileged to act 'willingly'. We then turn to the subject who thinks he is beguiling his prince with a 'show of love and obedience' – what Castiglione called a 'salutary deception'[25] – but who is in fact being manipulated. The final sentence is almost shockingly explicit: first the picture of the queen as a clever gamester and then the allusion to Henry VIII, the perfect picture, in Ralegh's phrase, of a merciless prince. We have come a long way from the gentle air of a summer's morn! Behind all the cultic shows of love, in reserve but ready to be used when necessary, lies force. And yet the recognition of such force is not for Harington the decisive perception: 'We did all love her,' he concluded, 'for she said she loved us, and much wisdom she showed in this matter.'[26] The realism and irony remain, but they are caught up in an appreciation of the mutual interest of both ruler and subject in the transformation of power relations into erotic relations, an appreciation of the queen's ability at once to fashion her identity and to manipulate the identities of her followers.

It is to a culture so engaged in the shaping of identity, in dissimulation and the preservation of moral idealism, that Spenser addresses himself in defining 'the general intention and meaning' of the entire *Faerie Queene*:

the end of all the book, he writes to Ralegh, 'is to fashion a gentleman or noble person in vertuous and gentle discipline'.[27] The poem rests on the obvious but by no means universal assumption that a gentleman can be so fashioned, not simply in art but in life. We will, in the remainder of this chapter, consider the implications of one episode in this educative discipline, the destruction of the Bower of Bliss in book 2, canto 12. After a perilous voyage, as readers of *The Faerie Queene* will recall, Guyon, the knight of Temperance, arrives with his companion, the aged Palmer, at the realm of the beautiful and dangerous witch Acrasia. After quelling the threats of Acrasia's monstrous guards, they enter the witch's exquisite Bower where, aided by the Palmer's sober counsel, Guyon resists a series of sensual temptations. At the Bower's center they spy the witch, bending over a young man, and, rushing in upon her, they manage to capture her in a net. Guyon then systematically destroys the Bower and leads the tightly bound Acrasia away.

Inevitably, we will slight other moments in Spenser's vast work that qualify the perspective established by this one, but we can at least be certain that the perspective is important: like Falstaff's banishment, Othello's suicide speech, and the harsh punishment of Volpone, the close of book 2 of *The Faerie Queene* has figured in criticism as one of the great cruxes of English Renaissance literature. The destruction of Acrasia's Bower tests in a remarkably searching way our attitudes toward pleasure, sexuality, the body; tests too our sense of the relation of physical pleasure to the pleasure of aesthetic images and the relation of both of these to what Guyon calls the 'excellence' of man's creation. By 'tests' I do not mean that the work examines us to see if we know the right answer – the poetry of *The Faerie Queene*, as Paul Alpers has demonstrated, continually invites us to trust our own experience of its rich surface[28] – rather, this experience tends to reveal or define important aspects of ourselves. Thus when C.S. Lewis, invoking the 'exquisite health' of Spenser's imagination, characterizes the Bower as a picture of 'the whole sexual nature in disease', of 'male prurience and female provocation', indeed of 'skeptophilia', the reader familiar with Lewis's work will recognize links to his criticism of erotic passages in *Hero and Leander* and *Venus and Adonis*, links to his conception of maturity and of mental and moral health. This is not to deny that Lewis's brilliant account describes disturbing qualities that any attentive reader may recognize in the Bower, but it may help us to understand why he writes that 'the Bower of Bliss is not a place even of healthy animalism, or indeed of activity of any kind', whereas Spenser depicts Acrasia and her adolescent lover reposing 'after long wanton joys' and even (following Tasso) pictures droplets of sweat trilling down Acrasia's snowy breast 'through langor of her late sweet toil'. What for Spenser is the place 'Where Pleasure dwells in sensual delights' is for Lewis the realm only of frustration; all sexual activity is in this way reserved for the Garden of Adonis and hence tied securely to reproduction.[29]

At the other extreme, Yeats dismisses the moral judgments in the canto as 'unconscious hypocrisy'. Spenser, he tells us, 'is a poet of the delighted senses, and his song becomes most beautiful when he writes of those islands of Phaedria and Acrasia'.[30] And here again the reader familiar with Yeats will recognize certain perennial interests and values. The point would be too obvious to belabor, were it not for the fact that much Spenser commentary of the past several decades treats the Bower of Bliss and comparable passages in Spenser as if they were technical puzzles to be solved, as if one could determine their meaning quite apart from their effect upon the reader: 'The main subject of the bower of Bliss is disorder in the human body, the general image or picture is of the cause of that disorder, the imagery used in painting this picture is all of disorder, and the laws of decorum are satisfied.'[31] A sympathetic response like Hazlitt's to the canto's 'voluptuous pathos, and languid brilliancy of fancy' or a residual uneasiness about the destruction are dismissed as absurd. Indeed the Romantic readers of the poem implicitly stand charged as either degenerates or moral incompetents. To be sure, criticism has convincingly shown that the intellectual tradition behind Guyon's act of moral violence included not only Puritanism (which must, in any case, be understood as far more than a hysterical rejection of the flesh) but a rich matrix of classical and medieval thought.[32] Moreover, it has demonstrated that the description of the Bower itself is not an isolated 'beauty' that Spenser, in growing uneasiness and bad faith, decided to crush, but an episode embedded in a narrative that is shaped throughout by the poet's complex moral intelligence. The Romantic critics who have been discredited by this scholarship, however, had the virtue of fully acknowledging the Bower's intense erotic appeal. It is frequently said in reply that Spenser has given us a picture of healthy sexual enjoyment in the Garden of Adonis where 'Franckly each paramor his leman knowes' (3.6.41); but the comparison fails to take into consideration the fact that the Garden of Adonis, that great 'seminary' of living things, has almost no erotic appeal. The issue is not whether sexual consummation is desirable in Spenser, but why the particular erotic appeal of the Bower – more intense and sustained than any comparable passage in the poem – excites the hero's destructive violence.

We are told that after an initial attractiveness the Bower becomes stultifying, perverted, and frustrating or that the reader's task, like the hero's, is to interpret the images correctly, that is, to recognize the danger of 'lewd loves, and wasteful luxury' embodied in the Bower. I believe that one easily perceives that danger from the beginning and that much of the power of the episode derives precisely from the fact that this perception has little or no effect on the Bower's continued sensual power:

> Upon a bed of roses she was layd,
> As faint through heat, or dight to pleasant sin,
> And was arayd, or rather disarayd,
> All in a vele of silke and silver thin,
> That hid no whit her alablaster skin,
> But rather shewd more white if more might bee.

(2.12.77)

'Pleasant sin' – the moral judgment is not avoided or suspended but neither does it establish its dominion over the stanza; rather, for a moment it is absorbed into a world in which the normal conceptual boundaries are blurred: languor and energy, opacity and transparency, flesh and stone all merge. Similarly, the close of the famous rose song –

> Gather the rose of love, whilest yet is time,
> Whilest loving thou mayst loved be with equall crime –

invites us momentarily to transvalue the word 'crime', reading it as the equivalent of 'passion' or 'intensity', even as we continue to know that 'crime' cannot be so transvalued. We can master the iconography, read all the signs correctly, and still respond to the allure of the Bower. It is, as we shall see, the threat of this absorption that triggers Guyon's climactic violence. Temperance – the avoidance of extremes, the 'sober government' of the body, the achievement of the Golden Mean – must be constituted paradoxically by a supreme act of destructive excess.

The Bower's dangerous attractiveness is in sharp contrast to the Cave of Mammon, where Guyon's experience, and ours, is remarkable for the complete absence of sympathetic response to the temptation. The hero's journey through the Cave, past the fabulous displays of riches, embodies one of the basic patterns in the life of a temperate man: to be constantly confronted with baits which are at once spectacular and curiously easy to resist. The consequences of succumbing to these temptations are horrible – nothing short of being torn to pieces – but the temperate man resists far less for fear of the evil consequences than out of genuine indifference. That is, Mammon's offers are only attractive to those who are going to fall – a tautology not at all alien to Spenser or to Protestant thought. Guyon faints not as an emblem of tension, the strain of resisting temptation, but from want of food and sleep.

In the Bower of Bliss, Guyon's 'stubborne brest gan secret pleasaunce to embrace' (2.12.45), and he does not merely depart from the place of temptation but reduces it to ruins. To help us understand more fully why he must do so in order to play his part in Spenser's fashioning of a gentleman, we may invoke an observation made in *Civilization and Its Discontents*: 'It is impossible,' writes Freud, 'to overlook the extent to which civilization is built up upon a renunciation of instinct, how much it presupposes precisely the nonsatisfaction (by suppression, repression, or some other means?) of powerful instincts . . . Civilization behaves toward sexuality as a people or a stratum of its population does which has subjected another one to its exploitation.'[33] Modern criticism would make the destruction of the Bower easy by labeling Acrasia's realm sick, stagnant, futile and joyless, but Spenser, who participates with Freud in a venerable and profoundly significant intertwining of sexual and colonial discourse, accepts sexual colonialism only with a near-tragic sense of the cost. If he had wished, he could have unmasked Acrasia as a deformed hag, as he had exposed Duessa or as Ariosto had exposed (though more ambiguously) the enchantress Alcina, but instead Acrasia remains enticingly seductive to the end. She offers not simply sexual pleasure – 'long wanton joys' – but self-abandonment, erotic aestheticism, the melting of the will, the end of all quests; and Spenser understands, at the deepest level of his being, the appeal of such an end. Again and again his knights reach out longingly for resolution, closure, or release only to have it snatched from them or deferred; the whole of *The Faerie Queene* is the expression of an intense craving for release, which is overmastered only by a still more intense fear of release.

The Bower of Bliss must be destroyed not because its gratifications are unreal but because they threaten 'civility' – civilization – which for Spenser is achieved only through renunciation and the constant exercise of power. If this power inevitably entails loss, it is also richly, essentially creative; power is the guarantor of value, the shaper of all knowledge, the pledge of human redemption. Power may, as Bacon claimed, prohibit desire, but it is in its own way a version of the erotic: the violence directed against Acrasia's sensual paradise is both in itself an equivalent of erotic excess and a pledge of loving service to the royal mistress. Even when he most bitterly criticizes its abuses or records its brutalities, Spenser loves power and attempts to link his own art ever more closely with its symbolic and literal embodiment. *The Faerie Queene* is, as he insists again and again, wholly wedded to the autocratic ruler of the English state; the rich complexities of Spenser's art, its exquisite ethical discriminations in pursuit of the divine in man, are not achieved in spite of what is for us a repellent political ideology – the passionate worship of imperialism – but are inseparably linked to that ideology.

To say that Spenser worships power, that he is our originating and preeminent poet of empire, is not, in the heady manner of the late '60s, to condemn his work as shallow, craven or timeserving. Rather, his work, like Freud's, bears witness to the deep complicity of our moral imagination even in its noblest and most hauntingly beautiful manifestations in the great Western celebration of power. Alongside Freud, we may invoke Virgil, whose profound faith in Aeneas's personal

65

and world-historical mission and whose adoration of Augustus are tempered but never broken by a bitter sense of all that empire forces man to renounce, to flee from, to destroy. The example of Freud is useful, however, because it helps us to grasp the relation of our response to the Bower to our own contemporary preoccupations, to perceive as well those qualities in Renaissance culture which we are at this moment in our history uniquely situated to appreciate.

If all of civilization rests, as Freud argues, upon repression, nevertheless the particular civilization we produce and inhabit rests upon a complex technology of control whose origins we trace back to the Renaissance. We are no longer inclined to celebrate this period as the lifting of a veil of childish illusion, nor are we concerned to attack it in the name of a nostalgic vision of lost religious unity. The great syncretic structures of the Renaissance humanists no longer seem as intellectually compelling or as adequate to the period's major works of art as they once did, and even the imposition upon nature of an abstract mathematical logic, which Cassirer celebrates so eloquently as the birth of modern science, seems an equivocal achievement. We continue to see in the Renaissance the shaping of crucial aspects of our sense of self and society and the natural world, but we have become uneasy about our whole way of constituting reality. Above all, perhaps, we sense that the culture to which we are as profoundly attached as our face is to our skull is nonetheless a construct, a thing made, as temporary, time-conditioned and contingent as those vast European empires from whose power Freud drew his image of repression. We sense too that we are situated at the close of the cultural movement initiated in the Renaissance and that the places in which our social and psychological world seems to be cracking apart are those structural joints visible when it was first constructed. In the midst of the anxieties and contradictions attendant upon the threatened collapse of this phase of our civilization, we respond with passionate curiosity and poignancy to the anxieties and contradictions attendant upon its rise. To experience Renaissance culture is to feel what it was like to form our own identity, and we are at once more rooted and more estranged by the experience.

If it is true that we are highly sensitive to those aspects of the Renaissance that mark the early, tentative, conflict-ridden fashioning of modern consciousness, then *The Faerie Queene* is of quite exceptional significance, for Spenser's stated intention is precisely 'to fashion a gentleman or noble person in vertuous and gentle discipline'. This mirroring – the conscious purpose of the work seeming to enact the larger cultural movement – may help to account for the reader's sense of encountering in Spenser's poem the process of self-fashioning itself. In the Bower of Bliss that process is depicted as involving a painful sexual renunciation: in Guyon's destructive act we are invited to experience the ontogeny of our culture's violent resistance to a sensuous release for which it nevertheless yearns with a new intensity. The resistance is necessary for Spenser because what is threatened is 'our Selfe, whom though we do not see, / Yet each doth in him selfe it well perceiue to bee' (2.12.47). We can secure that self only through a restraint that involves the destruction of something intensely beautiful; to succumb to that beauty is to lose the shape of manhood and be transformed into a beast.[34]

The pleasure offered by Acrasia must be rejected with brutal decisiveness, but how exactly does one distinguish between inordinate or excessive sexual pleasure and temperate sexual pleasure? Spenser does not, after all, wish to reject pleasure entirely: if Guyon's destruction of the Bower of Bliss suggests 'the extent to which civilization is built up upon a renunciation of instinct', Scudamour's seizure of Amoret in the Temple of Venus, recounted in book 4, canto 10, suggests the extent to which civilization is built upon the controlled satisfaction of instinct, upon the ability to direct and profit from the 'kindly rage' of desire. Pleasure can even be celebrated, as in the nameless supplicant's hymn to Venus, provided that its legitimating function, its 'end' both in the sense of purpose and termination, be properly understood:

> So all things else, that nourish vitall blood,
> Soone as with fury thou doest them inspire,
> In generation seeke to quench their inward fire.
>
> (4.10.46)

Spenser cannot deny pleasure, even the extreme pleasure suggested by 'rage', 'fury', and 'fire', a legitimate function in sexuality. Quite apart from the poet's own experience and observation, it may have been extremely difficult even for figures far more suspicious of the body than Spenser to imagine an entirely pleasureless generation of children (though, as we shall see later, such a doctrine found occasional expression), for there seems to have been widespread medical belief in early modern Europe that for conception to take place, both the male and the female had to experience orgasm.[35] Virtually all of Spenser's representations of sexual fulfillment, including those he fully sanctions, seem close to excess and risk the breakdown of the carefully fashioned identity:

> Lightly he clipt her twixt his armes twaine,
> And streightly did embrace her body bright,
> Her body, late the prison of sad paine,
> Now the sweet lodge of loue and deare delight:
> But she faire Lady ouercommen quight

Of huge affection, did in pleasure melt,
And in sweete rauishment pourd out her spright:
No word they spake, nor earthly thing they felt,
But like two senceles stocks in long embracement dwelt.

(3.12.45 [1590])

The distinction upon which self-definition rests at the close of book 2 – between temperate pleasure and inordinate pleasure – can only be understood in terms of a further distinction between a pleasure that serves some useful purpose, some virtuous end, and a pleasure that does not. Thus the denizens of the Bower acknowledge time solely as an inducement to the eager satisfaction of desire here and now, before the body's decay, and not as the agency of purposeful direction. That direction – expressed in *The Faerie Queene* as a whole by the idea of the *quest* – is for sexuality found in the power of love to inspire virtuous action and ultimately, with the sanctification of marriage, in the generation of offspring. Generation restores the sense of linear progression to an experience that threatens to turn in upon itself, reveling in its own exquisite beauty. A pleasure that serves as its own end, that claims to be self-justifying rather than instrumental, purposeless rather than generative, is immoderate and must be destroyed, lest it undermine the power that Spenser worships.

But this way of distinguishing temperate and inordinate pleasure is less stable than it first appears, for desire may be 'quenched' in generation but is not itself temperate. On the contrary, generation only takes place because all living beings – men and beasts – are 'priuily pricked with' Venus's 'lustfull powres' (4.10.45). All attempts to restrain these powers must be overcome for fruitful sexual union to occur: thus Scudamour must seize Amoret from the restraining and moderating figures – Womanhood, Shamefastness, Modesty, Silence, Obedience, and the like – who sit at the feet of Venus's image. The fashioning of a gentleman then depends upon the imposition of control over inescapably immoderate sexual impulses that, for the survival of the race, must constantly recur: the discriminations upon which a virtuous and gentle discipline is based are forever in danger of collapsing. Hence, I suggest, the paradox of the Knight of Temperance's seemingly intemperate attack upon the Bower of Bliss: Guyon destroys the Bower and ties Acrasia 'in chaines of adamant' – 'For nothing else might keepe her safe and sound' – in a violent attempt to secure that principle of difference necessary to fashion the self. 'Excess' is defined not by some inherent imbalance or impropriety, but by the mechanism of control, the exercise of restraining power. And if excess is virtually invented by this power, so too, paradoxically, power is invented by excess: this is why Acrasia cannot be destroyed, why she and what she is made to represent must continue to exist, forever the object of the destructive quest. For were she not to exist as a constant threat, the power Guyon embodies would also cease to exist. After all, we can assume that the number of people who actually suffer in any period from *melt-down* as a result of sexual excess is quite small (comparable to the number of cases of that spontaneous combustion depicted by Dickens), small enough to raise questions about the motives behind the elaborate moral weaponry designed to combat the supposed danger. The perception of the threat of excess enables institutional power to have a legitimate 'protective' and 'healing' interest in sexuality, to exercise its constitutive control over the inner life of the individual.

Self-fashioning, the project of Spenser's poem and of the culture in which it participates, requires both an enabling institution, a source of power and communal values – in *The Faerie Queene*, the court of Gloriana – and a perception of the not-self, of all that lies outside, or resists, or threatens identity. The destruction of the Bower is the fulfillment of the knight's quest – the institution has been glorified, the demonic other at once identified and destroyed – but the inherent contradictions in the relations between temperance and pleasure, restraint and gratification have been deferred rather than resolved. What appears for a moment as decisive closure gives way to renewed efforts, other quests, which, as we have already glimpsed in Scudamour, attempt to compensate for the limitations, the sacrifice of essential values, implicit in the earlier resolution.

In a remarkable study of how societies make 'tragic choices' in the allocation of scarce resources (e.g. kidney machines) or in the determination of high risks (e.g. the military draft), Guido Calabresi and Philip Bobbitt observe that by complex mixtures of approaches, societies attempt to avert 'tragic results, that is, results which imply the rejection of values which are proclaimed to be fundamental': these approaches may succeed for a time, but it will eventually become apparent that some sacrifice of values has taken place, whereupon 'fresh mixtures of methods will be tried, structured . . . by the shortcomings of the approaches they replace.'[36] These too will in time give way to others in a 'strategy of successive moves' that comprises an 'intricate game', a game that reflects the simultaneous perception of a tragic choice and the determination to 'forget' that perception in an illusory resolution. Driven by the will to deny its own perception of tragic conflict inherent in the fashioning of civility, *The Faerie Queene* resembles such an intricate game. Thus a particular 'move', here the destruction of the Bower, represents in effect a brilliant solution, constructed out of the most conventional materials and yet unmistakably original, of the uneasy, aggressive, masculine court identity fashioned by Wyatt: male sexual aggression – the hunt, the loathing, the desire to master – is yoked to the service of ideal values embodied in a female ruler, and it is through this service that identity is achieved. The conception obviously depends upon Queen Elizabeth's own extraordinary manipulation of a secular mythology infused with displaced religious veneration, yet Spenser manages to suggest that the 'vertuous and gentle discipline' he chronicles is not limited by its historical circumstances. Like Elizabeth herself, Spenser appeals to an image of female power – the benevolent and nurturing life force – that transcends a local habitation and a name. But this 'solution' has its costs that Spenser, as we have seen, represents with extraordinary power and that drive him to further constructions.

Each heroic quest is at once a triumph and a flight, an escape from the disillusionment glimpsed for a brief moment on the Mount of Contemplation and again at the close of the Mutabilitie Cantos. Spenser's knights live in the profound conviction that there is a moral task set for themselves by virtue of the power of Gloriana, a demonic object out there to be encountered and defeated. Each triumphant act of virtuous violence confirms this conviction, defending it from all that would undermine the rightness of the moral mission, all that would question the possibility of achieving a just, coherent, stable identity anchored in the ardent worship of power. But the destruction of the Bower of Bliss suggests the extent to which each self-constituting act is haunted by inadequacy and loss.

The experience I have just described is, insofar as the work retains its power, common to us all, embedded in each of our personal histories, though a protective cultural amnesia may have led us to forget it until we re-experience it in art. We need, at this level, bring nothing to the text but ourselves. Fuller understanding, however, requires that we confront not only personal history but the history of peoples. We must, as Clifford Geertz suggests, incorporate the work of art into the texture of a particular pattern of life, a collective experience that transcends it and completes its meaning.[37] If Spenser told his readers a story, they listened, and listened with pleasure, because they themselves, in the shared life of their culture, were telling versions of that story again and again, recording the texts on themselves and on the world around them. In this sense, it is not adequate for a cultural poetics to describe the destruction of the Bower of Bliss or any literary text as a *reflection* of its circumambient culture; Spenser's poem is one manifestation of a symbolic language that is inscribed by history on the bodies of living beings as, in Kafka's great parable, the legal sentences are inscribed by the demonic penal machine on the bodies of the condemned.

It is not possible within the scope of this chapter to outline the dense network of analogies, repetitions, correspondences and homologies within which even this one episode of Spenser's immense poem is embedded. But I can point briefly to three reiterations by the culture of important elements of the destruction of the Bower of Bliss: the European response to the native cultures of the New World, the English colonial struggle in Ireland, and the Reformation attack on images. The examples suggest the diversity of such reiterations – from the general culture of Europe, to the national policy of England, to the ideology of a small segment of the nation's population – while their shared elements seem to bear out Freud's master analogy: 'Civilization behaves towards sexuality as a people or a stratum of its population does which has subjected another one to its exploitation.'

In the texts written by early explorers of the New World, a long, arduous voyage, fraught with fabulous dangers and trials, brings the band of soldiers, sailors, and religious fathers – knight, boatman and palmer – to a world of riches and menace. The adventurer's morality is the morality of the ship, where order, discipline, and constant labor are essential for survival, and they are further united by their explicit religious faith and by an unspoken but powerful male bond. The lands they encounter are often achingly beautiful: 'I am completely persuaded in my own mind,' writes Columbus in 1498, 'that the Terrestrial Paradise is in the place I have described.'[38] So Spenser likens the Bower of Bliss to Eden itself, 'if ought with Eden mote compayre', and lingers over its landscape of wish fulfillment, a landscape at once lavish and moderate, rich in abundant vegetation and yet 'steadfast', 'attempred', and well 'disposed'. If these descriptive terms are shared in the Renaissance by literary romance and travelers' accounts, it is because the two modes of vision are mutually reinforcing: Spenser, like Tasso before him, makes frequent allusion to the New World – to 'all that now America men call' (2.10.72) – while when Cortes and his men looked down upon the valley of Mexico, they thought, says a participant, of Amadis of Gaule.[39] The American landscape has to European eyes the mysterious intimations of a hidden art, as Ralegh's description of the Orinoco suggests: 'On both sides of this river, we passed the most beautiful country that ever mine eyes beheld: and whereas all that we had seen before was nothing but woods, prickles, bushes, and thorns, here we beheld plains of twenty miles in length, the grass short and green, and in diverse parts groves of trees by themselves, as if they had been by all the art and labor in the world so made of purpose: and still as we rowed, the Deer came down feeding by the water's side, as if they had been used to a keeper's call.'[40]

Spenser, to be sure, has no need of the 'as if' – he credits art as well as nature with the making of the paradisal landscape – but this difference should not suggest too sharp a contrast between an 'artless' world described by the early voyagers and the poet's 'artificial' Bower. The Europeans again and again record their astonishment at the Indians' artistic brilliance: 'Surely I marvel not at the gold and precious stones, but wonder with astonishment with what industry and laborious art the curious workmanship exceedeth the matter and substance. I beheld a thousand shapes, and a thousand forms, which I cannot express in writing; so that in my judgment I never saw anything which might more allure the eyes of men with the beauty thereof.'[41]

But all of this seductive beauty harbors danger, danger not only in the works of art which are obviously idolatrous but in the Edenic landscape itself. The voyagers to the New World are treated, like Guyon and the Palmer, to mild air that 'breathed forth sweet spirit and holesom smell' (2.12.51), and they react with mingled wonder and resistance: 'Smooth and pleasing words might be spoken of the sweet odors, and perfumes of these countries,' writes Peter Martyr, 'which we purposely omit, because they make rather for the effeminating of men's minds, than for the maintenance of good behavior.'[42] Similarly, if the New World could be portrayed as a place 'In which all pleasures plenteously abownd, / And none does others happiness envye' (2.10.58), a Golden World, it could also serve – often in the same text and by virtue of the same set of perceptions – as a screen on to which Europeans projected their darkest and yet most compelling fantasies: 'These folk live like beasts without any reasonableness, and the women be also as common. And the men hath conversation with the women who that they been or who they first meet, is she his sister, his mother, his daughter, or any other kindred. And the women be very hot and disposed to lecherdness. And they eat also one another. The man eateth his wife, his children . . . And that land is right full of folk, for they live commonly 300 year and more as with sickness they die not.'[43] In 1582 Richard Madox, in Sierra Leone with Edward Fenton's expedition, heard from a Portuguese trader comparable stories of African customs: 'He reported that near the mountains of the moon there is a queen, an empress of all these Amazons, a witch and a cannibal who daily feeds on the flesh of boys. She ever remains unmarried, but she has intercourse with a great number of men by whom she begets offspring. The kingdom, however, remains hereditary to the daughters, not to the sons.'[44]

Virtually all the essential elements of the travel narratives recur in Spenser's episode: the sea voyage, the strange, menacing creatures, the paradisal landscape with its invisible art, the gold and silver carved with 'curious imagery', the threat of effeminacy checked by the male bond, the generosity and wantonness of the inhabitants, the arousal of a longing at once to enter and to destroy. Even cannibalism and incest which are the extreme manifestations of the disordered and licentious life attributed to the Indians are both subtly suggested in the picture of Acrasia hanging over her adolescent lover:

> And oft inclining downe with kisses light,
> For fear of waking him, his lips bedewd,

And through his humid eyes did sucke his spright
Quite molten into lust and pleasure lewd.

(2.12.73)

In book 6 of *The Faerie Queene* Spenser offers a more explicit version
of these dark imaginings;[45] here in book 2 the violation of the taboos
is carefully displaced, so that the major threat is not pollution but the
very attractiveness of the vision. Sexual excess has caused in Verdant
a melting of the soul,[46] and this internal pathology is matched by an
external disgrace:

His warlike armes, the idle instruments
Of sleeping praise, were hong vpon a tree,
And his braue shield, full of old moniments,
Was fowly ra'st, that none the signes might see.

(2.12.80)

The entire fulfillment of desire leads to the effacement of signs and hence
to the loss both of memory, depicted in canto 10 and of the capacity for
heroic effort, depicted in the figure of the boatman who ferries Guyon
and the Palmer to the Bower:

Forward they passe, and strongly he them rowes,
Vntill they nigh vnto that gulfe arryve,
Where streame more violent and greedy growes:
Then he with all his puisaunce doth stryve
To strike his oares, and mightily doth dryve
The hollow vessell through the threatfull wave,
Which, gaping wide, to swallow them alyve
In th'huge abysse of his engulfing grave,
Doth rore at them in vaine, and with great terrour rave.

(2.12.5)

The threat of being engulfed that is successfully resisted here is
encountered again at the heart of the Bower in the form not of
cannibalistic violence but of erotic absorption. Verdant, his head in
Acrasia's lap, has sunk into a narcotic slumber: all 'manly' energy, all
purposeful direction, all sense of difference upon which 'civil' order
is founded have been erased. This slumber corresponds to what the
Europeans perceived as the *pointlessness* of native cultures. It was as if
millions of souls had become unmoored, just as their ancestors had, it
was thought, somehow lost their way and wandered out of sight of the
civilized world. Absorbed into a vast wilderness, they lost all memory of
the true history of their race and of the one God and sank into a spiritual
and physical lethargy. It is difficult to recover the immense force which

this charge of idleness carried; some sense may be gauged perhaps from the extraordinary harshness with which vagabonds were treated.[47]

That the Indians were idle, that they lacked all work discipline, was proved, to the satisfaction of the Europeans, by the demonstrable fact that they made wretched slaves, dying after a few weeks or even days of hard labor. And if they were freed from servitude, they merely slid back into their old customs: 'For being idle and slothful, they wander up and down, and return to their old rites and ceremonies and foul and mischievous acts.'[48] That the European voyagers of the sixteenth century, surely among the world's most restless and uprooted generations, should accuse the Indians of 'wandering up and down' is bitterly ironic, but the accusation served as a kind of rudder, an assurance of stability and direction. And this assurance is confirmed by the vast projects undertaken to fix and enclose the native populations in the mines, in encomiendas, in fortified hamlets, and ultimately, in mass graves. A whole civilization was caught in a net and, like Acrasia, bound in chains of adamant; their gods were melted down, their palaces and temples razed, their groves felled. 'And of the fairest late, now made the fowlest place.'[49]

Guyon, it will be recalled, makes no attempt to destroy the Cave of Mammon; he simply declines its evil invitations which leave him exhausted but otherwise unmoved. But the Bower of Bliss he destroys with a rigor rendered the more pitiless by the fact that his stubborn breast, we are told, embraced 'secret pleasance'. In just this way, Europeans destroyed Indian culture not despite those aspects of it that attracted them but in part at least because of them. The violence of the destruction was regenerative; they found in it a sense of identity, discipline and holy faith.[50] In tearing down what both appealed to them and sickened them, they strengthened their power to resist their dangerous longings, to repress antisocial impulses, to conquer the powerful desire for release. And the conquest of desire had the more power because it contained within itself a version of that which it destroyed: the power of Acrasia's sensuality to erase signs and upset temperate order is simultaneously attacked and imitated in Guyon's destruction of the exquisite Bower, while European 'civility' and Christianity were never more ferociously assaulted than in the colonial destruction of a culture that was accused of mounting just such an assault.

One measure of European complicity in what they destroyed is the occurrence of apostasy or at least fantasies of apostasy. Bernal Diaz del Castillo tells one such story about a common seaman named Gonzalo Guerrero who had survived a shipwreck in the Yucatan and refused to rejoin his compatriots when, eight years later, Cortes managed to send word to him: 'I am married and have three children, and they look on me as a *Cacique* here, and a captain in time of war. Go, and God's blessing be with you. But my face is tattooed and my ears are pierced. What would the Spaniards say if they saw me like this? And look how handsome these children of mine are!'[51] The emissary reminded him that he was a Christian and 'should not destroy his soul for the sake of an Indian woman', but Guerrero clearly regarded his situation as an improvement in his lot. Indeed Cortes learned that it was at Guerrero's instigation that the Indians had, three years before, attacked an earlier Spanish expedition to the Yucatan.

We have, in the tattooed Spanish seaman, encountered an analogue to those disfigured beasts who try to defend the Bower against Guyon and, in particular, to Gryll, who, having been metamorphosed by Acrasia into a hog, 'repyned greatly' at his restoration. Such creatures give a local habitation and a name to those vague feelings of longing and complicity that permeate accounts of a sensuous life that must be rejected and destroyed. And if the Yucatan seems too remote from Spenser's world, we need only turn to our second frame of reference, Elizabethan rule in Ireland, to encounter similar stories. In Spenser's own *View of the Present State of Ireland*, probably written in 1596, Eudoxius asks, 'is it possible that an Englishman brought up naturally in such sweet civility as England affords could find such liking in that barbarous rudeness that he should forget his own nature and forgo his own nation? . . . Is it possible that any should so far grow out of frame that they should in so short space quite forget their country and their own names? . . . Could they ever conceive any such devilish dislike of their own natural country as that they would be ashamed of her name, and bite off her dug from which they sucked life?'[52] In reply, Spenser's spokesman, Irenius, speaks bitterly of those Englishmen who are 'degenerated and grown almost mere Irish, yea and more malicious to the English than the very Irish themselves' (48); these metamorphosed wretches even prefer to speak Irish, although, as Eudoxius observes, 'they should (methinks) rather take scorn to acquaint their tongues thereto, for it hath been ever the use of the conqueror to despise the language of the conquered and to force him by all means to learn his.'[53] Irenius locates the source of this unnatural linguistic betrayal, this effacement of signs, in the subversive power of Irish women. The rebel Englishmen will 'bite off her dug from which they sucked life' because another breast has intervened: 'the child that sucketh the milk of the nurse must of necessity learn his first speech of her, the which being the first that is enured to his tongue is ever after most pleasing unto him,' and 'the speech being Irish, the heart must needs be Irish.'[54] The evil metamorphosis caused by Irish wetnurses is completed by miscegenation: 'the child taketh most of his nature of the mother . . . for by them they are first framed and fashioned' (68). As the fashioning of a gentleman is threatened in book 2 of *The Faerie Queene* by Acrasia, so it is threatened in Ireland by the native women.

It is often remarked that the *View*, which Spenser wrote after his completion of *The Faerie Queene*, expresses a hardening of attitude, a harsh and bitter note brought on by years of tension and frustration. It may well reflect such a change in tone, but its colonial policies are consistent with those with which Spenser had been associated from his arrival in Ireland as Lord Grey's secretary in 1580, that is, from the time in which *The Faerie Queene* was in the early stages of its composition. When Spenser 'wrote of Ireland', Yeats comments, 'he wrote as an official, and out of thoughts and emotions that had been organized by the State.'[55] It was not only in his capacity as an official that Spenser did so: in art and in life, his conception of identity, as we have seen, is wedded to his conception of power, and after 1580, of colonial power. For all Spenser's claims of relation to the noble Spencers of Wormleighton and Althorp, he remains a 'poor boy', as he is designated in the Merchant Taylor's School and at Cambridge, until Ireland. It is there that he is fashioned a gentleman, there that he is transformed from the former denizen of East Smithfield to the 'undertaker' – the grim pun unintended but profoundly appropriate – of 3028 acres of Munster land. From his first acquisition in 1582, this land is at once the assurance of his status – the 'Gent'. Next to his name – and of his insecurity: ruined abbeys, friaries expropriated by the crown, plow lands rendered vacant by famine and execution, property forfeited by those whom Spenser's superiors declared traitors.

For what services, we ask, was Spenser being rewarded? And we answer, blandly, for being a colonial administrator. But the answer, which implies pushing papers in a Dublin office through endless days of tedium, is an evasion. Spenser's own account presses in upon us the fact that he was involved intimately, on an almost daily basis, throughout the island, in the destruction of Hiberno–Norman civilization, the exercise of a brutal force that had few if any of the romantic trappings with which Elizabeth contrived to soften it at home.[56] Here, on the periphery, Spenser was an agent of and an apologist for massacre, the burning of mean hovels and of crops with the deliberate intention of starving the inhabitants, forced relocation of peoples, the manipulation of treason charges so as to facilitate the seizure of lands, the endless repetition of acts of military 'justice' calculated to intimidate and break the spirit. We may wish to tell ourselves that a man of Spenser's sensitivity and gifts may have mitigated the extreme policies of ruthless men, but it appears that he did not recoil in the slightest from this horror, did not even feel himself, like his colleague Geoffrey Fenton, in mild opposition to it.[57] Ireland is not only in book 5 of *The Faerie Queene*; it pervades the poem. Civility is won through the exercise of violence over what is deemed barbarous and evil, and the passages of love and leisure are not moments set apart from this process but its rewards.

'Every detail of the huge resettlement project' in Munster, writes Spenser's biographer Judson, 'was known to him as it unfolded, including its intricate legal aspects, and hence his final acquisition of thousands of acres of forfeited lands was entirely natural'.[58] Natural perhaps, but equally natural that his imagination is haunted by the nightmares of savage attack – the 'outrageous dreadfull yelling cry' of Maleger, 'His body leane and meagre as a rake' and yet seemingly impossible to kill[59] – and of absorption. The latter fear may strike us as less compelling than the former – there is much talk, after all, of the 'savage brutishness and loathly filthiness' of native customs – but the Elizabethans were well aware, as we have already seen, that many of their most dangerous enemies were Englishmen who had been metamorphosed into 'mere Irish'. Spenser's own career is marked by conflicting desires to turn his back on Ireland forever and to plant himself ever more firmly in Munster;[60] if the latter course scarcely represented an abandonment of English civility, it may nonetheless have felt like the beginning of the threatened transformation. I do not propose that Spenser feared such a metamorphosis on his own behalf – he may, for all we know, have been obscurely attracted to some of the very things he worked to destroy, though of this attraction our only record is his poetry's fascination with the excess against which it struggles – only that he was haunted by the fact that it had occurred over generations to so many of his countrymen. The enemy for Spenser then is as much a tenacious and surprisingly seductive way of life as it is a military force, and thus alongside a ruthless policy of mass starvation and massacre, he advocates the destruction of native Irish identity.

Spenser is one of the first English writers to have what we may call a field theory of culture, that is, the conception of a nation not simply as an institutional structure or a common race, but as a complex network of beliefs, folk customs, forms of dress, kinship relations, religious mythology, aesthetic norms and specialized modes of production. Therefore, to *reform* a people one must not simply conquer it – though conquest is an absolute necessity – but eradicate the native culture: in the case of Ireland, eliminate (by force, wherever needed) the carrows, horseboys, jesters and other 'idlers'; transform the mass of the rural population from cowherds with their dangerous freedom of movement to husbandmen; break up the clans or sects; prohibit public meetings, councils and assemblies; transform Irish art, prohibiting the subversive epics of the bards; make schoolchildren ashamed of their parents' backwardness; discourage English settlers from speaking Irish; prohibit traditional Irish dress; eliminate elections of chiefs, divisible inheritance and the payment of fines to avoid capital punishment. And always in this immense undertaking, there is the need for constant vigilance and unrelenting pressure, exercised not only upon the wild Irish but upon the civilizing English themselves. 'So much,' writes Spenser, 'can liberty and ill example do' (63) that the threat of seduction is always present, and the first inroad of this seduction is misguided compassion: 'Therefore, by all means it must be foreseen and assured that after once entering into this course of reformation, there be afterwards no remorse or drawing back' (110). Pitiless destruction is here not a stain but a virtue; after all, the English themselves had to be brought from barbarism to civility by a similar conquest centuries before, a conquest that must be ever renewed lest the craving for 'liberty and natural freedom' (12) erupt again. The colonial violence inflicted upon the Irish is at the same time the force that fashions the identity of the English.

We have returned then to the principle of regenerative violence and thus to the destruction of the Bower of Bliss. The act of tearing down is the act of fashioning; the promise of the opening stanza of canto 12 – 'Now gins this goodly frame of Temperance / Fairely to rise' – is fulfilled at the close in the inventory of violence:

> But all those pleasant bowres and Pallace braue,
> *Guyon* broke downe, with rigour pittilesse;
> Ne ought their goodly workmanship might saue
> Them from the tempest of his wrathfulnesse,
> But that their blisse he turn'd to balefulnesse;
> Their groues he feld, their gardins did deface,
> Their arbers spoyle, their Cabinets suppresse,
> Their banket houses burne, their buildings race,
> And of the fairest late, now made the fowlest place.

(2.12.83)

If the totality of the destruction, the calculated absence of 'remorse or drawing back', links this episode to the colonial policy of Lord Grey which Spenser undertook to defend, the language of the stanza recalls yet another government policy, our third 'restoration' of the narrative: the destruction of Catholic Church furnishings. In the *Inventarium monumentorum superstitionis* of 1566, for example, we may hear repeated echoes of Guyon's acts:

> Imprimis one rood with Mary and John and the rest of the painted pictures – burnt . . .
>
> Item our rood loft – pulled down, sold and defaced . . .
>
> Item our mass books with the rest of such feigned fables and peltering popish books – burnt . . .
>
> Item 3 altar stones – broken in pieces . . .[61]

In 1572 Spenser, a student at Pembroke, could have witnessed a similar scene at nearby Gonville and Caius where the authorities licensed the destruction of 'much popish trumpery'. Books and vestments, holy water stoops and images were 'mangled, torn to pieces, and mutilated' – *discerpta dissecta et lacerata* – before being consigned to the bonfire.[62]

There is about the Bower of Bliss the taint of a graven image designed to appeal to the sensual as opposed to the spiritual nature, to turn the wonder and admiration of men away from the mystery of divine love. In the Bower the love survives only in the uncanny parody of the Pietà suggested by Verdant cradled in Acrasia's arms. It is not surprising then to find a close parallel between the evils of the Bower and the evils attributed to the misuse of religious images. Devotion to the representations of the Madonna and saints deflected men from the vigorous pursuit of the good, enticed them into idleness and effeminacy. With their destruction, as Hugh Latimer writes, men could turn 'from ladyness to Godliness'.[63] Statues of the virgin were dismembered by unruly crowds, frescoes were whitewashed over and carvings in 'Lady Chapels' were smashed, in order to free men from thralldom to what an Elizabethan lawyer calls, in describing the pope, 'the witch of the world'.[64]

But the art destroyed by Guyon does not pretend to image holy things; it is designed to grace its surroundings, to delight its viewers with its exquisite workmanship. Against such art there could be no charge of idolatry, no invocation of the Deuteronomic injunctions against graven images, unless art itself were idolatrous. And it is precisely this possibility that is suggested by Guyon's iconoclasm, for Acrasia's realm is lavishly described in just those terms which the defenders of poetry in the Renaissance reserved for imagination's noblest achievements. The Bower's art imitates nature, but is privileged to choose only those aspects of nature that correspond to man's ideal visions; its music is so perfectly melodious and 'attempred' that it blends with all of nature in one harmony, so that the whole world seems transformed into a musical 'consort'; above all, the calculation and effort that lie behind the manifestation of such perfect beauty are entirely concealed:

> And that which all faire workes doth most aggrace,
> The art, which all that wrought, appeared in no place.

'Aggrace' has virtually a technical significance here; Castiglione had suggested in *The Courtier* that the elusive quality of 'grace' could be acquired through the practice of *sprezzatura*, 'so as to conceal all art and make whatever is done or said appear to be without effort and almost without any thought about it.'[65]

Spenser deeply distrusts this aesthetic, even as he seems to pay homage to its central tenets; indeed the concealment of art, its imposition upon an unsuspecting observer, is one of the great recurring evils in *The Faerie Queene*. Acrasia as demonic artist and whore combines the attributes of those other masters of disguise, Archimago and Duessa.[66] Their evil depends upon the ability to mask and forge, to conceal their satanic artistry; their defeat depends upon the power to unmask, the strength to turn from magic to strenuous virtue. Keith Thomas notes that in the sixteenth and seventeenth centuries the Protestant 'emphasis upon the virtues of hard work and application . . . both reflected and helped to create a frame of mind which spurned the cheap solutions offered by magic, not just because they were wicked, but because they were too easy.'[67] *Sprezzatura*, which sets out to efface all signs of 'hard work and application', is a cult of the 'too easy', a kind of aesthetic magic.

But what can Spenser offer in place of this discredited aesthetic? The answer lies in an art that constantly calls attention to its own processes, that includes within itself framing devices and signs of its own createdness. Far from hiding its traces, *The Faerie Queene* announces its status as art object at every turn, in the archaic diction, the use of set pieces, the elaborate sound effects, the very characters and plots of romance. For the allegorical romance is a mode that virtually by definition abjures all concealment; the artist who wishes to hide the fact that he is making a fiction would be ill-advised to write about the Faerie Queene.

If you fear that images may make a blasphemous claim to reality, that they may become idols that you will be compelled to worship, you may smash all images or you may create images that announce themselves at every moment as things made. Thus did the sixteenth-century kabbalists of Safed circumvent the Hebraic injunction against images of the Godhead;[68] their visions are punctuated by reminders that these are merely metaphors, not to be confused with divine reality itself. So too did the more moderate Protestant Reformers retain a version of the Communion, reminding the participants that the ceremony was a symbol and not a celebration of the real presence of God's body. And so does Spenser, in the face of deep anxiety about the impure claims of art, save art for himself and his readers by making its createdness explicit. Images, to be sure, retain their power, as the sensuous description of the Bower of Bliss attests, and Spenser can respond to the charge that his 'famous antique history' is merely 'th'aboundance of an idle braine . . . and painted forgery' by reminding his readers of the recent discoveries, of 'The Indian Peru', 'The *Amazons* huge riuer', and 'fruitfullest *Virginia*':

> Yet all these were, when no man did them know;
> Yet haue from wisest ages hidden beene:
> And later times things more vnknowne shall show.
> When then should witlesse man so much misweene
> That nothing is, but that which he hath seene?
> What if within the Moones faire shining spheare?

What if in euery other starre vnseene
Of other worldes he happily should heare?
He wonder would much more: yet such to some appeare.

(2 Proem 3)

For a moment the work hovers on the brink of asserting its status as a newfound land, but Spenser immediately shatters such an assertion by invoking the gaze of royal power:

And thou, O fairest Princesse vnder sky,
In this faire mirrhour maist behold thy face,
And thine owne realmes in lond of Faery,
And in this antique Image thy great auncestry.

(2 Proem 4)

In an instant the 'other world' has been transformed into a mirror; the queen turns her gaze upon a shining sphere hitherto hidden from view and sees her own face, her own realms, her own ancestry. That which threatens to exist independent of religious and secular ideology, that is, of what we believe – 'Yet all these were, when no man did them know' – is revealed to be the ideal image of that ideology. And hence it need not be feared or destroyed: iconoclasm gives way to appropriation, violence to colonization. J.H. Elliott remarks that the most significant aspect of the impact of the new world upon the old is its insignificance: men looked at things unseen before, things alien to their own culture, and saw only themselves.[69] Spenser asserts that Faerie Land is a new world, another Peru or Virginia, only so that he may colonize it in the very moment of its discovery. The 'other world' becomes mirror becomes aesthetic image, and this transformation of the poem from a thing discovered to a thing made, from existence to the representation of existence is completed with the poet's turn from 'vaunt' to apology:

The which O pardon me thus to enfold
In couert vele, and wrap in shadowes light,
That feeble eyes your glory may behold,
Which else could not endure those beames bright,
But would be dazled with exceeding light.

(2 Proem 5)

The queen is deified precisely in the act of denying art's claim to ontological dignity, to the possession or embodiment of reality.

Such embodiment is the characteristic achievement of great drama, of Marlowe and supremely of Shakespeare, whose constant allusions to the fictionality of his creations only serve paradoxically to question the status of everything outside themselves. By contrast, Spenser's profoundly *undramatic* art, in the same movement by which it wards off idolatry,

81

wards off this radical questioning of everything that exists. That is, if art like Shakespeare's realizes the power we glimpsed in Wyatt, the power in Althusser's words, to 'make us "perceive" . . . from *the inside*, by an *internal distance*, the very ideology' in which it is held, Spenserean allegory may be understood as a countermeasure: it opens up an internal distance within art itself by continually referring the reader out to a fixed authority beyond the poem. Spenser's art does not lead us to perceive ideology critically, but rather affirms the existence and inescapable moral power of ideology as that principle of truth toward which art forever yearns. It is art whose status is questioned in Spenser, not ideology; indeed, art is questioned precisely to spare ideology that internal distantiation it undergoes in the work of Shakespeare or Marlowe. In *The Faerie Queene* reality as given by ideology always lies safely outside the bounds of art, in a different realm, distant, infinitely powerful, perfectly good. 'The hallmark of Spenserean narration,' Paul Alpers acutely observes, 'is confidence in locutions which are at the same time understood to be provisional.'[70] Both the confidence and the provisionality stem from the externality of true value, order, meaning. For Spenser this is the final colonialism, the colonialism of language, yoked to the service of a reality forever outside itself, dedicated to 'the Most High, Mightie, and Magnificent Empresse . . . Elizabeth by the Grace of God Queene of England Fraunce and Ireland and of Virginia, Defendour of the Faith.'

Notes

1. JACOB BURCKHARDT, *The Civilization of the Renaissance in Italy* (1860). For criticism of Burckhardt, see WALLACE FERGUSON, *The Renaissance in Historical Thought* (Boston: Houghton Mifflin, 1948), chaps. 7–11.
2. See PAUL O. KRISTELLER, *Renaissance Thought: The Classic, Scholastic, and Humanist Strains* (New York: Harper & Row [Harper Torchbooks], 1961); HANNA H. GRAY, 'Renaissance Humanism: The Pursuit of Eloquence', in *Renaissance Essays*, eds Kristeller and Philip P. Wiener (New York: Harper & Row [Harper Torchbooks], 1968), pp. 199–216. On relations between rhetoric and other fields, see ROSEMOND TUVE, *Elizabethan and Metaphysical Imagery* (Chicago: University of Chicago Press, 1947); JERROLD SEIGEL, *Rhetoric and Philosophy in Renaissance Humanism* (Princeton: Princeton University Press, 1968); NANCY S. STREUVER, *The Language of History in the Renaissance* (Princeton: Princeton University Press, 1970). On rhetoric in the English school curriculum, see T.W. BALDWIN, *William Shakespere's Small Latine and Lesse Greeke*, 2 vols (Urbana, Ill.: University of Illinois Press, 1944).
3. On the theatricality of Renaissance culture, see JEAN DUVIGNAUD, *Sociologie du théâtre: Essai sur les ombres collectives* (Paris: Presses Universitaires de France, 1965).
4. See NORBERT ELIAS, *The Civilizing Process*, p. 73: 'The problem of behavior in society had obviously taken on such importance in this period that even people of extraordinary talent and renown did not disdain to concern

themselves with it . . . Erasmus' treatise [*De civilitate morum puerilium*] comes at a time of social regrouping. It is the expression of the fruitful transitional period after the loosening of the medieval social hierarchy and before the stabilizing of the modern one.'

5. *The Covrte of Civill Courtesie . . . Out of Italian by S.R. Gent* (London, 1577). The full title is revealing: 'Fitly furnished with a pleasant port of stately phrases and pithy precepts: assembled in the behalf of all young Gentlemen, and others, that are desirous to frame their behavior according to their estates, at all times and in all companies: thereby to purchase worthy praise of their inferiors, and estimation and credit among their betters.'

6. STEPHEN GUAZZO, *The Civile Conversation*, trans. George Pettie and Bartholomew Young, ed. Sir Edward Sullivan, 2 vols (London: Constable, 1925), 1: 86ff; Castiglione, *The Book of the Courtier*, trans. Charles S. Singleton (New York: Anchor, 1959), p. 294.

7. PHILIBERT DE VIENNE, *The Philosopher of the Court*, trans. George North (London, 1575), p. 13. See C.A. MAYER, 'L'Honnête Homme. Molière and Philibert de Vienne's "Philosophe de Court",' *MLR* 46 (1951), pp. 196–217, and PAULINE SMITH, *The Anti-Courtier Trend in Sixteenth Century French Literature* (Geneva: Droz, 1966).

8. Philibert's Court Philosopher commends to his readers 'the understanding of all Arts and liberal Sciences, whereby we become right Courtiers' (p. 29). We must be skilled in music, dancing, and poetry; we should have 'some pretty sprinkled judgment in the commonplaces and practices of all the liberal sciences, chopped up in hotchpot together' out of which we may stock our conversation; likewise, we should have 'store of histories, to pass the time meet for any company' or, what is just as good, 'certain sudden lies and inventions of our own forging' (p. 30).

9. Cf. MACHIAVELLI, *The Prince*: 'if one could change one's nature with time and circumstances, fortune would never change' (p. 93). For Proteus, see A. BARTLETT GIAMATTI, 'Proteus Unbound: Some Versions of the Sea God in the Renaissance', in *The Disciplines of Criticism*, eds Peter Demetz, Thomas Greene and Lowry Nelson, Jr (New Haven: Yale University Press, 1968), pp. 437–75.

10. DANIEL JAVITCH, 'The Philosopher at Court: A French Satire Misunderstood', *Comparative Literature* 23 (1971), pp. 97–124. There is similar ambiguity about ROBERT LANEHAM's *Letter* (1575), ed. F.J. Furnivall (New York: Duffield, 1907).

11. Quoted in STEPHEN J. GREENBLATT, *Sir Walter Ralegh: The Renaissance Man and His Roles* (New Haven: Yale University Press, 1973), p. 24. The official occasion for this effusion is a letter to Robert Cecil about bills for the coats of the Queen's Guards.

12. Quoted in GREENBLATT, *Sir Walter Ralegh*, pp. 76–7.

13. *Memoirs of the Life of Robert Cary*, (ed.) John, Earl of Corke and Orrery (London: R. & J. Dodsley, 1759), p. 103.

14. 'On the Fortunate Memory of Elizabeth Queen of England', trans. James Spedding, in *The Works of Francis Bacon*, (eds) Spedding and Robert Ellis, 14 vols (London: Longman, 1857–74), 6: 317.

15. See DAVID M. BERGERON, *English Civic Pageantry, 1558–1642* (London: Edward Arnold, 1971); FRANCES A. YATES, *Astraea: The Imperial Theme in the Sixteenth Century* (London: Routledge & Kegan Paul, 1975); ROY STRONG, *The Cult of Elizabeth: Elizabethan Portraiture and Pageantry* (London: Thames & Hudson, 1977). For the queen's Tudor predecessor, see SYDNEY ANGLO, *Spectacle*,

Pageantry, and Early Tudor Policy (Oxford: Clarendon Press, 1969). For the 'Platonic politics' of the Stuart reigns, see STEPHEN ORGEL, *The Illusion of Power: Political Theater in the English Renaissance* (Berkeley: University of California Press, 1975).

16. Quoted in ALLISON HEISCH, 'Queen Elizabeth I: Parliamentary Rhetoric and the Exercise of Power', *Signs: Journal of Women in Culture and Society* 1 (1975), p. 39.

17. Accession speech, quoted in HEISCH, p. 33. Plowden and Coke, quoted in KANTOROWICZ, *The King's Two Bodies*, p. 13.

18. The religious element emerges most clearly in Elizabeth's conservative stance in the Vestarian Controversy.

19. Quoted in J.E. NEALE, *Elizabeth I and Her Parliaments, 1584–1601*, 2 vols (London: Jonathan Cape, 1965), 2: 119. Referred to in text as 'Neale'.

20. Godfrey Goodman, Bishop of Gloucester, *The Court of King James the First*, ed. J.S. Brewer, 2 vols (London: R. Bentley, 1839), 1: 163 (italics mine). We would do well to remember that in 1588, with widespread fear of assassination attempts, any royal appearance before a crowd was a courageous act.

21. *The Quenes maiesties passage through the citie of London to Westminster the day before her coronacion* [1559], ed. James M. Osborn (New Haven: Yale University Press, 1960), pp. 28, 46. On Queen Mary's accession, see *The Chronicle of Queen Jane and of Two Years of Queen Mary*, ed. John G. Nichols, Camden Society, 48 (London: Royal Historical Society, 1850), p. 14: 'The Queen's Grace stayed at Allgate Street before the stage where the poor children stood, and heard an oration that one of them made, but she said nothing to them.'

22. YATES, *Astraea*, comments, 'The bejewelled and painted images of the Virgin Mary had been cast out of churches and monasteries but another bejewelled and painted image was set up at court, and went in progress through the land for her worshippers to adore' (p. 79).

23. RALEGH, 'Now we have present made', in WALTER OAKESHOTT, *The Queen and the Poet* (London: Faber, 1960), p. 205. See ROY STRONG, *The Cult of Elizabeth and The Portraits of Queen Elizabeth I* (Oxford: Clarendon Press, 1963); E.C. WILSON, *England's Eliza* (Cambridge, Mass.: Harvard University Press, 1939). The richest compilation of materials remains *The Progresses and Public Processions of Queen Elizabeth*, ed. John Nichols, 3 vols (London: J. Nichols, 1823).

24. *The Letters and Epigrams of Sir John Harington*, ed. Norman E. McClure (Philadelphia: University of Pennsylvania Press, 1930), p. 122.

25. *The Book of the Courtier*, p. 294.

26. *Letters*, p. 125. 'I write from wonder and affection', he remarks (p. 126).

27. We may note that in 1589 (the date of the letter), Ralegh is perhaps the supreme example in England of a gentleman not born but fashioned.

28. PAUL J. ALPERS, *The Poetry of 'The Faerie Queene'* (Princeton: Princeton University Press, 1967), and 'How to Read *The Faerie Queene*', in *Essays in Criticism* 18 (1968), pp. 429–43.

29. C.S. LEWIS, *The Allegory of Love* (New York: Oxford University Press [first published 1936]), p. 332. Lewis's description of the Bower has been discussed by Graham Hough, *A Preface to 'The Faerie Queene'* (New York: Norton, 1963).

30. *Essays and Introductions* (London: Macmillan, 1961), p. 370.

31. N.S. BROOKE, 'C.S. Lewis and Spenser: Nature, Art and the Bower of Bliss', in *Essential Articles for the Study of Edmund Spenser*, ed. A.C. Hamilton (Hamden, Conn.: Archon Books, 1972), p. 28. Typical of much recent criticism is the observation by M. Pauline Parker that the Bower's 'painted golden ivy is used

where the real plant could have grown and should have grown', indeed the ivy is 'alive only with the horrible energy of corruption' (*The Allegory of 'The Faerie Queene'* [Oxford: Clarendon, 1960], pp. 42, 152).

32. See especially MERRITT Y. HUGHES, 'Spenser's Acrasia and the Circe of the Renaissance', *Journal of the History of Ideas* 4 (1943), pp. 381–99; ROBERT M. DURLING, 'The Bower of Bliss and Armida's Palace', *Comparative Literature* 6 (1954), pp. 335–47; JAMES NOHRNBERG, *The Analogy of 'The Faerie Queene'* (Princeton: Princeton University Press, 1976), pp. 490–513.

33. SIGMUND FREUD, *Civilization and Its Discontents*, trans. James Strachey (New York: Norton, 1962), pp. 44, 51.

34. For modern versions, see SAMUEL Z. KLAUSNER, 'A Collocation of Concepts of Self-Control', in *The Quest for Self-Control: Classical Philosophies and Scientific Research*, ed. Klausner (New York: Free Press, 1965), pp. 9–48.

35. NATALIE ZEMON DAVIS, ' "Women's History" in Transition: The European Case', *Feminist Studies* 3 (1976), p. 89 and the refs. in note 31.

36. GUIDO CALABRESI and PHILIP BOBBITT, *Tragic Choices* (New York: Norton, 1978), p. 195.

37. CLIFFORD GEERTZ, 'Art as a Cultural System', *Modern Language Notes* 91 (1976), pp. 1473–99.

38. CHRISTOPHER COLUMBUS, *Journals and Other Documents*, p. 287.

39. TASSO, *Gerusalemme Liberata* (book 15, stanzas 28ff.), relates the quest for the realm of Armida to Columbus's voyages. Spenser's Maleger carries arrows 'Such as the *Indians* in their quiuers hide' (2.11.21). BERNAL DIAZ DEL CASTILLO recalls the first reaction to the sight of the Aztec capital in *The Conquest of New Spain*, trans. J.M. Cohen (Baltimore: Penguin, 1963), p. 214. On Spenser and the New World, see ROY HARVEY PEARCE, 'Primitivistic Ideas in *The Faerie Queene'*, *Journal of English and Germanic Philology* 45 (1945), pp. 139–51; A. BARTLETT GIAMATTI, 'Primitivism and the Process of Civility in Spenser's Faerie Queene', in *First Images of America: The Impact of the New World on the Old*, ed. Fredi Chiappelli, 2 vols (Berkeley: University of California Press, 1976), 1: 71–82.

40. RALEGH, *The Discovery of Guiana*, ed. V.T. Harlow (London: Argonaut Press, 1928), p. 42.

41. PETER MARTYR, *The Decades of the New World*, trans. Michael Lok, in *A Selection of Curious, Rare, and Early Voyages and Histories of Interesting Discoveries chiefly published by Hakluyt* . . . (London: R.H. Evans and R. Priestly, 1812), p. 539.

42. *Ibid.*, p. 530.

43. *Of the newe landes*, in *The First Three English Books on America*, (ed.) Edward Arber (Birmingham: Turnbull and Spears, 1885), p. xxvii; cf. WILBERFORCE EAMES, 'Description of a Wood Engraving Illustrating the South American Indians (1505)', *Bulletin of the New York Public Library* 26 (1922), pp. 755–60.

44. Elizabeth Story Donno (ed.), *An Elizabethan in 1582: The Diary of Richard Madox, Fellow of All Souls*, Hakluyt Society, Second Series, No. 147 (London: Hakluyt Society, 1977), p. 183. The editor notes that 'in the older maps the mountains of the moon figure as a range extending across the continent from Abyssinia to the Gulf of Guinea.'

45. At 6.8.43, the cannibals who capture Serena consider raping her, but they are stopped by their priests.

46. Compare Redcrosse who, when he dallies with Duessa, is described as 'Pourd out in loosnesse on the grassy grownd, / Both carelesse of his health, and of his fame' (1.7.7).

47. On vagabonds, see FRANK AYDELOTTE, *Elizabethan Rogues and Vagabonds* (London: Frank Cass, 1913).
48. MARTYR, *Decades*, p. 628. On charges of idleness, see EDMUND S. MORGAN, *American Slavery, American Freedom: The Ordeal of Colonial Virginia* (New York: Norton, 1975).
49. Cortes 'had ordered that all houses should be pulled down and burnt and the bridged channels filled up; and what he gained each day was thus consolidated. He sent an order to Pedro de Alvarado to be sure that we never crossed a bridge or gap in the causeway without first blocking it up, and to pull down and burn every house' (BERNAL DIAZ, *Conquest*, p. 369).
50. I am indebted here to RICHARD SLOTKIN, *Regeneration through Violence: The Mythology of the American Frontier, 1600–1860* (Middletown, Conn.: Wesleyan University Press, 1973).
51. BERNAL DIAZ, *Conquest*, p. 60.
52. *A View of the Present State of Ireland*, ed. W.L. Renwick (Oxford: Clarendon Press, 1970), pp. 48, 64, 65. Our primary purpose is to explore aspects of Elizabethan policy in Ireland as a reiteration of a characteristic cultural pattern rather than to detail the direct influence of Ireland upon *The Faerie Queene*; for the latter, see M.M. GRAY, 'The Influence of Spenser's Irish Experiences on *The Faerie Queene*', *Review of English Studies* 6 (1930), pp. 413–28; PAULINE HENLEY, *Spenser in Ireland* (Folcroft, Pa.: Folcroft Press, 1920).
53. *View*, p. 67. Cf. LOUIS-JEAN CALVET, *Linguistique et colonialisme: Petit traité de glottophagie* (Paris: Payot, 1974) and STEPHEN J. GREENBLATT, 'Learning to Curse: Aspects of Linguistic Colonialism in the Sixteenth Century', in *First Images of America* 2: 561–80.
54. *View*, pp. 67–8. Children 'draweth into themselves together with their suck, even the nature and disposition of their nurses, for the mind followeth much the temperature of the body; and also the words are the image of the mind, so as they proceeding from the mind, the mind must be needs effected with the words' (p. 68).
55. YEATS, *Essays and Introductions*, p. 372.
56. R. DUDLEY EDWARDS, *Ireland in the Age of the Tudors: The Destruction of Hiberno-Norman Civilization* (London: Croom Helm, 1977); NICHOLAS P. CANNY, *The Elizabethan Conquest of Ireland: A Pattern Established, 1565–76* (Hassocks, Sussex: Harvester Press, 1976); DAVID BEERS QUINN, *The Elizabethans and the Irish* (Ithaca: Cornell University Press, 1966). For an apologetic account of Spenser's involvement, see PAULINE HENLEY, *Spenser in Ireland*; for an enigmatic indication of Spenser's personal profit from the Smerwick massacre, see ANNA MARIA CRINÒ, 'La Relazione Barducci-Ubaldini sull'Impresa d'Irlanda (1579–1581)', *English Miscellany* 19 (1968), pp. 339–67.
57. ALEXANDER C. JUDSON, *The Life of Edmund Spenser* (Baltimore: Johns Hopkins University Press, 1945), pp. 107–8.
58. *Ibid.*, p. 116. The reference to the 'fennes of Allan' in 2.9.16 indicates that it was written after Spenser acquired New Abbey, a ruined Franciscan friary in County Kildare, in 1582 (see JOSEPHINE WATERS BENNETT, *The Evolution of 'The Faerie Queene'* [Chicago: University of Chicago Press, 1942], p. 131n.).
59. It has been frequently noted that Maleger and his band resemble accounts in Spenser's *View* and in other reports on Ireland of Irish kerns.
60. We should perhaps note in this connection that Guyon leaves the Bower immediately after its destruction: 'But let vs hence depart,' says the Palmer, 'whilest wether serues and wind' (2.12.87).

61. Quoted in PHILIP HUGHES, *The Reformation in England*, 3 vols (New York: Macmillan, 1954), 3: 408.
62. JOHN VENN, *John Caius* (Cambridge: Cambridge University Press, 1910), p. 37. In a letter of the vice-chancellor, Dr Byng, to the chancellor, Lord Burghley, dated 14 December 1572, the 'trumpery' is catalogued: 'vestments, albes, tunicles, stoles, manicles, corporas clothes, with the pix and sindon, and canopie, besides holy water stoppes, with sprinkles, pax, sensars, superaltaries, tables of idolles, masse bookes, portuises, and grailles, with other such stuffe as might have furnished divers massers at one instant'. The Latin account is from JOHN CAIUS, *The Annals of Gonville and Caius College*, ed. John Venn, Cambridge Antiquarian Society Octavo Series no. 40 (Cambridge, 1904), p. 185. Caius adds that iconoclasts used hammers to smash certain objects.
63. Quoted in JOHN PHILLIPS, *The Reformation of Images: Destruction of Art in England, 1535–1660* (Berkeley: University of California Press, 1973), p. 80.
64. KEITH THOMAS, *Religion and the Decline of Magic* (London: Weidenfeld & Nicolson, 1971), p. 69.
65. *The Book of the Courtier*, trans. Singleton, p. 43. On *sprezzatura*, see WAYNE A. REBHORN, *Courtly Performances: Masking and Festivity in Castiglione's 'Book of the Courtier'* (Detroit: Wayne State University Press, 1978), pp. 33–40.
66. On demonic artists, see A. BARTLETT GIAMATTI, *Play of Double Senses: Spenser's Faerie Queene* (Englewood Cliffs, N.J.: Prentice Hall, 1975), pp. 106–33. We may observe that Spenser seems on occasion to invoke positive versions of self-concealing art:

> Then came the Bride, the louely *Medua* came,
> Clad in a vesture of vnknowen geare,
> And vncouth fashion, yet her well became;
> That seem'd like siluer, sprinckled here and theare
> With glittering spangs, that did like starres appeare,
> And wau'd vpon, like water Chamelot,
> To hide the metall, which yet euery where
> Bewrayd it selfe, to let men plainely wot,
> It was no mortall worke, that seem'd and yet was not.

> (4.11.45)

Spenser's suspicions of aesthetic concealment can be allayed by its use in a virtuous context, but we might also note that in this instance the device both hides and does not hide its own artifice. The art is designed to seem natural and yet at the same time to let men plainly know, through a kind of 'self-betrayal', that it is not natural. For conflicting arguments on the status of artifice in Spenser, see C.S. LEWIS, *The Allegory of Love*, pp. 326–33, and HANS P. GUTH, 'Allegorical Implications of Artifice in Spenser's *Faerie Queene*', *Publication of the Modern Language Association* 76 (1961), pp. 474–9.
67. KEITH THOMAS, *Religion and the Decline of Magic*, p. 275.
68. See GERSHOM SCHOLEM, *Sabbatai Sevi* (Princeton: Princeton University Press, 1973).
69. J.H. ELLIOTT, *The Old World and the New, 1492–1650* (Cambridge: Cambridge University Press, 1970).
70. PAUL ALPERS, 'Narration in *The Faerie Queene*', *English Literary History* 44 (1977), p. 27.

3 Suspended Instruments: Lyric and Power in the Bower of Bliss*

PATRICIA A. PARKER

In this essay, Patricia Parker combines the cultural analysis of new historicism with the gender analysis of feminism. Although Greenblatt argues that Guyon's reaction against the sensuality of the Bower expresses Spenser's 'pledge of loving service to the royal mistress', Parker claims that Guyon's violent destruction represents an attack on Queen Elizabeth's erotic Petrarchanism. As a new historicist, Parker considers not only the literary but also the social contexts for lyric evoked by the canto, and she defines the Petrarchan sonnet as a 'dominant cultural form'. Nevertheless, as simply a feminist, she resists approaching erotic or gender relations as a displacement of political relations – between subject and monarch. Although Elizabeth held class and political superiority over Spenser, his own masculine position within culture elicited an aggressive reaction against his subordination to a woman in power. Following Nancy Vickers' analysis of the sonnet sequence (included in this collection), Parker reads the 'sexual politics' of the episode as a 'male remastery' of Spenser's subordinated status. Parker uses psychoanalytic criticism to account for the danger that figures like Acrasia and Elizabeth pose for cultural models of masculinity.

In the midst of the Bower of Bliss, the culminating episode of Guyon's quest in Book II of *The Faerie Queene*, the Elfin knight and his Palmer guide gain a sight of the Bower's reigning Enchantress and Verdant, her male victim:

> His warlike armes, the idle instruments
> Of sleeping praise, were hong upon a tree,
> And his brave shield, full of old moniments,

---

* Reprinted from Patricia A. Parker, *Literary Fat Ladies: Rhetoric, Gender, Property* (London: Methuen, 1987), pp. 54–66.

Was fowly ra'st, that none the signes might see;
Ne for them, ne for honour cared hee,
Ne ought, that did to his advauncement tend,
But in lewd loves, and wastfull luxuree,
His dayes, his goods, his bodie he did spend:
O horrible enchantment, that him so did blend.

(II.xii.80)[1]

The immediate resonance of these 'idle instruments / Of sleeping praise',
suspended or 'hong' upon a tree, is the iconography of Venus and Mars –
with Verdant lying like the disarmed warrior in the lap of his paramour
before Vulcan, the formerly impotent voyeur husband, rushes in upon
them with his crafty 'net'. The suspension or hanging of these instruments
reiterates the suspensions of the Bower itself, and the hovering of Acrasia
as she cannibalistically 'pastures' her eyes upon her powerless subject.
But the instruments hung upon a tree also recall a very different and
specifically lyric context – one that will lead us toward the various strains
of lyricism that cross in this crucial Spenserian scene. This context is the
suspended song and suspended lyric instruments of the haunting Psalm
137:

> By the rivers of Babel we sate, and there we wept, when we
>   remembered Zion.
> We hanged our harpes upon the willowes in the middes thereof.
> When thei that led us captives required of us songs and mirth, when
>   we had hanged up our harpes, saying, Sing us one of the songs
>   of Zion.
> How shall we sing, said we, a song of the Lord in a strange land?
> If I forget thee, O Jerusalem, may my right hand forget to play.
> If I do not remembre thee, let my tongue cleve to the rofe of my
>   mouth . . .
> O daughter of Babel, worthie to be destroied, blessed shal he be [who]
>   rewardeth thee, as thou hast served us.
> Blessed shal be he that taketh and dasheth thy children against the
>   stones.[2]

That this biblical lyric of lament should sound in the midst of the
otherwise euphonious and *carpe diem* lyricism of the Bower of Bliss
– filled with songs and lyric traditions of its own – should not, on
reflection, be surprising. The psalm sings of abandoned instruments in
Babylonian exile and captivity: Verdant's instruments are suspended on
the tree of a 'Witch' only too easily assimilated to Babylon and its famous
Whore. Calvin, in his gloss on the psalm, speaks of its Babylon as a *locus
amoenus* very much like the Bower of Bliss – as a 'fair and fertile' place
'with charms which could corrupt effeminate minds' and 'tempt them to

forget their native inheritance'. Augustine speaks of its 'Babylon' as the pleasures of this world and of the 'willows' on which its lyric instruments are hung as ultimately barren rather than fruitful trees – an emblem of barrenness in the midst of apparent fertility that repeats the biblical dynamic of Spenser's principal subtext, the Garden of Armida in Tasso which stands upon a Dead Sea.[3] The invocation of the psalm not to forget – or to be punished with speechlessness and forcibly suspended song as a result – thus joins the Homeric, lotus-eating resonances of this Spenserian scene, and both figure the necessity of the withheld and vigilant mind, the reversal of Verdant's suspended instruments, which themselves provide a sign not of song refused but, more ominously, of song as in some other sense suspended.

The psalm behind Verdant's suspended instruments, however, also imports into this private and enclosed erotic scene the powerful political dimension this psalm has always had for singers conscious of the wider context of their singing, a resonance that might make it a powerful subtext for lyric poets in the era of Spenser, subject to a queen who very much demanded their voices. Hanging up one's instrument stands here as a sign of resistance, a refusal to hire out one's voice on the part of a people who otherwise sure can sing and dance. The specifically political force of this psalm continues in a contemporary reggae version of the impossibility of singing in Babylon, a version that chillingly suppresses the psalm's own violent ending – 'Blessed shal be he that taketh and dasheth thy children against the stones' – and ambiguously substitutes for it another very different psalm text, 'May the words of our mouths and the meditations of our hearts be *acceptable* in thy sight' (my emphasis).

The echo of this psalm's suspended instruments introduces if only elliptically into Spenser's scene the threat of the silencing, controlling or compromising of song, one that is biblical in its immediate reference but also, in Acrasia's leafy retreat, inevitably evokes a particularly pastoral lyric tension between power and song – that tension that opens Virgil's *Eclogues* with an allusion to the 'god' who has given the singer his 'ease'. Indeed, the other lyric context recalled in the stanza of Verdant's suspended instruments is this specifically pastoral one, hanging up one's instruments being not just the gesture of a Mars-like warrior abandoning the instruments of war, the hanging up of trophies as signs of victory, or the lament of a Dido-like abandoned lover (as in Spenser's 'Willow worne of forlorne Paramours' or 'Hang my harp on a weeping willow tree'), but also the suspending of instruments on trees in pastoral lyric, a suspension of song that may reflect the suspension Paul Alpers and others find characteristic of pastoral lyric itself.[4] In Sannazaro's *Arcadia*, one of the principal subtexts for Spenser's *Shepheardes Calender*, the hanging of the instrument of Pan upon a tree generates an entire history of pastoral lyric from Theocritus to Virgil and, by implication, to the poet-persona of the *Arcadia* itself.[5] The suspending of Pan's instrument there – in a way suggestive for a Spenserian episode that signals its debts to multiple predecessors – is an emblem of the interval before a new poet takes up these temporarily 'idle instruments' and turns them into the instruments of his own potency.

Within this specifically pastoral lyric tradition, Verdant's suspended instruments summon up a Spenserian echo as well, and one intimately bound up with the tensions within Spenser's lyric vocation. Readers of *The Shepheardes Calender* will remember that it opens with Colin Clout, Spenser's own pastoral persona, not just suspending but breaking his pastoral instrument. And it ends with Colin hanging his pipe upon a tree, in a gesture that more than one commentator has linked with a sense of the impotence of song, or the necessary compromising of lyric voice in a political context which would make only too appropriate a conflation of a recall of Psalm 137 with a reminder of Colin's own suspended instrument.[6] *Otium*, or idleness, is traditionally the attraction of pastoral, as it is also of the fatal Bower of Bliss; but the 'idleness' of the suspended instruments of Verdant suggests in their echo of Colin's gesture the potential impotence of poetry itself in a state in which it was scorned as a form of effeminacy, or idle 'toye', in contrast to more active, imperial pursuits.[7] In this context it was highly problematic whether there was any alternative to the opposed temptations of the idle Phaedria and the industrious Mammon of Book II – an opposition that Blake might later ridicule as a 'cloven fiction', but one that continued to dominate a whole post-Spenserian tradition of the potential impotence or irrelevance of the poetic vocation. The Romantics' Aeolian harp, we may remember, is one of the lyric descendants of this suspended instrument.

There is, however, yet another aspect of Verdant's suspended instruments that needs to be explored and, though it will emerge only after a brief excursus, another specifically lyric dimension of this episode and the defeat of its reigning queen. The pervasive phallic symbolism of Guyon's Odyssean journey to the Bower of Bliss makes it impossible to miss the fact that these suspended 'instruments' are also clearly *male* instruments and that the impotence their suspension betokens is an impotence that is sexual as well as martial or lyric.[8] A link between the instruments of war and the instruments of virility is, of course, part of the visual cliché of the iconography of Mars and Venus: we think of Botticelli's painting with its wreathed phallic lance, clearly no longer ready for immediate use as an instrument of war, though still serviceable as an instrument of a different kind.

The sense not just of lyric but of sexual contest within the stanza of Verdant's suspended instruments evokes a recall not only of Mars and Venus but of a whole series of subject males and dominating female figures, from Hercules and Omphale to Samson reclining in the lap of that Delilah who deprives him of his strength, a figure of the man dedicated to higher things who cannot, however, ultimately escape the power of women. The link between the latter emblem and Spenser's pair is made even stronger by the fact that Samson in sixteenth-century depictions was also represented as laying aside his warlike instruments. Spenser's scene manages to evoke the iconography of both Virgin Mother with her sleeping infant and the more sinister Pietà, a dead Adonis in the lap of a powerful maternal Venus. The emblem of Samson made impotent in Delilah's lap shares with the tableau of Verdant and Acrasia anxieties of a particularly oral kind, the reduction of the male subject to an infant, or *infans*. Acrasia, like Delilah throughout much of her pictorial history, is not just a temptress but an overpowering mother; and it is in this respect worth citing at least one Renaissance representation of that overpowering. Madlyn Millner Kahr, in *Feminism and Art History*, cites a late sixteenth-century drawing entitled 'Allegory of the Power of Woman', which shows in the foreground a woman nursing an infant in one arm, holding a royal scepter and golden chain in the other, and standing on the broken instruments – shield and sword – of male power; in the background are the women who tempted Solomon to idolatry (and hence, ultimately, into Babylon) and Delilah cutting off the hair, and strength, of Samson in her lap.[9]

The underlying threat of the story of Samson's abandoned instruments is, of course, the threat of castration. The hair mentioned in the case of Verdant is the just-beginning hair on his boyish face: if Acrasia is a Delilah, she has only a symbolic need for scissors. But the sense of castration pervades the entire scene, and the unavoidably phallic overtones of Verdant's removed and now useless 'instruments' bring to the scene an echo of the severed instruments of yet another boy – Attis, who after transgressing the demand of the Great Mother Cybele that he remain forever a boy, in a frenzy castrates himself, thus becoming not just an impotent Adonis to Cybele's Venus but also the prototype of the *Magna Mater's* Galli or eunuch servants. Attis is traditionally represented as an effeminate youth, wearing the distinctive Phrygian cap whose droop, as Neil Hertz has recently reminded us,[10] conveys an equivocal sense of both the possession and the lack of phallic power, as indeed the effeminately dressed porter of the Bower of Bliss wields his 'staff' for 'more [we may hear "mere"] formalitee' (II.xii.48.9), and reminds us of the Attis-like Aeneas at the court of Dido, another powerful female, his forgetfulness of outside world and higher task the Virgilian counterpart of the dangers of oblivion in Babylon.

The evocation of these pairs of dominant female and subject, even castrated, male in the episode of Verdant's suspended instruments works with other elements of the description to establish the Bower as a predominantly female space – whose enclosures suggest the *hortus conclusus* of the female body – and a place that might excite the knight to forget his own higher purpose, an act of submission that would suspend his 'instruments'. But the motif of male subjection within at least some of the plots suggested here – the case of Hercules, for example – is one in which the moment of male subjection is only one moment in a larger narrative progression. Though Guyon, unlike his prototype Odysseus, does not use his sword to overcome the Bower's witch, the culminating or phallic narrative 'point' (1.7) of his Odyssean journey substitutes, for homecoming to Penelope, the overpowering of a threatening Circe through the potent 'vertue' (41.9) of the Palmer's simultaneously phallic and Mosaic staff. Like the staff of Mercury to which it is kin, the staff is able both to recall souls from the symbolic Hades of subjection to female power and also to 'rule the *Furyes*, when they most do rage' (41.8), a hint perhaps of the relation between the establishment of civilization and the taming of the female from the story of yet another dangerously powerful queen.

But the echo of Cybele in particular gives a further dimension to this episode's suspended – and (in the case of Guyon) potentially suspended – instruments, both lyric and virile, one that involves not just the episode's narrative progression but a specific form of lyric tradition adumbrated within it. Cybele, the *Magna Mater* of imperial Rome, is one of *The Faerie Queene's* most ubiquitous figures for the presiding patroness of 'Troynovaunt' and hence for Elizabeth, the poem's allegorically shadowed queen, who was repeatedly represented (and self-represented) as the great 'Mother', and even nursing mother, of her subjects. Virgil's Roman version of the *Magna Mater* carefully removes the more oriental and threatening female aspects of her cult – including the castration of Attis and her subject males. But Spenser's allusions to Cybele include this more ambivalent complex, Cybele's 'franticke rites' (I.vi.15) as well as her maternal embodiment of order and civilization.[11] The Cybele–Attis iconography of the Isis Church episode of Book V of *The Faerie Queene*, with its Galli-like priests who 'on their mother Earths deare lap did lie' (V.vii.9), links the pair of Great Mother and castrated boy emblematically with the posture of the mother-queen of the Bower of Bliss and the reclining youth who has surrendered his 'instruments'. But, interestingly enough, the vision at Isis Church also comes within the larger story of the powerful Amazon Radigund's subjection of Artegall, who comes under her control by abandoning his sword (V.v.17), which she then breaks, causing his 'warlike armes' to be 'hang'd on high', suspended so that they 'mote his shame bewray', and forcing him to dress in 'womans weedes' (20–2). The echoes of the Verdant–Acrasia scene in Artegall's humiliating subjection to a woman also, however, include a stanza that makes explicit reference to Spenser's ruling queen, the exceptional powerful female dominant over her male subjects.

> Such is the crueltie of womenkynd,
>> When they have shaken off the shamefast band,
>> With which wise Nature did them strongly bynd,
>> T'obay the heasts of mans well ruling hand,
>> That then all rule and reason they withstand,
>> To purchase a licentious libertie.
>> But vertuous women wisely understand,
>> That they were borne to base humilitie,
> Unlesse the heavens them lift to lawful soveraintie.

$$\text{(V.v.25)}$$

Elizabeth here is so belatedly made an exception to the rule – indeed only in a single concluding alexandrine – that what emerges in the picture of the monstrosity of the subjection of male to female power makes one wonder whether, reading back from this episode to the hints of Attis's severed instruments in the Bower of Bliss, Elizabeth herself is not also 'shadowed' in the scene of suspended instruments, evocative both of male 'vertue' and of instruments of a more lyric kind.[12]

Recent Spenser criticism has increasingly drawn attention to the relation between the combination of eroticized Virgin and dominating mother in the figure of Acrasia and the typical self-presentation of Spenser's ruling queen.[13] Certainly, the *otium* and debased lyric 'toyes' of Acrasia's Bower echo the debased social situation of which Cuddie complains in lamenting the impotence of his own lyric instruments in the 'October' eclogue, implying that, at least in part, the predicament of the poet in the age of Elizabeth – his potentially impotent, or suspended, instrument – is that he is subject to powers that necessarily compromise his song. Cuddie's complaint resembles the lyric lament of the Muses themselves in another Spenserian intertext for Verdant's suspended instruments, *The Teares of the Muses*, whose complaint of internal exile (341) and of the 'idlenes' and brute sloth (99, 335) of the contemporary English context recall at once the language of the Bower of Bliss and the lament of suspended song in Psalm 137, which might indeed provide its most appropriate lyric epigraph. The episode of Guyon in the Bower has long been interpreted, following Milton, as the drama of an individual trial. But the affinities of its language with a lament published only a year later imports into the Bower itself a suggestion of that contemporary 'Babylon' in which the Muses' 'sweete instruments' (20) can no longer be heard and are finally broken, replaced instead by vain idle 'toyes' (325), a place where it is difficult to distinguish between 'Poets' and 'Sycophants' (471–2), or to save one's own lyric instruments from a subject's use.[14] Once again, in this lament, Elizabeth is made explicitly an exception, but in a fashion reserved until the end, and in a praise so exceptional that it too seems a second thought (571 ff.)

The iconography of subject male and dominant female in the scene of Verdant's suspended instruments brings us, then, to the last of the lyric traditions figured in this scene – not just the suspended lyricism of Psalm 137 or the pastoral topos of pipes hung on trees, but also the polarized structure of Petrarchan lyric, itself dependent on the polarity of male subject and elevated female figure, a polarity of which the suspended dyad of the subjected Verdant and dominant Acrasia offers an almost parodic visual emblem. This context for these suspended instruments necessarily returns us to our first – the suspension of song in an alien political context – for in both, as so much of recent Spenser criticism suggests, the relationship of lyric to society, in the terms of Adorno's famous essay, is one that cannot be overlooked.

It has long been recognized that the vogue for Petrarchan lyric in the era of Elizabeth was inseparable from the structure of a politics in which political and erotic codes interpenetrated to a remarkable degree, in which Elizabeth's courtiers related to their queen as Petrarch's to an often cruel mistress, and in which the male poet was 'subject' in both the political and in the Petrarchan lyric sense. Petrarchism was not just a lyric but also a dominant cultural form, a politicized lyric structure inscribed within the complex sexual politics of the exceptional rule of a woman in an otherwise overwhelmingly patriarchal culture. Stephen Greenblatt and others have noted the antagonism – or implicit contest of wills – always present within this Petrarchan politics of courtier-lover and tantalizing, dominant and even cruel mistress.[15] Greenblatt cites the example of Ralegh's playing a frenzied Orlando to Elizabeth's disdainful beloved; and Elizabeth figured as Ariosto's already highly Petrarchanized Angelica, who drives her courtier-knights mad, might also easily be shadowed as a dominating Acrasia artfully orchestrating both her own rival romance and her own Petrarchan poetics. The Bower of Bliss is a threatening female space not just because of its enervating *carmina* and etymologically related 'charms' but also in part because, while it arouses hopes of gratification, it does not clearly fulfill them or fulfills them only in an illusory or compromising way; in the stanza of Verdant's suspended instruments, the knight's slumber seems post-coital, but it is not at all clear from the syntax what his share has been in these delights ('There she had him now layd a slombering, / In secret shade, after long wanton ioyes'; 72.5–6). Bacon, for one, could easily assimilate Elizabeth's Petrarchan politics to the arts of 'the Queen in the blessed islands . . . who allows of amorous admiration but prohibits desire'.[16]

The antagonism within this politicized lyric structure, however, also left the way open for a male remastering of its dominant Petrarchan mistress. As Sir John Harington observed, the queen's male, Petrarch-like subjects could and would themselves make 'matter' out of their *Magna Mater*. Her subjects (both in the political and in the erotic sense) could make the queen in turn the 'subject' of their verse,[17] just as in the emblem of suspended pastoral instruments which Spenser echoes from Sannazaro, the origin of those instruments is in the death of Syrinx, in the transformed body of that female figure who becomes literally the enabling instrument of pastoral song.

The dynamics of this threatening female dominance and male remastery – the narrative dynamism of the overpowering of the Bower's Queen – is, however, already part of the sexual politics of Petrarchan lyric itself. Nancy Vickers, in *Writing and Sexual Difference*, describes the threat of dissolution or dismemberment that haunts the subject–object structure of the Petrarchan poetry of praise, in which the male subject is always potentially an Actaeon, torn apart after his vision of an unattainable Diana.[18] The canto of the Bower of Bliss bears a hint of this potential dismemberment as well as the castration of the male poet-lover in its reference both to Ida (II.xii.52) – sacred to Cybele and her Phrygian rites – and to Rhodope, where Orpheus, the male lyric poet *par excellence*, not only sang but was undone by women. Its suspended instruments obliquely recall the lyric contests not just between shepherd-singers hanging their pipes upon a tree or between sacred and secular lyric traditions (as is suggested in the echo of Psalm 137 in the midst of the Bower's very different lyricism) but also between male poet and female object of desire in Petrarchan lyric, a relationship of power translatable into both psychological and sociopolitical terms.

The vulnerable, subject status of the male lover within this Petrarchan lyric structure is countered by the mastery of the poet. In Petrarch himself, as Vickers suggests, the poet reverses the dangers of subjection and dismemberment by scattering the body of his mistress across his own *rime sparse* or scattered rhymes. In Spenser, the same stanza as evokes Ida and Rhodope in the Bower of Bliss makes reference to 'Thessalian *Tempe*, where of yore / Faire *Daphne Phoebus* hart with love did gore' (4–5). The reference is to the first, or lover, moment of the myth – the victimage of the male subject before a cruel and unattainable mistress. But it inevitably provokes consciousness of its second moment – the transformation of the body of Daphne into a laurel, the triumphant sign of Phoebus' poetic power, the *lauro* that in Petrarchan lyric punningly assimilates the body of *Laura* just as Syrinx becomes in her death (an event that, though it means a loss for her lover, also removes her threat) the instrument of Pan.

The Diana–Actaeon structure of Petrarchan lyric and its underlying dyadic antagonism were clearly part of the Petrarchan politics of a reign in which the Ovidian story had already been assimilated to relationships of power through a play on the Latin words *cervus/servus* ('stag' and 'slave') and a comparison of the fate of Actaeon to the perils of life at court.[19] Like the myth of Attis' permanently suspended instruments, the threat of the Actaeon persona of the Petrarchan lyric poet is, once again, castration – a threat that Spenser recalls in the 'Some would have gelt him' (VII.vi.50.3) of the story of the Actaeon-like Faunus in the *Cantos of Mutabilitie*. The same threat enters euphemistically into the Bower of Bliss when Guyon's quaintly named 'courage cold' (II.xii.68) begins to rise up at the sight of the naked bathing nymphs. The Actaeon–Diana story has been thought to be one of the many myths relating to the incest prohibition, the consequence of a forbidden view of the body of the mother; and certainly Guyon and the Palmer creep somewhat pruriently through the female brush ('couert groues, and thickets close'; 76) to gaze upon the simultaneously erotic and maternal 'Witch' of this scene before they destroy it. The infant posture of the sleeping Verdant, together with the echo of the silencing of song from Psalm 137, reflects as well the threat of speechlessness in this Petrarchan structure, as in the Circean metamorphosis of her male victims. Petrarch, the threatened poetic Actaeon of his own canzone 23, can utter his lyrics only because he has an Orpheus-like respite between a forbidden seeing and dismemberment, and through his respite is able to silence rather than be silenced, to scatter the body of Laura rather than be dismembered himself. In Spenser's episode, Verdant's suspended instruments – signs of his status as what Mariann Sanders Regan suggestively calls 'Lover infans'[20] – may figure a threat in which the potentially suspended instrument is poetic voice itself.

The split within the male subject of lyric that Regan represents as the split between Lover and Poet is matched in the episode of the Bower of Bliss by the splitting of the male figures of the scene between the subjected and symbolically castrated Verdant – his instruments hung like a sign of victory on Acrasia's tree – and the mastering Guyon, who by implication releases them. Ralegh presented the whole of *The Faerie Queene* not as the more usually cited outdoing of the narrative Ariosto but as an overgoing of the lyric Petrarch, written by a subject of a queen greater than Laura. But to become merely a Petrarch-like lyricist in praise of Elizabeth would be in some sense to become an imitative subject of the queen herself, held within a structure already appropriated as an instrument of power and presented elsewhere in *The Faerie Queene* as both paralyzed and paralyzing. In overgoing Petrarch in a poem that seems to repeat the Petrarchan lyric structure at a higher level, Spenser may also be subtly reversing the relation dictated by his own subject status. A gentleman by education only, himself dependent on the patronage system manipulated by the queen, might well conflate a visual icon reminiscent of a Petrarchan cruel mistress and her paralyzed male subject with echoes of the psalm of suspended instruments and potentially captive as well as captivating song. But, like Petrarch, the poet subject to his mistress is also capable of creating – or decreating – her, and Spenser at the end of Book II gives us an episode whose pervasive echoes of Aeneas at the court of Dido already evoke a text in which this moment of potential suspension is left behind by the narrative itself, and a female ruler is both surpassed and overruled.

Elizabeth was already identified by name with Dido or 'Elissa'. In the same legend which culminates in the overpowering of Acrasia, the Belphoebe who shadows Spenser's queen in her aspect as unattainable virgin or Petrarchan cruel mistress is introduced in a compound simile (II.iii.31). Its first part ('Such as *Diana* by the sandie shore / Of swift Eurotas . . .') makes her a reminiscence of Dido as she first appeared to the Aeneas she temporarily effeminated and forestalled. Its conclusion, however, compares her to 'that famous Queene / Of *Amazons* whom *Pyrrhus* did destroye', an allusion which not only anticipates the Amazonian Radigund who suspends the warlike instruments of Artegall but manages, as Louis Montrose reminds us,[21] to suggest at once an exceptional female power and its destruction or remastery. The destruction of the Bower of Bliss is as violent as the prophesied ending of Psalm 137, with its captive and suspended instruments. Paradoxically, as Stephen Greenblatt and others have observed,[22] the final act of the Knight of Temperance is an act of intemperate violence, destruction of the Bower as a place of dangerous female dominance as well as of a suspect and seductive lyricism. Though the Cave of Mammon in this book is left standing and Verdant is let go with a mere lecture, Acrasia herself is led away in triumph. As with the dyadic antagonism of Petrarchan lyric, there seems to be here, ironically, no temperate middle way, no alternative to the polarity of subject or be subjected.

The lyric appeal of the Bower of Bliss is the isolated moment of its *carpe diem* song and its suspended cynosure. Regan, in *Love Words*, offers a psychologized theory of amorous or Petrarchan lyric in which the 'charm' or 'spell' that holds the lover resembles the Lacanian Imaginary or Melanie Klein's primal dyad of mother and child. We do not need object-relations theory or Lacanian psychoanalysis to catch the spell-bound or oral fix of Verdant in the arms of a maternal Acrasia: indeed, the attempt to apply such contemporary theories to Renaissance texts often simply reveals the bluntness of our own instruments. And yet the simultaneous use and critique of Lacan in a famous essay by Laura Mulvey on the male gaze (in cinema)[23] might provide a suggestive supplement for students of this particular Spenserian episode, undergraduates and overgraduates alike. Mulvey describes the mediatory function of the female – and the threat of castration she represents – in the movement from the mother–child dyad, which Lacan terms the Imaginary, to the realm of the Symbolic, the name of the Father and the Law. The narrative of the overpowering and surpassing of Acrasia uncannily resembles the narrative progression of this Lacanian family romance. The raised and potent Mosaic 'staffe' of the Palmer (which makes possible a detour out of this enclosure) evokes both the Law and the Father at once and rescues Guyon as potential second Verdant or arrested boy from the fate of the latter's suspended instruments, from the posture of the speechless *infans* caught within a spellbinding female space.[24] What Mulvey goes on to say of the voyeuristic *scopophilia* of the male gaze recalls much of the striking voyeurism of the visitants who come to destroy the Bower of Bliss, and her description of the two ways of overcoming the threat of castration figured by the female has intriguing resonances both for the defeat of Acrasia and for the representation of Elizabeth, Spenser's Petrarchan mistress-queen. The first way, writes Mulvey, involves turning the dangerous female figure into an image entirely outside the narrative – as, for example, in the cult of the female star, a strategy that might shed light on the cult of Elizabeth as Astraea, or quite literally a 'star', transcendent embodiment of all the idealized Stella figures of Petrarchan lyric. This virgin star reigns outside the sublunar system as Gloriana is figured as outside *The Faerie Queene* or Elizabeth presented repeatedly as transcendent exception to the threatening dominant females within it.

The other means of escape from female power and the anxiety of castration, however, is a specifically narrative one, an overcoming through narrative of the 'extradiegetic tendencies' of woman as spectacle, whose 'visual presence tends to . . . freeze the flow of action in moments of erotic contemplation' – a visual freeze that resembles the moments of paralysis, astonishment, or stonification in Petrarchan lyric as well as the potentially suspending moments of centripetal gaze that A. Bartlett Giamatti and others have described within *The Faerie Queene*.[25] It is, in Mulvey's description, the active male protagonist, the gazer rather than the gazed upon, who neutralizes this dangerous suspension by specifically narrative means, by a re-enactment that repeats both the original trauma of the castrating female and the process of her overcoming. The sense of resolute narrative movement and of re-enactment as a form of control is conveyed in the canto of Acrasia by the resolutely 'forward' movement (II.xii.76.5) of Guyon's quest and by the aura of repetition and even *déjà vu* in its imitation of earlier literary scenes, which suggests that the victory over its threatening female is in a sense already won: Guyon's almost ritual re-enactment of Odysseus' resistance to the Sirens suggests that they are by no means as threatening the second time around.[26] In Mulvey's account, in a way reminiscent of Guyon's destruction of the Bower, this narrative process of overcoming is not only voyeuristic but sadistic, its violence a sign simultaneously of the form of the threat and of the imperative of asserting control. In Spenser, the 'suspended instruments' of Acrasia's male captives are recovered as the Bower itself is overcome, and as Guyon and his Mosaic guide move forward to the narrative 'point' or end of a Book of the Governor in which both a threatening female ruler and her suspect lyricism are finally mastered and surpassed.

Perhaps because of the notorious difficulty of defining it, lyric is frequently described in oppositional terms, by its relation or tension with something else – lyric cynosure as distinct from centrifugal movement, lyric as opposed to epic or narrative, and so on. *The Faerie Queene* seems to be exploring the implications of this opposition in its very form – narrative in its forward, linear quest and yet composed out of lyric stanzas that, like the enchantresses within it, potentially suspend or retard. It would be crude simply to transcode genre into gender here, though much of the history of lyric associates it with the female or the effeminate, and though Spenser's episode contains that confrontation which Horkheimer and Adorno saw as part of a revealing 'dialectic of enlightenment' between a questing Odysseus and Sirens evocative of both lyric and threatening female 'charm'. But Guyon's defeat of Acrasia seems to involve something more than one of the poem's many narrative defeats of a potentially suspended, centripetal, 'lyric' space, to be not just, as Greenblatt suggests, a repression of pleasure for the sake of an empire ruled by Elizabeth (who in this reading would be simply *opposed* to Acrasia) but more complexly an overgoing of the potentially paralyzing suspensions – unpleasure as well as pleasure – of a lyric form adapted to the domination of a woman.

Spenser's monarch was ultimately subject not only to the higher patriarchal authority of her God but to the allegorical fashioning of the poet who scattered her dread image into 'mirrours more then one' (III.Proem.5.6). The allusive structures and staging of the Bower of Bliss suggest repeatedly that what is at stake within it is a complex hierarchy – the defeat of the Sirens by female Muses who are in turn subject to the authority of Apollo; the subordination, in Renaissance lyric theory, of secular lyric and its motivations to the higher lyricism and higher epideictic object of the Psalms; the surpassing, in Virgilian epic, both of the lesser pastoral genre of the Petrarchan *Shepheardes Calender* and of the power of eros and female rule. Its reticulation of these hierarchies suggests not simply the imperial politics inherited from Virgil and conveyed through the episode's unmistakable echoes of contemporary colonial enterprise but the subtle gender politics inscribed within the contradictory structure of rule by a Queen whose name recalled not Aeneas but Elissa.

The Palmer's power to defeat all 'charmes' gives to this episode a sense, ultimately, of something suspect about all *carmina*, something Protestant as well as male about its anxieties, though the defeat of Acrasia's 'subtile web' (77) by the Vulcan-like Palmer's 'subtile net' (81) suggests a strategy more complex than simple straightforward 'enlightenment', a sense, as Keats put it, that only the poet's fine 'spell of words' can rescue from a 'dumb' and paralyzing 'charm' and, perhaps, from an enchantress. A poem, finally, as dedicated as Spenser's to the polysemous perverse could easily encompass the psychological dynamic of the overpowering of a potentially castrating female, the covert political allegory of the overgoing of a lyricism associated with Elizabeth, and a simultaneously aesthetic and moral uneasiness about the seductiveness of lyric 'charm', even if that charm is an inseparable part of the attraction of his own poetry, its own tantalizingly suspending instrument.

Notes

This essay is a revised version of the English Institute essay of the same title, published in MARJORIE GARBER (ed.), *Cannibals, Witches, and Divorce: Estranging the Renaissance* (Baltimore, 1987). I am grateful for the readings given it by MARY NYQUIST, in preparation for its original presentation at the English Institute in 1984, and by MAUREEN QUILLIGAN and RICHARD STRIER.

1. The edition used for this and all subsequent quotations from Spenser is *Poetical Works*, eds J.C. Smith and E. de Selincourt (London, 1912).
2. Geneva Bible (1560) version. I am indebted to JOHN HOLLANDER's valuable discussion of the different versions and pervasive poetic influence of this psalm in *The Oxford Anthology of English Literature*, ed. Frank Kermode *et al.* (New York, 1973), vol. I, pp. 534–42. For the influence of the psalms themselves on Renaissance lyric and lyric theory, see, *inter alia*, O.B. HARDISON, JR, *The Enduring Monument: A Study of the Idea of Praise in Renaissance Literary Theory and Practice* (Chapel Hill, NC, 1962), pp. 95–102, and BARBARA KIEFER LEWALSKI, *Donne's Anniversaries and the Poetry of Praise* (Princeton, NJ, 1973), pp. 11–41.
3. See CALVIN, *Commentaries on the Book of Psalms*, trans. James Anderson, 5 vols (Grand Rapids, Mich., 1949), pp. 189–90, and AUGUSTINE, *Expositions on the Book of Psalms*, trans. J. Tweed *et al.*, 6 vols (Oxford, 1847–57), p. 163. Armida's garden appears in TASSO's *Gerusalemme liberata*, 16. CALVIN's commentary doubles 'hanged our harpes' with singers themselves held 'in suspense', and this paralleling of the suspended instruments with a more properly psychological or spiritual 'suspension' in the singer is continued in the versions of Thomas Campion, Thomas Carew and Sir John Denham cited by HOLLANDER in *The Oxford Anthology*.
4. See, for example, the analyses in PAUL ALPERS, *The Singer of the 'Eclogues': A Study of Virgilian Pastoral* (Berkeley and Los Angeles, 1979), pp. 97 ff., 102, 134.
5. JACOPO SANNAZARO, *Arcadia*, ch. 10, prose.
6. See, for example, the discussion in RICHARD HELGERSON, *Self-Crowned Laureates* (Berkeley and Los Angeles, 1983), pp. 65–82; and LOUIS ADRIAN MONTROSE, ' "The perfecte paterne of a Poete": The Poetics of Courtship in *The Shepheardes Calender*', *Texas Studies in Language and Literature*, 21 (1979), pp. 34–67.
7. The Bower of Bliss episode twice uses 'toyes' for 'trifles' or 'trifling'. THOMAS WATSON, *Hekatompathia or Passionate Centurie of Love*, ed. S.K. Heninger, Jr (Gainesville, Fla., 1964), p. 5, speaks of poems themselves as 'idle toyes proceeding from a youngling [i.e. prodigal, errant] frenzy'. Sir John Harington,

Elizabeth's godson and translator of Ariosto, feared that, in becoming 'a translator of Italian toys', he was wasting his education and later bade farewell to his 'sweet wanton Muse'. See LUDOVICO ARIOSTO, *Orlando furioso*, ed. Robert McNulty, trans. Sir John Harington (Oxford, 1972), pp. 14–15; SIR JOHN HARINGTON, *Nugae Antiquae*, ed. Henry Harington (London, 1804), vol. I, p. 333; and HELGERSON's seminal discussion of these and other texts in relation to the profession of poetry in *Self-Crowned Laureates*.

8. The crossing of phallic with lyric instruments is of course not an exclusively Spenserian one, 'instruments' being itself a fertile source of sexual double entendre. Cloten in *Cymbeline* (II.iii.13–14), setting up with his musicians to woo Imogen, arranges his lyric entertainment in the hope that it will 'penetrate' ('Come on, tune: if you can penetrate her with your fingering, so: we'll try with tongue too').

9. See MADLYN MILLNER KAHR, 'Delilah', in Norma Broude and Mary D. Garrard (eds), *Feminism and Art History* (New York, 1982), p. 137, an essay first brought to my attention by Mary Nyquist. That the evocation of Samson and Delilah would not be inappropriate within a Renaissance *locus amoenus* such as the Bower of Bliss is suggested as well by Kahr's citation of the reclining Samson in the *Small Garden of Love*. Kahr's entire discussion of the oral and maternal aspects of this iconography is useful in juxtaposition with Spenser's scene. In one representation (*c.* 1508) by the great Dutch graphic artist Lucas van Leyden, Samson has laid his shield and halberd on the ground beside him, stressing his defenselessness as he sleeps in Delilah's lap; in another by the same artist (*c.* 1517–18), the abandoned weapon is a spiked club, perhaps a reference to the club of Hercules.

10. See NEIL HERTZ, 'Medusa's Head: Male Hysteria under Political Pressure', *Representations*, 1, 4 (1983), pp. 40–50.

11. See PETER HAWKINS, 'From Mythography to Myth-Making: Spenser and the *Magna Mater* Cybele', *Sixteenth Century Journal*, 12, 3 (1981), pp. 51–64. Hawkins reminds us that ISABEL RATHBORNE long ago conjectured that Cybele was one of the literary ancestors of Gloriana: see her *Meaning of Spenser's Fairyland* (New York, 1937), p. 35. I am indebted to Hawkins's discussion of Cybele for the more general sense here of a link with *The Faerie Queene*, II.xii.

12. The episode in Book V also makes clearer the role of Britomart in this regard. She is the 'martial maid' who defeats Radigund, but who, after the battle, softens from the counterpart of a warlike Amazon (V.v.29) into a waiting 'Penelope' (39) who then, as reigning 'Princess', the 'liberty of women did repeale, / Which they had long usurpt; and them restoring / To Mens subiection, did true Iustice deale' (42.3–7). More detailed examination of the Britomart–Radigund pairing in relation to the Acrasia canto would suggest the tissue of contradictions at work in the reign of a Queen so clearly an exception to the patriarchal norm and under whom the situation of other women remained unchanged. The monstrosity of the rule of women is attested to, among other documents, by JOHN KNOX's attack on female rulers in his *First Blast of the Trumpet against the Monstrous regiment of women* (1558) and, after Elizabeth's accession as a female ruler sympathetic to Protestantism, his condition conveyed in a letter to her minister William Cecil that he would do 'reverence' to the 'miraculouse worke of God's comforting his afflicted by an infirme vessell', but only if the Queen would acknowledge 'that the extraordinary dispensation of Godes great mercy maketh that lawfull unto

her, which both nature and Godes law denye' to other women. See JAMES E. PHILLIPS, 'The Background of Spenser's Attitude Toward Women Rulers', *Huntington Library Quarterly*, 5 (October 1941–July 1942), pp. 19–20.

13. See MAUREEN QUILLIGAN, *Milton's Spenser: The Politics of Reading* (Ithaca, NY, 1983), pp. 67 ff.; and LOUIS ADRIAN MONTROSE, ' "Shaping Fantasies": Figurations of Gender and Power in Elizabethan Culture', *Representations*, 1, 2 (1983), pp. 61–94.

14. The Muses' lament indicts the English nobility in phrases that directly recall the Bower of Bliss from the first installment of *The Faerie Queene* ('loathly idleness' (p. 335); 'base slothfulnesse' (p. 99); 'men depriv'd of sense and minde' (p. 156); together with an image of navigation that parallels that of the journey of Guyon and his Palmer guide: 'But he that is of reasons skill bereft, / And wants the staffe of wisdome him to say, / Is like a ship in the midst of tempest left / Withouten helme or Pilot her to sway' (pp. 139 ff.)).

15. See the influential discussion of the Bower of Bliss in STEPHEN GREENBLATT, *Renaissance Self-Fashioning* (Chicago, 1980), pp. 165 ff.

16. See FRANCIS BACON, 'On the Fortunate Memory of Elizabeth Queen of England', trans. James Spedding, in *The Works of Francis Bacon*, eds James Spedding and Robert Ellis (London, 1857–74), vol. VI, p. 317; and GREENBLATT, *Renaissance Self-Fashioning*, pp. 166–7. Elizabeth was also both a forbidding Virgin and, in the words of Thomas Wenden, a yeoman subject, an 'arrant whore'. See PETER STALLYBRASS, 'Patriarchal Territories: The Body Enclosed', in Margaret W. Ferguson *et al.* (eds), *Rewriting the Renaissance* (Chicago, 1986), p. 132.

17. See SIR JOHN HARINGTON's 'Remembrauncer', *Nugae Antiquae* (1779; repr. Hildesheim, 1968), vol. II, p. 211, cited in LOUIS ADRIAN MONTROSE, 'The Elizabethan Subject and the Spenserian Text', in Patricia Parker and David Quint (eds), *Literary Theory/Renaissance Texts* (Baltimore, 1986), p. 326, and Montrose's larger discussion there of the dynamic of subjection and remastery, esp. pp. 317–26.

18. NANCY VICKERS, 'Diana Described: Scattered Woman and Scattered Rhyme', in Elizabeth Abel (ed.), *Writing and Sexual Difference* (Chicago, 1982), pp. 265–79. I am indebted to Vickers's suggestive discussion of the 'scattering' of Laura and of the Orpheus-like respite between seeing and dismemberment. See below.

19. LEONARD BARKAN, 'Diana and Actaeon: The Myth as Synthesis', *English Literary Renaissance*, 10, 3 (1980), p. 328, notes the Latin pun and George Sandys's explication of the myth as illustrating 'how dangerous a curiosity it is to search into the secrets of Princes'. See SANDYS, *Ovid's 'Metamorphosis' Englished, Mythologiz'd and Represented in Figures* (Oxford, 1632), pp. 151–2.

20. See MARIANN SANDERS REGAN, *Love Words: The Self and the Text in Medieval and Renaissance Poetry* (Ithaca, NY, 1982), pp. 50–82.

21. See MONTROSE, 'Shaping Fantasies', p. 77. For a different discussion of the link between Elizabeth and Dido or Elissa, see STEPHEN ORGEL, 'Shakespeare and the Cannibals', in Marjorie Garber (ed.), *Cannibals, Witches, and Divorce: Estranging the Renaissance* (Baltimore, 1987), pp. 60 ff.

22. See, for example, GREENBLATT, *Renaissance Self-Fashioning*, p. 177.

23. LAURA MULVEY, 'Visual Pleasure and Narrative Cinema', *Screen*, 16, 3 (1978), pp. 6–18.

24. HELGERSON, in *Self-Crowned Laureates*, pp. 86–7, suggests as well a link between Verdant, 'the green youth', and Spenser.

25. See MULVEY, 'Visual Pleasure', pp. 12 ff.; and A. BARTLETT GIAMATTI, 'Spenser: From Magic to Miracle', in Herschel Baker (ed.), *Four Essays on Romance* (Cambridge, Mass., 1971).

26. GREENBLATT, *Renaissance Self-Fashioning*, p. 177, also notes this sense of implicit repetition or re-enactment, remarking on 'why Acrasia cannot be destroyed, why she and what she is made to represent must continue to exist, forever the object of the destructive quest. For were she not to exist as a constant threat, the power Guyon embodies would also cease to exist.' My analysis would also invoke this sense of re-encounter, but it would shift the emphasis more clearly to the specifically sexual politics of this episode.

Part Two
Poetry and the Early
Modern Subject

4 Diana Described: Scattered Woman and Scattered Rhyme*

Nancy J. Vickers

Nancy Vickers applies a feminist approach to Petrarch's lyrics by arguing that the representation of gender in literature has consequences for women readers. Defining Petrarch's portrayal of Laura as 'informing the Renaissance norm of a beautiful woman', Vickers claims that the sonnet form creates woman as a fetishized body without a voice. The 'poetics of fragmentation', which scatters Laura into a composite of details, also makes possible Petrarch's construction of his own poetic subjectivity. Using a psychoanalytic perspective, Vickers finds that Petrarch's use of the myth of Diana and Actaeon expresses a fear of dismemberment associated with incest prohibitions and the castration complex. In Petrarch's version of the myth, the continuity of lyric song is only made possible through the silencing of Diana; so male subjectivity is constructed through the dismemberment of Laura. Such an 'ideal' image of femininity instructs women readers and writers in the cultural value of their own silence.

The import of Petrarch's description of Laura extends well beyond the confines of his own poetic age; in subsequent times, his portrayal of feminine beauty became authoritative. As a primary canonical text, the *Rime sparse* consolidated and disseminated a Renaissance mode. Petrarch absorbed a complex network of descriptive strategies and then presented a single, transformed model. In this sense his role in the history of the interpretation and the internalization of woman's 'image' by both men and women can scarcely be overemphasized. When late-Renaissance theorists, poets and painters represented woman's body, Petrarch's verse justified their aesthetic choices. His authority, moreover, extended beyond scholarly consideration to courtly conversation, beyond the treatise on

* Reprinted from *Writing and Sexual Difference*, ed. Elizabeth Abel (Chicago: University of Chicago, 1982), pp. 95–109.

beauty to the after-dinner game in celebration of it. The descriptive codes of others, both ancients and contemporaries, were, of course, not ignored, but the 'scattered rhymes' undeniably enjoyed a privileged status: they informed the Renaissance norm of a beautiful woman.[1]

We never see in the *Rime sparse* a complete picture of Laura. This would not be exceptional if we were considering a single 'song' or even a restricted lyric corpus; gothic top-to-toe enumeration is, after all, more appropriate to narrative, more adapted to the 'objective' observations of a third-person narrator than to those of a speaker who ostensibly loves, and perhaps even addresses, the image he describes. But given an entire volume devoted to a single lady, the absence of a coherent, comprehensive portrait is significant.[2] Laura is always presented as a part or parts of a woman. When more than one part figures in a single poem, a sequential, inclusive ordering is never stressed. Her textures are those of metals and stones; her image is that of a collection of exquisitely beautiful disassociated objects.[3] Singled out among them are hair, hand, foot and eyes: golden hair trapped and bound the speaker; an ivory hand took his heart away; a marble foot imprinted the grass and flowers; starry eyes directed him in his wandering.[4] In terms of qualitative attributes (blondness, whiteness, sparkle), little here is innovative. More specifically Petrarchan, however, is the obsessive insistence on the particular, an insistence that would in turn generate multiple texts on individual fragments of the body or on the beauties of woman.

When the sixteenth-century poet Joachim Du Bellay chose to attack the French propensity for Italianizing, his offensive gesture against the Petrarchans (among whose number he had once prominently figured) culminated in just this awareness: in his final verses he proposed to substitute the unified celebration of female beauty for the witty clichés of Petrarchan particularization:

> De voz *beautez* je diray seulement,
> Que si mon oeil ne juge folement,
> Vostre *beauté* est joincte egalement
>> A vostre bonne grace:
>>> [...]
> Si toutefois Petrarque vous plaist mieux,
>>> [...]
> Je choisiray cent mille nouveautez,
> Dont je peindray voz plus grandes *beautez*
>> Sur la plus belle Idee.
>
>> ('Contre les Petrarquistes', ll. 193–6, 201, 206–8)

Of your *beauties* I will only say that, if my eye does not mistakenly judge, your *beauty* is perfectly joined to your good grace: . . . But if you still like Petrarch better . . . I will choose a hundred thousand new ways to paint your greatest *beauties* according to the most beautiful Idea.⁵

Du Bellay's opposition of 'beauties' and 'beauty' suggests the idiosyncratic nature of Petrarch's depiction of woman as a composite of details. It would surely seem that to Petrarch Laura's whole body was at times less than some of its parts; and that to his imitators the strategy of describing her through the isolation of those parts presented an attractive basis for imitation, extension and, ultimately, distortion. I will redefine that strategy here in terms of a myth to which both the *Rime* and the Renaissance obsessively return, a myth complex in its interpretation although simple in its staging. As a privileged mode of signifying, the recounting of a mythical tale within a literary text reveals concerns, whether conscious or unconscious, which are basic to that text.⁶ It is only logical, then, to examine Petrarch's use of a myth about seeing woman in order to re-examine his description of a woman seen. The story of Actaeon's encounter with the goddess Diana is particularly suited to this purpose, for it is a story not only of confrontation with forbidden naked deity but also with forbidden naked femininity.

In the twenty-third *canzone*, the *canzone* of the metamorphoses, Petrarch's 'I' narrates a history of changes: he was Daphne (a laurel), Cygnus (a swan), Battus (a stone), Byblis (a fountain), Echo (a voice), he will never be Jove (a golden raincloud), and he is Actaeon (a stag). He has passed through a series of painful frustrations, now experiences a highly specific one, and will never be granted the sexual fulfillment of a god capable of transforming himself into a golden shower and inseminating the object of his desire. His use of the present in the last full stanza, the Actaeon stanza, is telling, for it centers this *canzone* on the juxtaposition of what the speaker was and what he now is: 'Alas, what am I? What was I? The end crowns the life, the evening the day.'⁷ The end also crowns the song, and this song paradoxically abandons its speaker in the form of a man so transmuted that he cannot speak:

I' segui' tanto avanti il mio desire
ch' un dì, cacciando sì com' io solea,
mi mossi, e quella fera bella et cruda
in una fonte ignuda
si stava, quando 'l sol più forte ardea.
Io perché d'altra vista non m'appago
stetti a mirarla, ond' ella ebbe vergogna
et per farne vendetta o per celarse
l'acqua nel viso co le man mi sparse.
Vero dirò; forse e' parrà menzogna:
ch'i' senti' trarmi de la propria imago
et in un cervo solitario et vago

di selva in selva ratto mi trasformo,
et ancor de' miei can fuggo lo stormo.

(RS, 23. 147–60)

I followed so far my desire that one day, hunting as I was wont, I
went forth, and that lovely cruel wild creature was in a spring naked
when the sun burned most strongly. I, who am not appeased by any
other sight, stood to gaze on her, whence she felt shame and, to take
revenge or to hide herself, sprinkled water in my face with her hand.
I shall speak the truth, perhaps it will appear a lie, for I felt myself
drawn from my own image and into a solitary wandering stag from
wood to wood quickly I am transformed and still I flee the belling of
my hounds.

Petrarch's account of Actaeon's story closely follows the subtext that
obviously subtends the entire *canzone* – Ovid's *Metamorphoses*. Actaeon is,
as usual, hunting with friends. At noon, he stumbles upon a grove where
he sees Diana, chaste goddess of the hunt and of the moon, bathing
nude in a pool.[8] In the *Metamorphoses* she is surrounded by protective
nymphs, but Petrarch makes no mention of either her company or of
Actaeon's. He thus focuses the exchange on its principal players. Actaeon
is transfixed (a stance Petrarch exaggerates), and Diana, both in shame
and anger, sprinkles ('spargens') his face ('vultum') and hair ('comas')
with water. Although in the *Rime sparse* Diana is significantly silenced, in
the *Metamorphoses* she utters, 'Now you can tell ['narres . . . licet'] that
you have seen me unveiled ['posito velamine'] – that is, if you can tell
['si poteris narrare'].[9] Diana's pronouncement simultaneously posits
telling (description) as the probable outcome of Actaeon's glance and
negates the possibility of that telling. Her vengeful baptism triggers a
metamorphosis: it transforms Actaeon from horn to hoof into a voiceless,
fearful stag (*Metamorphoses* 3. 193–8). It is at this moment that Petrarch,
with his characteristic use of an iterative present, situates his speaker:
No other sight appeases me; 'I am transformed'; 'I flee.'[10] The speaker *is*
Actaeon, but, more important, he is a self-conscious Actaeon: he knows
his own story; he has read his own text; he is defined by it and even
echoes it in articulating his suffering. What awaits him is annihilation
through dismemberment, attack unto death by his own hounds goaded
on by his own devoted friends.

Seeing and bodily disintegration, then, are related poles in the Ovidian
context that Petrarch brings to his text; they also are poles Ovid conjoins
elsewhere. Actaeon's mythological antitypes in dismemberment, Pentheus
and Orpheus, are both textually and experientially linked to his story.[11]
His is the subtext to their suffering; he is the figure for their pain. In
Metamorphoses 3. 708–33, Pentheus gapes with 'profane eyes' upon the
female celebrants of the sacred rites of Bacchus, and they, urged by his

mother (the woman who sees him), tear his body limb from limb: 'Let the ghost of Actaeon move your heart,' he pleads, but 'she [his mother] knows not who Actaeon is, and tears the suppliant's right arm away.' In *Metamorphoses* 11. 26–7, Orpheus is so grief stricken at having irrevocably lost Eurydice by turning back to look at her that he shuns other women; falling victim to an explosion of female jealousy, he is dismembered and scattered, 'as when in the amphitheatre . . . the doomed stag is the prey of dogs'.

All three men, then, transgress, see women who are not to be seen, and are torn to bits. But the Orpheus–Actaeon analogy is particularly suggestive, for in the case of Orpheus, seeing and dismemberment are discrete events in time. The hiatus between them, the extended reprieve, is a span of exquisite though threatened poetry, of songs of absence and loss. Petrarch's 'modern' Actaeon is in that median time: he is fearful of the price of seeing, yet to be paid, but still pleased by what he saw. The remembered image is the source of all joy and pain, peace and anxiety, love and hate: 'Living is such heavy and long pain, that I call out for the end in my great desire to see her again whom it would have been better not to have seen at all' (*RS*, 312. 12–14). Thus he must both perpetuate her image and forget it: he must 'cry out in silence', cry out 'with paper and ink', that is to say, write (*RS*, 71. 6, 23. 99).

It is especially important to note that the productive paralysis born of this ambivalence determines a normative stance for countless lovesick poets of the Petrarchan generations. As Leonard Barkan has recently shown, 'From that source [Petrarch] Actaeon's story becomes throughout the Renaissance a means of investigating the complicated psychology of love.'[12] When Shakespeare, for example, lends a critical ear to Orsino in his opening scene to *Twelfth Night*, we hear what was by 1600 the worn-out plaint of a languishing lover caught precisely in Actaeon's double bind:

CURIO: Will you go to hunt, my lord?
ORSINO: What, Curio?
CURIO: The hart.
ORSINO: Why, so I do, the noblest that I have.
         O, when mine eyes did see Olivia first,
         Methought she purg'd the air of pestilence!
         That instant was I turn'd into a hart,
         And my desires, like fell and cruel hounds,
         E'er since pursue me.
                            (Act 1, sc. 1, ll. 16–23)

Subsequent imitation, no matter how creative or how wooden, bears witness to the reader's awareness of and the writer's engagement in the practice of 'speaking' in Actaeon's voice. A reassessment of Petrarch's use of Actaeon's fate to represent the status of his speaking subject, then, constitutes a reassessment of not just one poetic stance but of many. When we step back from the Petrarchans to Petrarch, the casting of the poet in this role (and, by extension, the beloved in that of Diana) is less a cliché than a construct that can be used to explain both the scattering of woman and of rhyme in his vernacular lyric. Here the 'metaphor of appearance', so central to the volume, is paired with the myth of appearance: the fateful first perception of Laura – an image obsessively remembered, reworked, and repeated – assumes a mythical analogue and mythical proportion.[13] What the reader must then ask is why that remembrance, like the rhyme ('rimembra'/'membra' [remember/members]) that invokes it, is one of parts: 'Clear, fresh, sweet waters, where she who alone seems lady to me rested her lovely body ['membra'], gentle branch where it pleased her (with sighing I remember)' (RS, 126. 1–5).[14]

Although traces of Diana are subtly woven into much of the imagistic texture that progressively reveals the composite of Laura, only one text refers to her by name:

Non al suo amante più Diana piacque
quando per tal ventura tutta ignuda
la vide in mezzo de le gelide acque,

ch' a me la pastorella alpestra et cruda
posta a bagnar un leggiadretto velo
ch' a l'aura il vago et biondo capel chiuda;

tal che mi fece, or quand' egli arde 'l cielo,
tutto tremar d'un amoroso gielo.

(RS, 52)

Not so much did Diana please her lover when, by a similar chance, he saw her all naked amid the icy waters,

as did the cruel mountain shepherdess please me, set to wash a pretty veil that keeps her lovely blond head from the breeze;

so that she made me, even now when the sky is burning, all tremble with a chill of love.

This simple madrigal based on the straightforward equation of the speaker's pleasure at seeing Laura's veil and Actaeon's pleasure at seeing Diana's body has, of late, received lengthy and suggestive comment. Giuseppe Mazzotta, in an analysis centered on Petrarch's 'language of the self', reads it in relation to a reversibility of 'subject and object'.[15] John Freccero places Petrarch's use of the 'veil covering a radiant face' motif within its traditional context (Saint Paul to Dante), that of a 'figure for the relationship of the sign to its referent'. He concludes that Laura's 'veil, bathed in the water like the naked goddess seen by Actaeon, functions as a fetish, an erotic signifier of a referent whose absence the lover refuses to acknowledge'. That act of substituting the veil for the body, previously linked by Freccero to the Augustinian definition of idolatry, ultimately associates the fragmentation of Laura's body and the 'non-referentiality' of Petrarch's sequence:

> One of the consequences of treating a signifier as an absolute is that its integrity cannot be maintained. Without a principle of intelligibility, an interpretant, a collection of signs threatens to break down into its component parts . . . So it is with Laura. Her virtues and her beauties are scattered like the objects of fetish worship: her eyes and hair are like gold and topaz on the snow, while the outline of her face is lost; . . . Like the poetry that celebrates her, she gains immortality at the price of vitality and historicity. Each part of her has the significance of her entire person; it remains the task of the reader to string together her gemlike qualities into an idealized unity.[16]

Freccero's analysis departs from a position shared by many contemporary Petrarch critics – that of the centrality of a dialectic between the scattered and the gathered, the integrated and the disintegrated.[17] In defining Petrarch's 'poetics of fragmentation', these same critics have consistently identified as its primary figure the particularizing descriptive strategy adopted to evoke Laura.[18] If the speaker's 'self' (his text, his 'corpus') is to be unified, it would seem to require the repetition of her dismembered image. 'Woman remains,' as Josette Féral has commented in another context, 'the instrument by which man attains unity, and she pays for it at the price of her own dispersion.'[19]

Returning to *Rime sparse* 52, some obvious points must be made: first, this text is read as an emblem of Petrarchan fragmentation; and second, it turns on a highly specific analogy ('I am pleased by Laura's veil as Actaeon was pleased by Diana's nakedness'; 'My fetish equals Diana's body'). It is the analogy itself that poses an additional problem. While the enunciation of 'I' 's fetishistic pleasure through comparison with Actaeon's voyeuristic pleasure might appear incongruous, it is both appropriate and revealing.

The Actaeon–Diana story is one of identification and reversal: Actaeon hunts; Diana hunts; and their encounter reduces him to the status of the hunted.[20] This fated meeting, this instant of midday recognition, is one of fascination and repulsion: it is a confrontation with difference where similarity might have been desired or even expected. It is a glance into a mirror – witness the repeated pairing of this myth with that of Narcissus (*Metamorphoses* 3. 344–510) – that produces an unlike and deeply threatening image.[21] Perceiving that image is, of course, prohibited; such a transgression violates proscriptions imposed on powerless humans in their relation to powerful divinities. Similarly, such a transgression violates proscriptions imposed upon powerless men (male children) in relation to powerful women (mothers):[22] 'This is thought,' writes Howard Daniel, 'to be one of many myths relating to the incest mechanism – punishment for an even accidental look at something forbidden.'[23] The Actaeon–Diana encounter read in this perspective re-enacts a scene fundamental to theorizing about fetishistic perversion: the troubling encounter of a male child with intolerable female nudity, with a body lacking parts present in his own, with a body that suggests the possibility of dismemberment. Woman's body, albeit divine, is displayed to Actaeon, and his body, as a consequence, is literally taken apart. Petrarch's Actaeon, having read his Ovid, realizes what will ensue: his response to the threat of imminent dismemberment is the neutralization, through descriptive dismemberment, of the threat. He transforms the visible totality into scattered words, the body into signs; his description, at one remove from his experience, safely permits and perpetuates his fascination.

The verb in the *Rime sparse* that places this double dismemberment in the foreground is determinant for the entire sequence – *spargere*, 'to scatter'. It appears in some form (most frequently that of the past-participial adjective *'sparso, -i, -a, -e'*) forty-three times; nineteen apply specifically to Laura's body and its emanations (the light from her eyes, the generative capacity of her footsteps) and thirteen to the speaker's mental state and its expression (tears, voice, rhymes, sighs, thoughts, praises, prayers, hopes). The uses of *spargere* thus markedly gravitate toward 'I' and Laura. The etymological roots of the term, moreover, virtually generate Laura's metaphoric codes: 'I' knows that the outcome of seeing her body is the scattering of his; hence he projects scattering on to her through a process of fetishistic overdetermination, figuring those part-objects in terms of the connotations of 'scattering': *spargere*, from the Latin *spargere*, with cognates in the English 'sprinkle' and 'sparkle' and in the Greek σπείρω – 'I disseminate.' Laura's eyes, as in the sequence of three *canzoni* devoted exclusively to them (*RS*, 71–3), are generative sparks emanating from the stars; they sow the seeds of poetry in the 'untilled soil' of the poet (*RS*, 71. 102–5), and they sprinkle glistening drops like clear waters. Her body parts metaphorically inseminate; his do not: 'Song, I was never the cloud of gold that once descended in a precious rain so that it partially quenched the fire of Jove; but I have certainly been a flame lit by a lovely glance and I have been the bird that rises highest in the air raising her whom in my words I honor' (*RS*, 23. 161–6). Desire directed in vain at a forbidden, distant goddess is soon sublimated desire that spends itself in song. That song is, in turn, the celebration and the violation of that goddess: it would re-produce her vulnerability; it would re-present her nakedness to a (male) reader who will enter into collusion with, even become, yet another Actaeon.[24]

Within the context of Petrarch's extended poetic sequence, the lady is corporeally scattered; the lover is emotionally scattered and will be corporeally scattered, and thus the relation between the two is one of mirroring. 'I', striking Actaeon's pose, tells us that he stood fixed to see but also to mirror Diana–Laura ('mirarla').[25] He offers to eliminate the only source of sadness for the 'lovely eyes', their inability to see themselves, by mirroring them (*RS*, 71. 57–60). And he transforms the coloration of the lady's flesh into roses scattered in snow in which he mirrors himself (*RS*, 146. 5–6). The specular nature of this exchange explains, in large part, the disconcerting interchangeability of its participants. Even the key rhyme 'rimembra/membra' reflects a doubling: twice the *membra* are his (*RS*, 15 and 23); once those of the lost heroes of a disintegrating body politic, a dissolving mother country (*RS*, 53); and twice hers (*RS*, 126 and 127). In reading the Diana–veil madrigal cited above, Mazzotta demonstrates this textual commingling, pointing out that Diana's body, in the first tercet, is completely naked ('tutta ignuda') in a pool of icy waters ('gelide acque') but, by the last line, her observer's body is all atremble ('tutto tremar') with a chill of love ('un amoroso gielo'). Mazzotta goes on to note that male/female roles often alternate in Petrarch's figurations of the speaker/Laura relationship: he is Echo to her Narcissus, Narcissus to her Echo; she is Apollo to his Daphne, Daphne to his Apollo, and so on.[26] The space of that alternation is a median one – a space of looks, mirrors and texts.

Actaeon sees Diana, Diana sees Actaeon, and seeing is traumatic for both. She is ashamed, tries to hide her body (her secret), and thus communicates her sense of violation. Her observer consequently knows that pleasure in the sight before him constitutes transgression; he educes that transgression, although thrilling (arousing), is threatening (castrating). Their initial communication is a self-conscious look; the following scenario fills the gap between them: 'I . . . stood to gaze on her, whence she felt shame and, to take revenge or to hide herself, sprinkled water ['mi sparse' – cf. Ovid, 'spargens'] in my face with her hand[s]. I shall speak the truth' (*RS*, 23. 153–6). She defends herself and assaults him with scattered water; he responds with scattered words: 'You who hear in scattered rhymes the sound of those sighs with which I nourished my heart during my first youthful error, when I was in part another man from what I am now' (*RS*, l. 1–4). Water and words, then, pass between them; hands and transparent drops cannot conceal her but do precipitate a metamorphosis, preventing a full sounding of what was momentarily seen. Threatened rhymes try to iterate a precious, fleeting image, to transmute it into an idol that can be forever possessed, that will be forever present.

But description is ultimately no more than a collection of imperfect signs, signs that, like fetishes, affirm absence by their presence. Painting

Laura in poetry is but a twice-removed, scripted rendering of a lost woman (body → introjected image of the body → textual body), an enterprise by definition fragmentary. 'I' speaks his anxiety in the hope of finding repose through enunciation, of re-membering the lost body, of effecting an inverse incarnation – her flesh made word. At the level of the fictive experience which he describes, successes are ephemeral, and failures become a way of life.

> Quella per cui con Sorga ò cangiato Arno,
> con franca povertà serve ricchezze,
> volse in amaro sue sante dolcezze
> ond' io già vissi, or me ne struggo et scarno.
>
> Da poi più volte ò riprovato indarno
> al secol che verrà l'alte bellezze
> pinger cantando, a ciò che l'ame et prezze,
> né col mio stile il suo bel viso incarno.
>
> Le lode, mai non d'altra et proprie sue,
> che 'n lei fur come stelle in cielo sparte,
> pur ardisco ombreggiare, or una or due;
>
> ma poi ch' i' giungo a la divina parte,
> ch' un chiaro et breve sole al mondo fue[,]
> ivi manca l'ardir, l'ingegno et l'arte.

(RS, 308)

She for whom I exchanged Arno for Sorgue and slavish riches for free poverty, turned her holy sweetness[es], on which I once lived, into bitterness, by which now I am destroyed and disfleshed [I destroy and disflesh myself].

Since then I have often tried in vain to depict in song for the age to come her high beauties, that it may love and prize them, nor with my style can I incarnate her lovely face.

Still now and again I dare to adumbrate one or two of the praises that were always hers, never any other's, that were as many as the stars spread [scattered] across the sky;

but when I come to her divine part, which was a bright, brief sun to the world, there fails my daring, my wit, and my art.

This text organizes itself upon a sequence of oppositions which contrast fullness (presence) with emptiness (absence). The speaker has exchanged Arno (Florence, mother country) for Sorgue (Vaucluse, exile); riches (although slavish) for poverty (albeit free); sweetness for bitterness; a body for dismemberment; and union for separation. The speaker's rhymes point to a past place (a body of water, 'Arno') and to two present, though fruitless ('indarno'), activities – he is at once stripped of flesh ('me ne . . . scarno') and would give flesh to her ('incarno'). He acknowledges his inability to re-create Laura's absent face, and yet he maintains that he still tries, 'now and again'. Her praises (that is, his poems) are but images he 'dare[s] to adumbrate', shadows 'scattered', like their source, across the sky. Daring, wit and art cannot re-present her to him, but they can evoke her parts 'one by one' and thus generate an exquisite sequence of verse (*RS* , 127. 85–91 and 273. 6). For it is in fact the loss, at the fictional level, of Laura's body that constitutes the intolerable absence, creates a reason to speak, and permits a poetic 'corpus'. As Petrarch's readers have consistently recognized, Laura and *lauro*, the laurel to crown a poet laureate, are one.[27]

Petrarch's poetry is a poetry of tension, of flux, of alternation between the scattered and the gathered. Laura's many parts would point to a unity, however elusive, named Laura; the speaker's ambivalent emotions are spoken by a grammatically constant 'io'. In the space of exchange, the only space the reader is given, permutation is possible; each part of her body can produce each aspect of his positive/negative reactions. A given text can expand any combination; infinite variety spawns infinite verse. Petrarch's particularizing mode of figuring that body, the product of a male-viewer/female-object exchange that extends the Actaeon/Diana exchange, thus reveals a textual strategy subtending his entire volume: it goes to the heart of his lyric program and understandably becomes the lyric stance of generations of imitators.

And yet such praise carries condemnation with it because it implies at least two interdependent consequences. First, Petrarch's figuration of Laura informs a decisive stage in the development of a code of beauty, a code that causes us to view the fetishized body as a norm and encourages us to seek, or to seek to be, 'ideal types, beautiful monsters composed of every individual perfection'.[28] Petrarch's text, of course, did not constitute the first example of particularizing description, but it did popularize that strategy by coming into fashion during the privileged early years of printing, the first century of the widespread diffusion of both words and images. It is in this context that Petrarch left us his legacy of fragmentation. And second, bodies fetishized by a poetic voice logically do not have a voice of their own; the world of making words, of making texts, is not theirs. The status of Laura's voice, however, resists easy or schematic characterization. Once dead, it should be noted, she can often address her sleeping, disconsolate lover; while she is alive, direct discourse from her is extremely rare. Her speech, moreover, undergoes a treatment similar to that of her body in that it ranks high on the list of her exquisitely reified parts: 'and her speech and her lovely face and her locks pleased me so that I have her before my eyes and shall always have wherever I am, on slope or shore' (*RS*, 30. 4–6).

Rime sparse 23, the *canzone* of the metamorphoses, strikingly dramatizes the complexity of both citing and stifling Laura's voice. Although each of its transformations repeats an Ovidian model, only three stress the active participation of the Lady. In the first she lifts the speaker's heart out of his chest, utters two exceptional sentences, and ultimately turns him (like Battus) into a stone; next, she reduces him (like Echo) into a repetitive voice; and finally, she transforms him (like Actaeon) into a stag. The Ovidian models are telling in that they all either limit or negate a voice: Mercury says to Battus, 'Whoever you are, my man, if anyone should ask you about some cattle, say that you have not seen them' (*Metamorphoses* 2. 692–4); Juno says to Echo, 'That tongue by which I have been tricked shall have its power curtailed and enjoy the briefest use of speech' (*Metamorphoses* 3. 366–7); and Diana says to Actaeon, 'Now you are free to tell ['narres . . . licet'] that you have seen me unveiled – if you can tell ['narrare']' (*Metamorphoses* 3. 192–3).[29]

The first model permits speech, but insists that it not be true, and, when disobeyed, denies it; the second, by reducing speech to repetition, eliminates its generative capacity; and the third, through irony, does away with it altogether. In Ovid's retelling of that third encounter, Diana is the only person to speak once Actaeon has had his first glimpse of her: *'narrare'* is her word; she pronounces it; she even repeats it. Although she cannot (would not?) prevent him from seeing, she can prevent him from telling. Consequently, that Petrarch erases both her speech and the verbal object of her interdiction (*narrare*) from his own narration is significant. A review of the evolution of the Diana/Actaeon sequence of *Rime sparse* 23, a text at many points explicit in its verbal echoing of Ovid, shows that 'I shall speak ['dirò'] the truth' initiates the primary and final versions of line 156: two intermediate variants read 'I tell ['narro'] the truth.'[30] What that rejected present, *narro*, affirms, in a mode perhaps too obvious to be acceptable even to Petrarch, is that his speaker as Actaeon does precisely what Diana forbids: ' "Make no word of this," ' said the 'powerful Lady' of a preceding stanza (*RS*, 23. 74, 35). Not only does Petrarch's Actaeon thus nullify Diana's act, he repeats her admonition in so doing; by the time we arrive at the end that 'crowns' his song, her speech has been written out and his has been written in. To the measure that he continues to praise her beauties, he persists in inverting the traditional economy of the mythical exchange; he persists in offending her: 'Not that I do not see how much my praise injures you [the eyes]; but I cannot resist the great desire that is in me since I saw what no thought can equal, let alone speech, mine or others'' (*RS*, 71. 16–21).

Silencing Diana is an emblematic gesture; it suppresses a voice, and it casts generations of would-be Lauras in a role predicated upon the muteness of its player.[31] A modern Actaeon affirming himself as poet cannot permit Ovid's angry goddess to speak her displeasure and deny his voice; his speech requires her silence. Similarly, he cannot allow her to dismember his body; instead he repeatedly, although reverently, scatters hers throughout his scattered rhymes.

Notes

An early version of this paper was shared with the University Seminar on Feminist Inquiry at Dartmouth College; I sincerely appreciate the time, attention and suggestions of its members. I am particularly indebted to Richard Corum, Jonathan Goldberg, Katherine Hayles, Marianne Hirsch, David Kastan, Stephen Orgel, Esther Rashkin, Christian Wolff and Holly Wolff for their contributions.

1. On this 'thoroughly self-conscious fashion', see ELIZABETH CROPPER, 'On Beautiful Women, Parmigianino, *Petrarchismo*, and the Vernacular Style', *Art Bulletin* 58 (1976): 374–94. Cropper shares many of the observations on Petrarchan descriptive technique outlined in the following paragraph (see pp. 385–86). I am indebted to DAVID QUINT for bringing this excellent essay to my attention.
2. Description is, of course, always fragmentary in that it is by nature enumerative. Petrarch, however, systematically avoids those structures that would mask fragmentation. On enumeration and the descriptive text, see ROLAND BARTHES, *S/Z* (Paris, 1970), pp. 120–2.
3. For lengthy discussions of these qualities of Petrarchan descriptions, see ROBERT DURLING, 'Petrarch's "Giovene donna sotto un verde lauro"', *Modern Language Notes* 86 (1971): 1–20, and JOHN FRECCERO, 'The Fig Tree and the Laurel: Petrarch's Poetics', *Diacritics* 5 (Spring 1975): 34–40.
4. On Petrarch's role in the popularization of this *topos*, see JAMES V. MIROLLO, 'In Praise of "La bella mano"': Aspects of Late Renaissance Lyricism', *Comparative Literature Studies* 9 (1972): 31–43. See also JAMES VILLAS, 'The Petrarchan Topos "Bel piede": Generative Footsteps', *Romance Notes* 11 (1969): 167–73.
5. Italics and translation mine.
6. For a recent summary and bibliography of the place of myth in the Renaissance text, see LEONARD BARKAN, 'Diana and Actaeon: The Myth as Synthesis', *English Literary Renaissance* 10 (1980).
7. *Petrarch's Lyric Poems: The 'Rime sparse' and Other Lyrics*, trans. and ed. Robert M. Durling (Cambridge, Mass., 1976), *canzone* 23, ll. 30–1; all further references to the *Rime sparse* will be included in the text with poem and line number in parentheses and with Durling's translation. For recent analyses of *Rime sparse* 23, see DENNIS DUTSCHKE, *Francesco Petrarca: Canzone XXIII from First to Final Version* (Ravenna, 1977), and ALBERT J. RIVERO, 'Petrarch's "Nel dolce tempo de la prima etade"', *Modern Language Notes* 94 (1979): 92–112.
8. For an extremely useful comparison of the Ovidian and Petrarchan narrations of this scene, see DUTSCHKE, *Francesco Petrarca*, pp. 200–9. On the relationship between midday and sexuality in this myth, see NICOLAS J. PERELLA, *Midday in Italian Literature: Variations on an Archetypal Theme* (Princeton, NJ, 1979), pp. 8–9.
9. Ovid, *Metamorphoses*, ed. and trans. Frank J. Miller, 2 vols (1921; London, 1971), bk 3, ll. 192–3; all further references to the *Metamorphoses* will be included in

the text with book and line number in parentheses. The quotations from this work are based upon but do not entirely reproduce Miller's edition.

10. On the use of the present tense in relation to Actaeon, see DURLING'S introduction to *Petrarch's Lyric Poems*, p. 28.
11. On the association of Actaeon and Orpheus, see *ibid.*, p. 29. On Actaeon and Pentheus, see NORMAN O. BROWN, 'Metamorphoses II: Actaeon', *American Poetry Review* 1 (November/December 1972): 38.
12. BARKAN, 'Diana and Actaeon', p. 335. On the use of this myth in medieval lyric, see STEPHEN G. NICHOLS, JR, 'Rhetorical Metamorphosis in the Troubadour Lyric', in *Mélanges de langue et de littérature médiévales offerts à Pierre Le Gentil, Professeur à la Sorbonne, par ses collègues, ses élèves, et ses amis*, eds Jean Dufournet and Daniel Poirion (Paris, 1973), pp. 569–85.
13. See GIUSEPPE MAZZOTTA, 'The *Canzoniere* and the Language of the Self', *Studies in Philology* 75 (1978): 277.
14. The connection between these verses and the Diana/Actaeon myth is noted by DURLING, *The Figure of the Poet in Renaissance Epic* (Cambridge, Mass., 1965), p. 73. See also my 'Re-membering Dante: Petrarch's "Chiare, fresche et dolci acque"', *Modern Language Notes* 96 (1981): 8–9.
15. See MAZZOTTA, 'The *Canzoniere*', pp. 282–4.
16. FRECCERO, 'The Fig Tree', pp. 38–9.
17. See, e.g., DURLING, introduction to *Petrarch's Lyric Poems*; FRECCERO, 'The Fig Tree'; and Mazzotta, 'The *Canzoniere*'.
18. For the phrase 'poetics of fragmentation', see MAZZOTTA, 'The *Canzoniere*', p. 274.
19. JOSETTE FÉRAL, 'Antigone or *The Irony of the Tribe*', trans. Alice Jardine and Tom Gora, *Diacritics* 8 (Fall 1978): 7. I am indebted to Elizabeth Abel for calling this quotation to my attention. See also DURLING, introduction to *Petrarch's Lyric Poems*, p. 21, and MAZZOTTA, 'The *Canzoniere*', p. 273.
20. See BARKAN, 'Diana and Actaeon', pp. 320–2, and BROWN, 'Metamorphoses II', p. 40.
21. See BARKAN, 'Diana and Actaeon', pp. 321, 343; BROWN, 'Metamorphoses II', p. 39; DURLING, introduction to *Petrarch's Lyric Poems*, p. 31; and MAZZOTTA, 'The *Canzoniere*', pp. 274, 282.
22. This myth has often been used to point to relationships of power through play on the words *cervus/servus, cerf/serf* (stag/slave); see BARKAN 'Diana and Actaeon', p. 328. The identification of Diana with women in political power is perhaps best exemplified by the frequent representation of Elizabeth I as Diana; see Barkan, pp. 332–5.
23. HOWARD DANIEL, *Encyclopedia of Themes and Subjects in Painting*, s.v. 'Actaeon' (London, 1971). Daniel's point is, of course, supported by the tradition identifying Actaeon's hounds with the Law, with his conscience: 'Remorse, the bite of a mad dog. Conscience, the superego, the introjected father or animal: now eating us even as we ate him' (BROWN, 'Metamorphoses II', p. 39); see also PERELLA, *Midday in Italian Literature*, p. 42. On Actaeon as 'unmanned' or castrated, see BARKAN, 'Diana and Actaeon', pp. 350–1.
24. See DANIEL, 'Actaeon'. On the casting of the male spectator (reader) in the role of the voyeur, see also John Berger, *Ways of Seeing* (New York, 1977), pp. 45–64, and LAURA MULVEY, 'Visual Pleasure and Narrative Cinema', *Screen* 16 (Autumn 1975): 6–18. On women conditioned by patriarchal culture to see themselves as 'sights', see JESSICA BENJAMIN, 'The Bonds of Love: Rational

Violence and Erotic Domination', in *The Future of Difference*, eds Hester
Eisenstein and Alice Jardine (Boston, 1980), p. 52, and BERGER, *Ways of Seeing*,
pp. 46–51.

25. I am, of course, alluding to the etymological associations and not the definition
of the verb *mirare* ('to stare').
26. MAZZOTTA, 'The *Canzoniere*', pp. 282–4. See also DURLING, introduction to
Petrarch's Lyric Poems, pp. 31–2.
27. For recent analyses of the play on Laura/*lauro*, see FRANÇOIS RIGOLOT, 'Nature
and Function of Paronomasia in the *Canzoniere*', *Italian Quarterly* 18 (Summer
1974): 29–36, and MARGA COTTINO-JONES, 'The Myth of Apollo and Daphne in
Petrarch's *Canzoniere*: The Dynamics and Literary Function of Transformation',
in *Francis Petrarch, Six Centuries Later: A Symposium*, ed. Aldo Scaglione
(Chapel Hill, N.C., 1975), pp. 152–76.
28. CROPPER, 'On Beautiful Women', p. 376.
29. On the Diana/Actaeon myth and 'the danger of losing the poetic voice', see
MAZZOTTA, 'The *Canzoniere*', p. 278; see also DURLING, introduction to *Petrarch's
Lyric Poems*, p. 28.
30. See DUTSCHKE, *Francesco Petrarca*, pp. 196–8.
31. For the problem of women writing within the constraints of the Petrarchan
tradition, see ANN R. JONES, 'Assimilation with a Difference: Renaissance
Women Poets and Literary Influence', *Yale French Studies* no. 62 (October 1981);
on the impact of another masculine lyric tradition on women poets, see
MARGARET HOMANS, *Women Writers and Poetic Identity: Dorothy Wordsworth,
Emily Brontë and Emily Dickinson* (Princeton, N.J., 1980), pp. 12–40.

LAURA MULVEY comments on the silencing of women in her rereading of a
different medium, film: 'Woman then stands in patriarchal culture as signifier
for the male other, bound by a symbolic order in which man can live out his
phantasies and obsessions through linguistic command by imposing them on
the silent image of woman still tied to her place as bearer of meaning, not
maker of meaning' ('Visual Pleasure', p. 7).

5 *Astrophil and Stella*: 'All Selfnesse He Forbeares'*

RICHARD C. MCCOY

Richard McCoy's *Sir Philip Sidney: Rebellion in Arcadia* (1979) was an early, influential study of Sidney's political career and literary works. It looked forward to new historicism in its assumption that social issues could determine the most personal of literary genres, including the sonnet. McCoy argues that Sidney's works pose a conflict between rebellious defiance of authority and obedient submission, a pattern which reflects his own difficulties with his sovereign, Queen Elizabeth. Sidney's defiance is characterized by McCoy as an embryonic questioning of the principle of monarchy which never becomes fully conscious. Unlike many new historicists, however, McCoy approaches *Astrophil and Stella* as a realm to some extent set off from politics, in which Sidney could explore these issue free from court pressures. Nevertheless, in McCoy's argument, historical forces determine the shape of subjectivity in the sonnet sequence: for Astrophil, 'selfnesse' remains inherently divided, in a 'clash between autonomy and submission', structured in terms of the relationship between sovereign and subject.

Since it first appeared, *Astrophil and Stella* has stirred biographical speculation. The links between the poems and the facts of Sidney's life have proved confusing for many readers, and some have sought to minimize the connection.[1] The principal resemblance is unavoidably obvious, however, for as William Ringler, the sonnets' recent editor, points out, 'Sidney went out of his way to identify himself as Astrophil and Stella as Lady Rich.'[2] Lady Rich was the former Penelope Devereux, sister to Essex, and the charge of several of Philip's close relations. She was presented at court in January 1581, the same month that Sidney

---

* Reprinted from Richard C. McCoy, *Sir Philip Sidney: Rebellion in Arcadia* (New Brunswick: Rutgers University Press, 1979), pp. 69–109.

returned from his rustication. On New Year's Day he had presented a 'whip garnished with small diamonds' to the Queen as a token of his deference to her judgment in the Anjou marriage question.[3] Penelope was engaged that spring to Lord Rich and married him in November. For his part, Sidney was extremely active in the affairs of court and Parliament, and he participated in several tournaments. It seems that he fell in love with the young lady shortly after her marriage and remained troubled by this adulterous preoccupation until his death, when he mentioned his concern to an attending chaplain.[4]

Astrophil and Stella was begun in 1582, and it developed into one of the most coherent sonnet sequences in English. Sidney deals with recent events and characters from his life, but he imposes a clear dramatic structure. *Astrophil and Stella* is not a documentary record of an affair, nor is it a 'versified diary'.[5] In fact, the rather remarkable feature of the sequence, as Ringler points out, is the numerous biographical omissions:

When we compare the known facts of Sidney's life during the years 1581–2 with the sonnets and songs of *Astrophil and Stella*, we are immediately struck with how much of his biography he left out of his poem. He tells us nothing about the disappointment of his hopes in being superseded as the Earl of Leicester's heir, nothing about his trip to Antwerp, nothing about his dominating interest in politics and international affairs – his friendship with the exiled Earl of Angus and the Portuguese pretender Don Antonio, and, most significant, nothing about his activities in opposition to the proposed marriage of the Duke of Anjou with the Queen.[6]

In short, no aspect of his political career intrudes, a surprising exclusion for a man of Sidney's ambitions. In *AS* 30, for example, the details of public affairs are carefully enumerated only to be renounced as matters indifferent to one in love:

> If French can yet three parts in one agree;
> What now the Dutch in their full diets boast;
> How Holland hearts, now so good townes be lost,
> Trust in the shade of pleasing Orange tree;
> How Ulster likes of that same golden bit,
> Wherewith my father once made it halfe tame;
> If in the Scottishe Court be weltring yet;
> These questions busie wits to me do frame;
> I, cumbred with good maners, answer do,
> But know not how, for still I thinke of you.
>
> (*AS* 30)

Like other heroes of Elizabethan sonnets, Astrophil banishes all other concerns in his love for Stella. Love becomes, in J.W. Lever's apt phrase, 'the supreme and inalienable individual experience',[7] diminishing all other values and dismissing rival claims. John Donne pushes the lover's prerogative to its celestial limits in his songs and sonnets, scorning other interests as trivial distractions. The belligerence that accompanies this erotic *contemptus mundi* is another connection between Sidney and Donne. The latter's 'Canonization' begins with a tone of contentious riposte frequently assumed by Astrophil, but Donne moves beyond the conflicts and equivocations of the earlier poetry to an irreproachable sanctimony, brazenly fusing the carnal and platonic. Sidney is distinctive both in his insistence on their split and in his emphasis on the troubling aspects of sexual desire. In his excellent study of Sidney's poetry, David Kalstone finds a persistent and 'sharply defined concern for the corrosive effects of love upon the heroic life'.[8]

Yet, while the virtue of love may be less absolute for Sidney, it still represents a profoundly absorbing experience. All the major thematic concerns of his other works are organized and contained within the bounds of this poetic courtship. This restriction of focus gives this work a clarifying force, the impact of which is well described by Theodore Spencer: 'Who Stella was, and whether or not Sidney as a man felt a genuine passion for her, are puzzling questions, but not worth much conjecture. All that matters is that she was a symbol around which were mustered a set of important emotions, emotions which were multiplied and intensified, sometimes perhaps even induced by Sidney's desire to express them.'[9] *Astrophil and Stella* not only depicts the vicissitudes of courtship and sexual desire; it also allows Sidney his clearest expression of other crucial issues. Romantic intrigue reveals the clash between autonomy and submission in a more clearly focused narrative, freed of all the troubling connections and details of Sidney's political career.

As I have shown, these connections are more explicit in his other works, and the conflict becomes more unwieldy. The larger narrative scope of the *Arcadia* allows Sidney to include more of his immediate concerns, and both versions expand to their own artistic detriment. Their problematic complexity subverts Sidney's control of his material. *Astrophil and Stella* presents a more restricted drama from which Sidney omits 'the full range of his interests and activities, but only [writes] about those directly connected with his love for Stella. His emotion may or may not have been recollected in tranquillity, but he was obviously in full command of himself and of his materials while he was writing. Everything in his poem is focused on his relations with Stella; everything in his experience during those months which did not directly relate to his central theme he ruthlessly excluded. Therefore, though the substance of his poem was autobiographical, mere fact was made subservient to the requirements of art.'[10] It is this 'ruthless exclusion' that makes *Astrophil and Stella* such a successful sequence. Sidney deals with the problem of control and autonomy in purely romantic terms. The politics here are exclusively sexual, and he examines them with a clarity, humor and assurance lacking in the other works.

The political aspect of love is immediately apparent in all of Sidney's writing. 'But alas,' Musidorus sighs, 'well have I found, that Love to a yeelding hart is a king; but to a resisting, is a tyrant' (*NA*, 115). The metaphor has several sources, some psychological and some historical. The Freudian explanation of love's contradictions is certainly pertinent here. In his excellent study of Freud's thought, Philip Rieff says that 'by "nature" (that is, originally) love is authoritarian; sexuality – like liberty – is a later achievement, always in danger of being overwhelmed by our deeper inclinations toward submissiveness and domination.'[11] In *The Allegory of Love*, C.S. Lewis sees a similar evolution in consciousness occurring historically, in the medieval emergence of courtly love. Lewis formulates his own 'law of transference which determined that all the emotion stored in the vassal's relation to his *seigneur* should attach itself to the new kind of love' for women.[12] 'The lover is always abject. Obedience to his lady's lightest wish, however whimsical, and silent acquiescence in her rebukes, however unjust, are the only virtues he dares to claim. There is a service of love closely modelled on the service which a feudal vassal owes to his lord. The lover is the lady's "man". He addresses her as *midons*, which etymologically represents not "my lady" but "my lord". The whole attitude has been rightly described as "a feudalisation of love".'[13]

Court poetry and court culture sustained these ambiguities in a highly self-conscious fashion, combining sexual impulse and submission with a refined erotic sensibility. The political aspect of love became even more explicit with various challenges to the code of courtly love. In the sixteenth century, a rebellious note sounds with sharp clarity, as Sir Thomas Wyatt rails against the constraints and indignities of erotic vassalage. His particular predicament also reveals disturbing links between sexual and court politics. Sidney's heroes follow this tradition of 'amorous insubordination'.[14] Astrophil is grieved and enraged by love's assaults on his integrity. Typically, the insurgence of desire is experienced as a loss of control. Before he succumbs to its tyrannous assaults, Musidorus warns Pyrocles that, 'if we will be men, the reasonable part of our soul is to have absolute commandment, against which if any sensual weakness arise, we are to yield all our sound forces to the overthrowing of so unnatural a rebellion' (*OA*, 19). Too rigid in its initial presumptions, this brittle self-government is easily subverted, and the heroes languish helplessly. They are now vulnerable to the intervention of various authority figures, and their autonomy is further threatened. It is a predicament the erotic and psychological aspects of which Sidney

handles with finesse in his love poetry, for, in *Astrophil and Stella*,
he keeps its troublesome political implications nicely generalized.

The problem of control comes up immediately, in the first sonnet,
with an account of Astrophil's difficulties. He begins this enterprise with
splendid confidence, but his mood quickly changes:

> Loving in truth, and faine in verse my love to show,
>> That the deare She might take some pleasure of my paine:
>> Pleasure might cause her reade, reading might make her know,
>> Knowledge might pitie winne, and pitie grace obtaine,
> I sought fit words to paint the blackest face of woe,
>> Studying inventions fine, her wits to entertaine:
>> Oft turning others' leaves, to see if thence would flow
>> Some fresh and fruitfull showers upon my sunne-burn'd braine.
> But words came halting forth, wanting Invention's stay,
>> Invention, Nature's child, fled step-dame Studie's blowes,
>> And others' feete still seem'd but strangers in my way.
> Thus great with child to speake, and helplesse in my throwes,
>> Biting my trewand pen, beating my selfe for spite,
>> 'Foole,' said my Muse to me, 'looke in thy heart and write.'
>
> *(AS 1)*

The octet offers a statement of poetic purpose. The traditional objectives
of instruction, 'knowledge', and delight ('pleasure') combine with a more
urgently affective goal. Poetic *energia*, 'inwardly working a stirre to the
mynde', could move Stella to some affirmative, reciprocal response.[15]
Thus, 'knowledge might pitie winne, and pitie grace obtaine.' His
procedures begin to fail when he embarks on an assiduous study of
the works of others. Instead of culminating in creative expression, this
imitative study leads to the parched sterility of a 'sunne-burn'd braine'.
Astrophil's difficulties are attributable to the kind of imitation Sidney
condemns in the *Apology*: poetry that sounds as though it were written
by 'men that had rather read lover's writings (and so caught up certain
swelling phrases . . .) . . . than that in truth they feel those passions,
which easily (as I think) may be betrayed by that same forcibleness or
energia'.[16]

Astrophil's problem is hardly a dearth of passion. On the contrary,
his affections are dangerously boxed in as a result of his fruitless
methodology, and their force is felt through the building pressures of
frustration. This force is baffled by a series of suspended climaxes, the
first two in the two quatrains and the third in the first tercet.[17] The results
of the first two are merely conditional, and the third ends in failure.
Instead of the 'fresh and fruitfull showers' anticipated in the second
quatrain, the result is stumbling and anguished agitation. The smooth,

orderly discipline of the octet leads to frustration and blockage, breaking down altogether in the sestet.

This breakdown becomes a kind of comic rout as the imagery takes a lively, antic turn: 'Invention, Nature's child, fled step-dame Studie's blowes.' The poem shifts from the confident erudition of humanism to the clumsy flight of a truant schoolboy. By the end, Astrophil has regressed even further as he is caught in the throes of childbirth. In this final climax, the movements are still more anguished and agitated and their purpose increasingly desperate. Only with the outburst of the last line is some sort of resolution obtained: ' "Foole," said my Muse to me, "looke in thy heart and write." '

The final line is not a plea for heartfelt sincerity or spontaneity; as several critics have shown, the heart as a shrine for the beloved's image and the proper source of invention is a conventional Petrarchan conceit. Neil Rudenstine thus argues that 'Astrophel's primary goal remains an objective one: not self-exploration and self-expression as ends in themselves, but the expression of personal feeling for the purposes of rhetorical persuasion.'[18] Yet this ignores the affective impact of the sestet and its final line, which allows an assertive outburst of feeling. David Kalstone is more responsive to this aspect when he points out that 'the substance of the line is entirely conventional. But the manner of its presentation is not: the violence and release of tension with which the poet is advised to look at Stella's image marks Sidney's version as quite special.'[19]

The release from tension felt in this final line is almost palpable, but the resolution is ambiguous. Astrophil had started by submitting to a program of poetic study, but its constraints prove oppressive and frustrating. The sestet traces the breakdown and escape from this other-directed discipline, but Astrophil still cannot express himself. The final command offers a sense of release from frustration and uncorks the flow of 'fresh and fruitfull showers', but it does so by imposing a simpler, more emphatic discipline. The sonnet traces a diminishing circular movement away from and back to control by others, a pattern typical in *Astrophil and Stella*.

The tone in the second sonnet is somewhat edgier and more belligerent, though many of the issues are the same:

> Not at first sight, nor with a dribbed shot
> > Love gave the wound, which while I breathe will bleed:
> > But knowne worth did in mine of time proceed,
> > Till by degrees it had full conquest got.
> I saw and liked, I liked but loved not,
> > I loved, but straight did not what Love decreed:
> > At length to Love's decrees, I forc'd, agreed,
> > Yet with repining at so partiall lot.

> Now even that footstep of lost libertie
>> Is gone, and now like slave-borne Muscovite,
>> I call it praise to suffer Tyrannie;
> And now employ the remnant of my wit,
>> To make my selfe beleeve, that all is well,
>> While with a feeling skill I paint my hell.

(AS 2)

The poem describes the process of falling in love as a gradual submission to 'Tyrannie'. Astrophil resists erotic vassalage, and submission is by no means automatic, proceeding by slow degrees. Indeed, Astrophil insists on maintaining the processes of choice while he mourns his lost liberty. Sidney echoes Wyatt here, recalling the latter's testy dignity and pathos. Even as he finds himself caught in love's snare, Wyatt insists that 'it was my choyse, yt was no chaunce.'[20] Astrophil's resistance is sustained throughout, despite its hopelessness, and the bitter conclusion offers no release from tension.

When others intervene, this tension can become explosive. Just as Philisides is pestered by the stereotypical Geron, so is Astrophil troubled by moralizing elders. Amusing personifications of Reason and Virtue urge Astrophil to cease his amorous follies in *AS* 4 and 10, and well-intentioned 'friends' remind him of his public duties in *AS* 14 and 21. Their ineffectual *remedia amoris* only exacerbate his afflictions and are brusquely dismissed. In *AS* 14, this meddlesome solicitude becomes the most grievous persecution:

> Alas have I not paine enough my friend,
>> Upon whose breast a fiercer Gripe doth tire
>> Then did on him who first stale downe the fire,
>> While Love on me doth all his quiver spend,
> But with your Rubarb words yow must contend
>> To grieve me worse, in saying that Desire
>> Doth plunge my wel-form'd soule even in the mire
>> Of sinfull thoughts, which do in ruine end?

(AS 14)

Astrophil presents himself as a combination of Prometheus and Saint Sebastian. Even as he undergoes excruciating torture at the hands of Love, his friend 'must contend / To grieve me worse, in saying that Desire / Doth plunge my wel-form'd soule even in the "mire"'. Astrophil's predicament is embodied by a striking metaphorical antithesis: the soul hovers between the purity and order of good 'form' and a slide into the 'mire'. The latter image suggests not only the filth of 'sinful thoughts' but a loss of shape and structure. Yet, despite this connotation of looseness, the 'mire' is also a place where one may be stuck or held fast as in a bog. Astrophil flees from one trap to another, out of the 'mire' into Love's 'fiercer Gripe', all holding him fast. Astrophil's reply clarifies the significance of this antithesis:

> If that be sinne which doth the maners frame,
>   Well staid with truth in word and faith of deed,
>   Readie of wit and fearing nought but shame:
> If that be sinne which in fixt hearts doth breed
>   A loathing of all loose unchastitie,
>   Then love is sinne, and let me sinfull be.
>
> (*AS* 14)

Love, he claims, imposes as much rigorous good form as his friend might wish; it frames and holds his 'wel-form'd soule' within good 'maners' and rigid bonds. Rather than leading to 'loose unchastitie', Love enforces 'fixt hearts' among its adherents. The verbs, participles and adjectives sustain the figurative opposition between the loose flow of impurity and the tight frame of love's discipline. They impart a certain subtlety to the otherwise heavy irony of the last line.

Behind Astrophil's posturing, there are more ambiguous ironies that undercut his declamatory triumph. Astrophil escapes his friend's moralistic abuse by insisting with real conviction on his virtue, yet he ends up submitting to the more ruthless discipline of Love. The pain of submission, lamented so dramatically at the sonnet's beginning, is obscured by the flurry of self-righteous assertion at the end. Yet for all his defiant bluster, Astrophil never establishes his autonomy. The odd circular movement of the opening sonnet is repeated here. One set of rules is escaped only to be supplanted by more restrictive regulations, and subordination is inescapable. In *AS* 14, Astrophil literally makes a virtue of this necessity. Thus, in the terms of the poem's latent metaphor, the velvet glove of good manners is drawn over authority's 'fiercer Gripe'.

In *AS* 18, Astrophil is more humble as he submits to 'Reason's audite'.

> With what sharpe checkes I in my selfe am shent,
>   When into Reason's audite I do go:
>   And by just counts my selfe a banckrout know
>   Of all those goods, which heav'n to me hath lent:
> Unable quite to pay even Nature's rent,
>   Which unto it by birthright I do ow:
>   And which is worse, no good excuse can show,
>   But that my wealth I have most idly spent.
> My youth doth waste, my knowledge brings forth toyes,
>   My wit doth strive those passions to defend,
>   Which for reward spoile it with vaine annoyes.

> I see my course to lose my selfe doth bend:
> I see and yet no greater sorow take,
> Then that I lose no more for Stella's sake.

(AS 18)

The poem combines the parables of the talents and the prodigal son, and each loss is dolefully itemized with no excuse offered. Wealth, youth, skills, knowledge, and ultimately the self are all sacrificed, and yet Astrophil's only regret is 'that I lose no more for Stella's sake'. The final line has a surprising double meaning: Astrophil is sorry that he has nothing better to lose for Stella as well as nothing left. All the goods relinquished are mere trifles compared to Stella's worth. The careful enumeration of 'Reason's audite' makes this sudden devaluation jarring, and the poem forges a paradoxical link between orderly assessment, sacrificial largesse and casual *sprezzatura*.

The poem's impact again derives, as it did in *AS* 14, from Sidney's inspired use of terms of action. In his analysis of *AS* 18, Robert Montgomery offers a perceptive account of this quality: 'the imagery itself may create a living world because it can suggest human action, not by explanation, but by offering a background of movement, gesture, and sensation. Sonnet 18 has an energy which may be explained partly by vocal tonalities and the kind of flexible structure of discourse we have already noted, but mainly by the fact that the imagery is driven towards physical movement.'[21] Sidney often reinforces this impression of movement by visualizing it, describing even a minor gesture as something literally seen; thus it is actualized and its importance increased. 'A series of strong verbs,' Montgomery explains, 'suggestive of physical movement and energy, accompany the logical development of the trope: "shent", "waste", "brings forth", "strive", "defend", "spoile", "bend". These are in no sense remarkable; they are commonplace, unobtrusive words, but Sidney concentrates them toward the movement of emotional crisis just before the grouping controlled by the repeated "I see." '[22] This highly visual sense of movement in *Astrophil and Stella* is a source of its animation and vitality. It also imparts a sharp perception of tension and conflict as passions are visualized in concrete actions.

One of the actions that deserves special attention is *bending*, appearing as it does in several contexts. 'I see my course to lose my selfe doth bend,' Astrophil tells us in *AS* 18. Here it implies a deviation and decline from the straightforward 'course' previously adhered to. In the next sonnet, bending is imposed twice, once in the first line and again in the last.

> On Cupid's bow how are my heart-strings bent,
> That see my wracke, and yet embrace the same?
> When most I glorie, then I feele most shame:
> I willing run, yet while I run, repent.

My best wits still their owne disgrace invent:
  My verie inke turnes straight to Stella's name;
  And yet my words, as them my pen doth frame,
  Avise themselves that they are vainely spent.
For though she passe all things, yet what is all
  That unto me, who fare like him that both
  Lookes to the skies, and in a ditch doth fall?
O let me prop my mind, yet in his growth
  And not in Nature for best fruits unfit:
  'Scholler,' saith Love, 'bend hitherward your wit.'

                                                          (*AS* 19)

The trope of the bow uses the imagery for clever effect: Astrophil's
heartstrings are tied on Cupid's weapon, thus embracing, and causing,
their own destruction. On closer inspection, the imagery makes less
sense because the strings of a bow should be pulled taut and straight.
Yet the sense of painful strain is still forcefully conveyed. The line recalls
a familiar image, used in both the correspondence and the *Arcadia*, a
parallel first noted by Rudenstine.[23] In all three contexts, the image is
one of tension that requires release: 'a bow too long bent . . . ,' Sidney
writes to Languet, 'must be unstrung or it will break.'[24]

In the next two lines, Astrophil's ambivalence is enacted in painful,
halting movements: 'When most I glorie, then I feele most shame: / I
willing run, yet while I run, repent.' These are like the crippled flights
of Pyrocles, who 'was like a horse, desirous to runne, and miserable
spurred, but so short rainde, as he cannot stirre forward' (*NA*, 95). For
Astrophil, forward movement is hobbled by shame and repentance, and
he stumbles helplessly in his quest for the celestial Stella: 'For though she
passe all things, yet what is all / That unto me, who fare like him that
both / Lookes to the skies, and in a ditch doth fall?' The bathos of the
star gazer who falls in the ditch recalls in witty and poignant fashion the
basic human dilemma set forth in the *Apology*: 'our erected wit maketh
us know what perfection is, and yet our infected will keepeth us from
reaching unto it.'[25] The poem's activities are all painfully constricted,
pulled back and forth, upward and downward by Astrophil's guilt and
misgivings.

In the sestet's second half, the mind is pliable, tender and youthful;
and it requires some support: 'O let me prop my mind, yet in his growth
/ And not in Nature for best fruits unfit.' The image has other echoes,
recalling the advice of Roger Ascham in *The Scholemaster*: 'if will, and
witte' are corrupted, Ascham warns, 'surelie it is hard with ientleness,
but unpossible with seuere crueltie, to call them back to good frame
againe. For, where the one, perchance maie bend it, the other shall surelie
breake it.'[26] Young spirits may be injured by too much severity, so Ascham

makes a case for more flexible discipline. *The Scholemaster* reflects
contemporary shifts in the conception of authority and obedience,
shifts discernible in Sidney's writing as well. There are still important
differences in their approaches. For Sidney, bending and breaking seem
to have the same destructive results: the mind must be 'unbent', the bow
unstrung, to release them from strain.

Yet despite this yearning for release, it does not occur. Instead
discipline is imposed on the young 'Scholler', Astrophil, by a magistral
personification of Love. Astrophil had pleaded for some edifying 'prop'
or frame for his delicate mind, whose pliancy and 'fruits' evoke an image
of a vine. Love comes to his aid, but this brings Astrophil back to where
he started. The prop must resemble 'Cupid's bow' around which he must
bend himself again. The poem's movement is again circular. Perhaps
the peremptory final line reflects a rueful and ironic appreciation of
pedagogy's subtler pressures. Ascham, after all, sought to bend a student's
will and wit less from simple lenience than a desire for increased
control. Sidney's hapless 'Scholler' discovers that bending is only a more
effective means of subjugation. In any case, there is no escaping from
this bending submission.

The middle section of *Astrophil and Stella* focuses more directly on
Astrophil's increasingly urgent desires. A decision seems to have been
made as attention shifts from equivocation and argument to their cause.
Nevertheless, a more direct focus on love and passion brings Astrophil
no closer to a resolution. Desire is assigned a kind of reified primacy in
these middle poems, and the tone is alternately flippant, even cavalier,
and anguished. The first attitude is assumed in *AS* 52, in which the strife
between Virtue and Love is resolved by a facetious variant on Solomon's
wisdom: 'Let Virtue have that Stella's selfe', but Astrophil and his ally,
Love, will take the body. The joking is less irreverently brash in *AS* 25,
but the point is the same:

> The wisest scholler of the wight most wise
>> By Phoebus' doome, with sugred sentence sayes,
>> That Vertue, if it once met with our eyes,
>> Strange flames of Love it in our soules would raise;

(*AS* 25)

The language of platonic ardor is satirically desublimated when Astrophil
exclaims in the final line that 'I do burne in love.'

Astrophil can also be serious in his assertion of desire. The superior
virtue of love is affirmed against its detractors in *AS* 31. Astrophil finds
a doleful companion in the moon, which also affords him a celestial
vantage point far from the arrogant jibes of court 'beauties'. The sestet
consists of a series of melancholy questions concerning love's afflictions:

Then ev'n of fellowship, ô Moone, tell me
  Is constant Love deem'd there but want of wit?
  Are Beauties there as proud as here they be?
Do they above love to be lov'd, and yet
  Those Lovers scorne whom that Love doth possesse?
  Do they call Vertue there ungratefulnesse?

(AS 31)

The combination of lyric pathos and reproach for courtly 'Vertue' represents an affecting vindication of the 'Lover's case'. Sidney depicts the same predicament in Song xi toward the end of the sequence, and he elicits the same strong sympathies for the hero's feelings.

Astrophil becomes still more assertive when debate is resumed in *AS* 56. This time he argues with 'Patience', whose 'leaden counsels' prove tedious. Astrophil demands reciprocity and fair treatment: 'No Patience, if thou wilt my good, then make / Her come, and heare with patience my desire, / And then with patience bid me beare my fire' (*AS* 56). The same demand is made in *AS* 64 in a more earnest and direct fashion. Rather than sparring with personified abstractions, Astrophil here refutes Stella herself in fond but deliberate terms:

No more, my deare, no more these counsels trie,
  O give my passions leave to run their race:
  Let Fortune lay on me her worst disgrace,
  Let folke orecharg'd with braine against me crie,
Let clouds bedimme my face, breake in mine eye,
  Let me no steps but of lost labour trace,
  Let all the earth with scorne recount my case,
  But do not will me from my Love to flie.
I do not envie Aristotle's wit,
  Nor do aspire to Caesar's bleeding fame,
  Nor ought do care, though some above me sit,
Nor hope, nor wishe another course to frame,
  But that which once may win thy cruell hart:
  Thou art my Wit, and thou my Vertue art.

(AS 64)

Her admonitions are swiftly dismissed; his claims on her affections, established. The mortifications invoked prove him Love's willing martyr. Moreover, like Pyrocles who withdraws from the company of all 'excellent men in learning and soldiery' (*OA*, 13), Astrophil renounces traditional male distinctions and professes indifference to 'Aristotle's wit' and 'Caesar's bleeding fame'. Nor does he 'care, though some above me sit' because all his ambition, wit and virtue are contained in Stella. It is one of his best performances, overwhelming her reproofs with a stunning self-justification.

Two other poems in this middle section are among the most seriously probing in the entire cycle. *AS* 61 and 62 explore the fundamental contradictions of love and the self, clarifying certain irreconcilable conflicts. The lover is fundamentally ambivalent in his relationship with the beloved because his feelings involve both self-assertion and self-denial. For Astrophil, these emotional contradictions prove agonizing. Earlier in the sequence, in *AS* 27, he had denied the suspicions of other courtiers who assumed 'that only I / Fawne on my self,' while confessing to 'one worse fault, Ambition. . . . / That makes me oft my best friends overpasse, / Unseene, unheard, while thought to highest place / Bends all his powers, even unto Stella's grace' (*AS* 27). The place of the self in this equivocal blend of bending and aspiration is left uncertain. In *AS* 61, Stella forces the issue by demanding a rejection of 'all selfnesse'. Sidney seems to have invented this splendid word, which covers a whole range of troublesome feelings.[27]

> Oft with true sighes, oft with uncalled teares,
>> Now with slow words, now with dumbe eloquence
>> I Stella's eyes assayll, invade her eares;
>> But this at last is her sweet breath'd defence:
> That who indeed infelt affection beares,
>> So captives to his Saint both soule and sence,
>> That wholly hers, all selfnesse he forbeares,
>> Thence his desires he learnes, his live's course thence.
> Now since her chast mind hates this love in me,
>> With chastned mind, I straight must shew that she
>> Shall quickly me from what she hates remove.
> O Doctor Cupid, thou for me reply,
>> Driv'n else to graunt by Angel's sophistrie,
>> That I love not, without I leave to love.

> (*AS* 61)

The paradoxical conclusion exposes the contradictions of her 'sophistrie' with its own conundrum: he will not love without leaving off or ceasing to love. The other possibility, that he will not love without leave or permission, is, for Astrophil, no less paradoxical than the first. Musidorus, whose speech in the *Arcadia* this echoes, elaborates on the impossibility of fulfilling such a command: 'I find my love shalbe proved no love, without I leve to love, being too unfit a vessell in whom so high thoughts should be engraved. Yet since the Love I beare you, hath so joyned it self to the best part of my life, as the one cannot depart, but that th'other will follow, before I seeke to obey you in making my last passage, let me know which is my unworthines, either of mind, estate, or both?' (*NA*, 158). In one sense the heroes' predicaments differ. Pamela might respect 'high' amorous sentiments, but she regards Dorus in his shepherd's disguise as an 'unfitt vessell'. By contrast, Stella's 'chast mind hates this love in me', recalling Christ's hatred of the sin and not the sinner. Both heroes are alike though in their insistence on the inseparable integrity of their feelings and identity. 'Selfnesse' cannot be split off from the self or, for those who deem it so, the sin from the sinner, without jeopardizing the lover's authenticity and even his life. The requirements of the courtly code, which 'so captives to his Saint both soule and sence', demand an impossible self-division and suppression. The system denies fulfillment or reciprocity.

In *AS* 62, such demands are explicitly criticized. When Astrophil accuses Stella of being 'unkind', he means that her attitude is both ungenerous and unnatural. He refutes her insistence on chaste love with another paradox: 'Alas, if this the only mettall be / Of Love, new-coind to helpe my beggery, / Deare, love me not, that you may love me more' (*AS* 62).

Astrophil's insistent self-justification seems to be having some effect, and the mood begins to change in *AS* 66 and 67 with the promise of 'Hope'. In the next, he dismisses Stella's efforts 'to quench in me the noble fire', and he contemplates her exertions with cool pleasure, thinking 'what paradise of joy / It is, so faire a Vertue to enjoy'. Stella finally relents in *AS* 69, submitting to his desires on one condition:

> For Stella hath with words where faith doth shine,
> Of her high heart giv'n me the monarchie:
> I, I, ô I may say, that she is mine.
> And though she give but thus conditionly
> This realme of blisse, while vertuous course I take,
> No kings be crown'd, but they some covenants make.
>
> (*AS* 69)

Their relationship is formulated in the hierarchical terms of sovereignty and subjection. Astrophil is elated at the sudden reversal of their positions. Before, in sonnets like *AS* 29 and 36, 40 and 42, he mourned his own enslavement and her tyranny; he considers rebellion in *AS* 47, but his resolve collapses as soon as she appears. In *AS* 69, their relationship abruptly changes, and Astrophil exults in his swift triumph. His cynical disregard for 'covenants' is entirely appropriate, for the balance of power is such that no true compromise is possible. Sovereignty is absolute, unbound by any genuine conditions, and Astrophil enjoys it very briefly. In order to enforce the 'vertuous course' she stipulates, Stella must simply resume control, and she does so almost immediately.

After a few more moments of silent elation in *AS* 70, Astrophil finds himself at a disadvantage, for Stella again demands the eradication of desire. Astrophil still insists on the inseparability of desire from self:

Who will in fairest booke of Nature know,
   How Vertue may best lodg'd in beautie be,
   Let him but learne of Love to reade in thee,
   Stella, those faire lines, which true goodnesse show.
There shall he find all vices' overthrow,
   Not by rude force, but sweetest soveraigntie
   Of reason, from whose light those night-birds flie;
   That inward sunne in thine eyes shineth so.
And not content to be Perfection's heire
   Thy selfe, doest strive all minds that way to move,
   Who marke in thee what is in thee most faire.
So while thy beautie drawes the heart to love,
   As fast thy Vertue bends that love to good:
   'But ah,' Desire still cries, 'give me some food.'

                                                            (*AS* 71)

The bookish metaphor introduces a subtle hint of pedantry into the
otherwise splendid declaration of the octet. Stella's 'faire lines' represent
an edifying, and rather tendentious, order. In the sestet the coercive
aspects become more apparent as Stella strives to uplift her admirers.
'And not content to be Perfection's heire . . .' Stella 'doest strive all minds
that way to move'. Astrophil is once again the victim of a disciplinary
design, aimed at imposing the 'sweetest soveraigntie / Of reason', as his
beloved seeks to bend his impulses into their proper shape. The final line,
one of Sidney's most forceful and deliberate non-sequiturs, provides the
only escape from the ruthless encroachments of Virtue. Desire, although
it can bring about an impasse and thwart Virtue's objectives, is still too
helpless to achieve its own ends. The final assertion is plaintive and
passive; the characterization, infantile. Desire is a helpless babe crying
for food, whose innocuous yearnings recall those proclaimed in *CS* 6:

   Sleepe Babie mine, Desire, nurse Beautie singeth:
   Thy cries, ô Babie, set mine head on aking:
   The Babe cries 'way, thy love doth keepe me waking.'

   Lully, lully, my babe, hope cradle bringeth
   Unto my children alway good rest taking:
   The Babe cries 'way, thy love doth keepe me waking.'

   Since babie mine, from me thy watching springeth,
   Sleepe then a litle, pap content is making:
   The babe cries 'nay, for that abide I waking.'

                                                            (*CS* 6)

AS 72 adopts a tone of easy and familiar intimacy in its address to
Desire. Stella requires Astrophil to renounce his truest friend and choose

more virtuous associates. 'Service and Honor', 'feare to offend', and 'care' are recommended. The deferential nature of all these virtues is clearly a significant link; even the more sublime attitudes, such as 'faith' and 'wonder with delight', impose humility. Desire must be banished because it prevents such ready submission, 'because thou wouldst have all'. It is too voracious and self-aggrandizing in its demands, for all its pathos. The clinging inseparability of Astrophil's desire from all his other feelings makes banishment impossible, and this indissoluble bond provokes the final lament. In this scheme, self-assertion is impossible, and desire is constrained by guilt, ambivalence and restrictions imposed from above.

Astrophil achieves a temporary respite from this quandary in the poems extending from Song ii to Song viii. Song ii begins with Astrophil suddenly positioned above his sleeping mistress, plotting to teach her a lesson:

> Have I caught my heav'nly jewell,
> Teaching sleepe most faire to be?
> Now will I teach her that she,
> When she wakes, is too too cruell.

> (*AS* ii. 1–4)

The poem somewhat luridly emphasizes her being offguard:

> See the hand which waking gardeth,
> Sleeping, grants a free resort:
> Now will I invade the fort;
> Cowards Love with losse rewardeth.

> But ô foole, thinke of the danger,
> Of her just and high disdaine:
> Nor will I alas refraine,
> Love feares nothing else but anger.

> (*AS* ii. 13–20)

Astrophil is hindered from raping her, apparently, only by his fear of her wrath. The complex inhibitions of earlier poems are supplanted here by rather simplistic calculations. Even her anger does not prevent him from stealing a kiss and regretting subsequently that he did not steal more. *AS* 73 returns to this situation, playfully trivializing Stella's indignation by making it a more piquant stimulus to his desires.

AS 75 is a rather sophomorically scandalous poem in which Astrophil exalts Edward IV as his hero. Sidney and his readers were well acquainted with the disreputable character of this king, whom the *Mirror for Magistrates* condemned for his 'surfeting and untemperate life', a life 'greatly given to fleshely wantonnesse'.[28] Praise for this man who chose to 'lose his Crowne, rather then faile his love' displays a somewhat heavy

137

frivolity. A more genuinely amusing poem is the next one, *AS* 76, which
again desublimates the platonist's sacred fires in very witty fashion.

> She comes, and streight therewith her shining twins do move
>   Their rayes to me, who in her tedious absence lay
>   Benighted in cold wo, but now appears my day,
>   The onely light of joy, the onely warmth of Love.
> She comes with light and warmth, which like Aurora prove
>   Of gentle force, so that mine eyes dare gladly play
>   With such a rosie morne, whose beames most freshly gay
>   Scortch not, but onely do darke chilling sprites remove.
> But lo, while I do speake, it groweth noone with me,
>   Her flamie glistring lights increase with time and place;
>   My heart cries 'ah', it burnes, mine eyes now dazled be:
> No wind, no shade can coole, what helpe then in my case,
>   But with short breath, long lookes, staid feet and walking hed,
>   Pray that my sunne go downe with meeker beames to bed.

(AS 76)

Stella's eyes, like the sun, dispel 'cold wo' from her lover's heart, so that
'now appeares my day, / The onely light of joy, the onely warmth of
Love'. All is 'rosie morne' in the octet, but in the sestet all this sweetness
and light get out of hand as things heat up too quickly. Sidney offers a
very droll, lively parody of conventional praise, literally animating his
beloved's attributes with irrepressible *energia*. The result is one of the
funniest poems in the sequence.

The third song presents an interesting hiatus in the midst of this
segment's sexual dalliance. The astonishing power of love and beauty is
the subject, and Astrophil marvels at their effects on the stones and trees,
birds and beasts of Grecian myth. The feats of Orpheus and Amphion are
alluded to, and love is said to move animals to strange acts of heroism.
Stella combines all these effects, and Astrophil is enthralled by the
beauty of her appearance and her song. This solemn celebration of her
miraculous powers affords a rare contemplative moment in the sequence.

The poem concludes with an odd paradoxical compliment. The
continued immobility of the 'birds, beasts, stones and trees' in the final
stanza is simply proof of deeper love. 'Know, that small Love is quicke,
and great Love doth amaze.' The lively, facile, active response belies
feelings that are shallow; 'great Love' overwhelms and immobilizes those
who genuinely feel it. If animals and objects are thus overwhelmed, what
wonder then that men 'with reason armed' are similarly 'charmed'.

The poem finally betrays a peculiar mistrust of poetry's effects. In
some ways, its conclusion recalls the contrast of *AS* 54, where 'Dumb
Swannes, not chatring Pies do Lovers prove.' At several points in *Astrophil
and Stella* (*AS* 6, 15, 28, 70 and 90), Sidney criticizes the glib fluency of

other poet–lovers, and he argues with no less fluency for the virtues of simplicity and silence. Both the ironic and highly conventional aspects of this pose have been pointed out by many critics. Poetic eloquence generally thrives under such attacks. In Song iii, however, the implied criticism goes deeper, beyond the problem of sincerity, to more basic issues. In his depreciation of 'quicke Love', Sidney seems to disparage *energia* itself, the lively 'stir to the mind' that poetry provokes. Indeed, the miraculous moving power of Orpheus and Amphion is their essential qualification as poets: 'as Amphion was said to move stones with his Poetry, to build Thebes, and Orpheus to be listened to by beasts'.[29] Yet here the responsive mobility their poetry arouses is deemed inferior to the rapt fixity Stella inspires.

On one level the conclusion of Song iii is simply a clever, complimentary rationalization, yet it has a deeper significance indicated by parallels with *AS* 38, another instance of brief, visionary transcendence:

> This night while sleepe begins with heavy wings
>   To hatch mine eyes, and that unbitted thought
>   Doth fall to stray, and my chiefe powres are brought
>   To leave the scepter of all subject things,
> The first that straight my fancie's error brings
>   Unto my mind, is Stella's image, wrought
>   By Love's owne selfe, but with so curious drought,
>   That she, me thinks, not onely shines but sings.
> I start, looke, hearke, but what in closde up sence
>   Was held, in opend sense it flies away,
>   Leaving me nought but wailing eloquence:
> I, seeing better sights in sight's decay,
>   Cald it anew, and wooed sleepe againe:
>   But him her host that unkind guest had slaine.

(*AS* 38)

Here too, Stella 'not onely shines but sings'. Astrophil attains this happy vision when his thoughts are 'unbitted' by sleep, and the cramped and painful vacillations of his waking hours are suspended for a time. The freedom of his mind in sleep is not unlike that achieved in poetry, for Astrophil finds that 'my chiefe powres are brought / To leave the scepter of all subject things'. In the *Apology*, Sidney distinguishes between fields that have 'the works of Nature for his principal object, without which they could not consist, and on which they so depend' and poetry, which disdains 'to be tied to any such subjection'.[30] Yet the phrase 'fancie's error' raises doubts about the legitimacy of this dream-vision before it even begins; once started, the dream cannot be held. 'Astrophel is completely incapable of sustaining it,' says Rudenstine of this visionary lapse; 'It arouses his desire, and his effort to possess the vision quickly dispels it.'[31]

Astrophil's failure reveals inherent ambiguities in this imaginative vision of perfection. In his analysis of the third song, Richard Young cites some pertinent remarks of Ficino: 'beauty pertains only to the mind, sight and hearing. Love, therefore, is limited to these three, but desire which rises from the other senses is called, not love, but lust or madness.'[32] *AS* 38 reveals the surprising vulnerability of these senses to the most disruptive desires. The singing, shining and disembodied image of Stella certainly appeals to these higher faculties, yet her beauty provokes simple lusts as the image turns into a seductive succubus. Once again, the rarefied aspirations of Neo-platonism are undercut.

The dream-vision of Philisides in the *Old Arcadia* reveals similar contradictions. Its prelude is an innocent, peaceful slumber:

> Free all my powers were from those captiving snares,
> Which heav'nly purest gifts defile in muddy cares.
> Ne could my soul itself accuse of such a fault
> As tender conscience might with furious pangs assault.

> (*OA*, 335. 29–32)

The verse is replete with paradox and guilt. Conscience is both 'tender' and 'furious', its fury springing from its tenderness, and the soul coils back on itself in tight, reflexive harshness. The greatest contradiction involves the source and nature of this vision. Presumably, 'those captiving snares' are the subject of 'defile', and 'heav'nly purest gifts' are the object. The syntax allows, however, and even encourages, an inversion, suggesting that such heavenly sights may infect the viewer with 'muddy cares'. This disturbing prospect seems confirmed by the consequences of Philisides' vision. This glimpse of his beloved's perfection, however platonically exalted, is the occasion of his fall. The mind is 'made of heav'nly stuff' and it is freed from 'fleshly bondage' in sleep (*OA*, 336. 10–11), but it still remains captive to the flesh and its desires.

These problems do not arise in *The Apology for Poetry*. There, the 'erected wit' is freed from the 'clayey lodgings' and 'dungeon of the body' by poetic imagination, and the mind ascends 'to as high a perfection as our degenerate souls . . . can be capable of'.[33] The virtue of poetry consists in this freedom from 'subjection' to the limits of sense and fact. Poetry also derives power from its appeal to the emotions, for it can arouse both an active and a contemplative appreciation of its ideals, moving men to desire to do good: 'And that moving is of a higher degree than teaching, it may by this appear, that it is well nigh the cause and the effect of teaching. For who will be taught, if he be not moved with desire to be taught? and what so much good doth that teaching bring forth . . . as that it moveth one to do that which it doth teach?'[34] Only once, in a rather cryptic and offhand fashion, does Sidney explicitly concede any difficulties with this scheme, difficulties that arise from the

choice of subject. When mundane things are idealized, the poet might
finally 'make the too much loved earth more lovely'.[35]

Sidney's poetry reveals a much deeper distrust of the imagination,
a distrust fairly typical in the Renaissance. Greville summarizes the
case against the imagination in *A Treatise on Human Learning*:

> So must th'imagination from the sense
> Be misinformed, while our affections cast
> False shapes, and formes on their intelligence,
> And to keepe out true intromissions thence
> Abstracts the imagination, or distasts
> With images preoccupately plac'd.
>
> Hence our desires, fears, hopes, love, hate, and sorrow
> In fancy make us heare, feele, see impressions,
> Such as out of our sense they doe not borrow,
> And are the efficient cause, the true progression
> Of sleeping visions, idle phantasmes waking,
> Life, dreams; and knowledge, apparitions making[36]

Although Sidney's explicit speculations are much more positive,
his poetry shows the mind's vulnerability to corrupting 'affections'.
Astrophil's predicament dramatically shows a conflicted relationship
between 'erected wit' and 'infected will'. In fact, the fusion of affect and
perception in poetic vision always seems to weight the conflict in favor of
desire. Astrophil is undone, in a sense, by *energia*, by his own hyperactive
responsiveness. In *AS* 38 his beloved's perfections move him too strongly
and his emotional reactions ('I start, looke, hearke') are literally too
'quicke'. The poetry is too lively to contain its own effects, and desire
disrupts the dream: the satisfactions promised in the *Apology* are
frustrated by the conflicts of the poetry.

Despite his depreciation of 'quicke Love', Astrophil is hyperkinetic in
the poems immediately following the third song. In *AS* 84 and 85, he is
riding to meet her for a secret assignation. This is the peak of narrative
activity in the sequence following Stella's 'conditional' surrender. The first
of these poems carries to nearly absurd lengths his zeal for racing about:

> Highway since you my chiefe Pernassus be,
> And that my Muse to some eares not unsweet,
> Tempers her words to trampling horses feet,
> More oft then to a chamber melodie;
> Now blessed you, beare onward blessed me
> To her, where I my heart safeliest shall meet.
> My Muse and I must you of dutie greet
> With thankes and wishes, wishing thankfully.

(*AS* 84)

In the sestet, blessings are showered on the road whose comparison with Parnassus links poetry with some rather dubious aspirations. The highway's inspirational virtue consists in its providing both a means for their rendezvous and an occasion for thinking about it.

In *AS* 85 Astrophil's sense of urgency and excitement increases still further when he spots the house:

> I see the house, my heart thy selfe containe,
>> Beware full sailes drowne not thy tottring barge:
>> Least joy, by Nature apt sprites to enlarge,
>> Thee to thy wracke beyond thy limits straine.
> Nor do like Lords, whose weake confused braine,
>> Not pointing to fit folkes each undercharge,
>> While everie office themselves will discharge,
>> With doing all, leave nothing done but paine.
> But give apt servants their due place, let eyes
>> See Beautie's totall summe summ'd in her face:
>> Let eares heare speech, which wit to wonder ties,
> Let breath sucke up those sweetes, let armes embrace
>> The globe of weale, lips Love's indentures make:
>> Thou but of all the kingly Tribute take.
>
> (AS 85)

The language resembles that of Troilus in its fear of strain beyond limits. Emotion threatens to overwhelm him amid the confusion and anxiety of his headlong rush. The sestet depicts a labored effort to regain self-control. Mastery still proves a precarious achievement. Various tasks are methodically parceled out to the senses, and while the pleasures anticipated are kingly, their enjoyment requires rigid discipline and care. Only thus can composure be restored.

Song iv brings these events to consummation:

> Onely joy, now here you are,
> Fit to heare and ease my care:
> Let my whispering voyce obtaine,
> Sweete reward for sharpest paine:
> Take me to thee, and thee to me.
> 'No, no, no, no, my Deare, let be.'
>
> (AS iv. 1–5)

Sexual urgency increases with Astrophil's whispering pleas, and the *carpe diem* theme is given point by the jostling rhythms:

> This small light the Moone bestowes,
> Serves thy beames but to disclose,

So to raise my hap more hie;
Feare not else, none can us spie:
Take me to thee, and thee to me.
'No, no, no, no, my Deare, let be.'

That you heard was but a Mouse,
Dumbe sleepe holdeth all the house:
Yet a sleepe, me thinkes they say,
Yong folkes, take time while you may:
Take me to thee, and thee to me.
'No, no, no, no, my Deare, let be.'

Niggard Time threats, if we misse
This large offer of our blisse,
Long stay ere he graunt the same:
Sweet then, while each thing doth frame:
Take me to thee, and thee to me.
'No, no, no, no, my Deare, let be.'

(*AS* iv. 19–36)

For all its dramatic immediacy, the scene here is still very generalized
and conventional. The protracted courtship of Astrophil and Stella
culminates in a kind of jolly Chaucerian fabliaux. The dramatic
personalities of each character are here transformed to caricature: with
Astrophil, all voluble, charming insistence; with Stella, redundant denial.
Sexual frustration had complicated the lineaments of character, but now
they are generalized and simplified by satisfaction. The joke, of course,
is that Stella's denial finally turns into assent, Astrophil having forced
this from her with a combination of petulant threat, sly double entendre,
and simple attrition.

Sweet alas, why strive you thus?
Concord better fitteth us:
Leave to Mars the force of hands,
Your power in your beautie stands:
Take me to thee, and thee to me.
'No, no, no, no, my Deare, let be.'

Wo to me, and do you sweare
Me to hate? But I forbeare,
Cursed be my destines all,
That brought me so high to fall:
Soone with my death I will please thee.
'No, no, no, no, my Deare, let be.'

(*AS* iv. 43–54)

The consequences and significance of this reversal are still not clear, and some critics have imposed a decorum and distance on Song iv more restrictive than it calls for. Kalstone sees the 'sweet flowers on fine bed too' as an invitation to pastoral pleasures;[37] Ringler lumps Songs iv and xi together, placing Astrophil outside Stella's window in each of them.[38] Whatever figurative associations the flowers may bring to this scene, the 'fine bed' is at its center; and if any further evidence is required that Astrophil is inside Stella's bedroom, the embrace of the penultimate stanza – 'Leave to Mars the force of hands' – seems to provide it. The closeness of the scene and mood suggest that the conclusion's ellipsis is prompted by decorum of another, more courtly sort – protection of a lady's reputation.

Nevertheless, there is still no change or development in their relationship. The tone of witty evasion and the lack of any follow-up prevent that. What could have been the dramatic climax of the entire sequence is muted by a blend of levity and inconsequence. Stella's capitulation is decorously passed over, and her surrender has no profound significance. Their relationship never moves beyond a simple test of wills, and Astrophil obtains no other satisfaction than this momentary triumph.

His triumph is indeed brief. In *AS* 86, the sequence lapses abruptly into quarrelsome disappointment and guilt:

> Alas, whence came this change of lookes? If I
> Have chang'd desert, let mine owne conscience be
> A still felt plague, to selfe condemning me:
> Let wo gripe on my heart, shame loade mine eye.
>
> (*AS* 86)

Once more the balance of power shifts back to Stella. His conscience and her reproaches make Astrophil her 'slave', swiftly plunging him to 'hell'. The belligerence of Song v is transparent bluster, becoming meekly plaintive in the final stanza, and Stella's praises are lovingly proclaimed in the sixth and seventh songs.

Song viii is the first in a series of alternative endings; in it the evanescent pleasures of their affair are conclusively renounced. Pastoral retirement and the past tense soften the pain of relinquishment. The song puts an end to the conflict of wills. Tranquillity and reconciliation prevail in this small pastoral world, and erotic antagonisms are subdued, for a time. The poetry gracefully allows the two lovers to have it both ways. While Astrophil's advances are repelled, Stella's denial is subtly inverted to imply its opposite:

> There his hands in their speech, faine
> Would have made tongue's language plaine;

But her hands his hands repelling,
Gave repulse all grace excelling.

Then she spake; her speech was such,
As not eares but hart did tuch:
While such wise she love denied,
As yet love she signified.

(*AS* viii. 65–72)

Even if her speech does not signify the more direct assent of Song iv, it still offers sublime affirmation. Promising him the first place in her heart, Stella swears that 'All my blisse in thee I lay; / If thou love, my love content thee, / For all love, all faith is meant thee' (*AS* viii. 89–91).

Unfortunately, the lovers are blocked from consummation by 'Tyran honour', but their mutual submission to this higher tyranny dispels their earlier inequality. Previously, Astrophil had been Stella's slave, but now they are reconciled through shared thralldom. Their bond is reaffirmed in *AS* 87, where it is said that Stella suffers as much as he does under 'iron lawes of duty'. Their mutual frustration affords the only possible union.

Song viii provides a resolution that is attractive and dramatically satisfying, reconciling several fundamental conflicts, but the sequence does not stop here. Instead the poems continue for another long stretch, disrupting this mood of equanimity and reverting to old problems. In Song x, Astrophil seeks solace in meditation on Stella's charms, but the result is entirely devoid of Petrarch's contemplative reverence.

Thought therefore I will send thee,
    To take up the place for me;
    Long I will not after tary,
    There unseene thou maist be bold,
    Those faire wonders to behold,
    Which in them my hopes do cary.

Thought see thou no place forbeare,
    Enter bravely every where,
    Seaze on all to her belonging;
    But if thou wouldst garded be,
    Fearing her beames, take with thee
    Strength of liking, rage of longing.

(*AS* x. 13–24)

The exertions of the 'erected wit' are lurid and aggressively dissolute. These fantasies of ravishment are followed by image of yielding lips, 'opening rubies, pearles deviding' (*AS* x. 30). In this erotic revery, Astrophil is restored to his 'most Princely power . . .'

> When I blessed shall devower,
> With my greedy licorous sences,
> Beauty, musicke, sweetnesse, love
> While she doth against me prove
> Her strong darts, but weake defences.
>
> Thinke, thinke of those dalyings,
> When with Dovelike murmurings,
> With glad moning passed anguish,
> We change eyes, and hart for hart,
> Each to other do imparte,
> Joying till joy make us languish.

(*AS* x. 31–42)

All these voluptuous fantasies end, however, in swooning delirium. Such license clearly makes Astrophil uneasy:

> O my thought my thoughts surcease,
> Thy delights my woes increase,
> My life melts with too much thinking;
> Thinke no more but die in me,
> Till thou shalt revived be,
> At her lips my Nectar drinking.

(*AS* x. 43–8)

He is disappointed that these pleasures were merely fanciful and yearns for a genuine kiss. Yet there is also a fear of 'melting' dissolution in the midst of unrestrained indulgence as old fears of 'loose unchastitie' are revived. The tenth song moves beyond the conflicts and hesitating preliminaries to explicit fulfillment of desire. The evanescent vision of Stella glimpsed in *AS* 38 is forcefully held and fully developed through embrace to sated ecstasy. And yet the poem is undone by its own libertine excesses leading to melancholy distress. The agonized self-reproach and exaggerated guilt of the next poem, *AS* 93, are a natural sequel to Song x:

> I have (live I and know this) harmed thee,
> Tho worlds quite me, shall I my selfe forgive?
> Only with paines my paines thus eased be,
> That all thy hurts in my hart's wracke I reede;
> I cry thy sighs; my deere, thy teares I bleede.

(*AS* 93)

AS 93 through 99 all concern themselves with night, sadness, and isolation. In *AS* 94, Astrophil is nearly stupefied by sorrow:

Griefe find the words, for thou hast made my braine
So darke with misty vapors, which arise
From out thy heavy mould, that inbent eyes
Can scarce discerne the shape of mine owne paine.

(AS 94)

He simply chooses to dwell in darkness in AS 99. For a time, Stella
continues to share in his pain and affliction, and their empathy is
portrayed in AS 100 through 103, but all this changes in the eleventh
song:

'Who is it that this darke night,
Underneath my window playneth?'
It is one who from thy sight
Being (ah) exild, disdayneth
Every other vulgar light.

'Why alas, and are you he?
Be not yet those fancies changed?'
Deere when you find change in me,
Though from me you be estranged,
Let my chaunge to ruine be.

(AS xi. 1–10)

Astrophil's fidelity is indeed unshakable, and Stella, who is now eager to
be rid of him, prescribes the conventional *remedia amoris*: 'well in absence
this will dy', and 'time will these thoughts remove.' She lumps 'reason's
purest light' with the distractions of 'new beauties', cynically presuming
that either one or both will be effective in shaking off his irksome
constancy. Astrophil, however, is not so capriciously changeable. Stella
finally becomes exasperated and brusquely dismisses him:

'Peace, I thinke that some give eare:
Come no more, least I get anger.'
Blisse, I will my blisse forbeare,
Fearing (sweete) you to endanger,
But my soule shall harbour there.

'Well, be gone, be gone I say,
Lest that Argus eyes perceive you.'
O unjustest fortune's sway,
Which can make me thus to leave you,
And from lowts to run away.

(AS xi. 36–45)

The eleventh song and the sonnet before it, *AS* 104, stand together as a
vindication of Astrophil's love. The 'envious wits' of the court mock him
for his hapless devotion. They exult in their gossip, 'and puffing prove
that I / Do Stella love', but Astrophil flings this discovery back in their
faces: 'Fooles, who doth it deny?' Song xi establishes the same claim
with a tone of desperate pathos, but it is no less reproachful than the
more belligerent sonnet. Stella's fickle aversion to Astrophil links her
with the shallow, fashionable 'fooles' of the court; neither she nor they
can comprehend the deeper significance of Astrophil's love, for both are
prompted by the most conventional motives and concerns.

For some, this moment in the sequence is a triumphant climax.
Although Astrophil's despair verges toward recalcitrance in its allegiance
to 'night over day, dark over light, passion over reason', Rudenstine argues
that 'in the context of the sequence, Astrophil's ritual style lends him an
important dignity and preserves him from mere frenzy or whining.'[39]
In the eleventh song, Stella's abrupt repudiation places Astrophil at
an advantage because 'his love is presented in terms of its fidelity, its
capability of withstanding time and absence, whereas hers has clearly
consisted of little more than those "fancies" that have already changed.'[40]
His inability to control his feelings, for which he has been continually
upbraided, by various authority figures and Stella herself, is now the
source of virtue. Her rectitude seems by contrast merely priggish and
hypocritical in its concern with reputation. The ceremonial tone of these
closing sonnets and their assertion of unflagging constancy are seen as
effective ways of achieving closure.

Others, however, have found little solace in these poems of complaint.
David Kalstone feels that the 'special ferocity' of Astrophil's sorrow
prevents solution.[41] In his view, the narrative action dissolves in bitter
disappointment and then 'merely ends'.[42] A 'fitting conclusion' must be
sought elsewhere, and Kalstone, like many other readers of *Astrophil and
Stella*, finds it in two sonnets 'long printed as part of the sequence', but
now detached from it.[43]

The first renounces desire as:

> Thou blind man's marke, thou foole's selfe chosen snare,
>> Fond fancie's scum, and dregs of scattred thought,
>> Band of all evils, cradle of causelesse care,
>> Thou web of will, whose end is never wrought.

(CS 31)

The second evokes the solemn biblical tones of religious transcendence:

> Leave me ô Love, which reachest but to dust,
>> And thou my mind aspire to higher things:
>> Grow rich in that which never taketh rust:
>> What ever fades, but fading pleasure brings.

Draw in thy beames, and humble all thy might,
  To that sweet yoke, where lasting freedomes be:
  Which breakes the clowdes and opens forth the light,
  That doth both shine and give us sight to see.
O take fast hold, let that light be thy guide,
  In this small course which birth drawes out to death,
  And thinke how evill becommeth him to slide,
  Who seeketh heav'n, and comes of heav'nly breath.
Then farewell world, thy uttermost I see,
Eternall Love maintaine thy life in me.

(CS 32)

A grave Latin tag is appended to the latter sonnet: *Splendidis longum valedico nugis.* As Kalstone concedes, there is no sixteenth-century textual basis for the inclusion of these two sonnets in *Astrophil and Stella*, and Ringler, who places them at the end of *Certain Sonnets*, maintains they were written long before Sidney composed *Astrophil and Stella*.[44] Still, their air of resolute conviction draws many readers to this conclusion. J.W. Lever sees in them 'Sidney's final attitude to romance', and he regards 'Leave me o Love' as the paragon of poetic maturity in Sidney's development: 'Released from its perplexities, his genius leapt forward and made this sonnet perhaps his greatest poetic triumph,' one in which 'the facility of his early work was transformed into power under perfect control.'[45]

There is another final maneuver that has received less attentive acclaim. *AS* 107 seeks a more practical solution to Astrophil's troubles, a solution less dramatic than despairing constancy or fierce renunciation. Astrophil's constancy begins to seem unhealthy in *AS* 106, for his fixation becomes an incurable affliction:

But heere I do store of faire Ladies meete,
  Who may with charme of conversation sweete,
  Make in my heavy mould new thoughts to grow:
Sure they prevaile as much with me, as he
  That bad his friend, but then new maim'd, to be
  Mery with him, and not thinke of his woe.

(*AS* 106)

In *AS* 107, Astrophil seems to be striving to move beyond this wretchedness:

Stella since thou so right a Princesse art
  Of all the powers which life bestowes on me,
  That ere by them ought undertaken be,
  They first resort unto that soueraigne part;

149

> Sweete, for a while give respite to my hart,
>> Which pants as though it still should leape to thee:
>> And on my thoughts give thy Lieftenancy
>> To this great cause, which needs both use and art,
> And as a Queene, who from her presence sends
>> Whom she imployes, dismisse from thee my wit,
>> Till it have wrought what thy owne will attends.
> On servants' shame oft Maister's blame doth sit;
>> O let not fooles in me thy workes reprove,
>> And scorning say, 'See what it is to love.'

$$(AS\ 107)$$

Astrophil renews his address to Stella directly, asking this time for release from bondage. This is a highly formalized, almost legalistic appeal, carefully outlining the terms and conditions of their relationship. Astrophil seeks to alter the absolute nature of his subordination, establishing some claims of his own against her 'powers' as 'Princesse'. He pleads for the partial freedom and practical authority of 'thy Lieftenancy', so that, once his wit is dismissed from her, he can turn his attention to another 'great cause'. The phrase is intriguingly cryptic; whereas some assign specific biographical significance, Ringler argues that this ' "great cause" more probably refers to public service in general.'[46] In this laconic, glancing fashion, Sidney begins to return to the world of public and political concerns after deliberately banishing them from his protracted meditation on love. At the same time, he attempts one of the more explicit formulations of sexual politics, defining precisely the issues of power and autonomy. Within the constraints of Petrarchan tradition, Astrophil asks for the provisional power of a 'Lieftenancy', a compromise between dominance and defeat. Yet this limited solution is apparently impossible. In the last poem, *AS* 108, 'most rude dispaire my daily unbidden guest . . . makes me then bow downe my head.' Astrophil is firmly held by the inescapable bonds of oxymoronic anguish: 'That in my woes for thee thou art my joy. / And in my joyes for thee my only annoy.' The final note is one of complete submission to romantic convention.

Once again a balance of power between sovereignty and submission proves impossible. The curve of his fictive courtship is drawn to more extreme postures of transcendence or noble pathos. Yet here, in *Astrophil and Stella*, Sidney handles these alternatives with an assurance and awareness unmatched in his other works. The sequence is a triumph of courtly wit and *sprezzatura* that can accommodate the tensions of sexual politics. Conflict is internalized and reduced to purely romantic concerns, and less is finally at stake. When the conflicts expand in the more open and inclusive narratives of the *Arcadia*, they become harder to comprehend or negotiate, revealing the limitations of wit. In *Astrophil and Stella*, contradiction and frustration are more readily accepted, and wit maintains its extraordinary composure and control.

Notes

1. See JACK STILLINGER, 'The Biographical Problem of *Astrophel and Stella', Journal of English and Germanic Philology*, 59 (1960), p. 626, and ROBERT KIMBROUGH, *Sir Philip Sidney* (Boston: Twayne, 1971), pp. 121–3.
2. *The Poems of Sir Philip Sidney*, ed. William A. Ringler, Jr (1962; rpt. Oxford: Clarendon, 1967), p. xliv.
3. *Ibid.*, p. 440.
4. JEAN ROBERTSON, 'Sir Philip Sidney and Lady Penelope Rich', *Review of English Studies*, 15 (1964), pp. 296–7.
5. *Poems*, RINGLER, p. xliv.
6. *Ibid.*, p. 447.
7. J.W. LEVER, *The Elizabethan Love Sonnet* (London: Methuen, 1956), p. 141.
8. DAVID KALSTONE, *Sidney's Poetry* (1965; rpt. New York: Norton, 1970), p. 106.
9. THEODORE SPENCER, 'The Poetry of Sir Philip Sidney', *ELH* 12 (1945), p. 270.
10. *Poems*, RINGLER, p. 447.
11. PHILIP RIEFF, *Freud: The Mind of the Moralist*, New York: Anchor Doubleday, 1961, p. 175.
12. C.S. LEWIS, *The Allegory of Love* (Oxford: Oxford University Press, 1968), p. 18.
13. *Ibid.*, p. 2.
14. LOUIS B. SALOMON, *The Rebellious Lover in English Poetry*, Philadelphia: University of Pennsylvania Press, 1931, p. 1.
15. George Puttenham quoted by RINGLER, in *Poems*, p. 459.
16. SIR PHILIP SIDNEY, *An Apology for Poetry, or The Defence of Poetry*, ed. Geoffrey Shepherd (Manchester: Manchester University Press, 1973), pp. 137–8.
17. See ROBERT L. MONTGOMERY'S analysis of this sonnet in *Symmetry and Sense* (Austin: University of Texas Press, 1961), p. 84.
18. NEIL L. RUDENSTINE, *Sidney's Poetic Development* (Cambridge: Harvard University Press, 1967), p. 200.
19. KALSTONE, *Poetry*, pp. 126–7.
20. SIR THOMAS WYATT, *Collected Poems*, ed. Kenneth Muir (Cambridge: Harvard University Press, 1963), p. 111.
21. MONTGOMERY, *Symmetry and Sense*, p. 89.
22. *Ibid.*, p. 90.
23. RUDENSTINE, *Poetic Development*, p. 18.
24. *The Correspondence of Sir Philip Sidney and Hubert Languet*, ed. Stuart A. Pears (London: William Pickering, 1945), p. 36.
25. SIDNEY, *Apology*, p. 101.
26. ROGER ASCHAM, *The Scholemaster*, in *English Works*, ed. William Aldis Wright (Cambridge: Cambridge University Press, 1904), pp. 200–1.
27. Mona Wilson quoted by RINGLER, in *Poems*, p. 478.
28. Quoted by RINGLER, in *Poems*, p. 481.
29. SIDNEY, *Apology*, p. 96.
30. *Ibid.*, pp. 99–100.

31. RUDENSTINE, *Poetic Development*, p. 234.
32. RICHARD B. YOUNG, 'English Petrarke', in *Three Studies in the Renaissance: Sidney, Jonson, Milton* (New Haven: Yale Studies in English, 138, 1958), p. 70.
33. SIDNEY, *Apology*, p. 104.
34. *Ibid.*, p. 112.
35. *Ibid.*, p. 100.
36. SIR FULKE GREVILLE, *Poems and Dramas*, ed. Geoffrey Bullough (New York: Oxford University Press, 1945), p. 157.
37. KALSTONE, *Poetry*, p. 176.
38. *Poems*, RINGLER, p. xlv.
39. RUDENSTINE, *Poetic Development*, p. 267.
40. *Ibid.*, p. 268.
41. KALSTONE, *Poetry*, p. 177.
42. *Ibid.*, p. 178.
43. *Ibid.*
44. *Poems*, RINGLER, pp. 423–4.
45. LEVER, *Love Sonnet*, pp. 82, 91.
46. *Poems*, RINGLER, p. 490.

6   A Room Not Their Own: Renaissance Women as Readers and Writers*

Margaret W. Ferguson

With Maureen Quilligan and Nancy Vickers, Margaret Ferguson edited *Rewriting the Renaissance: The Discourses of Sexual Difference in Early Modern Europe* (1986), which brought into view the on-going revision of traditional views of this era by feminist scholars. In this essay, Ferguson employs a materialist feminist perspective in her analysis of the social constructions of gender which restricted female speech and writing. Ferguson considers the economic origins of the ideal of chastity, as well as the larger systems of meaning which equated female speech with sexual promiscuity. She finds significant differences in the reactions to this ideology by upper-class as opposed to non-upper-class women writers. In its cultural materialist approach, the essay assumes that individuals, including women, are deeply influenced by social institutions, here the church and the family, and yet that some women did contest, in a significant way, the dominant cultural teaching about them. The end of the essay considers how the emergence of 'a lyric "I" capable of articulating female passion' challenged a Petrarchan tradition based on the silence of women.

> Sexuality is to feminism what work is to marxism: that which is most one's own, yet most taken away.
>
> (Catherine A. MacKinnon,
> 'Feminism, Marxism, Method, and the State:
> An Agenda for Theory')

The title and initial inspiration for this essay came from observing an odd parallel between two women writers' descriptions of an alienating experience of reading what men have had to say about the female sex. The first passage occurs in Virginia Woolf's 1929 essay *A Room of One's Own*; the second comes from Christine de Pizan's *The Book of the City*

---

* Reprinted from *The Comparative Perspective on Literature*, eds Clayton Koelb and Susan Noakes (Ithaca: Cornell University Press, 1988), pp. 93–116.

of Ladies. That text, which was written in 1405, has still never been published in book form in its original language; it was published in English, however, during Henry Tudor's reign, and it has recently been republished in a new English translation, no doubt because the social movement known as women's liberation is having effects on the interconnected institutions of higher education and academic publishing.[1]

Virginia Woolf did not know Christine de Pizan's book or that this French contemporary of Joan of Arc, after being widowed at twenty-five, supported herself by her pen; paradoxically, however, Woolf's very ignorance of Pizan's work supports the general argument both authors make about the suppression or misrepresentation of women in the accounts of history constructed by men. As a prelude to their efforts to rewrite such accounts, both authors describe an experience of feeling themselves expropriated by a misogynistic discursive tradition. Woolf recalls a morning when she sat in her room looking at 'a blank sheet of paper on which was written, in large letters, Women and Fiction, but no more'.[2] Oppressed by that blank page, she leaves the room and goes to the British Museum, a larger but, as it turns out, even more oppressive space. Entering it, she stands for a moment stupefied beneath the vast dome, feeling, she says, as if she 'were a thought in the huge bald forehead which is so splendidly encircled by a band of famous names' (26). She goes to the catalogue, and after being nearly overwhelmed by the number of titles to be found under the heading 'Woman', she chooses some dozen volumes and spends the next four hours, isolated in her stall, taking notes on them. By lunchtime, she is in a state of listless depression. All the contradictory jottings she has made coalesce suddenly into an image she finds herself sketching on her notebook page, an image of a heavily built, great-jowled, small-eyed man named Professor von X who is writing a monumental work to be titled 'The Mental, Moral, and Physical Inferiority of the Female Sex' (31).

Christine de Pizan describes a similar experience in the first section of her *Book of the City of Ladies.* Sitting alone in her study, 'surrounded by books on all kinds of subjects' and dwelling on 'the weighty opinions of various authors' whom she has studied for a long time, Pizan seeks to relax for a moment by reading something light. 'By chance,' she writes, 'a strange volume came into my hands, not one of my own but one which had been given to me'; seeing that the volume is by one Maltheolus, she smiles, for she had heard that it 'discussed respect for women'.[3] Before she can read through it to amuse herself, however, her mother calls her to supper, and she is able to return to the book only the next morning. Again seated alone in her study, she peruses Maltheolus's book. The result of her morning's reading is that 'a great unhappiness and sadness welled up in my heart, for I detested myself and the entire feminine sex, as though we were monstrosities in nature.'[4] The cause of her grief is not just Maltheolus's book, which has turned out to be a bitter satire on women, but the realization that Maltheolus's opinions are shared by philosophers, poets and orators. 'It seems,' she laments, 'that they all speak from one and the same mouth. They all concur in one conclusion: that the behavior of women is inclined to and full of every vice.'[5] Pizan's book-filled study becomes, in this passage, a prisonlike space, an echo chamber in which the woman writer and reader falls into a state of lethargic anomie as she hears a chorus of authoritative male voices anatomizing the faults of her sex:

> I was so transfixed by this line of thinking that it seemed as if I were in a stupor. Like a gushing fountain, a series of authorities . . . came to mind, along with their opinions on [the] topic of [woman]. And I finally decided that God formed a vile creature when He made woman, and I wondered how such a worthy artisan could have deigned to make such an abominable work which, from what they say, is the vessel as well as the refuge and abode of every evil and vice.[6]

More than five hundred years separate Christine de Pizan from Virginia Woolf; the parallel between their autobiographical accounts of being textually defined by men serves, first of all, to indicate the historical continuity in certain aspects of the Western sex-gender system.[7] The parallel also serves to ironize the title of Woolf's essay and the well-known proposal to which that title refers: the proposal that a woman must have a room of her own and five hundred pounds a year to be able to write freely. But Woolf herself was unable to write that morning when she went to the British Museum, despite her possession of her own room and the relative economic independence it symbolizes. Although she, like Pizan, belongs to that historically small and privileged group of women who have actually had a room of their own, neither can find therein a refuge from her culture's definitions of her sex; nor can either escape the historically specific socioeconomic arrangements to which the apparently transhistorical discourse of misogyny indirectly points.

My specific focus in this essay is on how certain literate women in the era between 1400 and 1700 both reproduced and contested social constructions of female nature which alienated them not only from their sexuality but also from that special form of productive activity which is writing. The phrase 'social constructions' refers to a complex of social processes – some discursive, some not – which work to transform anatomical sex difference into concepts of gender that have distinct effects on one's economic status, one's status in the system of law, and one's general range of behavioral options. Such processes of social construction, and the relations of mutual determination among them, are very difficult to reconstruct analytically; not only do they vary over time and according to geographical region, but the evidence we have for them is inherently problematic, consisting as it does chiefly of coded representations – pictorial and textual – and of highly incomplete documentary material from such sources as court records, parish registers, company account books and guild ordinances.[8]

In this essay I shall be concerned chiefly with the effects of discursive modes of social construction and, even more narrowly, with the effects, on specific women writers, of patently ideological discourses that construct an 'ideal' of womanhood on the (flawed) ground of female nature as it was culturally defined. Those texts that overtly prescribe certain kinds of female behavior make up a small segment of the broader discursive territory that scholars have named the *querelle des femmes* and traced in legal, medical, political, educational and literary works (among others). Such works were produced and disseminated in many languages from the fifteenth through the seventeenth centuries in Europe.[9] The overtly prescriptive segment of this general discursive territory provides particularly interesting, if always partial, evidence about the economic and institutional structures that shaped women's social being during this period. The evidence is partial not only in the general sense of being incomplete but also in the specific sense of being more incomplete with respect to lower-class women than to women of the middle and upper classes. Although the set of prescriptions about female behavior I shall be examining arguably had significant, if uneven, effects on women of all social classes – on their very access to literacy, for instance – it is clear that the prescriptions were mainly articulated by educated men and aimed at controlling the behavior of relatively privileged women.[10] Such prescriptive texts – comprising, among other things, conduct books, sermons and educational treatises – were often reprinted and translated into several vernacular languages; this 'international' body of textual material worked, Peter Stallybrass has argued, to produce 'a normative "Woman" within the discursive practices of the ruling élite'.[11] That woman was defined as a private rather than a public being, and the three 'especiall vertues' she was most insistently required to possess – as Robert Greene epitomizes them in his book on 'faeminine perfection', *Penelope's Web* (1587) – were chastity, silence and obedience.[12] Of these three, by far the most important from a socioeconomic point of view was chastity. But for Renaissance women writers, as we shall see, the issue of chastity was intricately bound up with the problem posed by the (ideological) logic that made silence an equivalent of bodily purity. To see how women writers were affected by that strange equation, we need first to examine the 'fetish', as Virginia Woolf called it, of female chastity.

'Chastity', Woolf writes in the section of *A Room of One's Own* devoted to the tragic biography of an imagined sixteenth-century woman named Judith Shakespeare, 'may be a fetish invented by certain societies for unknown reasons,' but she adds, 'it had then, it has even now, a religious importance in a woman's life, and has so wrapped itself round with nerves and instincts that to cut it free and bring it to the light of day demands courage of the rarest' (51). For Woolf, the fetish of chastity was a major obstacle, perhaps *the* major obstacle, to women's ability to work as writers. Her use of the term *fetish* is fascinating, as is her airy suggestion that this particular one was 'invented' for 'unknown reasons': she knew, of course, that two major nineteenth-century male theorists had appropriated the notion of the fetish from its original religious context and used it in their elaboration of strong (and strongly incompatible) theories of causation. Freud's concept of the fetishization of the phallus, and Marx's concept of the fetishization of the commodity, are indeed suggestive for an understanding of the problem of female chastity.[13] Marx's concept is directly relevant insofar as female chastity was a commodity bought and sold on the marriage market during the early modern era. Nonetheless, neither psychoanalytic nor Marxist theory has to date done much to explain the fetish of female chastity; nor have many feminist scholars gone deeply into the problem, though it would seem to be a major historical instance of that 'alienation' of female sexuality which Catherine MacKinnon takes to be the prime object of feminist theory.[14]

It is, of course, easy enough to provide a functionalist sociological rationale for the requirement of chastity in the era of the transition from feudal to capitalist social formations in the West. As Angeline Goreau remarks in the Introduction to her collection of writing by and about seventeenth-century women, the 'insistence' on female chastity had its roots

> in concrete economic and social circumstance: under the patriarchal, primogenital inheritance system, the matter of paternity could most emphatically *not* be open to question . . . As the aristocracy's chief means of consolidating and perpetuating power and wealth was through arranged marriage, the undoubted chastity of daughters was a crucial concern. To be of value on the marriage market, girls had to deliver their maidenheads intact on the appointed day: a deflowered heiress could be disinherited, since her virginity was an indispensable part of her dowry; by its loss, she would deprive her father of the possibility of selling her to a husband whose family line she could perpetuate. Legally, a woman's chastity was considered the property of either her father or her husband. A father could sue his daughter's seducer for damages; a husband could sue his wife's lover for trespassing on his property – and many did, with success.[15]

This is a succinct and useful account of the socioeconomic rationale for chastity in women of the upper classes and even in the middle classes that were emerging during this era in the countries of Western Europe and in England; still, the economic rationale does not fully explain why chastity was required so insistently of *all* women, irrespective of their class status; nor does it explain the psychological and ideological logic according to which female silence was prescribed as a necessary sign of the (invisible) property of female chastity. It was that chain of signification which Renaissance women had to examine and challenge in order to write at all, much less to publish their words and thereby enter – albeit not with their bodies – that 'public' realm in which the property of their chastity was felt to be most at risk.

Let me further set the stage for their drama of transgressive utterance, as it might be called, by citing first some relatively simple and then some more complex examples of how the equation between silence and chastity was formulated in the prescriptive literature of the Renaissance. 'It is proper,' Francesco Barbaro wrote in 'Speech and Silence', a chapter of his treaties *On Wifely Duties* (1417), 'that not only the arms but indeed also the speech of women never be made public; for the speech of a noble woman can be no less dangerous than the nakedness of her limbs.'[16] If one accepts the logic of this argument, which is bolstered by a citation of Plutarch's *Coniugalia praecepta*, Barbaro's paradoxical conclusion will not be surprising: women, he says, 'should believe they have achieved [the] glory of eloquence if they will honor themselves with the outstanding ornament of silence'.[17] The formulation is by no means unique to Barbaro. In England over two centuries later, in Richard Braithwait's *The English Gentleman; and the English Gentlewoman*, for instance, a similarly paradoxical formulation appears: 'Silence in a woman is a moving rhetoricke, winning most when in words it wooeth least . . . More shall we see fall into sinne by speech then silence.'[18] The sin Braithwait has in mind, we may presume, is lust; as Peter Stallybrass observes, the 'connection between speaking and wantonness was common to legal discourse and conduct books. A man who was accused of slandering a woman by calling her a "whore" might defend himself by claiming that he meant "whore of her tonge", not "whore of her body." '[19]

So far, the cultural equation between chastity and silence (which defends against the perception of a 'natural' equation between female sexual desire and loquacity) seems fairly straightforward. One can grasp easily enough the economic and psychological rationales for construing a woman's closed mouth as a sign for that vaginal closure which secured her as a man's private property. As the English translator of Benedetto Varchi's *Blazon of Gelousie* put it, a wife was a 'high-pris'd commoditie of love'; when that 'commoditie chanceth to light into some other merchants hands, and that our private Inclosure proveth to be a Common for others, we care no more for it'.[20] Shakespeare's Othello articulates a similar sentiment:

> O curse of marriage,
> That we can call these delicate creatures ours,
> And not their appetites. I had rather be a toad
> And live upon the vapor of a dungeon
> Than keep a corner in the thing I love
> For others' uses.[21]

Matters become more complex, however, when we note that some passages in the prescriptive literature valorize silence over 'literal' chastity. The English translator of Varchi's *Blazon*, for instance, adds this marginal gloss to his text:

> Maides must be seene, not heard, or selde or never,
> O may I such one wed, if I wed ever.
> A Maide that hath a lewd Tongue in her head,
> Worse than if she were found with a Man in bed.[22]

Reversing the hierarchy that underpins the legal defense in which the phrase 'whore of her tongue' is a lesser slander than 'whore of her body', this little quatrain opens a problematic space between literal and figurative modes of unchastity. That space is opened in a different way by a passage in Richard Allestree's *The Ladies Calling*, which construes female loquacity as a 'symptom' not of physical wantonness but rather of an error Allestree seems unable to define except by a series of odd metaphors. '[T]his great indecency of loquacity in women,' he writes, is 'a symptom of a loose, impotent soul, a kind of incontinence of the mind.' Allying loquacity to curiosity (through their shared association with 'indecency'), he suggests that a metaphorical form of unchastity somehow *causes* physical defilement: 'Every indecent curiosity . . . is a deflowering of the mind, and every the least [*sic*] corruption of them gives some degree of defilement to the body too.'[23]

Such formulations open a Pandora's box of questions about how literate Renaissance women themselves perceived the nature of the transgression they committed when they engaged in that *figurative* mode of speech which is writing. Among those questions – which translate and simplify the moments of oblique and often anxious interrogation I shall shortly examine in texts by Renaissance women – are the following: What are the symbolic equivalences between acts of speech and acts of writing? Could not writing be construed in opposition to public speech rather than in conjunction with it?[24] Why – to rephrase that question in words borrowed from an anonymous seventeenth-century 'defender of her sex' – do 'censuring critics . . . measure [a woman's] tongue by [her] pen, and condemn [her] for a talkative by the length of [her] poem'?[25] Just how like a penis *is* a woman's tongue? Did authoritative classical and early Christian injunctions against women's public speech, especially Saint Paul's oft-invoked stipulations that women should 'keep silence in the churches' (1 Cor. 14:34) and 'learn in silence' (1 Tim. 2:11), clearly define a woman's act of writing (especially for a 'private' audience) as sinful? And how did the injunction against female public speech apply to women's relation to an institution unknown to Saint Paul, namely publication through print? Finally, and most generally, in what way does female utterance – oral, written or printed – constitute a threat to the 'rights of men'?

That last question underlies the moments of defensive rhetoric that appear in almost every text I have found by a Renaissance woman. Some lines by the English poet Anne Finch, Countess of Winchilsea (1667–1720), can serve to illustrate the gesture whereby women writers defensively anticipated being criticized for writing and warded off such criticism by disclaiming an intent to publish:

> Did I, my lines intend for publick view,
> How many censures, wou'd their faults persue.
> $[\,.\,.\,.\,]$
> True judges, might condemn their want of witt,
> And all might say, they're by a Woman writt.
> Alas! a woman that attempts the pen,
> Such an intruder on the rights of men,
> Such a presumptuous Creature, is esteem'd
> The fault, can by no virtue be redeem'd.
> They tell us, we mistake our sex and way;
> Good breeding, fassion, dressing, play
> Are the accomplishments we shou'd desire;
> To write, or read, or think, or to enquire
> Wou'd cloud our beauty, and exaust our time,
> And interrupt the Conquests of our prime;
> While the dull mannage, of a servile house
> Is held by some, our outmost art, and use.[26]

The New England poet Anne Bradstreet (1612–1672) makes a similar gesture of apologetic self-defense in the prologue poem of her book *The Tenth Muse Lately Sprung Up in America*, a collection of lyrics published – ostensibly without her consent – in London in 1650:

> I am obnoxious to each carping tongue,
> Who sayes my hand a needle better fits,
> A Poet's Pen all scorne, I should thus wrong;
> For such despite they cast on female wits:
> If what I doe prove well, it won't advance.
> They'l say its stolne, or else, it was by chance.[27]

I cite these passages by Finch and Bradstreet to illustrate the most obvious – but by no means the least interesting – way in which female writers reacted to the cultural ideal of the chaste, silent and obedient woman. In such passages – and they are legion – we see the author herself at once reproducing the ideological injunction against female public expression and querying it by the very fact that she *is* writing and imagining public criticism, even in works that disclaim her intent to publish.

In what follows I shall examine in somewhat more detail two other modes of reaction on the part of women writers to the ideologeme of female chastity, silence and obedience.[28] The first and apparently more conservative reaction, most common among highly religious women writers of the upper classes, involves an anxious effort to justify female self-expression, a certain disobedience to (secular) male authority, without challenging the supreme value of female chastity. In the course of interrogating the extension of the rule of chastity to the question of female speech and obedience, however, such women writers often expose significant contradictions in the rule itself, or rather, in its articulation by different social groups for different institutional purposes. In particular, as we shall see, a theological concept of female chastity, an institutional equivalent of which was the Catholic convent, could be deployed against the concepts of chastity required – for secular purposes even when they were formulated as theological ones – by the institution of marriage.

In contrast to those women writers who accepted the value of female chastity even if they did so in ways that had potentially subversive social implications, a few Renaissance women overtly defied social and literary conventions alike by celebrating female erotic passion. Such women generally lived and published in urban centers and were, significantly, *not* nobly born or nobly married. Membership in the landed gentry was seldom conducive to women's writing about their sexual experience.

To illustrate that mode of justifying female self-expression which proceeds without (overtly) challenging the value of female chastity, I shall adduce two examples, one French and one English: Christine de Pizan and Elizabeth Cary. Throughout her *Livre de la cité des dames* but especially in the concluding section devoted to the stories of female martyrs, Pizan challenges the idea that women's chastity is signified by silence; in so doing, she obliquely justifies her own act of writing as a 'legitimate' form of disobedience to that masculine authority represented by secular patriarchal rulers and even by Saint Paul. Her book, which revises Augustine's *City of God*, Boccaccio's *De claris mulieribus*, Ovid's *Metamorphoses*, and (for the saints' lives) Vincent of Beauvais's *Speculum historiale*, among many other sources, both represents and enacts a challenge to Saint Paul's injunction against female teaching. She derives her revisionary authority, within her fictional frame of a dream vision, from the three allegorical virtues, Reason, Rectitude and Justice, who encourage her to rectify men's false accounts of women by constructing her 'city' – both the text itself and the imaginary place it represents. Many of Christine's portraits of female martyrs stress the heroines' learning and powers of speech. Saint Catherine, for instance, is so well versed in 'the various branches of knowledge' that her arguments for the existence of God render a hostile pagan emperor mute with admiration. He summons a host of philosophers to debate with her; in a clear allusion to the gospel account of the boy Christ's questioning of the teachers in the Jerusalem temple (Luke 2:45–8), Catherine confounds the philosophers with her questions, dispelling her interlocutors' initial scorn about being gathered for an occasion so trifling as a debate 'with a maiden'. Her eloquent reasoning persuades the philosophers to convert to Christianity; the emperor, however – another figure for a male audience – not only remains unpersuaded by Catherine's words but is so enraged by them that he initiates a series of tortures that eventually lead to her death along with those she has converted.[29]

An even more striking and disturbing narrative of powerful but ultimately self-destructive – though soul-saving – female eloquence occurs in the story of Pizan's own patron saint. Her name, a female version of Christ's, assumes special significance in a narrative that not only has strong autobiographical overtones but also works a telling revision on the New Testament. Saint Christine is presented as a beloved daughter of God and also, like the Church and the allegorized bride of the Song of Songs, a spouse of Christ; as the narrative progresses, however, with Christine actively performing miracles and enduring torments, she becomes a sister to or even a female substitute for the Son. The story begins with her smashing her cruel earthly father's gold and silver idols; after undergoing horrendous tortures at his hands, she is delivered to a trio of equally cruel male judges. Rescued several times by God, Christ and various angels, she performs miracles that include walking on water and raising a man from the dead. Her most notable power, however, seems to be her ability to convert thousands of men by what the text calls her 'words and signs' (238); and it is no accident that her final torture, which occurs after she has been accused of witchcraft, consists of having her tongue cut out not once but twice – a vivid emblem for the censoring of female speech. The censorship, however, miraculously fails: after the first mutilation, she continues to speak 'even better and more clearly than before of divine things and of the one blessed God', who responds to her prayers with the gift of his voice, saying, 'Come, Christine, my most beloved and elect daughter, receive the palm and everlasting crown and the reward for your life spent suffering to confess My name' (239). Hearing this voice, the pagan judge orders the executioners to cut Christine's tongue even shorter so she 'could not speak to her Christ'. The second mutilation provides the martyr with an astonishing instrument of revenge: she 'spat this cut off piece of her tongue into the tyrant's face, putting out one of his eyes. She then said to him, speaking as clearly as ever, "Tyrant, what does it profit you to have my tongue cut out so that it cannot bless God, when my soul will bless Him forever . . . ? And because you did not heed my words, my tongue has blinded you, with good reason"' (239–40). The tongue, through divine authority, acquires the license to disobey and wound those earthly father figures who would censor it. But the price of this license is high, both in Christine's story and in the others Pizan tells of women beheaded, racked and debreasted for their devotion to God.[30] If, on the one hand, the martyr stories suggest that powerful female speech need *not* be associated with the idea of sexual sin, they suggest, on the other hand, that the female body itself must be sacrificed in exchange both for divine grace and for eloquence.

Elizabeth Cary (1585?–1639) in her play *The Tragedie of Mariam, the Faire Queene of Jewry* (1613) provides another exemplary meditation on the vexed relationship between female speech and chastity. Like Pizan, Cary both interrogates and in some sense affirms the ideological link between unruly female bodies and unruly tongues. Some of the parallels between their ideological positions derive, no doubt, from the fact that Cary, the daughter of a wealthy lawyer, secretly converted to Catholicism early in what proved to be an unhappy arranged marriage to a Protestant aristocrat. Scholars surmise that she wrote *Mariam* in the first years of her marriage; her choice of plot, drawn from Josephus's *Jewish Antiquities*, would seem to have autobiographical significance, since the story involved an unhappy interfaith and cross-class marriage between the royal Jewish woman Mariam and the less nobly born and non-Jewish Herod.[31]

Cary's closet drama, the first original play to be published in English by a woman, is indebted not only to *Jewish Antiquities* but also to Mary Sidney's translation of Robert Garnier's *Marc Antoine*; it bears, moreover, such striking resemblances to Shakespeare's *Othello* that it may well have either influenced or been influenced by that tragedy.[32] In the opening scene, Mariam soliloquizes about her ambivalent reactions to the (rumored) death of Herod in Rome. She hates Herod for having murdered her brother and grandfather to acquire the Judean throne through marriage to her, but she also loves him enough to regret his death. Brooding on the parallels between her current situation and that of a male hero, Mark Antony, when he lamented Pompey's death, she recalls, in particular, her prior 'public' speech act of criticizing Antony for hypocrisy:

How oft have I with publike voice run on?
To censure Rome's last Hero for deceit:

Because he wept when Pompeis life was gone,
Yet when he liv'd, hee thought his Name too great.

(1.1.1–4)

These lines immediately link the idea of female speech with transgression
('run on') and with punishment ('censure'). The question mark after the
first line seems at first glance merely an oddity of seventeenth-century
rhetorical punctuation. The question itself, however, voiced at the
threshold of the play by a heroine whose 'unbridled speech' (3.3.1186)
eventually plays a major role in provoking Herod to kill her on the
grounds of adultery, is by no means simply rhetorical. Note first that to
construe it as a rhetorical question at all, we must 'run on' over the line's
end and its punctuation. The structure of the verse creates for the reader
a slight but significant tension between pausing, to respect the seemingly
self-contained formal and semantic unit of the first line, and proceeding,
according to the dictates of the syntactic logic that retroactively reveals
the first line to have been part of a larger unit. The verse thereby works
to fashion a counterpoint between formal and semantic strains: we pause
on the theme of running on, we run on to encounter the theme of censure.
Deploying the strategy of the 'pregnant' beginning most famously used
in *Hamlet*, Cary's opening lines epitomize a dilemma of 'choice' that
recurs, for the heroine and others, throughout the play: the irony is that
such choices frequently turn out, in retrospect, not to have involved
genuine ethical alternatives at all.

A key example of such a non-choice is provided at the end of the
Chorus's speech in act 3, a speech that builds its ethical injunction for
Mariam by articulating an abstract doctrine of wifely duty. The doctrine
entails an extraordinarily strict definition of the wife's duty to remain in
the private sphere and a correspondingly extreme definition of woman's
'publike language' as a phenomenon equivalent to prostitution:

Tis not enough for one that is a wife
To keepe her spotles from an act of ill:
But from suspition she should free her life,
And bare herself of power as well as will.
Tis not so glorious for her to be free,
As by her proper selfe restrain'd to bee.

[...]

That wife her hand against her fame doth reare,
That more than to her Lord alone will give
A private word to any second eare,
And though she may with reputation live.
Yet though most chast, she doth her glory blot,
And wounds her honour, though she killes it not.

When to their Husbands they themselves doe bind,
Doe they not wholy give themselves away?
Or give they but their body not their mind,
Reserving that though best, for others pray?
No sure, their thoughts no more can be their owne,
And therefore should to none but one be knowne.

Then she usurpes upon anothers right,
That seeks to be by publike language grac't;
And though her thoughts reflect with purest light,
Her mind if not peculiar [one's private property] is not chast.
For in a wife it is no worse to finde,
A common body, then a common minde.

(3.3.1219–25, 1231–48)

This speech constructs the wife as a property of her husband no less absolutely than does the common law doctrine of coverture, which holds that 'the very being or legal existence of the wife is suspended during marriage, or at least is incorporated and consolidated into that of the husband: under whose wing, protection and cover, she performs everything.'[33] The play, however, works in many ways to question the logic of this view of the wife, a view that clearly condemns female authorship (figured as an illicit desire for 'glory' and 'fame'), and by implication denies this very play-text's right to exist.[34]

One way in which the play interrogates the censoring authority of the Chorus is by defining the heroine's dilemma as one not adequately 'covered' by the ethical rule the Chorus defines and applies to Mariam in its final stanza:

And every mind though free from thought of ill,
That out of glory seekes a worth to show:
When any's eares but one therewith they fill,
Doth in a fort her purenes overthrow.
Now Mariam had, (but that to this she bent)
Been free from feare, as well as innocent.

(3.3.1249–54)

These lines suggest that Mariam could have avoided her tragic fate had she refrained from speaking her mind to anyone other than her husband. The ethical choice the Chorus presents is between speaking publicly to many or speaking privately to one. But this construction of behavioral options doesn't fit Mariam's situation, since, as subsequent plot developments show, it is partly *because* she speaks freely to her husband that she loses her life. 'I cannot frame disguise, nor never taught / My face a looke dissenting from my thought,' she says to Herod, refusing to smile when he bids her to (4.3.1407–8). It is, however, not only her habits of speech that bring her downfall. The problem is that she both speaks too freely and refuses to give her body to Herod: she swears an oath, in fact, never to sleep with him again after she learns that he has commanded her death in the event of his own during an absence from Judea (3.3.1136–7).

The problem of her sexual withholding is only indirectly addressed by the Chorus in the form of the (apparently) rhetorical question, 'When to their Husbands they themselves doe bind, / Doe they not wholly give themselves away?' By the end of its speech, the Chorus has evidently suppressed altogether the crucial issue of Mariam's denial of Herod's rights to her body, focusing instead, as we have seen, on the condemnation of public speech. The Chorus thus anticipates the logic of Herod's own condemnation of his wife: 'Shee's unchaste / Her mouth will ope to any stranger's ear' (4.7.1704–5). This powerful (and anatomically bizarre) way of equating physical and verbal license casts Mariam's fault as one of double excess or openness, whereas what the play actually shows is that her verbal openness is linked to sexual closure. Her behavior entails a property crime in certain ways more threatening to the institution of marriage than adultery because she takes to a logical extreme, and deploys against the husband, the ideal of female chastity. As the Chorus later says, she refuses to 'pay' her marriage debt (4.8.1935).

Inadequate as it is to cover the complex facts of Mariam's situation and ethical stance, the Chorus's 'law' against female public speech seems nonetheless to be partly upheld by the final unfolding of the plot. Mariam is represented, through a messenger's account of her last moments, as a woman who has finally learned to bridle her tongue. Taunted by her mother on the way to her death, she remains silent, and she dies after saying 'some silent prayer' (2026). The wickedness associated with the female tongue is now symbolically transferred from Mariam to her mother, who takes Mariam's place as the object of Herod's censoring wrath: 'Why stopt you not her mouth?' Herod asks the messenger, referring to the mother's taunts (1979). We remember that he has just exercised his power to stop Mariam's mouth.

In what seems the play's most complex and ambivalent irony, Herod begins to value Mariam's eloquence immediately after her death. 'But what sweet tune did this faire dying Swan / Afford thine ears: tell all, omit no letter,' he says (5.1.2008–9). Frantically interrogating the messenger who has witnessed the execution, Herod asks – in words that resemble those of another patriarchal tyrant, King Lear – 'Is there no tricke to make her breathe again?' (2031). Again he asks the messenger to repeat every precious word she said. 'Oh say, what said she more? each word she sed / Shall be the food whereon my heart is fed' (2111–12).

It is significant that Cary imagines Herod valuing Mariam's eloquence only when her body – site of unresolvable ideological conflicts – has been removed from the scene. 'Her body is divided from her head,' the messenger announces, and with this detail and others Cary adds to Josephus's narrative, the play constructs Mariam's death as an allegorical Christian martyrdom. It is possible to read the play's ending as a symbolic act of authorial self-punishment that affirms the value of female silence even as – and partly because – it deploys the discourse of theology to exalt Mariam as a martyred innocent. On this interpretation, the play would 'repent', as it were, for its various moments of mimetic transgression, its representations of not only Mariam's 'unbridled' thoughts and speech but also those of other female characters (most notably Herod's sister Salome) who variously question the logic – and justice – of the patriarchal social system. It is, however, also possible to see in the play's ending – particularly in its handling of the scene of Herod's remorse – a wishful reformation of the tyrannical patriarchal power he represents, a reformation that draws on those currents in contemporary theological and political thought which contested the absolutist doctrine of sovereignty and that 'strengthening' of patriarchal ideology which attended it.[35] Mariam's defiance of Herod's authority as both king and husband should be understood, I am suggesting, in the context of those discourses of 'minority dissent', both Catholic and Protestant, that justified resisting a sovereign (or a husband) if his commands conflicted with God's. 'Your husbands over your soul have no authority and over your bodies but limited power,' states a Catholic *Treatise on Christian Renunciation* addressed to women readers.[36] Mariam enunciates a version of the same argument: 'They can but my life destroy, / My soule is free from adversaries power' (4.8.1843–4).

By drawing on contemporary discourses of minority religious dissent for her characterization of Mariam, Cary, like Christine de Pizan, ambivalently sanctions a certain disobedience and freedom of speech for women; in so doing, both authors implicitly interrogate the idea of woman as the 'property' of men: both, indeed, show women taking possession of their bodies insofar as they refuse to give them to (earthly) fathers or husbands. Neither, however, does more than hint, under the sign of an ethical negative, at the possibility that women might take *positive* possession of their sexuality. Pizan, for instance, justifies an illegitimate incestuous love on the grounds that the pagan queen in question, Semiramis, lived at a time when 'there was still no written law, and people lived according to the law of Nature, where all people were allowed to do whatever came into their hearts without sinning';[37] and Cary has her wicked character Salome, who plays an Iago-like role in shaping Mariam's downfall, voice the 'sinful' idea that women ought to have the same legal privilege men have to divorce an unloved mate when a new passion arises.[38] As if to counter the potentially subversive implications of such textual moments, however, both Pizan and Cary present their readers with images of valued heroines whose freedom to speak is bought, as it were, by their willingness to relinquish their (chaste) bodies to a paternal God.

A more overt challenge to the ideologeme of female chastity, silence and obedience is offered, as I have suggested, by those few Renaissance women writers who, by virtue of their non-aristocratic birth and unconventional marital status, were unusually well positioned to question social as well as literary rules of proper female behavior. Veronica Franco, a Venetian courtesan; Louise Labé, a Lyonnais ropemaker's daughter whose marriage to another ropemaker did not prevent her from having a notorious love affair (for which, among other things, she was denounced by Calvin); and Aphra Behn, an English woman of obscure birth who, after the early death of her Dutch merchant husband, supported herself by writing poems, novels and plays (which were produced on the London stage) and by working as a spy. All three of these women wrote and oversaw the publication of love poetry that revised Petrarchan conventions to create a lyric 'I' capable of articulating female passion. As Ann R. Jones wryly observes of Labé's *Oeuvres* (1555) – and the comment applies as well to Franco's *Terze rime* (1575) – a female beloved who says, 'I am here; I too burn and freeze; I am yours,' offers a disconcerting challenge to that poetry of 'male deprivation and fantasy' generated by Petrarchan lovers addressing their silent ladies.[39]

I have space here to comment only on Behn, whose poem 'The Disappointment' can serve to illustrate the kind of challenge Jones has in mind, which she and other feminist critics have begun to analyze in the works of Labé and Franco.[40] Behn is of particular interest to English-speaking readers because, as Virginia Woolf remarked, she was the first English-woman to earn her living by her pen (*Room of One's Own*, 67). She remains, however, relatively unknown except to specialists: a late eighteenth-century edition of the *Dictionary of National Biography* excoriated her as one whose wit, 'having been applied to the purposes of impiety and vice, ought to be . . . consigned if possible to eternal oblivion'.[41] That judgment, which prevailed during most of the eighteenth and nineteenth centuries, was repeatedly voiced during Behn's own lifetime as well, provoking her to defend herself in the Preface to her play *The Lucky Chance* with words that provide an interesting gloss on 'The Disappointment'. In the prose passage, Behn seeks to vindicate her right to write after proclaiming her innocence of the 'crime' of immoral representation:

> All I ask, is the Priviledge for my Masculine Part the Poet in me (if any such you will allow me) to tread in those successful Paths my

Predecessors have so long thriv'd in, to take those Measures that both
the Ancient and Modern Writers have set me, and by which they have
pleas'd the World so well; If I must not, because of my Sex, have this
Freedom, but that you will usurp all to your selves; I lay down my
Quill, and you shall hear no more of me, no not so much as to make
Comparisons, because I will be kinder to my Brothers of the Pen than
they have been to a defenceless Woman . . . I value Fame as much as
if I had been born a Hero; and if you rob me of that, I can retire from
the ungrateful world and scorn its fickle Favours.[42]

What is fascinating about this passage, to my mind, is that Behn here
defines the poet in her as her masculine part and seeks freedom for 'him'
in language that strikingly reproduces – in the form of the wounded
threat to 'retire' from the world and be silent – her society's vision of
a woman's proper role. Behn's prose self-defense thereby presents an
ideologically confusing argument for the woman's right to write: she
should have this freedom not because she intrinsically merits it but
because the masculine part in her deserves to tread those paths that 'his'
literary predecessors have successfully trod. In her dramatic and poetic
practice, however, Behn frequently constructs a less contradictory and
theoretically bolder argument for a public female voice. She often does
so not by simply following in her male precursors' footsteps but rather
by parodically revising conventions, both social and literary, from a
perspective explicitly defined as 'female'. This is what she does in 'The
Disappointment', a poem that tells the story of a pastoral Petrarchan
lover who pursues his bright-eyed lady in the time-honored fashion
but finds himself in an embarrassing situation when, after she has
properly repulsed his advances, his mistress suddenly steps out of her
conventional role and faintingly offers herself to him. The male lover is,
however, unable to rise to this surprising occasion:

> In vain th'enraged youth essayed
> To call its fleeting vigor back;
> No motion 'twill from motion take;
> Excesse of love his love betrayed.
> In vain he toils, in vain commands:
> The insensible fell weeping in his hand.

The nymph is understandably confused by this turn of events and,
reviving from her amorous trance, reaches out her hand to touch 'that
fabulous Priapus / That potent God, as poets feign'.[43] These lines suggest
that the object of Behn's irony is the tradition of male love poetry –
which includes the French and English subgenre of the impotence or
'Imperfect Enjoyment' poem[44] – as well as the body of the imagined
lover. And in stanza 12 Behn comically undermines the tradition by

169

making her nymph reassume the conventional female attributes of disdain and blushing shame. (Her blushes are described with bawdy pseudoanatomical precision as displacement of blood upward from the 'hinder place'.) In this poem, however, the Petrarchan mistress comes to resemble Daphne, who flees Apollo only because she has suffered a disappointment, not because she wishes to resist. Resistance to eros, prescribed for women by the codes of both society and Petrarchan poetry, is subversively relocated in Behn's little drama on to the male body itself.

In the poem's final stanza, an authorial 'I' emerges from the third-person narration and deliberately reveals itself as a gendered consciousness:

> The nymph's resentments none but I
> Can well imagine or condole:
> But none can guess Lysander's soul,
> But those who swayed his destiny.

By indicating her special knowledge of and sympathy for the nymph, the author coyly implies that she and her heroine are one. The moment of gendered authorial 'unveiling' acquires, however, a special ironic force in Behn's poem, which not only unveils the authorial 'I' as a female but also unveils – exposes in a comic light – the very idea and even the anatomical instrument of male potency, biological and literary. Instead of retiring into the silent private space culturally defined as the woman's proper room, Behn writes eloquently and loquaciously of a man's most private secret – and of how a woman felt about it. The poem offers a witty protest against – and an unconventional analysis of – the normative Renaissance definition of woman as chaste, silent and obedient.

In so doing, Behn's poem dramatizes a danger envisioned by many male humanist writers: the danger is that simply by being exposed to 'humayne letters', by acquiring the ability to *read* the works of men, women may well 'learn to be subtile and shameless lovers, connying and skilful Writers, of Ditties, Sonnettes, Epigrames, and Ballades'. The text I am quoting here is Giovanni Bruto's *La institutione di una fanciulla nata nobilmente* – an educational treatise that paradoxically (but also symptomatically) advises against educating women at all: 'It be not mete . . . for a Maiden to be . . . trained up in learning of humayne arts, in whome a vertuous demeanor and honest behaviour, would be a more sightlier ornament than the light or vaine glorie of learning.'[45] Bruto's argument exposes a problem that lies at the heart, I think, of the general Renaissance discursive project of prescribing (and proscribing) female behavior, verbal and sexual. The problem has to do with female literacy itself, a phenomenon defined and assessed in highly contradictory ways by male writers – servants of churches and states – who sought to shape readers' behavior through textual instruction and also to prevent their readers from using their literacy for 'unlicensed' ends. One such end was usurping the authority claimed by members of the emerging international group of male intellectuals whose work as diplomats, courtiers, and educators played an important role in the transition from feudal to capitalist societies in the West.[46]

Literacy was a double-edged sword, and it is no accident that humanist and Protestant propaganda for the value of literacy was 'pitched less enthusiastically', as David Cressy remarks, toward women than toward men – and more toward men of the upper classes than toward those of the lower ones.[47] It is also no accident that our knowledge of literacy rates in the early modern period is severely hampered by the fact that reading was frequently taught separately from writing. French synodal regulations and episcopal ordinances of the Counter-Reformation Church, for instance, often insist that girls, unlike boys, should be taught not to write but only to read (and to sew).[48]

In the larger study for which the present essay is a preliminary sketch, I hope to explore the ways literacy, in theory and in practice, constituted a major site of social conflict in the early modern period (as it still does today in the relations between 'First' and 'Third' World countries). Believing that the topic is as important for students of Comparative Literature as it is for our fellow comparatists in the field of social anthropology, I shall define literacy not as a self-evident phenomenon but – in John Guillory's formulation – as a 'complex of social facts that corresponds to all of the following questions: who reads? who writes? in what determinate circumstances? for whom?'[49]

Defining literacy thus, I shall hope to come to a better understanding of the role that our precursors in the field of education played in constructing, and representing, that 'complex of social facts'. Consider, for example, the following passage from Richard Allestree's *The Ladies Calling* (1675), which translates, for new social purposes, Saint Paul's injunctions against female public speech. The apostle, Allestree remarks,

> expressly enjoins women *to keep silence in the church*, where he affirms that it is a shame for them to speak: and though this seems only restrained to the ecclesiastical assemblies, yet even so it reaches home to the gifted women of our own age, who take upon them to be teachers . . . But besides this, he has a more indefinite prescription of silence to women . . . *Let women learn in silence* . . . The Apostle seems to ground the phrase, not only on the inferiority of the woman in regard of the creation and the first sin, but also on the presumption that they needed instruction, towards which silence has always been reckoned an indispensible qualification . . . If some women of our age think they have outgone that novice state the Apostle supposes, and want no teaching, I must crave leave to believe, they want that very first

171

principle which should set them to learn, i.e. their knowledge of their own ignorance.[50]

Allestree's passage shows that men as well as women were able to interrogate the logic of extending Paul's ancient prescription to a different historical situation. The passage also suggests, however, that the male writer's investment in his own authority helps shape a new rationale for the necessity of female silence. Recognizing that the Pauline prescription is 'indefinite', Allestree at once opens and seeks to close that Pandora's box of questions to which I referred earlier in this essay – a box in which truths that seem self-evident are revealed, if only intermittently and partially, to be (one hopes) contestable.

Notes

For their generous help with earlier versions of this essay, I would like to thank Mary Anne Ferguson, David Kastan, Joseph Loewenstein and Mary Poovey. I am also grateful for comments from the members of a colloquium on feminist literary theory held at the Johns Hopkins University in November 1986, at which a draft of this paper was discussed.

1. PIZAN's *Livre de la cité des dames* was translated in 1521 by Brian Ansley (*Boke of the Cyte of Ladies*) and was retranslated by EARL JEFFREY RICHARDS (New York: Persea, 1982). Richards's translation, from which quotations in the body of this essay are taken, is based on the manuscript in the British Library, Harley 4431, one of some twenty-five manuscript versions of the text. The only printed version of the French original is based on the Bibliothèque Nationale Fonds français 607 codex and is available, unfortunately, only in the form of a University Microfilms International dissertation (Ann Arbor, Mich.) by MAUREEN CHENEY CURNOW, 'The *Livre de la cité des dames* of Christine de Pisan: A Critical Edition', 3 vols (PhD diss., Vanderbilt University, 1975). Curnow's French text, therefore, does not always correspond exactly with Richards's translation.

2. WOOLF, *A Room of One's Own* (1929; rpt New York: Harcourt Brace Jovanovich, 1957), 25. All quotations are from this edition.

3. RICHARDS, 3; CURNOW, 2:616–17: 'Un jour comme je fusse seant en ma celle avironnee de plusieurs volumes de diverses mateires, mon entendement a celle heure aucques travaillié de reccuillir la pesenteur des sentences de divers aucteurs par moy longue piece estudiés . . . entre mains me vint d'aventure un livre estrange, non mie de mes volumes . . . [C]elluy parloit bien a la reverence des femmes.'

4. RICHARDS, 5; CURNOW, 2:620: 'me sourdi une grant desplaisance et tristesce de couraige en desprisant moy meismes et tout le sexe feminin, si comme ce ce fust monstre en nature.'

5. RICHARDS, 4; CURNOW, 2:618: '[Il] semble que tous parlent par une meismes bouche et tous accordent une semblable conclusion, determinant les meurs femenins enclins et plains de tous les vices.'

6. RICHARDS, 4–5; CURNOW, 2:619–20: 'En ceste pensee fus tant et si longuement fort fichiee que il sembloit que je fusse si comme personne en etargie, et me venoyent audevant moult grant foyson de autteur[s] ad ce propos que je ramentevoye en moy meismes l'un aprés l'autre, comme se fust une fontaine resourdant. Et en conclusion de tout, je determinoye que ville chose fist Dieux quant il fourma femme, en m'esmerveillant comment si digne ouvri[e]r daigna oncques faire tant abominable ouvrage qui est vaissel, au dit d'iceulx, si comme le retrait et herberge de tous maulx et de tous vices.'

7. Feminist anthropologists use the notion of the sex-gender system to describe how a given culture transforms the fact of anatomical sexual difference into a system of ideologically coded meanings and practices. See GAYLE RUBIN, 'The Traffic in Women', in *Toward an Anthropology of Women*, ed. Rayna R. Reiter (New York: Monthly Review Press, 1975), 156–210, esp. 150, 161; and also LOUIS MONTROSE, '*A Midsummer Night's Dream* and the Shaping Fantasies of Elizabethan Culture: Gender, Power, Form', in *Rewriting the Renaissance*, eds Margaret W. Ferguson, Maureen Quilligan and Nancy Vickers (Chicago: University of Chicago Press, 1986), 70.

8. There is a large and heterogeneous body of scholarship on the changes that occurred in the sex-gender system, particularly the structure of the family, during the early modern era. LAWRENCE STONE's monumental *The Family, Sex and Marriage in England, 1500–1800* (London: Weidenfield & Nicholson, 1977), which advances, among other theses, the idea that the Protestant Reformation in England saw a 'new emphasis on the home and on domestic virtues', has been challenged on many counts but remains central to scholarly debate. For a discussion of Stone's work in the context of recent scholarship, see R.B. OUTHWAITE, Introduction to his edition of *Marriage and Society: Studies in the Social History of Marriage* (New York: St Martin's Press, 1981). For bibliographic information on the documentary sources available for studying women in the Renaissance, see Joan Kelly, 'Did Women Have a Renaissance?', *Women, History, and Theory: The Essays of Joan Kelly* (Chicago: University of Chicago Press, 1984), 49–50; and the essays on women's work by MERRY E. WIESNER and JUDITH C. BROWN, in *Rewriting the Renaissance*, 191–205, 206–24. That volume also contains an extensive bibliography on recent research on women in the early modern era.

9. See, for a useful survey of the discussions of women in various disciplinary discourses, IAN MACLEAN, *The Renaissance Notion of Woman* (Cambridge: University of Cambridge Press, 1980).

10. See PETER STALLYBRASS, 'Patriarchal Territories: The Body Enclosed', *Rewriting the Renaissance*, 123–42, for a discussion of the prescriptive literature on women in the context of the larger Renaissance discursive project of 'behavior modification' analyzed by NORBERT ELIAS in *The History of Manners*, vol. 1 of his *The Civilizing Process*, trans. E. Jephcott (New York: Pantheon, 1978). See also SUZANNE W. HULL, *Chaste, Silent & Obedient: English Books for Women, 1475–1640* (San Marino: Huntington Library, 1984).

11. STALLYBRASS, 'Patriarchal Territories', 127. For information on the translation of books addressed to female readers (who were presumed to be unable to read foreign tongues), see HULL, *Chaste, Silent & Obedient*, 25–8 and passim.

12. Greene's treatise is cited in HULL, *Chaste, Silent & Obedient*, 173.

13. See Freud's essay 'Fetishism' (1927), *The Standard Edition of the Complete Psychological Works of Sigmund Freud*, ed. James Strachey *et al.*, 24 vols

(London: Hogarth Press, 1953–74), 21:149–56; and, for a useful discussion of the development of his theory of fetishism and its role as a 'proof' of the castration complex, JULIET MITCHELL, *Feminism and Psychoanalysis* (New York: Random House, 1975), 84–5. On MARX's theory of fetishism, see *A Dictionary of Marxist Thought*, ed. Tom Bottomore (Cambridge: Harvard University Press, 1983), 165–6.

14. The quotation from MacKinnon's article is from *Feminist Theory: A Critique of Ideology*, eds Nannerl G. Keohane, Michelle Z. Rosaldo and Barbara C. Gelpi (Chicago: University of Chicago Press, 1982), 1.

15. *The Whole Duty of a Woman: Female Writers in Seventeenth-Century England* (Garden City, NY: Doubleday, 1985), 9–10.

16. Quoted from FRANCESCO BARBARO, *On Wifely Duties*, trans. Benjamin G. Kohl, in *The Earthly Republic: Italian Humanists on Government and Society*, eds Kohl and Ronald G. Witt, with Elizabeth Welles (Philadelphia: University of Pennsylvania Press, 1978), 205. The original, from the chapter 'De verbis ac taciturnitate', is in *De re uxoria*, ed. A. Gnesotto, *Atti e memorie della R. Accademia di scienze, lettere ed arti di Padova* (Padova: Tipografia Giovanni Battista Randi, 1915–16), 6–105: 'Unde non modo lacertos, sed ne sermones quidem mulieris publicos esse conveniet. Nec enim minus hujusmodi feminae vox quam membrorum nudatio verenda est' (76).

17. KOHL, 206; GNESOTTO, 77: 'Itaque bene dicendi gloriam se assecuturas existiment, si praecipuo silentii ornamento scipsas honestaverint.'

18. Braithwait's treatise (London, 1641) is cited in CATHERINE BELSEY, *The Subject of Tragedy: Identity and Difference in Renaissance Drama* (London: Methuen, 1985), 179. Belsey also cites (180) John Dod and Robert Cleaver, *A Godly Form of Household Government* (London, 1641): 'Now silence is the best ornament of a woman, and therefore the law was given to the man, rather then to the woman, to shew that he should be the teacher, and she the hearer.'

19. STALLYBRASS, 'Patriarchal Territories', 126.

20. The quotation is from one of the supplemental notes Richard Tofte added to his translation of VARCHI's *Lezione su la Gelosia* (Lyons, 1550). Tofte's translation was published in London in 1615. STALLYBRASS, 'Patriarchal Territories', 128, quotes the passage.

21. Quoted from *The Tragedy of Othello*, ed. Alvin Kernan (New York: NAL, 1863), 102–3 (3.3.267–72).

22. Cited in STALLYBRASS, 'Patriarchal Territories', 126.

23. *The Ladies Calling* (London, 1673), quoted in GOREAU, *The Whole Duty*, 55, 11.

24. LEONARDO BRUNI, for instance, insists that rhetoric 'in all its forms . . . lies absolutely outside the province of women' but later in the same educational treatise recommends that women study great classical orators in order to learn eloquent expression in their *writing* (*De studiis et litteris*, a letter to Battista da Montefeltro Malatesta written in 1405 and translated in W.H. WOODWARD, *Vittorino da Feltre and Other Humanist Educators: Essays and Versions* (1897; rpt. ed. E. Rice, New York: Bureau of Publications, Teachers' College, Columbia University, 1963), 126, 128). Writing, for Bruni, appears to be somehow excluded from the category of 'rhetoric in all its forms', but as MARGARET L. KING and ALBERT RABIL, JR, observe in their introduction to *Her Immaculate Hand: Selected Works by and about the Woman Humanists of Quattrocento Italy* (Binghamton, NY: Center for Medieval and Early Renaissance Studies, State University of New York at Binghamton, 1983), women were in fact barred

from those forms of writing employed by humanists in their capacity as public officials, secretaries or diplomats.

25. The quotation, from *The Female Advocate: or, An Answer to a Late Satyr Against Pride, Lust and Inconstancy of Woman*, Written by a Lady in Vindication of Her Sex (London, 1686), is in GOREAU, 13.

26. 'The Introduction', *The Poems of Anne, Countess of Winchilsea*, ed. Myra Reynolds (Chicago: University of Chicago Press, 1913), 4–5.

27. *The Complete Works of Anne Bradstreet*, eds Jospeh R. McElrath, Jr, and Allen P. Rabb (Boston: Twayne, 1981), 7. See PATRICIA CRAWFORD, 'Women's Published Writing, 1600–1700', in *Women in English Society, 1500–1800*, ed. Mary Prior (London: Methuen, 1985), 214, 218, for information about the circumstances of the publication of Bradstreet's poems; her British publisher, as if acting out the male role of skeptical critic sketched in the Prologue, wondered whether Bradstreet's poems were truly her own work.

28. I adapt the term *ideologeme* from FREDRIC JAMESON, *The Political Unconscious: Narrative as a Socially Symbolic Act* (Ithaca: Cornell University Press, 1981), 87–8 and passim. Jameson uses the term to denote minimal ideological 'units' that manifest themselves 'either as a pseudoidea – a conceptual or belief system, an abstract value, an opinion or prejudice – or as a protonarrative'. Although he deploys the term to analyze conflicts among social classes, it seems equally appropriate for analysing gender conflicts.

29. The story is in RICHARDS, 219–22; CURNOW, 3:978–82. The French versions of the passages I quote are: 'comme grant clergesce et aprise es sciences que elle estoit' (979) and 'pour disputer a une pucelle' (979).

30. Saint Christine's story is in RICHARDS, 234–40; CURNOW, 3:1001–10. The originals of the passages cited are: 'les parolles et signes' (1006); 'mais mieulx que devant et plus cler parloit ades des choses divines et beneyssoit Dieu' (1008); 'Viens Christine, ma tres amee et tres elitte fille et reçoy la palme et la couronne pardurable et le guerdon de ta passionable vie en la confession de mon nom' (1008–9); 'si luy couppassent si pres que tant ne peust parler a son Crist' (1009); 'Tirant, que te vault avoir couppee ma langue adfin que elle ne beneysse Dieu, quant mon esperit a tousjours le beneystra . . . Et pource que tu ne congnois ma parolle, c'est bien raison que ma langue t'ait aveuglé' (1009).

31. Cary's play was written sometime between 1603 and 1612, when it was licensed in the Stationers' Register; it appeared in quarto in 1613, printed by Thomas Creede for Richard Hawkins, and bore on the title page the statement 'Written by that learned, vertuous, and truly noble Ladie, E.C.' This edition, of which there are several copies extant, was reprinted by the Malone Society (London, 1914) with an introduction by A.C. Dunstan. He explains the evidence for identifying the 'E.C.' of the title page with that Elizabeth Cary (or Carey or Carew) who was the daughter of Lawrence Tanfield and Elizabeth Symonds and the wife of Sir Henry Cary, after 1620 Viscount of Falkland. My quotations are from Dunstan's edition, which is full of textual problems I have not sought to correct. The autobiographical resonance of the play is obvious when one reads it in conjunction with the *Life* of Cary by one of her daughters, who became a nun in a French convent after her mother's separation from Sir Henry in 1625. The relationship between the *Life* (printed for the first and last time in an edition by Richard Simpson [London: Catholic, 1861]) and the play is discussed by ELAINE BEILIN, 'Elizabeth Cary and *The Tragedy of Mariam*', *Papers on Language and Literature* 16 (Winter 1980), 45–64.

32. The uncertainty about the dating of both *Mariam* and *Othello* makes it impossible to say which influenced which; I could make a plausible case, however, for *some* direct influence. The parallels in plot and phrasing are more extensive than critics have noticed. The topic has indeed hardly been discussed, though it's hinted at by Theobald in his editorial gloss on the famous 'base Indian' or 'base Iudean' crux (*Othello* 5.2.421); arguing for the latter reading he cites Cary's Herod, who, lamenting his killing of his wife on a false charge of adultery, berates himself for throwing his precious 'Jewell' away (5.1.2061). See *A New Variorium Edition of Shakespeare*, ed. Horace Howard Furness (Philadelphia: J.B. Lippincott, 1886), 327.

33. SIR WILLIAM BLACKSTONE, *Commentaries of the Laws of England, Book the First* (Oxford, 1875), 442, quoted in MARY POOVEY, *The Proper Lady and the Woman Writer* (Chicago: University of Chicago Press, 1984), 6–7.

34. ANGELINE GOREAU errs, I think, in taking the speech as a simple expression of Cary's own beliefs and an illustration of 'the social hegemony of "modesty"'; the oversimplification arises in part because Goreau considers the speech out of its dramatic context (she defines it as 'a poem') and without reference to Cary's own activity of writing. See her essay 'Two English Women in the Seventeenth Century: Notes for an Anatomy of Feminine Desire', in *Western Sexuality: Practice and Precept in Past and Present Times*, eds Philippe Ariès and André Bejin, trans. Anthony Forster (from the French edn of 1982) (Oxford: Blackwell, 1985). For a provocative discussion of the speech see BELSEY, *The Subject of Tragedy*, 171–5.

35. See LAWRENCE STONE, 'The Reinforcement of Patriarchy', Chap. 5 of *The Family, Sex and Marriage*; and JONATHAN GOLDBERG, 'Fatherly Authority: The Politics of Stuart Family Images', in *Rewriting the Renaissance*, 3–32. See also his *James I and the Politics of Literature: Jonson, Shakespeare, Donne, and Their Contemporaries* (Baltimore: Johns Hopkins University Press, 1981). If Cary's play does indeed reflect as well as obliquely criticize a form of patriarchal ideology specific to James's reign, then it would be worth exploring the parallels between Mariam and two historical queens whose images posed problems for James: Elizabeth Tudor and Mary Stuart.

36. Quoted by MARIE BOWLANDS, 'Recusant Women 1560–1640' in *Women in English Society*, 165. Cf. the radical Protestant KATHERINE CHIDLEY's statement in her *Justification of the Independent Churches of Christ* (London, 1641): 'I pray you tell me what authority the unbeleeving husband hath over the conscience of his beleeving wife. It is true he hath authority over her in bodily and civill respects but not to be a Lord over her conscience' (26). See also SANDRA K. FISCHER, 'Elizabeth Cary and Tyranny', in *Silent But for the Word*, ed. Margaret P. Hannay (Kent: Kent State University Press, 1985), 225–37.

37. RICHARDS, 40; CURNOW, 2:680: 'adonc n'estoit point de loy escripte: ains vivoyent les gens a loy de nature, ou il loisoit a chacun sans mesprendre de faire tout ce que le cuer luy apportoit.'

38. See SALOME's soliloquy in *Mariam*, 1.4, where she eloquently queries the sexual double standard and vows to be the 'custome breaker' who will 'shewe my Sexe the way to freedomes doore' (319–20).

39. JONES, 'Assimilation with a Difference: Renaissance Women Poets and Literary Influence', *Yale French Studies* 62 (1981), 135–53; quotation 146.

40. See, e.g., ANN JONES, 'City Women and Their Audiences: Louise Labé and Veronica Franco', in *Rewriting the Renaissance*, 299–316; MARGARET F. ROSENTHAL,

'Veronica Franco: The Courtesan as Poet in Sixteenth-Century Venice' (Ph.D. diss., Yale University, 1985); and FRANÇOIS RIGOLOT, 'Gender vs Sex Difference in Louise Labé's Grammar of Love', in *Rewriting the Renaissance*, 287–98.

41. Cited by FIDELIS MORGAN in her Introduction to APHRA BEHN, *The Lucky Chance*, ed. Morgan (London: Methuen, with the Royal Court Theatre, 1984), n.p. For the history of Behn's reputation, see ANGELINE GOREAU, *Reconstructing Aphra: A Social Biography of Aphra Behn* (New York: Dial, 1980).
42. Quoted from *The Works of Aphra Behn*, ed. Montague Summers, 6 vols (1915; rpt. New York: Benjamin Blom, 1967), 3:187.
43. The Disappointment', *Works*, 6:178–82, quotations 180 (stanza 11).
44. There is much irony in the fact that Behn's poem was originally printed as the Earl of Rochester's; his 'The Imperfect Enjoyment', like other poems in this subgenre (which goes back to Ovid's *Amores* 3.7), treats impotence from a purely male point of view. On Behn's revisionary strategies in this poem see JUDITH KEGAN GARDINER, 'Aphra Behn: Sexuality and Self-respect', *Women's Studies* 7 (1980), 67–78; and for a discussion of the Restoration 'obsession' with impotence, see JAY ARNOLD LEVINE, 'The Dissolution: Donne's Twofold Elegy', *ELH* 28, 4 (Dec. 1961), 303.
45. Bruto's treatise (Anvers, 1555) was translated by Thomas Salter (London, 1579); the quotation is from JONES, 'City Women', 300.
46. See ANTONIO GRAMSCI, 'The Intellectuals', in his *Selections from the Prison Notebooks*, ed. and trans. Quintin Hoare and Geoffrey Nowell Smith (New York: International, 1971), 5–23. See also, on the humanist intellectuals as servants of the emerging nation states of the early modern period, WLAD GODZICH, 'The Culture of Illiteracy', *Enclitic* 8 (Fall 1984), 27–35.
47. CRESSY, *Literacy and the Social Order* (Cambridge: Cambridge University Press, 1980), 128.
48. See FRANÇOIS FURET and JACQUES OZOUF, *Lire et écrire: L'Alphabétisation des français de Calvin à Jules Ferry*, 2 vols (Paris: Minuit, 1977), 1:85. Cf. also MARGARET SPUFFORD, *Small Books and Pleasant Histories: Popular Fiction and Its Readership in Seventeenth-Century England* (Cambridge: Cambridge University Press, 1981), 25.
49. GUILLORY, 'Canonical and Non-canonical: A Critique of the Current Debate' *ELH* 54 (1987), 485. See also Guillory, *Cultural Capital: The Problem of Literary Canon Formation* (Chicago: University of Chicago Press, 1993).
50. Quoted from Goreau, *The Whole Duty*, 55.

7 Mediation and Contestation: English Classicism from Sidney to Jonson*

DON E. WAYNE

In *Penshurst: The Semiotics of Place and the Poetics of History* (1984), Don Wayne analysed the work of Ben Jonson in terms of the transition from feudalism to capitalism illuminated by Marxist historians. The essay printed below summarizes some of Wayne's principal conclusions about Jonson's position at a time of conflicting ideologies. Although Jonson has been labelled a conservative because of his bitter satires of London commercialism, Wayne uses a cultural materialist perspective to argue that Jonson's classicism was a 'contestatory discourse' which enunciated 'a new conception of the subject'. As a poet–commoner, Jonson constructed a literary *persona* authorized not by the system of status but by an ideology of merit and achievement based on classicist norms of reason and nature. This allowed him to question the feudal, aristocratic ethos associated with his patrons, including the Sidney family. Jonson's mode of 'individualism' also reveals its limits, however, since this new ideology inevitably implicated him in the aggressive competition of the emerging literary marketplace.

If society sees itself and, in particular, sees itself as *seen*, there is, by virtue of this very fact, a contesting of the established values of the regime.

(Jean-Paul Sartre)

I

Classicism has often been regarded in the twentieth century as a conservative, if not totalitarian, orientation in literature. Those who have noted the reductive or repressive tendencies of classicism, with varying degrees of reproof, constitute a diverse and distinguished group that

---

* Reprinted from *Criticism* 25 (Detroit: Wayne State University Press, 1983), pp. 211–37.

includes such names as Auerbach, Lovejoy, Bakhtin, Sartre and Barthes. Auerbach associates classicism with the rise of absolute monarchy and suggests that it threatened to undermine the humanist sense of historical perspective that had been developing in European culture since the time of Dante. For Bakhtin, classicism represents a type of 'authoritative discourse' in which the fundamentally *dialogic* structure of human communication – expressive of a historical, sociolinguistic diversity within a culture – is suppressed: 'In neoclassicism, this double-voicing becomes crucial only in low genres, especially in satire.' However, in a later note to the same text, Bakhtin points to the necessity of historicizing such categorical judgments: 'When analyzing a concrete example of authoritative discourse . . . it is necessary to keep in mind the fact that purely authoritative discourse may, in another epoch, be internally persuasive [by the latter, he means a semantic structure that is not finite but open, in which the listener or reader is an active participant in the production of meaning].' Bakhtin is thinking here of the novel, but I suggest that his caveat applies as well to his own earlier comments on neoclassicism. The critical studies of French classicism written by Sartre and Barthes in the politically charged intellectual atmosphere of post-war Paris are well known. Barthes' is the more radical critique; but Sartre's account is, on the whole, more balanced in its assessment of the writer's situation in the seventeenth and eighteenth centuries. Also well known, and closer to home, is Lovejoy's essay relating classicism and deism in which an outline of Enlightenment ideology is set forth, the first and last categories of which are 'Uniformitarianism' and 'a negative philosophy of history'.[1]

It should already be evident from my remarks on Bakhtin that I mean to propose an alternative to the prevailing, negative view of classicism held by intellectual historians and social critics, and that I propose to do so from the standpoint of a historical approach to the analysis of discourse, genre and ideology. The basis for a more adequate historicization of classicism can be found in the work of some of the above mentioned critics themselves, most notably in Sartre. At the very least, we need to distinguish between classicism as an emergent cultural phenomenon and as a hegemonic 'period style'. I shall focus here on the earliest manifestations of literary classicism in English poetry.

To the extent that there is a classical component to English Renaissance literature prior to Ben Jonson,[2] it is evident at the level of the *signified*, but rarely is it a facet of the *signifier*. English humanists may have been diligent in their employment of classical subject matter, but, save perhaps for experiments in quantitative prosody, they tended to be less interested in classical forms.[3] In non-dramatic literature as in the visual arts, allegory – even when it entailed allusion to classical mythology – tended to override any sustained interest in the formal principles of classicism. English resistance to classicism was, in part, a consequence of Protestant and nationalist rejection of forms identified with Italian Popery. But it was also, and perhaps principally, an aspect of the retrospective feudalism through which Tudor ideology rationalized the dynasty's claim to legitimacy. The more overt, spectatorial forms of such legitimation included the persistence of the Gothic style in architecture; the building of 'sham' castles in which crenelation served a symbolic rather than a practical military function; the emphasis in painting on heroic portraits of the ruling élite and of their real or imagined ancestors; the vogue for heraldry; and, of course, the elaborate ritual of the Accession Day tilts.[4] We find the literary analogs of this tendency in pastoral romance like Sidney's *Arcadia* and in the deliberate archaism of Spenser.

The self-conscious medievalism of Tudor culture sought expression in forms and images that represented history as an unbroken tradition and a providential succession – with all the important connotations of rightful inheritance the latter term implied for sixteenth-century Englishmen. By contrast, for the classicist, who looked back beyond the actual or mythic feudal past to the 'golden age' of antiquity, *succession* was a far less important component of the representational code than were the principles of *identity* and *uniformity*, principles shared by classicism with its claim to the timeless validity of ancient forms (and the ethical norms that these were held to embody) and by the new science in its search for universal laws of nature. Ben Jonson's poetry is founded on these principles and, as such, constitutes a significant break with the sixteenth-century tradition of English humanism. In this respect, Jonson may indeed be said to be less historical – less preoccupied, that is, with a version of English history – than were Sidney, Spenser or Shakespeare in the history plays. Perhaps, too, the shift toward a truly classical mode of representation in the work of Jonson both reflected and helped to sustain the absolutist doctrines of James I. But a precise analysis of how classicism may have served as a code for legitimating absolute authority and power is not within the scope of the present essay. At the same time, it is by no means inconsistent to acknowledge this ideological function and to claim, as I do in what follows, that classicism at its inception was a contestatory discourse.[5]

For an analysis of Jonson's relation to the previous generation of English poets, the poetry of Sir Philip Sidney provides an especially interesting basis of comparison since Sidney is a mediatory figure for Jonson in more than one respect: as a poet and literary theorist, and as the heroic and legendary member of an aristocratic family that Jonson counted among his patrons. Sidney's *Astrophil and Stella* already exhibits a significant modification of the lyric tradition in which it is written. As David Kalstone has pointed out, a number of the poems in this sonnet cycle reveal a disturbed awareness of the limitations of the Petrarchan mode as an embodiment of a *mythos* and an *ethos* upon which to model behavior in the Elizabethan court: 'What had begun as an ideal of conduct had ended as an imperative of courtly affectation.'[6] Yet, these reservations notwithstanding, the consciousness assumed by Sidney in the *persona* of Astrophil is a heroic and a mythopoeic consciousness. Any changes that are traceable in Astrophil's attitude, as the drama of his relationship to Stella unfolds, occur within this heroic frame. Early in the sequence, Astrophil identifies himself with the suffering of Prometheus and associates his 'sinfull' love with this benefactor of mankind's noble theft of the celestial fire:[7]

> Alas have I not paine enough my friend,
>> Upon whose breast a fiercer Gripe doth tire
>> Then did on him who first stale downe the fire,
> While *Love* on me doth all his quiver spend . . .
> If that be sinne which in fixt hearts doth breed
>> A loathing of all loose unchastitie,
>> Then Love is sinne, and let me sinfull be.
>>>> (Sonnet 14, ll. 1–4, 12–14)

Even in the final poem, where hope has given way to 'most rude dispaire', Astrophil is still identified with the element of fire:

> When sorrow (using mine owne fier's might)
>> Melts downe his lead into my boyling brest,
>> Through that darke fornace to my hart opprest,
> There shines a joy from thee my only light. . . .
>>>> (Sonnet 108, ll. 1–4)

The poems are also filled with images of knightly service and combat and, whatever their ambiguities in other respects, thus remain consistent with that aspect of the courtly lyric tradition that has been described as 'a feudalisation of love'.[8]

The most important mythological figure in any of the Renaissance sonnet sequences is, of course, that of Eros, Cupid or Love. For Plato, writes Ernst Cassirer, 'Eros belongs to a middle realm of being. He stands between the divine and the human, between the intelligible and sensible worlds, and he must relate and join them to each other.'[9] The association of love and intellect, as developed in the writings of Ficino and other Neoplationists of the Italian Renaissance, is a frequent theme of Elizabethan poetry. In Spenser's *Amoretti* and in the *Fowre Hymnes*, Love is a beautifully elaborated yet still conventional Neoplatonic figure for the union of reason and desire in the human soul. But in *Astrophil and Stella*, such a union is rendered problematic, especially in those poems where Astrophil struggles with the irony of Love's double connotation as 'Desire' and 'Vertue' (see e.g. Sonnets 71, 72).

This ironic treatment of Love is a facet of what Richard C. McCoy describes as the 'sexual politics' of Sidney's literary works, involving an unresolved dialectic between the desire for autonomy and the duty of submission.[10] It is also, I believe, a symptom of the anxiety that was widespread among the Elizabethan aristocracy concerning their ancestry.[11] For among the functions of the dynamic and liminal force of Eros in the Neoplationic cosmos is that of relating the present to an exemplary past. Jerome Mazzaro is right in calling attention to this aspect of the doctrine of love within the English Petrarchan tradition; but he overlooks the irony in Sidney's handling of the theme. Mazzaro claims that the English sonneteers were possessed of a 'mythic consciousness' which 'like Ficinian "consciousness" . . . required the mind to divide itself into two – past and present – and to confront itself with the vehicle of a patterned past as the metaphoric tenor for its present mood and then by more knowledge to overcome the separation.'[12] His description is illuminating up to a point, but the last phrase is puzzling. For what or where is the 'more knowledge' that will finally 'overcome the separation'? Mazzaro understands the way in which the Petrarchan lyric embodies a dialectic between past and present, but he tends to overestimate the resolutive power of what he calls 'mythic consciousness' in the Elizabethan age. It is unlikely that Sidney and his aristocratic audience could have hoped to overcome the separation between themselves and an idealized past. Ideologically, what they hoped to secure through the power of representation was a relation to the past based on notions of resemblance and continuity rather than on identity in any absolute sense.[13] The continuity of the principle of Eros in the parallel between Petrarch/Laura and Astrophil/Stella was one way of constituting and retaining a cultural and social identification with the past, and with at least a portion of the European nobility (the latter was a motive of special importance to Sidney and to the faction at court led by Robert Dudley who saw themselves as part of an international movement of Protestant chivalry).

The relation between past and present in Sidney's verse is a self-consciously metaphorical or symbolic one, and this self-consciousness is evidence of the degree to which the poet feels the separation as intensely as he does the connection with the past. Kalstone writes: 'The voice of Astrophel is almost the opposite of Petrarch's: recognizing conflicts where Petrarch enforces harmonies; tentative and critical where Petrarch is sure about the relation of beauty and philosophic meditation.'[14] But although Sidney can criticize by pointing to the inadequacies of the Petrarchan mode, he can suggest no alternative because the ideological constraints of his social position preclude the assumption of a more personal or 'original' voice than that afforded by the Petrarchan *persona*, however modified it may be. Petrarch's love for Laura thus continues to function typologically as a moment against which Astrophil compares his own feelings for Stella; and the figure of Eros continues to serve Sidney as a poetic and cognitive device for mediating relationships of conflict and contradiction not only in love but in all aspects of an Elizabethan courtier's life.

Recent commentators have analyzed with great acuity the relationship between the allegory of love in *Astrophil and Stella* and Sidney's frustrated personal ambitions at court.[15] No doubt, the psychological conflict produced by these circumstances contributed to Sidney's straining against the Petrarchan conventions and, perhaps, against the authority and power represented by the person of the Queen. Certainly, the poetic medium through which Sidney articulated this conflict brought renewed vigor to the genre of the sonnet. But the particular decorum which he was so careful to observe in transforming social and political ambition into romantic desire is an indication of the extent to which his muse continued to obey an aristocratic and quasi-feudal *ethos*.

II

We tend to think of Sidney and of Spenser as representatives of a Renaissance tendency toward the refinement of poetic artifice, and of Jonson as reacting against this tradition by insisting on the placing of 'matter' above eloquence. But it is important to realize that the priority Jonson appears to have given to content was part of a broader concern throughout his work with the nature of literary and linguistic forms. The changes he brought to bear on the literary conventions of the previous generation were no less radical than the more startling experiments of Donne. This may not be immediately evident from our perspective today because the message-transferring function of language which Jonson emphasized has long since become the dominant one in our culture. Therefore, the principles he advocated are likely to seem to us unpoetic, if not downright anti-poetic. But in its own time Jonson's poetic theory and his practice as a poet were innovative. Moreover, the innovations involved had as much to do with poetic form as with thematic content.[16]

Jonson's avowed aim of reorienting poetry in such a way that words would serve as the agencies of 'matter' was carried out through a constant effort to define and to codify formal devices. Throughout his plays, poems and masques the fixation on the theme of authority and on authority figures has its direct formal counterpart in his insistence on rules or codes in grammar, in orthography and punctuation, in art and in public morality. Jonson's language and the literary genres in which he chooses to write imply the possibility, indeed the *inevitability*, if one uses language correctly, of an immediate access to knowledge of all kinds. His

poem 'Why I Write Not of Love', which opens *The Forrest*, can be read
not only as a middle-aged man's pathetic farewell to Eros, but as a final
rejection of the Petrarchan tradition and of the Neoplatonic doctrines
linking all knowledge to an idealized and romantic conception of sexual
desire. In Jonson's classical style metaphor is eschewed, matter takes
precedence over eloquence, instruction over delight, and the poet lays
claim to a more precise identification with antiquity on the grounds
that it can be known and can become a pattern for the present directly,
through study and imitation. In this view the role of metaphor is
rationalized, placed in the service of instruction which is the function
of the poet in the present as it was, according to Jonson, in the past.
Metaphor is no longer the means of overcoming a separation between
the 'patterned past' and the present; it is now only one technical device
among others whereby the poet–scholar can transmit his knowledge of a
pattern that is taken to be natural and universal and, therefore, to be *true*
for the present as well as the past.

Jonson's classicism was motivated in part by a calculated strategy of
self-assertion. Quite early in his career we find him proclaiming himself
the first true classicist among English poets, and this not only in his
attacks on other playwrights during the so-called 'war of the theatres',
but in the poems as well. In an epistle addressed in 1600 to Elizabeth,
Countess of Rutland, he writes:

> Then all, that have but done my Muse least grace,
>   Shall thronging come, and boast the happy place
> They hold in my strange poems, which, as yet,
> Had not their forme touch'd by an English wit.[17]

> *(The Forrest*, XII, ll. 79–82)

The self-conscious distinction Jonson grants his 'strange poems' is made
more striking by the fact that Elizabeth was the daughter of Sir Philip
Sidney whose own poetic skill in the older mode is alluded to in the
poem. Here, as elsewhere, Jonson pays homage to Sidney, homage that
is perhaps sincere but also obligatory given the status of Sir Philip and
the nature of Jonson's relation to the family. An epigram to the same
Countess of Rutland begins:

> That Poets are far rarer births than kings,
>   Your noblest father proved: like whom, before,
> Or then, or since, about our Muses' springs,
>   Came not that soule exhausted so their store.

Yet the poem ends on a curious turn. Elizabeth wrote poetry herself,
and Jonson's praise of her father is complicated by the assertion that
if he were alive and could look upon his daughter's poems

He should those rare, and absolute numbers view.
As he would burne, or better farre his booke.

(Epigrammes, LXXIX)

Later, in 1619, Jonson told Drummond that 'the Countess of Rutland was nothing inferior to her father S.P. Sidney in Poesie' (*Conversations*, ll. 213–14). We don't know what those 'rare, and absolute numbers' composed by the Countess of Rutland were like. But the descriptive phrase is suggestive, and, assuming Jonson wasn't merely engaging in flattery, we may surmise that he was praising her verse for qualities that were closer than her father's to Jonson's own classical standards.

This is, of course, speculation. But it is sustained by what we know of Jonson's attitude toward the previous generation of English poets. In the *Discoveries* he is more openly critical of Spenser than of Sidney.[18] But the comparison of Sidney's poetry with that of his daughter was perhaps a delicate way in which Jonson could pass judgment on Sir Philip and thereby uphold his own convictions regarding poetic form.

We may detect an anxiety of influence here. But insofar as Jonson's reading of Sidney was concerned, I suspect that the anxiety was brought on as much by the social aspects of the relationship as by the filtiation of poet to poet. After all, Jonson was a poet-commoner serving aristocratic patrons like the Sidneys who had helped to establish the norms of Elizabethan court culture in the previous generation. Jonson's deviation from those norms was a way for him, in turn, to establish an independent poetic, psychological and social identity. In comparing the Countess of Rutland's 'absolute numbers' to her father's poetry, Jonson expressed his own demand for a more rigorous adherence to classical models and asserted his own authority in matters of aesthetic judgment.

There is a sense, to be sure, in which Jonson's aesthetic shared with the new philosophy what one study terms 'a view of Nature even more static and fixed than that of medieval Europe'.[19] But before we dismiss classicism as dogmatic or unhistorical, we ought to recognize that for the poet, as for the philosopher and the scientist of the early seventeenth century, the appeal to a universal 'order of things' was an assertion of the right to think and to speak with relative freedom. This was especially true of those who were not aristocratic 'amateurs' but who wrote as professionals. For Jonson and his contemporaries the assertion of such freedom could not yet have resulted from a fully formed, conscious egalitarianism. Nevertheless, within the ideological limits of the time it constituted a legitimation of the ontological status of the writer as an independent subject in spite of his subjection to others within the prevailing social order.[20] In a still rigidly hierarchical social system, it was the appeal to rigor in method and to an authority in knowledge based on the norms of Nature and Reason, that gave the writer a certain freedom and transcendence. While he remained dependent on the king and the nobility, and while he may have consciously adhered to the ideology of those he served (as did Jonson), the writer nonetheless, and often in spite of himself, became the means of calling that ideology into question.

In England as elsewhere in seventeenth-century Europe, the condition of this new kind of writer, the professional, was inherently one of tension and conflict. Sartre's description of the situation is instructive:

> Only the governing classes can allow themselves the luxury of remunerating so unproductive and dangerous an activity [as writing], and if they do so, it is a matter both of tactics and of misapprehension. Misapprehension for the most part: free from material cares, the members of the governing élite are sufficiently detached to want to have a reflective knowledge of themselves. They want to retrieve themselves, and they charge the artist with presenting them with their image without realizing that he will then make them assume it. A tactic on the part of some who, having recognized the danger, pension the artist in order to control his destructive power. Thus, the writer is a parasite of the governing 'élite'. But, functionally, he moves in opposition to the interests of those who keep him alive. Such is the original conflict which defines his condition.
>
> *(What is Literature?*, pp. 75–6)

Neither the writer nor his patrons need have been conscious of this conflict at the time for it to have defined their relationship. Yet it is difficult to imagine the professional writer, even at this early stage, suffering from a 'misapprehension' equivalent to that of his patrons. There is certainly evidence in Jonson's writing that he was aware of the nature of the conflict, that he recognized, perhaps with some anguish, the dilemma of having his function as a poet and, consequently, his freedom depend on the subjection of that function to the power of others. Critics have often cautioned against thinking of Jonson's poems of praise or his court masques in terms of flattery. They point out that poets who wrote in praise of kings and lords did so out of a sense of moral conviction and social responsibility, and in the belief that they were providing their patrons with learned counsel. The principle is stated by Jonson in the form of a dignified ratio: 'Learning needs rest: Sovereignty gives it. Sovereignty needs counsell: Learning affords it' (*Discoveries*, ll. 65–6). But while we need to be alerted to the dangers of anachronism, we cannot pass so easily over the issue of flattery. It is no anachronism to say that even as the seventeenth-century poet claimed the poetic license to instruct, he was obliged to hold up a flattering mirror to his patron. Jonson goes to great lengths to disclaim the role of flatterer; but at times he protests too much, and one senses that he was oppressed by a keen awareness that what status he did possess depended on such a function.

In light of this relation of dependency, Jonson's response to the poetry of the previous generation, especially the poetry of the courtly amateurs among whom Sidney was pre-eminent, takes on special significance. The 'strange poems' Jonson claimed to have first brought to the English carried with them in their very formal constraints (that is, in the stress on 'matter' over eloquence, on imitation, on judgment and decorum) the fundamental principle that truth was unchanging. The capacity to represent this truth was situated in the mind of the individual who trained himself to decipher the classical forms. This meant not only the ability to employ classical subject matter allegorically, which had already been essential in the poetry and art of the sixteenth century, but it required as well a precise understanding of the decorous use of poetic device and genre. For a poet in Jonson's situation to proclaim himself a classicist was to adopt a literary *persona* that allowed him to go beyond the existing hierarchical system for grounding social and psychological identity, to derive his truth and his being from a prior order, a natural order first codified in the texts of antiquity.

III

Moreover, although it may have been personally motivated, Jonson's strategy of claiming a measure of freedom from an existing system of authority and power by appealing to a prior one had potentially far-reaching effects. The defining characteristics of classicism as both style and epistemology were such that any implicit assertion of personal transcendence on Jonson's part became immediately extendable to those readers or members of the theatre audience who shared his understanding and his judgment. Jonson acknowledged such an élite among his interlocutors, addressing them as 'hearers', 'readers', or 'understanders', and distinguishing them from the mere 'spectators' whom he described as coming to the theatre 'to see, and to be seen'.[21] This was a different élitism from the *noblesse* or *gentilesse* of the Middle Ages, concepts that grounded hereditary privilege and status on a Christian foundation of ethical duty and on chivalric rituals sanctioned by the Church.[22] Jonson's conception was not necessarily less Christian in its underlying assumptions, but it was more directly founded on reason than revelation. In this respect, his neoclassicism was, like the new philosophy, potentially if not intentionally egalitarian.

The rules or laws governing classical form were understood as immutable and universal, as was the human capacity to discern them, that is, the capacity for reason. No one was deprived of such capacity by nature, but many were impeded in its exercise by the corruptive effects of one or more of the passions. Jonson's diagnosis of the moral ills of his age is in this respect closely allied to Bacon's notion of the 'distempers of learning' that infect men's minds. 'The human understanding,' writes

Bacon, 'is no dry light, but receives an infusion from the will and affections; whence proceed sciences which may be called "sciences as one would". For what a man had rather were true he more readily believes . . . Numberless, in short, are the ways and sometimes imperceptible, in which the affections color and infect the understanding' (*New Organon*, I, xlix). A similar conception provides the basis of the psychology of 'humors' according to which Jonson drew the characters in his satires. It is also given as the root of sinfulness in an epode focused on the roles of reason and passion in human nature:

> For either our affections doe rebell,
>   Or else the sentinell
> (That should ring larum to the heart) doth sleepe,
>   Or some great thought doth keepe
> Backe the intelligence, and falsely sweares
>   They're base, and idle feares
> Whereof the loyall conscience so complaines.
>   Thus, by these subtle traines,
> Do severall passions still invade the minde,
>   And strike our reason blinde.[23]

While this view is certainly Christian in essence, it is important to distinguish it from the traditional notion that humanity was depraved and all of earthly nature in decay since the fall from Paradise. As caustic and disdainful as Jonson could be in his satires, his understanding of human nature was on the whole more optimistic than the doctrine of the decay of nature.[24] Implicit in Jonson's adoption of classical forms was the notion that the governance of reason is potentially available to *all* human beings. Thus while classicist principles of uniformity and universal law could be placed in the service of absolutist political doctrines, it is also the case that neoclassicism complemented the new science in anticipating the democratic aspects of Enlightenment ideology. We are not duty-bound to celebrate this rationalist, progressivist ideology uncritically; but we do need to remind ourselves that the liberal, humanist ideals on the basis of which classicism is denounced as a conservative, uniformitarian world view are themselves ushered in by the classicist strain within Renaissance humanism.

I am not suggesting that Jonson was a democrat in disguise, but I do believe that his conservative and legitimist pronouncements mask a deep sense of injustice concerning his own position in society. Given the social context in which he proclaimed himself a classicist, the forms he employed to that end were not as conservative as they might otherwise seem. Nor were the ideas that the classical forms brought with them. In the epistle to *Volpone*, where Jonson addresses the intellectual élite of the universities, he makes explicit his concern not just with classical form but with doctrine:

> . . . I have labored, for their instruction and amendment, to reduce *not only the ancient forms*, but manners of the scene: the easiness, the propriety, the innocence, and last, *the doctrine, which is the principal end of poesie, to inform men in the best reason of living* . . . (my emphasis)

The ethical doctrine implied here is hardly subversive, but the norms of Reason and Nature on which it is founded are potentially so. At times, this critical potential surfaces from within the apparent conservatism of the 'ancient forms'. So, for example, in an epigram 'To Sir William Jephson', Jonson writes:

> Thou wert the first, mad'st merit know her strength,
>   And those that lack'd it, to suspect at length,
> 'Twas not entayl'd on title. That some word
>   Might be found out as good, and not *my Lord*.
> That *Nature* no such difference had imprest
>   In men, but every bravest was the best:
> That blood not mindes, but mindes did blood adorne:
>   And to live great, was better, than great born.
> (Epigrammes, CXVI, ll. 5–12)

The idea of nobility based on 'merit' rather than on 'title' has classical origins in the Stoic philosophy. It also appears earlier in English literature, but rarely, if ever, with the force of personal conviction and the precision that Jonson gives it in his handling of the epigrammatic *point* in the poem to Jephson.[25] Moreover, while an aristocrat might conjoin intellectual merit with blood as necessary conditions of *nobilitas*, he would not conceive of them in the oppositional relationship that Jonson sets forth here.[26]

The breaking through of this critical attitude, in both the form and content of Jonson's classicism, suggests that he had at least an intuitive understanding of the 'misapprehension' at the center of his relationship with patrons like the Sidneys. I maintain that this awareness lends complexity, even irony to Jonson's poems of praise because it produces a tension within the poetry, a tension between conflicting ideologies. The conflict is resolved in a tenuous way by the surface order and regularity of Jonson's epideictic rhetoric. But this resolution is itself the outcome of a complex strategy of rationalization. What is rationalized is the poet's sense of an inequity concerning his own position in relation to that of his patron, and therefore, his recognition of a contradiction with respect to the legitimating purpose to which his poems are put. In my view, the most distinctive quality of Jonson's poems addressed to patrons is the way in which the sense of contradiction manages to come through in

spite of the social function Jonson was required to perform, and in spite
of his own rationalizing efforts to protect himself from failing to perform
that function.

In examining the ideological aspects of the extraordinary outpouring
of literature during the Tudor and Stuart periods, we need to be wary
of generalizations concerning the differences between 'aristocratic' and
'bourgeois' modes of thought. Cultural change is a complex phenomenon,
involving an interplay of endogenous and exogenous processes. The
humanist ideal of intellectual merit, which had been assimilated into
an aristocratic, courtly culture under the Tudors,[27] is eventually pushed
to its limits in Jonson. To paraphrase Sartre again, Jonson makes his
patrons *assume* the image which he is obliged to reflect for them. His
ode to Philip Sidney's nephew William, on the occasion of the latter's
having reached his majority in 1611, is a case in point. The poem, though
courteous in tone, is an exhortation to this young and unaccomplished
Sidney, and can be read as a covert warning to the family:

> Your blood
> So good
> And great, must seeke for new,
> And studie more:
> Not weary, rest
> On what's deceased.
> For they, that swell
> With dust of ancestors, in graves but dwell . . .
>
> So may you live in honor, as in name,
> If with this truth you be inspir'd.

(The Forrest, XIV, ll. 33–40, 51–2)

There is a strong implication in the poem that the poet has earned the
right to speak with authority on this ceremonial occasion because his
own mastery of classical form (exemplified here in one of the first odes
in English) and classical doctrine is proof that he, at least, lives 'in honor'
if not 'in name'. The irony is compounded by the fact that it is the voice
of the poet–commoner, Ben Jonson, through which the life of honor
associated with the noble name *Sidney* speaks in this poem.

While Jonson remains intellectually and politically conservative, his
insistence on a rationalist basis to all discourse, poetry included, and
to all social intercourse, points the way to new doctrines of sovereignty
and of social organization in England. Although he did not, or could
not, abandon Renaissance notions of hierarchy, his texts do give forceful
articulation to the idea of intellectual merit as the standard of an
individual's worth.

IV

But what complicates Jonson's poetry even further is that it already reveals the limits of the emerging ideology before it has come to full fruition. We may take the connotations of the opposition between 'merit' and 'title' in the poem to Jephson, and resonances of the same distinction elsewhere in Jonson's works, as an example of what I mean. Advancement on the basis of 'merit' is a doctrine that reflects the self-conscious individualism which we conventionally associate with the Renaissance. Individualism is, in turn, related to competition as a motive force in human affairs. In England, as the centers of culture shifted from the monastery and the university to the court and the city, competition for favor and patronage became an essential aspect of intellectual activity. Like flattery, competition was now a more or less inescapable fact of life for the poet.

But where the cultural form of this conflict at court is sublimated and refined in allegorical lyric and romance, competition among the new professional writers in the city is more openly individualistic. The infamous 'war of the theatres' involving Jonson, Dekker and Marston at the turn of the century is evidence to that effect. Moreover, even where Jonson bestows praise on a fellow poet or playwright, his encomium often turns on the theme of envy. One senses that for Jonson the recognition of merit and honor it brings is a result of comparison and competition. Therefore, to praise another is an act filled with anxiety and ambivalence.[28] As with the role of flattery in the poet's relation to his patron, we need to understand such competition among poets in its proper historical context. But I don't believe we can dismiss the anxiety that is apparent in the poetry as a distortion produced by our own historical perspective. Nor can Jonson's defensive posture be explained solely as an intra-psychic disorder, an aspect of the 'anal eroticism' that Edmund Wilson has described in a well-known essay. Jonson's aggressively competitive relation to other poets may be a matter of personal temperament, but it is a temperamental response forged by historical and social conditions.

Here, again, comparison with Sidney is fruitful. As a poet, the competition in which Jonson found himself was fundamentally different from the courtly struggle for place and power that is sublimated in the romantic sexuality of *Astrophil and Stella*. Sidney could refer with characteristic nonchalance to the *Arcadia* as 'my toyful book', and to the *Defence of Poetry* as 'this ink-wasting toy of mine'; his Astrophil can say, in mock remorse, 'My youth doth waste, my knowledge brings forth toyes.'[29] There is, of course, a good deal of tongue-in-cheek irony in these remarks, Sidney being ultimately as serious in his conception of the office of the poet as Jonson. Still, his amused rhetorical self-irony is revealing of the extent to which poetry was a necessary, but hardly a sufficient condition of Sidney's identity and of his station in life. To excel in the art of poetry was for him one of the many outward signs of an inner quality that ostensibly originated in birth and breeding. By contrast, for Jonson poetry was a singular means of achieving identity and status. In this regard Spenser, whose social origins are much closer to Jonson's than to Sidney's, provides something of a precedent. But it is not likely that Spenser, who began writing poetry at about the time Jonson was born, could have set out to make a career primarily as a poet. It took what Spenser had actually achieved by the 1590s, coupled with the legitimacy officially conferred on poetry by its most eminent champion Philip Sidney, for Jonson not only to claim for the poet the status of an 'arbiter of nature' (George Puttenham had claimed as much) but to attempt to live in accordance with that claim.[30]

Poetry's ascendancy as an honorable profession cannot be separated from the ideological value it had come to serve both in the theatres and in the occasional verses and masques written for the monarch and the court. The historical conditions that made it possible for Jonson to claim greater autonomy for poetry and to seek to define his own social identity as a poet, entailed, too, a change in the status of the object of what he liked to refer to as his 'studies'. In addition to its other attributes, culture was now becoming a commodity. The poet's skill and his learning had begun to assume the form of intellectual property in a client system of exchange that was rapidly turning into a marketplace. In reading Jonson we can sense the strain generated by these circumstances. The intensity of competition for a share of the new but, as yet, limited literary market is suggested by the proprietary tone of Jonson's frequent and worried references to plagiarists and poet-apes. And, in a more deeply disturbing way, it is evident in the anxiety already mentioned as to how his own work measures up against the poetry of contemporaries whom he praises such as Donne, Francis and John Beaumont, Drayton and, of course, Shakespeare. Jonson's persistent disavowal of the flattery of patrons and of the envy of fellow poets suggests that the opposite was in fact the case, or, at least, that he suspected it might be the case and wished to persuade himself as well as his reader that it was not.

Remarkably, Jonson shows a certain awareness of the extent to which in his time intellect and craft were coming to be thought of as private property, and the product of the intellect as a commodity. Despite his satires on acquisitiveness, he is not averse to employing the metaphor of accumulated wealth for the process that leads to accomplishment and honor. So much is evident in the following passage from 'An Epistle to Sir Edward Sackville, Now Earle of Dorset' (c. 1624), where coincidentally, and yet, as might be expected, the figure of Philip Sidney stands as the model:

> . . . he must feele and know, that will advance.
> Men have beene great, but never good by chance,
> Or on the sudden. It were strange that he
> Who was this morning such a one, should be
> *Sydney* e're night! . . .

> 'Tis by degrees that men arrive at glad
> Profit in aught; each day some little adde,
> In time 'twill be a heape; this is not true
> Alone in money, but in manners too.
> Yet we must more than move still, or goe on,
> We must accomplish: 'tis the last key-stone
> That makes the arch.

(Underwood, XIII, ll. 123–37)

Since this passage is nearly a direct translation of classical sources, the money imagery borrowed from Plutarch and the keystone that makes the arch from Seneca, we must be careful not to confuse the type of 'profit' it evokes with more modern senses of the term. There is little evidence here of a specifically bourgeois conception of capital accumulation and commodity exchange. If anything, the positive value attached to the term 'heape' is more likely to be associated with a recrudescent feudalism than with the incipient capitalist ideology with its doctrine of *use*; in this context, the effect of 'heape' is precisely the opposite of its negative effect in the phrase 'proud, ambitious heaps' (l. 101) in 'To Penshurst'. The contrast is made all the more interesting by the fact that the name Sidney is associated with both of these antithetical contexts. But aside from this inconsistency, what is most striking about the passage from the epistle to Sackville is that the regular ('by degrees') storing up of 'money' is an image there for the acquisition of 'manners', i.e. virtuous qualities which bring, in turn; honor and the recognition of others.[31] The equation may be borrowed from classical sources, but it is especially significant that Jonson should elect to employ it in a poem that reflects as much upon his own self-image as it does on the benefactor to whom he offers praise and thanks.

Elsewhere, the economic imagery used to describe virtue and talent is indeed more clearly related to early capitalist institutions of finance and trade. The conclusion of a commendatory poem on William Browne's *Brittania's Pastorals* (1616) reads:

> And, where the most reade bookes, on Authors' fames,
> Or, like our Money-Brokers, take up names

On credit, and are cossen'd; see, that thou
By offring not more sureties, then enow,
Hold thyne owne worth unbroke: which is so good
Upon th' *Exchange of Letters*, as I would
More of our writers would like thee, not swell
With the *how much* they set forth, but th' *how well*.

(*Ungathered Verse*, XXI, ll. 9–16)

Despite the distinction between quality and quantity in the last line, and the pejorative references to 'Money-Brokers' followed by the contrastive pun in 'Hold thyne owne worth unbroke', it is ultimately the phrase 'Exchange of Letters' that sets the tone and establishes the metaphorical, not to mention the real, context of the entire piece.

The market metaphor in the poem to William Browne is derived from a relatively recent sense of the term 'Exchange',[32] and is already an index of the commoditization of culture. Another poem, in praise of Chapman's translation of Hesiod's *Works and Days* (1618), carries the logic of such imagery a step further. After a series of metaphors describing Chapman's translations of Homer and Hesiod as the transporting of Greek treasure to English shores, the poem concludes:

If all the vulgar Tongues, that speake this day
Were asked of thy Discoveries; they must say,
  To the Greeke coast thine only knew the way.
Such Passage hast thou found, such Returnes made,
As, now, of all men, it is called thy Trade:
And who make thither else, rob, or invade.

(*Ungathered Verse*, XXIII, ll. 7–12)

The central image here is not only that of voyage and discovery, but of capturing a particular market on the 'Exchange of Letters'. In his edition of Jonson's poems, George Parfitt glosses 'Returnes' as a 'mercantile image which refers to the profit on an investment in a voyage'. The idea of intellectual property and proprietary interest in the fruits of intellectual labor are clearly stated in the last two lines.

Such imagery exposes a painful contradiction that is generally characteristic of Jonson's work: that is, while merit based on intellectual accomplishment is the means through which the poet–commoner asserts his freedom, and while the accomplishment is held to be an external sign of the interior quality of the man, the recognition of such merit depends finally on the same system of rationalized commodity exchange that Jonson satirizes in its more obvious acquisitive forms. This correlation is obscured by the manner in which worth is delineated in Jonson's poems of praise. The usual mode of description is through negative and comparative constructions. When value is described affirmatively it is in a highly abstracted form; virtues like integrity, honesty, intellectual ability are imputed, but more often than not justification of the quality comes in the form of a comparison. Satirized figures therefore take on special importance in Jonson's works because they constitute images of the Other against which a socially sanctioned ethical and behavioral norm is maintained.

The qualities that most often distinguish good from bad in his poems are the cardinal humanist virtues of honesty and integrity. Ironically, it may be Jonson's fidelity to the logic of this ethic that drives him, consciously or unconsciously, to reveal a certain overlap in the criteria of value that govern the behavior of those who are the objects of both his satire and his praise. Since for Jonson the good poet must, by definition, also be the good man, he could only demonstrate his rightful title to the office and function of poet by making his own work the concrete embodiment of the qualities of honesty and integrity. This he accomplished more through the structure and the rhetoric of his texts than at the level of statement, and this despite the fact that we tend to think of Jonson's poetry as a 'poetry of statement'. To the extent that Jonson's vaunted empiricism is observable in the poems of praise as well as in the satiric works, it is found primarily not in what is stated about those who are praised but in the imagery employed to make the statement and in the rhetorical stance adopted toward the addressee. The effect of the logic inherent in his rhetorical strategy is a dislocation of the tidy order of distinctions between virtue and vice that he otherwise appears to expound. In sum, the integrity of the body of the text on which Jonson staked his identity as poet depended on the revelation of a loss of integrity in the system of values that the text was supposed to transmit.

Jonson's poems succeed both in exposing the arbitrary, if not irrational basis of the traditional doctrines according to which a man of quality was identified, and, at the same time, in providing a disturbing glimpse of the consequences attendant upon the loss of such intrinsic and spontaneously recognized criteria of nobility and honor. In the 'Epistle, to Sir Edward Sackville' the metaphor comparing the acquisition of manners to the acquisition of money is attenuated by the lines

> Yet we must more than move still, or goe on,
> We must accomplish: 'tis the last key-stone
> That makes the arch.

Yet the question remains as to what distinguishes the stage of accomplishment from the process of accumulation that leads up to it; what *is* the keystone that completes the arch? Presumably, it is an activity or use to which the acquired manners are put. Jonson harks back to the traditional Aristotelian ethic adopted by Sidney: 'For, as Aristotle saith, it is not *gnosis* but *praxis* must be the fruit' (*Defence of Poetry*, p. 91). But, whereas for Sidney's generation *praxis* was still determined by a code of honor, in the reign of James I the code lost much of its power to compel belief. The thirty-nine years from the accession of James to the execution of Charles I illustrate what Lawrence Stone refers to as 'Tawney's Law': i.e. 'that the greater the wealth and more even its distribution in a given society, the emptier become titles of personal distinction, but the more they multiply and are striven for'.[33] The important distinction here is not an ethical but a pragmatic one. It is not a question of the superior moral fiber of the Elizabethan nobility as compared with the men elevated by the Stuarts. Rather, it is a matter of an ideology being unable to keep pace with changing socioeconomic conditions.

In the sixteenth century the claims of many noble families to title and to quality on the basis of primogeniture were highly questionable. Yet, despite his anxiety in this regard, Philip Sidney apparently believed that the pedigree his father had purchased from the heralds was authentic.[34] And, what is more important, he and his contemporaries behaved as though the outward signs of honor were indeed a proof of authenticity. By Ben Jonson's time, however, the inflation of honors had reached the stage at which belief in the correlation between 'honor' and its outward signs was strained to the breaking point. In his satires, Jonson could represent the confusion of material and spiritual value as an aberration. Yet Volpone's assertion that money is 'virtue, fame, / Honor, and all things else', only reflects what was rapidly becoming a new norm governing social *praxis* in England.[35]

This attitude, satirized by Jonson, eventually receives formal codification in Hobbes' famous assertions that 'Desire of Power, of Riches, of Knowledge, and of Honor [may all] be reduced to the first, that is Desire of Power', and that 'the *Value*, or Worth of a man, is as of all other things, his Price'.[36] For Jonson and his contemporaries, the alternative to such a cynical reduction was to retain some notion of an inherent spiritual value manifesting itself in forms of *praxis* that would constitute authentic outward signs of merit. The problem remained, however, as to how to validate such outward signs in the face of the steady disintegration of the homogeneous tradition of revealed doctrine which had previously served to provide the necessary criteria of validation. Jonson's solution typifies one of the major strains of thought in the literature of his age, a blending of Christian-humanism and Stoicism that is evident as well in Shakespeare's later plays. But, in contrast to Shakespeare, Jonson's insistence on rigorous imitation of his classical sources suggests a deep-felt need to find an authoritative basis for a revision of the Elizabethan courtiers' code of honor. Such a revision would entail a shift away from the feudal ethic which, however attenuated, is still central to Sir Philip Sidney's self-image,[37] toward a conception of honor in which reason reigns unequivocally over desire, and heroic *virtù* is replaced by the concept of virtue as an inner plenitude and integrity of being.

No doubt this ideological shift towards an ethic and a didactic aesthetic derived from study and imitation of the ancients entails a certain loss of historical perspective. Yet if we think of an emergent classicism like Jonson's strictly in terms of Lovejoy's categories, we ourselves run the risk of reducing a rather complex dialectic at a crucial moment in cultural history to an abstract principle – that is, we end up reproducing the very ideology we set out to criticize (and, indeed, the categorical methods of Lovejoy, of the early Barthes, and of other critics of classicism are, in their own ways, 'classical' in this sense!).

Seen from within, that is, in terms of its avowed premises, classicism appears as Lovejoy described it: anti-historicist and uniformitarian. But viewed in the context of a more inclusive historical frame, these very characteristics of classicism at its inception become their own opposites. They are recognized as strategies for confronting and contesting an older, outmoded structure of behavior and belief, and for enunciating a new conception of the subject. It is ironic, though hardly paradoxical, that classicism's reliance on a uniform, static notion of Nature was an inherently historical gesture. It marked the introduction of a potential difference (if not of diversity in the more modern, liberal conception) into the prevailing sense of quality that depended on inherited titles and property and on revealed rather than rationally derived doctrines.

Notes

An earlier version of this essay was presented at the 1982 MLA convention in a special session on 'Literary Text and Social Text in Late Sixteenth-Century Nondramatic Literature'.

1. ERICH AUERBACH, *Mimesis* (1946; rpt. Princeton: Princeton Univ. Press, 1968), pp. 321, 389–90; M.M. BAKHTIN, 'Discourse in the Novel', in *The Dialogic Imagination*, ed. Michael Holquist, trans. Caryl Emerson and M. Holquist (Austin: Univ. of Texas Press, 1981), pp. 325, 344–6; JEAN-PAUL SARTRE, *What is Literature?*, trans. Bernard Frechtman (1947; rpt. New York: Harper Colophon Books, 1965), pp. 85–6; ROLAND BARTHES, *Writing Degree Zero*, trans. Annette Lavers and Colin Smith (1953; trans. London: Cape, 1967); ARTHUR O. LOVEJOY, 'The Parallel of Deism and Classicism', in *Essays in the History of Ideas* (Baltimore: Johns Hopkins Univ. Press, 1948), pp. 78–98; see, too, DONALD WESLING's recent essay 'Augustan Form: Justification and Breakup of a Period Style', *Texas Studies in Literature and Language*, 22 (1980), 394–428, to whose strictures the present study is intended not as a rejoinder but as something of a qualification. I have deliberately omitted the name of MICHAEL FOUCAULT from this discussion because the eccentricities of his analysis of the relation between 'classical' and 'Renaissance' discourse, in *The Order of Things* (New

York: Pantheon, 1972), would require more detailed consideration than is possible here; I share the view of FREDRIC JAMESON, *The Political Unconscious* (Ithaca: Cornell Univ. Press, 1981), p. 47, that structuralist or semiotic method can be appropriated to a historicizing and dialectical criticism of the kind practiced by Sartre; also relevant in this context are Jameson's comments in *Marxism and Form* (Princeton: Princeton Univ. Press, 1971), pp. 379–80, on Paul Bénichou's study of French classicism, *Man and Ethics*, trans. Elizabeth Hughes (1948; trans. Garden City, N.Y.: Anchor Books, 1971).

2. O.B. HARDISON, JR, 'The Two Voices of Sidney's *Apology for Poetry*', *English Literary Renaissance*, 2 (1972), 94, detects in Sidney's discussion of the existing state of English poetry a different attitude from the earlier parts of the *Apology*, a shift from 'the Platonizing, idealizing tradition of humanist poetics to the critical and rationalistic poetic of neoclassicism'.

3. For an account of these experiments in quantitative verse and of Sidney's involvement in them, see WILLIAM A. RINGLER, JR's commentary in his edition of *The Poems of Sir Philip Sidney* (Oxford: Clarendon Press, 1962), pp. xxxiii–xxxiv and 389–93. All subsequent citations from Sidney's poems refer to this edition.

4. MARK GIROUARD, *Robert Smythson and the Architecture of the Elizabethan Era* (South Brunswick, NJ: A.S. Barnes, 1967), pp. 169–72; ERIC MERCER, *English Art 1553–1625*, vol. 7 of the Oxford History of English Art (Oxford: Clarendon Press, 1962), pp. 86, 150; FRANCES A. YATES, 'Elizabethan Chivalry: The Romance of the Accession Day Tilts', in *Astraea: The Imperial Theme in the Sixteenth Century* (London: Routledge & Kegan Paul, 1975).

5. For an example of the developing interpenetration of absolutist and proto-democratic ideologies in the culture of the early Stuart court, see NORMAN COUNCIL's recent analysis of the masque, *Prince Henry's Barriers*, on which Jonson and Inigo Jones collaborated in 1609, in 'Ben Jonson, Inigo Jones, and the Transformation of Tudor Chivalry', *ELH*, 47 (1980), 259–75.

6. DAVID KALSTONE, *Sidney's Poetry: Contexts and Interpretations* (Cambridge, Mass.: Harvard Univ. Press, 1967), p. 180.

7. Prometheus is invoked here primarily as a figure of heroic suffering; but Sidney is probably alluding also to Renaissance typologies in which Prometheus is thought of as the prototype of an active human intellect, and in which the celestial fire of the pagan myth is sometimes associated with the Christian notion of divine inspiration. One of Erasmus' earliest dialogues in defense of classical studies, *The Antibarbari* [printed in 1520, but revised from earlier drafts], trans. Margaret Mann Phillips, in *Collected Works of Erasmus*, vol. 23, ed. Craig R. Thompson (Toronto: Univ. of Toronto Press, 1978), refers to Prometheus as a figure for the union of human and divine wisdom: 'Why among the holy doctors is one more learned, another more eloquent? . . . The answer is obviously that the Spirit whom we worship does not find the same learning in all. For he increases what our industry has produced, he promotes our studies, he sustains our efforts. If it be right to bring in the fables of the poets at this point, we ought to imitate Prometheus, who when he wanted life for his clay image dared to seek it from the stars, but only when he had already applied every means available to human skill' (p. 117); SIR WALTER RALEGH writes in his *History of the World* (London, 1614): 'and Aeschylus affirmeth, that by the stealing of Jupiters fire, was meant, that the knowledge of Prometheus reached to the Starres, and other celestiall bodies. Againe, it is

written of him, that he had the art so to use this fire, as thereby he gave life
to Images of Wood, Stone, and Clay: meaning that before his birth and being,
those people among whom hee lived, had nothing else worthy of men, but
externall forme and figure' (Bk II, Ch. vi, Sec. 4, p. 266); cf. SPENSER, *Faerie
Queene*, II, x, 70, and BACON, *Wisdom of the Ancients*, in *The Works of Francis
Bacon*, ed. James Spedding, Robert Ellis, and Douglas Heath (London:
Longman, 1870), VI, 745–53. Sidney's *A Defence of Poetry*, in *Miscellaneous
Prose*, ed. Katherine Duncan-Jones and Jan Van Dorsten (Oxford: Clarendon
Press, 1973), contains no mention of Prometheus; but in his Christian-Platonist
notion that 'the skill of each artificer standeth in that *idea* or fore-conceit of the
work, and not in the work itself', in his comparison of the poet to the Christian
god, 'the heavenly Maker of that maker' (p. 79), and in his observation that
'both Roman and Greek gave such divine names unto it [poetry], the one of
prophesying, the other of making' (p. 99), Sidney may imply the figure of
Prometheus, the arch-maker, whose name (Gk, *forethought*) is Latinized and
Christianized as 'Providence' by some Renaissance authors (see, e.g., Bacon,
loc. cit.); cf. DON CAMERON ALLEN, *Mysteriously Meant: The Rediscovery of Pagan
Symbolism and Allegorical Interpretation in the Renaissance* (Baltimore: Johns
Hopkins Press, 1970), pp. 175–6, 193, and *passim*.

8. EDUARD WECHSSLER, quoted in C.S. LEWIS, *The Allegory of Love* (Oxford: Oxford
    Univ. Press, 1938), p. 2; MARK ROSE, *Heroic Love* (Cambridge, Mass: Harvard
    Univ. Press, 1968), observes that 'the glamor of love melancholy was in part
    the result of a curious semantic confusion. Early Latin translators of Greek
    manuscripts connected the Greek word *eros* with the Latin words *herus* and
    heros, and consequently believed that their authors meant to associate love
    with heroism and magnanimity' (pp. 11–12).
9. ERNST CASSIRER, *The Individual and the Cosmos in Renaissance Philosophy*, trans.
    Mario Domandi (Philadelphia: Univ. of Pennsylvania Press, 1972) pp. 132, 134.
10. RICHARD C. McCOY, *Sir Philip Sidney: Rebellion in Arcadia* (New Brunswick:
    Rutgers Univ. Press, 1979), Ch. 3.
11. Such anxiety is more openly expressed in SIDNEY'S *Defence of the Earl of
    Leicester*, in *Miscellaneous Prose*, ed. Duncan-Jones and Van Dorsten, which
    is both a reply to an anonymous libel of his uncle that appeared in 1584, and
    a calculated defense of Sidney's own hereditary status. The latter function is
    hardly concealed by the rather awkward disclaimer that '[I] truly am glad
    to have cause to set forth the nobility of that blood whereof I am descended,
    which, but upon so just cause, without vainglory could not have been uttered'
    (p. 134).
12. JEROME MAZZARO, *Transformations in the Renaissance Lyric* (Ithaca: Cornell Univ.
    Press, 1970), p. 145.
13. In *Penshurst: The Semiotics of Place and the Poetics of History* (Madison: Univ. of
    Wisconsin Press, 1984), I analyze the deliberate and self-conscious strategy
    of anachronism employed by Sidney's father, Sir Henry Sidney, in his building
    program at Penshurst from the 1560s through the 1580s. Henry Sidney did not
    try to conceal the fact that his family had only recently acquired title to the
    estate; but his additions to the older buildings were designed to represent the
    principles of continuity and legitimate succession.
14. KALSTONE, p. 150.
15. See McCOY, *Sir Philip Sidney: Rebellion in Arcadia, passim*; and ARTHUR
    MAROTTI, ' "Love is Not Love": Elizabethan Sonnet Sequences and the Social

Order', *ELH*, 49 (1982), 396–428; I have benefitted, too, from a paper by ANN ROSALIND JONES and PETER STALLYBRASS, 'The Politics of *Astrophil and Stella'*, *SEL* 24 (1984), pp. 53–68; also relevant here, though not focusing primarily on *Astrophil and Stella*, are LOUIS ADRIAN MONTROSE, 'Celebration and Insinuation: Sir Philip Sidney and the Motives of Elizabethan Courtship', *Renaissance Drama*, NS 8 (1977), 3–35, and MARGARET FERGUSON, 'Sidney's *A Defence of Poetry*: A Retrial', *Boundary* 2, 7 (Winter 1979), 84–5.

16. RALPH COHEN, 'Innovation and Variation: Literary Change and Georgic Poetry', in *Literature and History*, Clark Library Papers by Ralph Cohen and Murray Krieger (Los Angeles: William Andrews Clark Memorial Library, 1974), p. 6, argues that the first criterion that distinguishes innovation from imitation (as variation) 'is that the poets and, subsequently, the contemporaneous critics that comment upon them *identify* the innovations'. Jonson's reference, as early as 1600, to 'my strange poems', discussed below, is a case in point.

17. Except where stated otherwise, citations from Jonson's works refer to *Ben Jonson*, ed. C.H. Herford, Percy and Evelyn Simpson, 11 vols (Oxford: Clarendon Press, 1925–52), with spelling modernized in places.

18. 'Spencer, in affecting the Ancients, writ no language: Yet I would have him read for his matter; but as Vergil read Ennius' (*Discoveries*, ll. 1806–8).

19. STEPHEN TOULMIN and JUNE GOODFIELD, *The Discovery of Time* (New York: Harper & Row, 1965), p. 74. On Jonson's 'bias against change', see Jonas Barish, *The Antitheatrical Prejudice* (Berkeley: Univ. of California Press, 1981), pp. 143–6.

20. Jonson's ability to lay claim to such status owed much to the example of Sidney whose *Defence of Poetry* 'is also a defense of the speaking subject' (Ferguson, p. 62).

21. This distinction occurs frequently in Jonson. The last quoted phrase is from the dedication 'To the Reader' which followed upon the failure in the theatre of *The New Inn* (1629); for a related discussion, see BARISH, pp. 132–54.

22. Cf. JOHN B. MORRALL, *The Medieval Imprint* (Harmondsworth: Penguin Books, 1970), pp. 107–14.

23. *The Forrest* XI, ll. 21–30; cf. *Every Man in His Humor* (Quarto, 1601), ll, ii, 1–34, and *Discoveries*, ll. 30–2.

24. See *Mercury Vindicated from the Alchemists at Court* (1616), in *Ben Jonson: The Complete Masques*, ed. Stephen Orgel (New Haven: Yale Univ. Press, 1969), p. 221, where a more homely Prometheus than that invoked by Sidney is called upon by Nature, who is 'young and fresh', and told 'to show [the masquers] they are the creatures of the sun,/ That each to other/ Is a brother,/ And Nature here no stepdame, but a mother.'

25. MAROTTI, p. 418, cites earlier manifestations of the idea, in Spenser's commendatory sonnet to the translation of Nenna's *Nennio*, and as far back in English literature as Chaucer's 'Wife of Bath's Tale'. See, too, the adages collected under the category of 'Nobilitie' in SIR THOMAS ELYOT's *The Bankette of Sapience* [1534], facsimile rpt. in Elyot, *Four Political Treatises* (Gainesville: Scholar's Facsimiles and Reprints, 1967), pp. 176–7. My point is not that the idea of nobility based on 'merit' originates with Jonson, but that his manner of expressing it in the poem to Jephson is more direct and more personally contentious than the earlier instances which either dramatize the principle (as in the story told by Chaucer's Wife of Bath, or in the speeches of Marlowe's

Tamburlaine) or present it in a more abstract, aphoristic mode (as in the above mentioned texts by Elyot and Spenser).

26. In SIDNEY's *Arcadia* (Bk I, Ch. 2), Kalander asserts: 'I am no herald to enquire of mens pedigrees, it sufficeth me I know their vertues.' Both CURTIS BROWN WATSON, *Shakespeare and the Renaissance Concept of Honor* (Princeton: Princeton Univ. Press, 1960), p. 77, and MERVYN JAMES, *English Politics and the Concept of Honor 1485–1642*, Past and Present Supplement 3 (Oxford: Past and Present Society, 1978), p. 64, take this statement too literally as an expression of Sidney's personal views; neither acknowledges the fictive context in which the assertion occurs. In other respects, James' study is an exemplary account of how the concept of honor was modified under the Tudors to give 'parity, or even priority, to virtue over lineage, learning over arms, and "nobility dative" conferred by the state over hereditary nobility', a development in which the circle of Sir Philip Sidney played an important part (p. 59). But if Sidney did assert the priority of virtue over lineage, it was probably more a token of his didactic espousal of humanist ideas than a sign of indifference to the matter of ancestry (cf. Watson, p. 78). William Harrison, a man of lower birth than Sidney but of apparently more conservative views, registers the same shift in values in his description of contemporary notions of gentility: 'Gentlemen be those whom their race and blood, *or at the least their virtues*, do make noble and known' (my emphasis); see HARRISON's *Description of England* [1587], ed. George Edelen (Ithaca: Cornell Univ. Press, 1968), p. 113. It is significant that Harrison connects 'virtues' to 'race and blood' not by the inclusive conjunction *and* but by the mark of an alternative *or*, and that he adds the further qualifying phrase 'at the least'. The necessary connection of 'virtues' with 'race and blood' is thus attenuated by suggesting 'virtues' as an alternative qualification for the title of gentleman. In comparison with Jonson's poem to Jephson, Sidney's pronouncement is patronizing and in keeping with his position; and Harrison's statement has a peculiarly grudging tone that is explained, perhaps, by his ensuing description in sardonic and somewhat exaggerated terms of how any man of means might 'for money have a coat of arms bestowed upon him by the heralds' (p. 114).

27. See JAMES, pp. 58–72.

28. I have discussed this problem in 'Poetry and Power in Ben Jonson's *Epigrammes*: The Naming of "Facts" or the Figuring of Social Relations?' *Renaissance and Modern Studies*, 23 (1979), 79–103.

29. Letter to Robert Sidney, 18 October 1580, *The Prose Works of Sir Philip Sidney*, ed. Albert Feuillerat (Cambridge: Cambridge Univ. Press, 1962), III, 132; *A Defence of Poetry*, in *Miscellaneous Prose*, p. 121; *Astrophil and Stella*, Sonnet 18.

30. With regard to the above remarks on Spenser, see ELEANOR ROSENBERG, *Leicester: Patron of Letters* (New York: Columbia Univ. Press, 1955), p. 348, and DANIEL JAVITCH, *Poetry and Courtliness in Renaissance England* (Princeton: Princeton Univ. Press, 1978), pp. 160–1; cf. RICHARD HELGERSON, 'The Elizabethan Laureate: Self-Presentation and the Literary System', *ELH*, 46 (1979), 193–220; for PUTTENHAM's assertions see *The Arte of English Poesie* (1589) (facsimile rpt. Kent, Ohio: Kent State Univ. Press, 1970), p. 25.

31. In a similar fashion, BACON writes in his essay 'Of Ceremonies and Respects', *Essayes or Counsels Civill and Morall* (1625): 'But if a man mark it well, it is in praise and commendation of men as in gettings and gains: for the proverb is

true, *That light gains make heavy purses*; for light gains come thick, whereas great come but now and then' (*Works*, VI, 500).

32. *OED* entries for 'the Exchange' and 'the Burse' indicate that the terms were first employed in this sense after the opening of the Royal Exchange in London, built by Sir Thomas Gresham in 1566.

33. LAWRENCE STONE, *The Crisis of the Aristocracy 1558–1641* (Oxford: Clarendon Press, 1965), p. 128.

34. ROGER HOWELL, *Sir Philip Sidney: The Shepherd Knight* (Boston: Little, Brown, 1968), p. 18.

35. In the 1650s Gervase Holles looked back, with self-conscious irony, on a member of his own family who inveighed against such 'temporall simony in the reign of James I, but who, having 'observed merit to be no medium to an honorary reward . . . was perswaded to ware his money as other men had done.' GERVASE HOLLES, *Memorials of the Holles Family 1493–1656*, ed. A.C. Wood, Camden Soc., 3rd ser., 55 (London: Camden Society, 1937), 99.

36. THOMAS HOBBES, *Leviathan* (1651), ed. C.B. Macpherson (Harmondsworth: Pelican Books, 1968), pp. 139, 151.

37. On the tensions inherent in Sidney's attitude toward the chivalric code of honor, see HIRAM HAYDN, *The Counter-Renaissance* (1950; rpt. New York: Grove Press, 1960), Ch. 9; and McCoy, pp. 182–3.

Part Three
Seventeenth-century Poetry and History

8 George Herbert and Coterie Verse*

CRISTINA MALCOLMSON

Cristina Malcolmson uses traditional historical research to delineate the social rituals of upper-class literary coteries. She argues that the religious lyrics of Herbert's *Temple* did not originate as private meditations but as entries into the poetic debates that characterized his family circle. Following the work of Arthur Marotti in *John Donne: Coterie Poet*, this essay challenges the assumption in New Criticism that the individual poet was the source of creativity, since the 'answer-poem' took its shape within a community of writers. The coteries were headed by wealthy noblemen who could offer their clients access to evenings of entertainment as well as political alliances and patronage. The essay analyses Herbert's poetry in relation to lesser-known poetic exchanges between his patron, William Herbert, and other clients. Herbert is found to be constructing a 'double identity', linked with the structure of *The Temple*, which allowed him both to pursue patronage through the social rituals of his family and to preserve a sense of religious integrity which he believed to be classless.

When George Herbert announced his relationship to the English literary tradition, it was largely a family affair. His imitations of Sir Philip Sidney's poems and of the sonnet sequence itself were responses not only to a legendary literary figure but to a relative, the most famous member of the Sidney–Herbert clan. This family was known for its writers and patrons of the arts, but also recognized as a significant political and Protestant faction. Lawrence Stone characterizes a landed family as 'a dense network of lineage and kin relationships', whose members were involved in 'a reciprocal exchange of patronage, support and hospitality in return for attendance, deference, respect, advice and loyalty'. George

* Reprinted from *George Herbert in the Nineties: Reflections and Reassessments*, eds Jonathan F.S. Post and Sidney Gottlieb (George Herbert Journal, 1995), pp. 159–84.

Herbert's decision to make good on Sidney's claim that one's lyric powers could best be dedicated to God, a credo that Sidney did not follow himself, was impelled by sincere devotional commitment as well as the knowledge that, in order for Herbert to maintain himself as a gentleman, he needed the support of Sidney's nephew, William Herbert, the Earl of Pembroke.[1]

In this essay, I will argue that what we call Herbert's sacred parody originated in a specific context of poetic debate popular among the Herbert clan, as well as other literary coteries.[2] This contest in verse was an upper-class fashion as well as a convention which writers could learn and appropriate for their own purposes. To answer a poem was to request entrance into the upper-class circle that had produced it, and to take on its air of gentility. The point of the debate was to demonstrate one's verbal skills, not to express a personal opinion, and writers often displayed their training in the universities and the Inns of Court by arguing on both sides of the question. The debate was competitive not only because it took its cue from disputations in logic, but because writers matched wits with friendly rivals, or vied for the attention of prospective patrons. George Herbert's criticism of erotic love poetry was a more sustained version of the position taken by several poets. Sidney, Donne, Edward Herbert, Benjamin Rudyerd and Shakespeare argued for and against secular love, at times by renouncing it for sacred devotion. George Herbert entered the debate through his sacred parody, and 'Jordan' was his emblem both before and after he gave up his plans for a secular career. In this essay, I will consider the devotional lyrics in *The Temple* not as a set of private meditations, but as part of Herbert's lifelong performance within the Herbert circle.[3]

The publication of Herbert's English verse

Because of Herbert's upper-class status, he withheld most of his poetry from commercial publication during his lifetime.[4] I believe that he regularly presented his devotional lyrics to a select, élite group. Some critics have argued that Herbert's English lyrics were not known to others in any significant way until the publication of *The Temple* after his death in 1633. Underlying these arguments is the assumption that social performance within a patronage network and the expression of religious conviction are mutually exclusive. I plan to show that *The Temple* was conceived within the context of the Herbert family coterie and alluded continually to it; that George Herbert almost certainly sang or recited his religious lyrics in the family homes at Chelsea and in Wiltshire; and that it is possible that some of his manuscripts circulated.

Critical opinion has been divided on the question of the privacy of Herbert's English verse. F.E. Hutchinson claims that Herbert's English poems must 'have been circulated in manuscript, as he enjoyed some reputation as a poet many years before his death'. Rosemund Tuve argues that George Herbert's poem 'A Parodie' was a musical imitation of William Herbert's 'Soules Joy', and that both songs were meant to be performed during the musical entertainments at Wilton House, 'A network of ties we are largely unaware of made poets answer each other's poems, try out each other's modes.' She assumes that Herbert visited Pembroke's Wilton House regularly during his residence in Wiltshire (1628–33), and urges us to realize that 'Herbert as a poet could not have taken lightly such a kinsman's friendship.'[5]

On the other hand, Amy Charles argues that George Herbert 'was not generally known for his English poems' during his life because copies of the poems in commonplace books derive from printed versions, published after his death. She admits that there may have been 'small groups of amateur musicians (particularly in Salisbury) to whom he had perhaps sung some of his English lyrics', but she does not explicitly include his family in this group. Joseph Summers states that Herbert 'seems to have felt his "love poems" to be in some ways too private to be generally read within his lifetime', and Summers attributes this to Herbert's conviction that:

> an effect of sincerity was essential to the poems he wrote . . . 'sincerity' is likely to become a problem if one thinks of poems not primarily as constructions or social gestures but as true accounts of experience and as expressions of personal commitment.

For Summers, these expressions are not simple recordings of private experience but require 'a suspicious mastery of rhetorical conventions'. Nevertheless, such a view contrasts strikingly with Tuve's claim that 'A Parodie' was written precisely as a social gesture intended for entertainments at Wilton.[6]

Charles and Summers discount the evidence that Hutchinson offers to support his claim that Herbert presented his religious poetry to others. In *The Translations of Certain Psalms into English Verse* (1625), Francis Bacon dedicates his volume to George Herbert because of his ability in religion and verse. Charles's comments imply that she believes that Bacon knew only Herbert's Latin verse:

> In the absence of any manuscript evidence of the circulation of Herbert's English poems during his lifetime, there is no ground for assuming that Bacon had read any of Herbert's English poems or that it was the English poems that led to his dedicating the translation of *Certaine Psalmes* (1625) to Herbert. Bacon's acknowledgement of Herbert's part in translating *The Advancement of Learning* into Latin refers to Herbert's fitness in 'Divinitie, and Poesie,' no more; the

compliment could apply to English verse or to Latin verse, published or unpublished.[7]

Despite Charles's reasoning, there is more; Bacon's wording of his dedication suggests that he is referring not to Herbert's Latin poetry, but to his religious poetry, including the English lyrics:

> The paines, that it pleased you to take, about some of my Writings, I cannot forget: which did put me in minde, to dedicate to you, this poore Exercise of my sicknesse. Besides, it being my manner for Dedications, to choose those that I hold most fit for the Argument, I thought, that in respect of Divinitie, and Poesie, met, (whereof the one is the Matter, the other the Stile of this little writing) I could not make better choice.[8]

The phrase 'Divinitie, and Poesie, met' suggests not two separate skills, but rather Herbert's worth as a religious poet, and his fitness as a judge of sacred verse. Indeed, the 'Argument' of Bacon's *Certaine Psalmes* is most like Herbert's religious poems in *The Temple*: the Psalmist's personal experience of 'Divinitie' versified into English. Both in 'Matter' and 'Style', Herbert's English devotional poetry suits Bacon's description much more exactly than any of the Latin poetry.[9]

Charles and Summers also do not consider the strong evidence that Herbert composed music for his religious lyrics in order to perform them. Helen Wilcox gathers this evidence in 'Herbert's Musical Contexts: From Countrey-Aires to Angels Musick'.[10] Walton states that Herbert 'compos'd many *divine Hymns* and *Anthems*, which he set and sung to his lute or *Viol*'.[11] The anonymous author of the preface to *Select Hymns, Taken out of Mr Herbert's Temple* (1697) implies that certain tunes were available for particular lyrics before Herbert's death, and that the tunes were sung in some public way: 'Mr Herbert's *Poems* have met with so general and deserv'd Acceptance' yet 'few of them have been Sung since his Death, the Tunes not being at the Command of ordinary Readers.'[12] Aubrey's account of Herbert's life supports the view that Herbert composed settings for his poems:

> When he was first maried he lived a yeare or better at Dantesey House. H. Allen, of Dantesey, was well acquainted with him, who has told me that he had a very good hand on the Lute, and that he sett his own Lyricks or sacred poems.[13]

H. Allen's testimony sounds like it is based on personal experience, and that he heard Herbert's 'very good hand' play on his lute the settings composed for the sacred poems. It is likely in fact that Herbert sang these poems just in the way Tuve suggests, before those people in the homes where he lived or visited: his mother's house in Chelsea and the three homes in Wiltshire: Dauntsey House, Bainton House, and Wilton House, the seat of the Earl of Pembroke. The Herberts at Chelsea and Wilton were themselves skilled at music and frequently arranged for musical performances at their houses. According to Aubrey, Herbert's step-father set up an elaborate music room at Chelsea: 'Sir John was a great lover of Musick . . . The House is vaulted all underneath: which meliorates the sound of the Musique.' Aubrey also reports that Francis Bacon was a frequent visitor to the house in Chelsea.[14] It is probable that Bacon and many others heard Herbert sing his sacred lyrics. Herbert's poem 'The Posie' supports this view, since it refers to various kinds of 'poesie', all of which are meant to be heard or read by others:

> This on my ring,
> This by my picture, in my book I write:
> Whether I sing,
> Or say, or dictate, this is my delight.

(ll. 5–8)

The last two quoted lines refer to musical presentation, recitation or dictation to a scribe, and all imply some kind of audience.

In addition, the poems may also have been circulated in manuscript among a narrow circle of Herbert's family and friends. Copies of poems in the commonplace books can prove that the work of a poet circulated, but, if there are no copies in the commonplace books, this does not prove conclusively that the poetry was kept private. There is no evidence for the circulation of 'Upon Appleton House' by Marvell, yet it is more than likely that Thomas Fairfax received a copy of this poem.[15] The presentation of a copy of 'A Parodie' to the Earl of Pembroke is equally probable. We have Herbert's first sonnets because Walton printed them in his biography; there is no manuscript nor reference to them in commonplace books, although Herbert gave them to his mother in 1609. Therefore, copies of his poems could have been given to his family and close friends, and nevertheless not show up in contemporary commonplace books.[16]

In *Scribal Publication in Seventeenth-Century England*, Harold Love discusses a very limited form of circulation that would have been attractive to Herbert, given his aversion to print. In this case, a text is 'communicated within a closed circle of readers on the understanding it is not allowed to go beyond the circle'. One purpose for such limited circulation was to exclude the possibility that the text would appear in manuscript collections, and eventually in print. Love refers to a situation that would have had special relevance for Herbert and his family, 'Nashe in the 1590s seems to have been acting as an agent for the booksellers Richard Jones and Thomas Newman in obtaining scribally published texts by writers of the Sidney–Pembroke circle for unauthorized print publication.'[17]

My argument is that Herbert's religious lyrics were known by his family and friends, and that the genre of sacred parody used by Herbert in *The Temple* was a variation on the answer poem characteristic of poetic coteries. This context is explicitly visible in particular poems by Herbert: 'The Answer', 'The Posie', 'The Parodie', 'The Quip'. I believe it influenced a great many of Herbert's religious lyrics, including the Jordan poems and the verses on mutual love between God and man. It is clear that Herbert did not want to be well known through his devotional poems: he did not allow his poems to circulate as widely as possible. Yet since the members of his family were his major patrons, it is essential to consider the possibility that Herbert's lyrics were composed with performance or circulation in mind. If they were presented even in a limited way, then the lyrics must be included in accounts of his pursuit of patronage.

The family debate

William Herbert, Earl of Pembroke, socialized with his clients through the game of literary-exchange, and writers sought to enter the circle through their offerings. Poetic contest marked family entertainments, the establishing of friendships, and the request for patronage. E.F. Hart has argued that the 'answer-poem' thrived in the 'rich cultural life' of the court and the exclusive communities of the country-house. According to J.W. Saunders, a circle of amateur poets served as a 'finishing school' by 'preparing its members, through mutual competition and co-operation, for the service of the monarch'. A wealthy, prestigious nobleman like Pembroke attracted a circle of 'satellite' courtiers, who sought the rewards of court patronage through his influence. Henry Lawes composed music for the poems that were a social and musical recreation in William Herbert's household, and Lawes owed his position in the court to Pembroke. George Herbert originally intended to follow this path.[18]

The relationship between poetry and a public career can be clarified through a man very much like George Herbert, who sought Pembroke's support by writing verses against secular love. The poetic exchange between William Herbert and Benjamin Rudyerd signaled their friendly rivalry and social intimacy, but veiled Rudyerd's dependence on Pembroke for his position in the court and parliament. The poems collected and published in 1660 by John Donne's son were circulated earlier in manuscript form, and the title identifies the answer poem as the genre defining the exchange: *Poems Written by the Right Honorable William Earl of Pembroke Lord Steward of his Majesties Houshold. Whereof Many of which are answered by way of Repartee, by Sr Benjamin Ruddier, Knight.*[19]

Poetic contest structures the 'repartee' through a long set of verses debating love, poems which are debates in themselves, and William Herbert's version of the most answered poem of the time, Marlowe's 'Passionate Shepherd to his Love'.[20] This 'genteel' performance also marks a political alliance between a Protestant 'Earl' and a Protestant 'Knight', Pembroke's spokesman in the Commons. As an educated younger son of the gentry, Rudyerd required Pembroke's patronage in order to receive the office of Surveyor of the Court of Wards and Liveries under King James, and for his seat in Parliament for the boroughs of Portsmouth and Wilton, under the purview of William Herbert.[21] The ritual of the answer poem helped Rudyerd secure his public position, at the same time that it established a partial, temporary sense of equality with the Earl.

William Herbert, Benjamin Rudyerd and John Donne were members of the same coterie located in the Inns of Court in the 1590s, but Donne never seems to have became Pembroke's client.[22] Nevertheless, Donne played a significant role in the 'repartee' that made up the volume by Rudyerd and Herbert. Donne's presence as a poet is strong enough in the collection that he was often identified in manuscripts as their author.[23] William Herbert's 'Soules Joy' is a musical, simpler version of 'Valediction: Forbidding Mourning':

> Soules joy, now I am gone,
>   And you alone,
>   (Which cannot be,
> Since I must leave my selfe with thee,
>   And carry thee with me)
>   Yet when unto our eyes
>   Absence denyes
>   Each others sight,
> And makes to us a constant night,
>   When others change to light;
>   *O give no way to griefe,*
>   *But let beliefe*
>   *Of mutuall love,*
>   *This wonder to the vulgar prove*
>   *Our bodyes, not wee move.*[24]

Both 'Soules Joy' and 'Valediction; Forbidding Mourning' refer to the separation of the lovers, their spiritual union through mutual love, and their ascension above the 'laity' or 'vulgar'. Donne's reputation determines our assumption that Pembroke's poem is an imitation of Donne; it is possible that the process of patronage led Donne to write his poem in answer to Pembroke in an attempt to secure a position similar to Rudyerd's.[25] Neither poet was the originator of this subject

for verse: both poems as well as Hoskyns' 'Absence' are responses
to Sidney's meditations on absence in *Astrophil and Stella*.[26] Authorial
originality was not the goal for these writers, but rather skillful wit
and sophisticated argument.

The writers within the Herbert circle vied with each other over the
same conventions and genres that make up *The Temple*: imitations and
parodies of Petrarchan verse, the valediction poem, the paradox, ditties,
posies, the pastoral lyric, and the 'echo' poem. Edward Herbert, as well
as Shakespeare, wrote poems in praise of the dark lady. Both Edward
Herbert's 'Ode upon a Question Moved', and Donne's 'The Ecstasy' were
responses to Sidney's 'Eighth Song' in *Astrophil and Stella*. Donne and
Edward Herbert exchanged and answered each other's poems regularly:
Donne's 'The Progress of the Soul' (1601) influenced Edward Herbert's
'State-Progress of Ill' (1608), which Donne answered in a verse letter in
1610. George Herbert's 'Church Militant' resembles these poems. The
relationship between Donne and Edward Herbert may have been more
a matter of friendship than patronage; nevertheless, it is likely that
Donne also imagined that the alliance might lead to further support
from Edward's mother, Magdalen, or from her relative, Pembroke.[27]

George Herbert was influenced not only by the genres used in the
Herbert circle; for this coterie, love poetry had always been tied to its
renunciation. The contrast between secular and sacred love was a fully
conventional aspect of poetic debate. Sidney wrote *Astrophil and Stella*
and 'Leave me, O Love'. Donne argues for love in one poem and against
it in the next; his religious poetry compares love for his mistress and
for God. Edward Herbert uses the 'Ditty' as a love poem six times in
his volume of poems, but the first use, and the second poem in the
collection, is addressed to God rather than a mistress. He also includes
four 'Echo' poems, the last of which redirects their previous romantic
use into a sacred parody, which exchanges a pastoral landscape for the
inside of a church.[28] Again, we may assume that Edward imitates George,
but this is simply because of our acceptance of the literary canon as it
is formulated. It is possible that both George and Edward imitate other
poets, like Benjamin Rudyerd.

The poetic repartee between Pembroke and Rudyerd may have
provided a model for George Herbert's response to his patron's love
poetry. Their poems include an exchange about the value of erotic love,
in which Rudyerd argues against and Pembroke for it:

> R: Base Love, the stain of Youth, the scorn of Age,
>   The folly of a Man, a Womans rage . . .
> P: Go on, and laugh at Loves commanding fire,
>   Till you cannot your scorched self retire.[29]

The contest is reminiscent of the debate about love held between
Musidorus and Pyrocles in Sidney's *Arcadia*. This debate shapes the
volume collecting their verse, since most of Rudyerd's contributions
repeat his original arguments against love. It is also interesting that the
gentleman Rudyerd argues for restraint and the nobleman Herbert for
erotic desire; Rudyerd and Herbert may be playing the parts of humanist
courtier and unruly prince. Rudyerd instructs Herbert on the duties of
the noble man, through Rudyerd's poetic renunciations of love and
satires on women. The debate is a playful, but serious contest, according
to this passage by Rudyerd:

> Not like a Skeptic equally distract,
> Nor like a Sophister of sleights compact,
> Nor to vie Wit (a vanity of youth)
> Nor for the love of Victory, but Truth,
> The lists again I enter, bold assur'd,
> Within my Causes right, strongly immur'd.

Despite this love of truth, the collection also contains an example of
Rudyerd's love poetry.[30] Apparently Rudyerd was more interested in
vying wit than he would admit in the passage quoted above. This
confirms that conviction was less important in this exchange than the
display of verbal and argumentative skill.

The practice of rhetorical debate structured upper-class poetic
interchange during this period. The answer poem is the versified
equivalent of the disputed question used in Renaissance education.
Students were taught to generate elaborate and witty defenses for
opposing positions.[31] The practice of disputation was central to both
the grammar schools and the universities. At Westminster School every
Saturday, the students, which included George Herbert between 1604
and 1608, would 'declaim on a set original theme, and one inveighs
against another in speeches'.[32] At Oxford and Cambridge, such practices
were even more widespread: disputations would occur every Monday,
Wednesday and Friday from one to three o'clock, and also mark
Commencement exercises.[33] The disputed question also equipped the
prospective lawyers at the Inns of Court for their careers and underlay
much of the wit contests so popular there. At a Christmas festival at the
Middle Temple recorded by Benjamin Rudyerd, a 'Tuff-taffeta speech'
was presented, and immediately followed by a 'Fustian answer' in which
all figures of speech were used but nothing substantial was said.[34] Such
comedy satirizes the student's education but also emphasizes the extent
to which verbal contest was a daily practice in Renaissance schooling and
entertainment.

George Herbert's answer

The disputed question and the Herbert family poetic contest structure
the sonnets which George Herbert wrote the year he entered Cambridge.
They launch him into the poetic debate that characterized his family:

> My God, where is that ancient heat towards thee,
>   Wherewith whole showls of *Martyrs* once did burn,
>   Besides their other flames? Doth Poetry
> Wear *Venus* Livery? only serve her turn?
> Why are not *Sonnets* made of thee? and layes
>   Upon thine Altar burnt? Cannot thy love
>   Heighten a spirit to sound out thy praise
> As well as any she? Cannot thy *Dove*
> Out-strip their *Cupid* easily in flight?
>   Or, since thy wayes are deep, and still the same,
>   Will not a verse run smooth that bears thy name?
> Why doth that fire, which by thy power and might
>   Each breast doth feel, no braver fuel choose
>   Than that, which one day Worms may chance refuse?[35]

Like the answering speech in a disputation, this poem 'inveighs' against
the love poetry of Sidney, William Herbert, Edward Herbert, Donne
and Shakespeare. Like the answer poems of Benjamin Rudyerd, it also
requests attention for itself and its witty ability to handle the issue. It
seeks out that limited equality available to one who answers well, no
matter what the status of the participants. At stake is not only the virtue
of sacred rather than secular love poetry, but the disputed question,
should a man marry, or, is there any virtue in women?[36] To simulate the
debate, the poem pairs erotic and religious analogues in order to reveal
the primacy of the latter. Like the competition between 'thy *Dove*' and
'their *Cupid*' (ll. 8–9), Herbert and his God 'out-strip' love poets and their
women by appropriating flames, altars and passion, and restoring them
to the praise and worship of God. Although the poet announces his piety,
he also displays his own 'adult' wit through his jokes about the secular
poet's prostitution of his powers: 'Doth Poetry / Wear *Venus* Livery? only
serve her turn? / Why are not *Sonnets* made of thee? and layes / Upon
thine Altar burnt? Cannot thy love / Heighten a spirit to sound out thy
praise / As well as any she?' Herbert 'turns' a phrase here for the glory
of God, but also to register his verbal sophistication. The competitive
display of wit is matched by a strong antagonism against women,
especially in the last lines, when the love between man and women is
reduced to a misguided attachment to decaying flesh: 'Why doth that
fire, which by thy power and might / Each breast doth feel, no braver

fuel choose / Than that, which one day Worms may chance refuse?' This hostility against the female body is quite conventional in debates about love, especially within the Herbert circle. Edward Herbert's 'To His Mistress for Her True Picture' is addressed to Death, and rebukes the speaker's attachment to earthly lovers in terms reminiscent of Herbert's sonnets:

And do not think, when I new beauties see,
They can withdraw my settled love from thee.
Flesh-beauty strikes me not at all, I know: . . .
        Be the nut brown,
The loveliest colour which the flesh doth crown,
I'll think it like a Nut – a fair outside,
Within which worms and rottenness abide.[37]

In Donne's elegy on 'The Autumnal', traditionally assumed to be addressed to Herbert's mother Magdalen, he proves his skill in using the form of the paradox by praising an older women more highly than a younger, but nevertheless the skull beneath the skin appears like a *memento mori*:

No *Spring*, nor *Summer* beauty hath such grace,
    As I have seen in one autumnall face . . .
But name not Winter-faces, whose skin's slacke;
    Lanke, as an unthrifts purse; but a soules sacke;
Whose eyes seeke light within, for all here's shade;
    Whose mouthes are holes, rather worne out, than made . . .
Name not these living Deaths-heads unto mee . . .[38]

The display of wit and aggression against women in Herbert's early sonnets take their cue from the renunciation of physical love characteristic of love poets during this period, and from the debate about women popular in the schools and pamphlets of the time.[39] Perhaps Herbert's sonnets express more actual conviction than those by other poets; nevertheless, they are just as fully coterie performances. Walter Ong has analyzed the agonistic quality of Renaissance education and remarked on its characteristic hostility and virulence.[40] The answer poem hides this hostility within its genteel wit, but the attempt to triumph and to achieve recognition remains the same.

The wit contest in an exchange of verses between Donne and Herbert reveals that religious poetry was as appropriate in coterie performance as secular verse. According to Helen Gardner, Donne wrote a Latin poem on his seal to Herbert and Herbert replied in 1615 at the time of Donne's ordination and as Herbert was pursuing a successful academic career. Donne's poem alludes to shared religious interests, wishes Herbert well in his plans for secular preferment, and perhaps attempts to deepen an alliance with a young man who had better connections than Donne:

> The Crosse (my seal at Baptism) spred below,
> Does, by that form, into an Anchor grow.
> Crosses grow Anchors; Bear, as thou shouldst do
> Thy Crosse, and that Crosse grows an Anchor too . . .
> Under this little seal great gifts I send,
> [Wishes], and prayers, pawns and fruits of a friend.
> And may that Saint which rides in our great Seal,
> To you, who bear his name, great bounties deal.[41]

According to Helen Gardner, the 'great Seal' refers to 'the George that hangs from the Garter on the seated figure of the King on the reverse of the Great Seal'.[42] Donne associates George Herbert through his name with the monarchy, and identifies the King as the source for Herbert's future preferment. This reference indicates that Herbert's desires for secular office were quite clear to those who knew him. The poem also suggests that just as Donne bestows his gift on Herbert, so he asks for some help with his influential relations. Herbert's reply acknowledges the alliance, but partially through a display of wit that attempts to equal or perhaps surpass Donne's own. Both poems play on the link between the cross and the anchor, but Herbert's compact seven lines show up Donne's more expansive twenty-two; Latin was, of course, Herbert's forte, rather than Donne's:

> Although the Crosse could not Christ here detain,
> Though nail'd unto't, but he ascends again,
> Nor yet thy eloquence here keep him still,
> But onely while thou speak'st; This Anchor will.[43]

Witty and terse, the poem pins down its reworking of Donne's conceit through its half-line on the anchor. The English translation, perhaps by Herbert, praises Donne's preaching ability at the same time that it suggests indirectly some conflict between Christ's word and Donne's own. The poem clearly accepts Donne's good wishes and connects the spiritual hope of the anchor with the firmness of their friendship: 'Let the world reel, we and all ours stand sure, / This holy Cable's of all storms secure' (ll. 6–7). Yet the poem's reworking of Donne's conceited style also displays the younger poet's ability to answer back, and to be more obscure and more condensed than Donne himself.[44]

'Jordan' (I) constructs itself as an entry into another wit battle, and its jaunty rhetorical questions are presented as if to imagined opponents:

> Who sayes that fictions onely and false hair
> Become a verse? Is there in truth no beautie?

Is all good structure in a winding stair?
May no lines passe, except they do their dutie
  Not to a true but painted chair?

(ll. 1–5)

Like Herbert's first sonnets, each rhetorical question is meant to score a point. The poem may honor truth rather than artifice; nevertheless each line spryly proves its verbal power through turning a phrase. This plain style will not be artless, since it uses metaphor (the 'false hair' of empty tropes), puns ('become' as turn into or be appropriate to), and allegory (the 'lines' which bow before the chair of overly elaborate literary authority). The purification associated with the 'Jordan' allusion does not require abjuring rhetorical figures but rather puts them into the service of religious truth. Wit, the poem claims, is most becoming in a sacred poem.

Like Herbert's first sonnets, this poem begins with questions and ends with a concluding answer. The last stanza stages an imaginary truce between the debaters:

Shepherds are honest people; let them sing:
Riddle who list, for me, and pull for Prime:
I envie no mans nightingale or spring;
Nor let them punish me with losse of rime,
  Who plainly say, *My God, My King.*

To each his own style, according to the speaker, but his words prove that the plain style he adopts will be as indirect as any other, though far more condensed and pointed than the pastoral allegory still practiced by a few. 'Pull for Prime' is a riddling figure for the very pastoral songs he debunks as pretentiously and superficially riddling: since the phrase comes from Primero and refers to drawing for the winning card, these poets are imagined as vying to produce the best pastoral poem, or version of primavera. The speaker appears to be less interested in contest: 'I envie no mans nightingale or spring'; yet his last phrase again scores a point through its riddling ambiguity. Does '*My God, My King*' mean my God is my King, and therefore I abjure the court style? or does it mean that the speaker will praise both God and King, speak of religion and country, without the unwieldy self-protective artifice of pastoral allegory? Like the rest of the poem, the phrase pretends to be straightforward, but it outwits those who think plainness is equivalent to simple-mindedness.

'A Parodie'

Herbert originally intended to identify himself through the family debate as the 'Herbert' who wrote lyric poetry exclusively about sacred love, but nevertheless poetry just as witty and inventive as the verses by other members of the family, or perhaps even more so. But several poems in *The Temple* testify to a change over time in his attitude toward the answer poem, and his relationship to the family debate. This new attitude did not result in a withdrawal from that debate; one of Herbert's late poems is an answer to Pembroke's poem 'Soules Joy' quoted above. But the tone and the placement of the poem in *The Temple* reveal that Herbert approached such a contest in a new way later in his life. 'A Parodie' uses the methods of the answer poem to evoke the spiritual communion between God and the soul rather than between human lovers:

> Souls joy, when thou art gone,
> And I alone,
> Which cannot be,
> Because thou dost abide with me,
> And I depend on thee;
>
> Yet when thou dost suppresse
> The cheerfulnesse
> Of thy abode,
> And in my powers not stirre abroad,
> But leave me to my load:
>
> O what a damp and shade
> Doth me invade!
> No stormie night
> Can so afflict or so affright,
> As thy eclipsed light.

(ll. 1–15)

Given the association of Pembroke's verse with the poetry of John Donne and Edward Herbert, all of whom considered 'mutual love', it is clear that George Herbert's famous and compelling representations of spiritual intimacy owe more to his family circle than has previously been noticed. 'A Parodie' responds not only to Pembroke's 'Soules Joy'; it takes its position in a complex of poems including Sidney's meditations on absence, Hoskyn's 'Absence', Donne's 'Valediction: Forbidding Mourning', 'The Ecstacy', and Edward Herbert's 'Ode upon a Question Moved'.

Although 'A Parodie', like the poems of Rudyerd, rebukes Pembroke's fascination with the erotic, the tone of aggressive contest characteristic of Herbert's early poems and the form of the parody in general is absent here.[45] The speaker interestingly takes on the role of the woman in the valediction poem, and confesses the grief and sense of separation felt by the one who is left behind.[46] The significance of this careful avoidance of contentiousness can be clarified by the poem that precedes 'A Parodie' in

The Temple. 'The Posie' considers the very kind of wit contest inherent to the Herbert family ritual of answering. The poem does not renounce such verbal battles, but suggests that they must be entered with a different spirit:

> Let wits contest,
> And with their words and posies windows fill:
> *Lesse then the least*
> *Of all thy mercies,* is my posie still.
>
> This on my ring,
> This by my picture, in my book I write:
> Whether I sing,
> Or say, or dictate, this is my delight.
>
> Invention rest,
> Comparisons go play, wit use thy will:
> *Lesse then the least*
> *Of all Gods mercies,* is my posie still.

A posie was a short motto engraved on windows, or imprinted on personal objects, like rings and books, which often represented an intimate relationship or expressed a secret about an individual. Pembroke and Rudyerd composed posies; Edward Herbert's posie, 'In a Glass Window for Inconstancy' may have been answered by Donne's 'Valediction: Of my Name in the Window'. Like the device or *impresa*, the posie was a public symbol for a private or personal experience.[47]

George Herbert's 'The Posie' is autobiographical because it refers to the ritual of the answer poem enacted by 'A Parodie' which follows it. The motto in the poem has also been identified by Nicholas Ferrar, in the prefatory note to *The Temple*, as Herbert's own: 'We conclude all with his own Motto, with which he used to conclude all things that might seem to tend any way to his own honour; *Lesse then the least of Gods mercies'* (pp. 4–5). The humility of the motto may suggest the renunciation of rituals of honor: Ferrar's account suggests instead that it allowed Herbert to participate in them while preserving a sense of religious integrity. The poem does not renounce poetry or its social rituals: 'whether I sing, / Or say, or dictate, this is my delight' (ll. 7–8).

Most critics have recognized that the motto in the poem would have special significance for Herbert. It is spoken by Jacob: 'I am not worthy of the least of all the mercies and of all the truth, which thou hast shewed unto thy servant; for with my staff I passed over this Jordan.'[48] 'Jordan' was the personal 'device' which represented for Herbert the purification of ambition, especially that associated with literary creation.[49] But critics have not noticed that the next words of Jacob are equally important:

'Deliver me, I pray thee, from the hand of my brother, from the hand of Esau.' Jacob speaks these words after he has been informed of the approaching troops of his relative, with whom he has competed for the 'honors' of the family literally from birth, and now he asks for divine help in this troublesome encounter. We might remember as well that Jacob's meeting with Esau is preceded by his wrestling with the angel of God, during which he is given the new name of Israel: 'for as a prince hast thou power with God and with men, and hast prevailed'.

The motto 'lesse then the least of all Gods mercies' conferred on the poet a double identity which allowed him to be both a Herbert and something else. In his contests with and 'parodies' of his family relations and their client-poets, Herbert could hint at that devotional identity, that new name, in a public, but distanced way. The 'temple' within preserved a separate area in the self, a space ideally purified of family rivalry and personal ambition.[50] It was both a protective and a disciplinary enclosure, since it required that 'comparisons go play' (l. 10); that is, that poetic imitation, including the use of similes, be free from the impulse to triumph over another. It demanded that 'invention rest' (l. 9); that imaginative creativity be less important than the truth, and that the 'finding out' of topics occur without the disquiet of personal ambition. Similarly, the motto 'is my posie still' because it did not change despite the social need for cleverness, and because it provided a measure of stillness or quiet in the midst of public rivalry. Again, 'The Posie' does not imply that Herbert gave up singing or reciting the lyrics before an audience. Like a 'posie' that represented an intimate relationship, the poems referred in public to a personal devotional experience.

The sequence of both Herbert manuscripts of *The Temple* testify to the crucial role that the answer poem played in Herbert's literary career. When he revised the earlier Williams manuscript into the later Bodleian manuscript, he replaced one example of coterie verse with another. Near the end of the sequence, before the group on 'last things' that ends 'The Church', Herbert placed 'A Parodie', his most focused answer to William Herbert, in the original position of 'Invention', his most focused answer to Sir Philip Sidney.[51] The significant and analogous positions of the two poems were gestures toward the family literary circle. This revision demonstrates that the Sidney–Herbert coterie was fundamental to the original project of *The Temple*, and that it remained so throughout Herbert's life.

The modern assumption that religious verse can only be sincere when it is private misrepresents the role of poetry in the seventeenth century and interferes with our understanding of the social context of Herbert's verse. For the Herbert coterie, poetry was a social ritual evoked by and participating in an upper-class world that included evenings of entertainment and the exchange of verse, as well as the forging of political alliances and client–patron relations. What we have identified as literary aspects of the verse – the use of wit, allusions to other poets like Sidney, the critique of erotic poetry – should be reassessed as social gestures. Herbert's engagement in social ritual does not make his poetry any less religious than previously imagined, but perhaps less modern.[52]

Notes

1. LAWRENCE STONE describes the extended family in *The Family, Sex and Marriage in England, 1500–1800* (London: Weidenfeld & Nicolson, 1977), pp. 85, 89. ARTHUR MAROTTI has made evident the 'forms of competitive versifying' that made up 'a system of transactions within polite or educated social circles', and I am indebted to his account, in *John Donne: Coterie Poet* (Madison: Univ. of Wisconsin Press, 1986), pp. 12–13 and throughout. My thoughts on Herbert and patronage have been significantly influenced by my discussions with MICHAEL E. SCHOENFELDT and by his book *Prayer and Power: George Herbert and Renaissance Courtship* (Chicago: Univ. of Chicago Press, 1991). He does not discuss William Herbert as a patron for George Herbert at any length. Sidney was William Herbert's uncle, and William Herbert was George Herbert's fourth cousin, therefore George Herbert was Sidney's fourth cousin once removed. For the unstable status of younger sons of the gentry, see JOAN THIRSK, 'Younger Sons in the Seventeenth Century', *History*, 54 (1969) and my essay 'George Herbert's *Country Parson* and the Character of Social Identity' in *Studies in Philology*, 80 (1988), pp. 245–66. Both George Herbert and his brother Henry Herbert owed their best positions to the Earl of Pembroke: see BRIAN O'FARRELL, *Politician, Patron, Poet: William Herbert, Third Earl of Pembroke, 1580–1630* (Unpublished dissertation, Univ. of California, Los Angeles, 1966), pp. 207, 215–16, 275, 291 (n. 194); MICHAEL G. BRENNAN, *Literary Patronage in the English Renaissance: The Pembroke Family* (London and New York: Routledge, 1988), pp. 139, 153–4, 194–7; RICHARD DUTTON, *Mastering the Revels* (Iowa City: Univ. of Iowa Press, 1991) pp. 228, 233–6, 246–8. JOSEPH H. SUMMERS, in *George Herbert: His Religion and Art* (Cambridge: Harvard Univ. Press, 1968), notes that 'As an adolescent and an adult, Herbert probably read the poetry of the Sidney–Herbert connection for politic as well as literary reasons' (p. 31).

2. LOUIS L. MARTZ coined the illuminating term 'sacred parody' in *The Poetry of Meditation* (New Haven: Yale Univ. Press, 1954), pp. 186, 261, 271. The term 'coterie poetry' is often used to refer primarily to the exchange and copying of manuscripts, but the coteries themselves included social gatherings in which poetry was recited or presented with musical accompaniment. See especially E.F. HART, 'The Answer-Poem of the Early Seventeenth-Century', *Review of English Studies*, n.s. 7 (1956), pp. 19–29. On upper-class poetic exchange, see MAROTTI, pp. 3–24; J.W. SAUNDERS, *The Profession of English Letters* (London: Routledge & Kegan Paul, 1964), pp. 31–48; HERBERT GRIERSON, 'Bacon's Poem, *The World*: Its Date and Relation to Certain Other Poems', in *Cross-Currents in Seventeenth-Century Literature* (New York: Harper, 1958), pp. 221–37; and HAROLD LOVE, *Scribal Publication in Seventeenth-Century England* (Oxford: Clarendon Press, 1993).

3. Many recent studies have called into question the assumption that Herbert's poetry was private. But these studies have claimed that Herbert's poetry voices social or cultural issues either explicitly or implicitly. I am arguing that the verse is public because it was written as an entry into a debate within a limited and elite social circle, and that the convention of upper-class poetic debate determined Herbert's responses to poetry, both before and after he gave up a secular career. For recent studies on the relationship between Herbert's poetry and society, see SIDNEY GOTTLIEB, 'The Social and Political Backgrounds of George Herbert's Poetry' in *'The Muses Common-Weale': Poetry and Politics in the Seventeenth Century*, eds Claude Summers and Ted-Larry Pebworth (Columbia: Univ. of Missouri Press, 1988), pp. 107–18; LEAH SINANOGLOU MARCUS, *Childhood and Cultural Despair: A Theme and Variations in Seventeenth-Century Literature* (Pittsburgh: Univ. of Pittsburgh Press, 1978); SCHOENFELDT, *Prayer and Power: George Herbert and Renaissance Courtship*; RICHARD STRIER, 'Sanctifying the Aristocracy: "Devout Humanism" in François de Sales, John Donne, and George Herbert', *Journal of Religion*, 69 (1989), pp. 36–58; and CLAUDE J. SUMMERS and TED-LARRY PEBWORTH, 'Herbert, Vaughan, and Public Concerns in Private Modes', *George Herbert Journal*, 3 (1979–80), pp. 1–21.

4. See J.W. SAUNDERS, 'The Stigma of Print: A Note on the Social Bases of Tudor Poetry', *Essays in Criticism*, 1 (1951), 139–64, and *The Profession of English Letters*, pp. 31–48.

5. *The Works of George Herbert*, ed. F.E. Hutchinson (1941; corr. rpt. Oxford: Clarendon Press, 1941), pp. xxxix–xi. All citations to Herbert's work will be to this edition. ROSEMUND TUVE reconstructs the musical evenings in the Herbert family, but discounts their 'emulative' aspect, in ' "Sacred Parody" of Love Poetry, and Herbert' in *Essays by Rosemund Tuve*, ed. Thomas P. Roche, Jr (Princeton: Princeton Univ. Press, 1970), pp. 235–9.

6. AMY M. CHARLES, *A Life of George Herbert* (Ithaca: Cornell Univ. Press, 1978), pp. 78–89; JOSEPH H. SUMMERS, 'Sir Calidore and the Country Parson', in *Like Season'd Timber: New Essays on George Herbert*, eds Edmund Miller and Robert DiYanni (New York: Peter Lang, 1987), pp. 213–14.

7. CHARLES, *A Life of George Herbert*, p. 78.

8. *The Translation of Certain Psalmes into English Verse* by the Right Honourable, Francis Lo. Virulam, Viscount St. Alban (London, 1625), A3, A3ᵛ.

9. The question of the circulation of the Latin poetry is much more vexed than one would expect, given the assertions of Amy Charles and W. Hilton Kelliher that the Latin poems were far more public than the English verse. In the three collections of Latin poetry unpublished during Herbert's lifetime, *Musae Responsoriae*, *Lucus* and *Passio Discerpta*, there is clear evidence of circulation of only two poems, Epigram XXV originating in *Musae Responsoriae* but finally appearing in *Lucus*, and 'Triumphus Mortis' in *Lucus*. Kelliher in fact believes that Epigram XXV circulated on its own. Just like the English lyrics, there is no evidence of references in commonplace books nor in manuscript miscellanies during Herbert's lifetime to any other poem in *Musae Responsoriae* or *Lucus*, and none at all to the poems in *Passio Discerpta*. It is assumed that *Musae* circulated because of the public nature of the subject matter and Herbert's dedications to King James, Prince Charles and Bishop Andrewes. Certainly this suggests that the English lyrics might also have circulated without references in commonplace books, especially given the signs of coterie influence. See W. HILTON KELLIHER's 'The Latin Poetry of George Herbert' in

The Latin Poetry of English Poets, ed. J.W. Binn (London: Routledge & Kegan Paul, 1974) p. 39. See also *Works*, ed. Hutchinson, pp. 384–439.

10. HELEN WILCOX, 'Herbert's Musical Contexts', in *Like Season'd Timber*, pp. 43–5. Wilcox concludes, 'Our knowledge of how Herbert performed his poems, or intended them for performance, is likely to remain speculative.'

11. IZAAK WALTON, *The Lives of John Donne, Sir Henry Wotton, Richard Hooker, George Herbert & Robert Sanderson*, ed. George Saintsbury (London: Oxford Univ. Press, 1927), p. 303.

12. *Select Hymns, Taken out of Mr Herbert's Temple*, Augustan Reprint Society, no. 98 (Los Angeles: Univ. of California Press, 1962), A2.

13. JOHN AUBREY, *Brief Lives*, ed. Oliver Lawson Dick (London: Secker & Warburg, 1949), p. 137.

14. Bodleian Library, MS 2, folio 53, 56. Aubrey describes the musical evenings at the house in Chelsea (folio 56). See also Tuve, ' "Sacred Parody" '.

15. I owe these points about Marvell and the commonplace books to ANN BAYNES COIRO, who has examined Milton's relationship to coterie circulation and publication in 'Milton and Class Identity: the Publication of *Areopagitica* and the 1645 *Poems*', *Journal of Medieval and Renaissance Studies*, 22 (1992), pp. 261–89.

16. *The Index of English Literary Manuscripts* lists a copy of Herbert's 'A Parodie' in a manuscript volume of Donne's poetry, collected '*c.* 1632', but the poem in the manuscript is actually Pembroke's 'Soules Joy' which Herbert imitated. The *Index* also lists a copy of Herbert's 'The 23rd Psalm' with musical setting in Henry Lawes's autograph songbook compiled in the mid-seventeenth century. Since Lawes came from Wilton, was Pembroke's client, and set his poetry to music, it is quite possible that Lawes knew George Herbert's poem from musical evenings at Wilton, and provided his own musical setting. See PETER BEAL, *Index of English Literary Manuscripts* (London: Mansell; New York: Bowker, 1980) vol. 1, pt. 2, pp. 203, 208.

17. LOVE, *Scribal Publication*, pp. 43–4, 70–2.

18. On upper-class poetic exchange, see note 2 above, including Hart, p. 21, and SAUNDERS, *The Profession of English Letters*, pp. 41–4. WILLA MCCLUNG EVANS discusses Lawes and Pembroke in *Henry Lawes: Musician and Friend of Poets* (New York: The Modern Language Association of America, 1941), pp. 23–4, 35–46. Clients of William Herbert also included Thomas Adams, Christopher Brooke, William Browne, Samuel Daniel (his tutor), John Earle, Ben Jonson, William Shakespeare and George Wither. Pembroke inherited the patronage networks established by his mother, Mary Sidney Herbert, and to some extent, those developed by the Earl of Leicester, the Earl of Essex and Sir Philip Sidney. On these circles, see MARGARET HANNAY, *Philip's Phoenix: Mary Sidney, Countess of Pembroke* (New York: Oxford Univ. Press, 1990); MARY ELLEN LAMB, *Gender and Authorship in the Sidney Circle* (Madison: Wisconsin, 1990); O'FARRELL; and BRENNAN. The patronage circle around Lucy, Countess of Bedford is analogous; see BEN JONSON's poem 'To Lucy, Countess of Bedford, with Mr Donne's Satires'.

19. *Poems Written by the Right Honorable William Earl of Pembroke Lord Steward of his Majesties Houshold. Whereof Many of which are answered by way of Repartee, by Sr Benjamin Ruddier, Knight* (London: Matthew Inman, 1660). For commentary on the accuracy of the text, see the edition by G.E. Onderwyser, *Poems Written by the Right Honorable William Earl of Pembroke*. Augustan Reprint Society, #79 (Los Angeles: William Andrews Clark Memorial Library, 1959).

20. WILLIAM HERBERT, *Poems*, p. 38.
21. O'FARRELL, pp. 143–5, 153–8, 163–74; Brennan, pp. 155–6, 166, 173, 180, 187; *Memoirs of Sir Benjamin Rudyerd, Knt.* ed. James Alexander Manning (London: T. & W. Boone, 1841), pp. 18–23, 28. George Herbert writes that he plans to correspond with 'my Lord, or Sir Benjamin Ruddyard' to help him secure the position of Cambridge orator (p. 370). The 'Lord' is almost certainly Pembroke.
22. TED-LARRY PEBWORTH identifies the members of this coterie, and states that Pembroke became patron to several members after 1601, in 'John Donne, Coterie Poetry, and the Text as Performance', *SEL*, 29 (1989), pp. 62–3. Donne sought Pembroke's assistance in obtaining the deanship of St Paul's in 1621 through a poem in praise of Sidney and his sister, but it is unclear whether Donne received the support he was seeking. Despite Donne's patronage by Magdalen Herbert by 1607, he was never an explicit client of Pembroke's. On Donne's relationship with William and Magdalen Herbert, see DAVID NOVARR, *The Disinterred Muse* (Ithaca: Cornell Univ. Press, 1980), pp. 150–7; MAROTTI, pp. 186, 284–5; and O'FARRELL, pp. 214–15. Given Donne's great financial need and his exchange of verse with Pembroke, the lack of a client-relationship is surprising. The scandal of Donne's marriage may have deterred Pembroke, although Pembroke's affairs were far more disreputable. It is possible that Pembroke became a patron to Donne after the 'cleansing' experience of ordination.
23. MAROTTI, p. 333.
24. From 'Poems attributed to John Donne' in *The Poems of John Donne*, vol. I, ed. Herbert J.C. Grierson (Oxford: Oxford Univ. Press, 1912), pp. 429–30. I quote from this text because the text in Pembroke's *Poems* (p. 24) is shortened and garbled. See Tuve, ' "Sacred Parody" ', pp. 239–40.
25. The same question of precedence arises in terms of Donne's sonnet 'Death Be Not Proud', and the poem by his patron, Lucy, Countess of Bedford, 'Death be not proud, thy hand gave not this blow'. Marotti argues that Donne's valediction poems might have been shown to a few friends, like other poems of mutual love, but that they primarily represent Donne's relationship with his wife (p. 169). I cannot agree; the clear connections between 'Valediction: Forbidding Mourning' and 'Soules Joy' imply quite strongly that these were not private accounts of experience, but coterie performances, and perhaps even answer poems.
26. *Astrophil and Stella*, 105, 106. On Hoskyns' 'Absence', see PHILIP J. FINKELPEARL, *John Marston of the Middle Temple* (Cambridge: Harvard Univ. Press, 1969), pp. 73–4.
27. See Edward Herbert's 'To Her Eyes', 'To Her Hair', 'Sonnet of Black Beauty', and 'Another Sonnet to Black It Self', in *The Poems English and Latin of Edward Lord Herbert of Cherbury*, ed. G.C. Moore Smith (Oxford: Clarendon Press, 1923), pp. 54–9. On the exchange between Donne and Edward Herbert, see MAROTTI, pp. 195–202, and EUGENE HILL, *Edward, Lord Herbert of Cherbury* (Boston: Twayne Publishers, 1987), pp. 66–103. Hill points out the link between 'The Progress of the Soul' and 'State-Progress of Ill' (pp. 67–9), and argues that Herbert's 'An Ode upon a Question Moved' followed and commented upon Donne's 'Ecstacy' (pp. 95–103). Hutchinson associates 'The Church Militant' with Donne's 'The Progress of the Soul' (p. 543). On Magdalen Herbert's patronage of Donne, see NOVARR, p. 89, and MAROTTI, pp. 343–4. Later in

his life, the tables turned, and Donne lent money to Sir John Danvers; see
Edmund Gosse, *The Life and Letters of John Donne* (Gloucester, Mass.: Peter
Smith, 1959), II, 248.

28. Edward Herbert, *Poems*, 'Ditty', pp. 1, 12, 40, 41, 44, 47, 84; 'Echo' poems,
    pp. 40, 69, 70, 72.
29. William Herbert, *Poems*, pp. 8, 13.
30. William Herbert, *Poems*, pp. 13, 34, 53, 55.
31. On the disputed question, see Joel Altman, *The Tudor Play of Mind: Rhetorical
    Inquiry and the Development of Elizabethan Drama* (Berkeley: Univ. of California
    Press, 1978); and the 'General Introduction' in John Donne, *Paradoxes and
    Problems*, ed. Helen Peters (Oxford: Clarendon Press, 1980), pp. xxviii–xxxviii.
32. From the official schedule for Eton and Westminister during this period,
    quoted by T.W. Baldwin in *William Shakspere's Small Latine and Lesse Greeke*,
    vol. I (Urbana: Univ. of Illinois Press, 1944), p. 358. See also Altman, pp. 43–53.
33. Mark H. Curtis, *Oxford and Cambridge in Transition, 1558–1642* (Oxford:
    Clarendon Press, 1959), pp. 88–90; Rosemary O'Day, *Education and Society
    1500–1800* (New York: Longman, 1982), p. 112.
34. Rudyerd, *Memoirs*, p. 12. See also Finkelpearl, pp. 48–61. Rudyerd's phrase
    'Fustian Answer' suggests that 'answering' originated in debate, and was not
    restricted to 'answer' poems.
35. Herbert's gift of his early sonnets to his mother does not take them out of
    the network of patronage and poetic exchange; he refers to her as 'My clan's/
    Especial guardian' in *Memoriae Matris Sacrum: The Latin Poetry of George
    Herbert*, trans. Mark McCloskey and Paul R. Murphy (Ohio Univ. Press, 1965),
    p. 153. For a different interpretation of this gift, see E. Pearlman's excellent
    'George Herbert's God', *ELR*, 13 (1983), 88–112.
36. Altman, pp. 41–2, 49–50; Donne, *Paradoxes and Problems*, pp. 21–2, 89–90.
37. Edward Herbert, *Poems*, pp. 76–7.
38. John Donne, *The Elegies and the Songs and Sonnets*, ed. Helen Gardner (Oxford:
    Clarendon Press, 1965), p. 27, lines 1–2, 37–40, 43.
39. I am indebted to Kevin Dunn, who pointed out to me the wit displays
    about women in Donne's paradoxes and problems, which, like the poems,
    work out positions in the debate about women. Discussing the issue was a
    social pastime much like the answer poem; see Peters, pp. xxxi–xxxvi, and Ben
    Jonson's poem, 'That Women are but Mens Shaddowes'. On rhetorical debate
    and the controversy about women, see Linda Woodbridge, *Women and the
    English Renaissance: Literature and the Nature of Womankind, 1540–1620* (Urbana:
    Univ. of Illinois Press, 1984) and the introduction to Edmund Tilney, *The
    Flower of Friendship: A Renaissance Dialogue Contesting Marriage*, ed. Valerie
    Wayne (Ithaca: Cornell Univ. Press, 1992), pp. 1–93.
40. Walter J. Ong, 'Latin Language as a Renaissance Puberty Rite', *Studies in
    Philology*, 56 (April 1959), pp. 103–24; and *Fighting for Life: Contest, Sexuality,
    and Consciousness* (Ithaca: Cornell Univ. Press, 1981).
41. John Donne, *Divine Poems*, ed. Helen Gardner (Oxford: Clarendon Press,
    1952), pp. 52–3, 111–12, 138–47. See also Novarr, pp. 103–7. Neither Gardner
    nor Novarr concludes that Donne's poem could have been written with
    patronage in mind; I think it is unwise to discount it, given the prestige of
    the Herbert family and Donne's difficult financial situation. Novarr does
    conclude that Donne sought patronage even after his ordination, pp. 150–7.

42. DONNE, *Divine Poems*, p. 112.
43. DONNE, *Divine Poems*, pp. 144–5. On Donne's use of Latin, see NOVARR, p. 106.
44. Gardner suggests that Herbert may have written the translation, which appeared, along with the Latin poem, in Walton's *Life of Herbert*, 1658. Both Gardner and Novarr discuss the conceited wit of Donne's poem; Gardner points out in Herbert's verses a change in form, tone and style between what she sees as a part written in 1615 – an 'obscurely worded conceit' – and a section written after Donne's death in 1631 – 'warm in tone; they reveal a deep affection' (pp. 146–7). Such a change is analogous to the transition in style I am describing in this essay.
45. I do not agree with Tuve's conclusion that 'Herbert's title will not bear the meaning which the word *parody* has in seventeenth-century dictionaries of the learned or vernacular tongues . . . These, like our own use of the word, stress the element of mockery, burlesque or at the least some sidelong denigrating comment on the original author's sense' ('Sacred "Parody" of Love Poetry, and Herbert', pp. 208–9). Tuve claims that the word is used only in a musical sense, to refer to ' "replacement of text for a known tune" ', (p. 212), and that the poems by Pembroke and Herbert were sung to the same music. It is clear, however, from Herbert's early sonnets that he was quite proficient at denigrating love poets. I believe that he uses the term in order to evoke expectations of aggressive satire in order to deflate them. See the discussion of this issue in SIDNEY GOTTLIEB's 'The Two Endings of George Herbert's "The Church" ', in *A Fine Tuning: Studies of the Religious Poetry of Herbert and Milton*, ed. Mary A. Maleski (Binghamton, NY: Medieval and Renaissance Texts and Studies, 1989), p. 75, note 21.
46. PEARLMAN discusses Herbert's turn from masculine to feminine models of behavior (p. 101).
47. *A History of Private Life*, vol. III, *Passions of the Renaissance*, ed. Roger Chartier (Cambridge: Harvard Univ. Press, 1989), pp. 231–3.
48. Genesis 32:10. On 'Jordan', see especially TUVE, *A Reading of George Herbert* pp. 194–6; and STANLEY E. FISH, *Self-Consuming Artifacts* (Berkeley: Univ. of California Press, 1972), pp. 156–223, still among the best discussions of the dynamics of Herbert's verse.
49. I use the word 'device' in order to suggest that 'Jordan', though associated with religious purity, was nevertheless a witty invention, and that it was meant to represent Herbert personally, just as mottos or emblems were used to represent other members of the upper-classes.
50. DEBORA SHUGER offers an intriguing analysis of the structure of *The Temple* in terms of William Perkins' notion of dual persons, a split between a private self and a public persona, in *Habits of Thought in the English Renaissance: Religion, Politics, and the Dominant Culture* (Berkeley: Univ. of California Press, 1990), pp. 91–119.
51. 'Invention' became 'Jordan' (II); both are elaborate imitations of the first poem of Sidney's *Astrophil and Stella*. In the Williams manuscript, 'Invention' precedes 'Perfection', the original version of 'The Elixir', and both poems come before the sequence on 'last things' that ends 'The Church'. In the Bodleian manuscript, the combination of 'Invention' and 'Perfection' is revised into 'The Posie', 'A Parodie', 'The Elixir' and 'A Wreath', all of which comment on the earthly things of poetry and performance. For a different account of these

manuscript revisions, see GOTTLIEB, 'The Two Endings of George Herbert's "The Church" ', pp. 57–76.

52. I thank Deborah Dyson, Sanford Freedman, Sidney Gottlieb, Lillian Nayder and Jonathan Post, who generously reviewed this essay for me. The question and answer session at the conference 'George Herbert in the Nineties: Reflections and Reassessments' was an invaluable help in formulating these issues, and I thank everyone involved.

9 Puritanism and Maenadism in *A Mask**

RICHARD L. HALPERN

Richard Halpern analyses Milton's *Mask* in terms of a Marxist or cultural materialist account of history. Instead of focusing on the subversion of dominant culture, however, Halpern notes that the Puritan bourgeoisie, despite their position as only the 'emerging' ruling class, instituted powerful systems of control, especially in domestic life. Halpern's methodology could also be called materialist feminist because of his attention to the conditions of women in the transition from feudalism to capitalism, and because of his claim that the struggle over the mode of reproduction was complexly interrelated to the struggle over the mode of production. Halpern considers allusions to the Greek figures of Dionysus and the maenads in order to argue that Milton's use of myth constructs the Lady as primarily a threat to men rather than as being threatened by them. Married chastity becomes the ideological ideal that saves the Puritan home from the real dangers in the poem: an undomesticated female sexuality and a rural collectivity which is both working-class and 'foreign'.

> Christianity gave Eros poison to drink; he did not die of it but he degenerated into vice.
>
> (NIETZSCHE, *Beyond Good and Evil*)

Despite the suggestions of union that inhere in the very word *wedding*, it was no secret by Milton's time that the nuptial passage was rather fraught. The vast apparatus of ceremonial and mythical harmony that Renaissance humanists applied to it only threw its tensions, both sexual and political, into greater relief.[1] It was John Milton's privilege to live through these tensions with such disastrous intensity that his art could

---

* Reprinted from *Rewriting the Renaissance*, eds Margaret W. Ferguson, Maureen Quilligan and Nancy Vickers (Chicago: Chicago University Press, 1986), pp. 88–105.

illuminate them in a particularly telling way. Milton composed *A Mask* in 1634, eight years before his first marriage. Yet Milton seems particularly interested in the hymeneal associations of the masque form, even though this takes the paradoxical shape of a masque in praise of chastity. Milton's ideological project in *A Mask*, I will argue, is to trace the line that leads from virginity to married chastity. In one sense, of course, this is only to retrace a line drawn by Spenser. Milton not only invokes the Britomartian machinery at times but superimposes the line of marriage on to that of romance, so that the hero's quest represents the (incomplete) movement from virgin to bride. What makes it possible for Spenser to formulate this identity, however, and what therefore keeps Milton's project from becoming perfunctory, was the increasing tendency of the marital line to wander. The formal structure of romance – which throve on the tension between the straight and teleological line of the quest, on the one hand, and the curved and anarchic line of error, on the other – perfectly suited a situation in which new historical circumstances threatened the efficacy of marriage as an institution for containing women.

Along with his ideological theme, Milton inherits a field of literary instruments: specifically, a mythopoesis that tends to congeal into Neoplatonic and Christian allegory. The syncretic mythology of *A Mask*, and the ponderous symbolism of its action, draw on techniques common to both the Spenserian epic and the Jonsonian masque. Yet Milton's allegory lacks the coherence of its literary forebearers. *A Mask* seems to want to wed the Christian and classical virtues in a way that is appropriate to its hymeneal form. But the mythical vehicle keeps exceeding the allegory that it is supposed to express and thus subverts its coherence. The ambivalence of myth produces a surplus or residue of meaning that cannot be contained by allegory; hence Milton's masque begins to wander from its official ideological stance.

The surplus meaning of myth, which subverts the linearity of Milton's allegorical narrative, provides a privileged intersection of form and ideology in *A Mask*, where mythical contradictions are substituted for ideological ones. Nowhere is this more evident than in the Dionysian mythology that the masque half-invokes in order to suppress. The supremely ambivalent figure of Dionysus bursts the containment of his allegorical role, thereby revealing significant contradictions in Milton's sexual ideology.

I

Dionysus makes his only explicit appearance in Comus's genealogy, the significance of which is easily read within the masque's dominant, allegorical code.

Bacchus that first from out the purple grape,
Crushed the sweet poison of misused wine
After the Tuscan mariners transformed
Coasting the Tyrrhene shore, as the winds listed,
On Circe's island fell (Who knows not Circe
The daughter of the Sun? whose charmed cup
Whoever tasted, lost his upright shape,
And downward fell into a groveling swine)
This nymph that gazed upon his clustering locks,
With ivy berries wreathed, and his blithe youth,
Had by him, ere he parted thence, a son
Much like his father, but his mother more,
Whom therefore she brought up and Comus named.

(46–58)[2]

Both Circe and Bacchus are magical, both are associated with beasts and bestiality, intemperence, intoxication, promiscuous sexuality. Comus's lineage sets him in stark contrast to Milton's virginal, temperate Lady and indicates the grotesque animalism that awaits her if she falls prey to his wiles.

The threat to the Lady is clear; and yet something seems awry, for Circe's sexual magic is directed only against men. Bacchus may make a more sensible adversary, if we recall the lustful, vinous father of Mirth in *L'Allegro*, the language of which Comus echoes in his first dance. And yet, in *Lycidas* and later, Milton seems more interested in the very different legend of Orpheus's dismemberment by the maenads, or female followers of Dionysus. Because the maenad – a figure who, as we shall see, plays a role in *A Mask* as well – never attacks women but only beasts or men, a curious situation arises. Both of Comus's parents represent dangers that cannot overtake the Lady; rather, they would make her the bearer of a threat to men.

The thematic oppositions of *A Mask* are therefore questioned from its inception. That Dionysus should help begin this process is only appropriate, as in Hellenic culture he was the god of contradictions, embodying not so much a specific mythic or ritual content as a set of operations: Dionysus is a liminal god who either mediates or collapses or overthrows the structural oppositions on which Attic culture was based, oppositions that include male and female, citizen and slave, culture and nature, Greek and barbarian.[3] As even this partial list suggests, however, these are structures of domination as well as opposition. In *The Bacchae* and elsewhere, Dionysus overturns the oppressive structures that establish a dominant culture of Greek male citizens on the one hand, and, on the other, a world of slaves, women, barbarians and nature, which, through domination or exclusion, constitute the collective otherness of Greek culture.[4] Dionysus embodies the breaking in or revolt of this cultural otherness. Maenadic worship directed its inverting energies against both the Attic state and the household. Practiced solely by women, the central ritual practice of maenadism was *omophagia*, or the eating of raw meat, which rejected cooking both as the basis of the state religion[5] and as the duty of a wife. Omophagia exemplified the thoroughgoing primitivism of maenadism, which, by reverting from culture to nature, temporarily evaded the patriarchal structures of both *polis* and *oikos*. Hence the wearing of animal skins, for example, abjured the traditional wifely tasks of weaving and spinning, and ecstatic dancing through the wood temporarily released women from the isolation and imprisonment of the Greek household.

In its animalism and its ecstatic dancing, maenadism presages Comus's orgiastic revels. Yet, as depicted by Euripides and others, maenadism was also chaste; bacchants did not drink wine or engage in sexual activity.[6] The amorous and cup-bearing Comus derives from a comic Bacchism that must be distinguished from the austere practices of maenadism, although it is precisely a function of Dionysian ambivalence that the god can encompass both chastity and promiscuity, asceticism and intoxication. Both strains emerge in Comus's seduction speech:

> It is for homely features to keep home,
> They had their name thence: coarse complexions
> And cheeks of sorry grain will serve to ply
> The sampler, and to tease the housewife's wool.
> What need a vermeil-tinctured lip for that
> Love-darting eyes, or tresses like the morn?
>
> (747–52)

The insinuating and aristocratic rhetoric of the cavalier poet, which expresses the promiscuity of comic Bacchism, also uncovers a maenadic theme: Dionysus will free the housewife from her spinning. By collapsing liberation into yet another seduction, Milton signals the dominance of the comic over the tragic Dionysus. Yet the ghost of maenadism still haunts the masque. When the heavenly spirit, disguised as the shepherd Thyrsis, fables his recent encounter with Comus's band, he patterns his tale after Orpheus's encounter with the maenads:

> I sat me down to watch upon a bank
> With ivy canopied, and interwove
> With flaunting honeysuckle, and began
> Wrapt in a pleasing fit of melancholy
> To meditate my rural minstrelsy,
> Till fancy had her fill, but ere a close

> The wonted roar was up amidst the woods,
> And filled the air with barbarous dissonance.
>
> (543–50)

The phrase 'barbarous dissonance' reappears in the invocation to book 7 of *Paradise Lost*, whose explicit subject is Orpheus's dismemberment. Milton thus specifies the implied subtext of this earlier scene, which offers a menace to the male poet and not to the female protagonist.

Bacchus is introduced to reinforce the distinction between the Lady and Comus, which in turn expresses oppositions between temperance and intemperance, chastity and promiscuity. The logical as well as the practical substance of Milton's ethic rests on the discreteness of categories, to which the Lady gives dramatic expression by refusing Comus's advances. The univocal signification of allegory also reinforces this discreteness. But by embracing both sexual abstinence and excess, the Dionysian mode threatens to collapse the ruling antithesis of Milton's masque. For if aggressive virginity characterizes maenadism, then the Lady is already somehow Bacchic. A subterranean connivance between Comus and the Lady tends to undercut their ostensible opposition.

The formal disruption of *A Mask* both expresses and substitutes for a conceptual *aporeia*: virginity and promiscuity turn out to be doubles, not antitheses. The basis of this specular or imaginary reversal is, however, neither psychological nor semiological but ideological and political. More specifically, it derives from the contradictory place of women within Puritan sexual ideology, particularly with respect to the concepts of virginity and chastity. Roberta Hamilton has observed that the cultural prestige of women rose in England in the transition from Catholicism to Protestantism, even as their material condition declined in the virtually simultaneous transition from feudalism to capitalism.[7] One sign of this increased cultural prestige was the replacement of the Catholic ideal of female virginity with the Protestant ideal of chastity, that is, of a monogamous marital relationship. For the Puritans, woman was no longer a vessel of sin, a whore of Babylon whose sexuality was fearful and deadly, but a 'helpmeet' for men, secondary in authority and yet primary as an embodiment of domestic purity. The reasons for this change are several: one was the Puritans' rather uncanny understanding of the importance of family life as a sphere for political and religious indoctrination; another was the Puritan doctrine of the priesthood of all true believers, which by its very logic demanded a rough equality for women.

This new cultural prestige helped Milton to choose a woman as the hero of his masque, a choice he was not again inclined to make after his marriage to Mary Powell. Yet the tension between the logic of feminine equality and the desire to impose a patriarchal family structure was one

of the primary contradictions within Puritanism, expressing itself in the
conflict between patriarchal Presbyterianism and radical sectarianism,
the latter of which often supported both female and sexual liberation.

The sectarians attacked the Puritan family most directly by holding
that a wife who was a true believer could divorce a heretical or
atheistical husband. In *Tetrachordon*, Milton himself writes that 'the
wife also, as her subjection is terminated in the Lord, herself being the
redeemed of Christ, is not still bound to be the vassal of him who is the
bondslave of Satan.'[8] Milton's language recalls the conflict between the
Lady and Comus in his masque. Yet Milton was palpably uncomfortable
with this position and more generally held that the husband could
unilaterally divorce the wife.

Katherine Chidley gave a more spirited defense of woman's
independence in 1641: 'I pray you tell me,' she says, 'what authority [the]
unbelieving husband hath over the conscience of his believing wife; it is
true he hath authority over her in bodily and civil respects, but not to
be a lord over her conscience.'[9] In the same key, Milton's Lady warns
Comus,

> Thou canst not touch the freedom of my mind
> With all thy charms, although this corporal rind
> Thou hast immanacled, while heaven sees good.

(662–4)

The Lady, of course, is not yet a wife, although the masque intends
that she eventually become one.[10] Yet in her speeches and those of her
brothers, the words *virginity* and *chastity* are interchangeable, reflecting
the Puritan belief that they are related and sequential virtues: the virginal
girl becomes the chaste wife.[11] But the reasoning of the radical sectarians
may also obtrude itself here.[12] If Christian liberty allows the virginal girl
to refuse her seducer, might it not also allow the married woman to
refuse her husband?

The dispute between Presbyterians and radical sectarians realized
certain tensions that were always inherent in Puritan sexual ideology. In
particular, the relation between virginity and chastity was more difficult
than it might initially seem. In a purely empirical sense, of course, both
stand opposed to sexual promiscuity by imposing a partial or total
limitation on sexual activity. And the practice of patrimonial inheritance
required both virginity and chastity, in sequence, to insure the legitimacy
of the male line. Here it is a question of who controls, owns or deploys
female sexuality. The virginity of the pubescent or unmarried girl, held as
untainted goods for the future husband or owner, comprises a passive
virginity that suits a system of patriarchal control. Not only did the
Puritan husband own his wife's sexuality in marriage, he owned it in
advance.

Sectarian doctrine on divorce, however, suggested that a woman could, under certain circumstances, recoup her own person and sexuality. This repudiation of the husband's ownership I will call active virginity, a mode of sexual revolt at least as old as Lysistrata. If matrimonial monogamy, or chastity, is the dominant form of sexual control, then both promiscuity and active virginity violate it, although in different ways. Hence the uncanny doubling of apparent opposites in *A Mask*. The virtuous resistance of the Lady may become revolt if it is not relinquished at the proper moment. In excess, both virginity and sexuality overturn domestic rule.

Of course, the maenad was not the only figure for the fierce virgin available to Renaissance poetry. Amazons and the nymphs of Diana also withold their sexuality in ways that make them independent, strange, and frightening to men. All of these figures mark the point at which virginity ceases to denote submission and begins to denote revolt, at which purification becomes danger. In all of these cases, moreover, active virginity is marked by wandering, which contrasts with the stasis of domestic life. Here spatial containment figures political containment, and the freedom of the wilderness illuminates the structures of domestic space. Renaissance gynecological theory reproduced this figure by holding that the female uterus was an independent animal prone to wander from its proper place if not stabilized by regular insertion of the husbandly penis.[13] The virgin's wandering uterus is not unlike Diana, or the maenad, wandering through the hills, while the chaste or housewifely uterus, by contrast, is pinned in its place. It is one of the ironies of Milton's masque, then, that Comus captures and binds the wandering Lady. If, in one sense, this serves as a prelude to Bacchic perversion, in another it tames maenadic eccentricity. Comus seems to betray his father's epithet *Lyaeus*, 'the looser' or 'the releaser'.

A question may arise: if *A Mask* works to reject or suppress the figure of the maenad, why does it extol the other fierce virgins? When the Second Brother asks what power can protect his supposedly helpless sister, his Elder Brother replies, in language that recalls Spenser's Britomart,

'Tis chastity, my brother, chastity:
She that has that, is clad in complete steel,
And like a quivered nymph with arrows keen
May trace huge forests, and unharboured heaths,
Infamous hills, and sandy perilous wilds,
Where through the sacred rays of chastity,
No savage fierce, bandit, or mountaineer
Will dare to soil her virgin purity.

(419–26)

He then invokes the goddess Diana, who, he says,

> set at nought
> The frivolous bolt of Cupid, gods and men
> Feared her stern frown, and she was queen o' the woods.
>
> (444–6)

The mythological panoply of the virgin queen, as it had been applied to Elizabeth, accompanies the usual explicit threat to men and the almost obligatory hints of castration or male sexual impotence. Since Acteon fared no better than Pentheus, one might ask why a masque that can celebrate Diana balks at the Greek Dionysus.

While Diana and the maenad both evade the household regime, their differing modes of doing so make the one tolerable and the other not. Diana's nymphs are virgins from birth; they simply abjure the domestic sphere while leaving it intact. Diana may be the patroness of virginity, but she also doubles as the patroness of childbirth. As consecrated figures, her nymphs are set off from the mass of women; the mythology surrounding Elizabeth, for example, regularly emphasized her singularity or uniqueness. By contrast, maenadism does not ignore the household; it ruptures it from within, as its votaries are wives and household slaves. For Puritanism, virginity before marriage is fine; virginity instead of marriage is less fine; but virginity within marriage, conceived as an explosive release from the domestic sphere, posed a grave threat at a time when the household was crucial as an arena for control but when sectarians were beginning to formulate dangerous ideas about a woman's right to release herself from wedlock. For Milton, then, the maenad mythologically embodies the logic of Christian liberty as it applied to women. The poet's anxiety takes the form of a figure who threatens not only the corporeal integrity of men but also the integrity of the household as an arena for patriarchal control.

'Licence they mean when they cry liberty,' writes Milton in his twelfth sonnet, attacking those who misunderstood his divorce tracts. Bacchus, also known as Liber, marks the point at which, from Milton's perspective, Liber-ty exceeds its proper limits and becomes license. From another perspective, we may say that he marks the point at which liberty fulfills itself beyond the bounds set by Puritanism. Nathaniel Henry argued thirty years ago that Milton's twelfth sonnet is directed not against conservative Presbyterians offended by Milton's radicalism but against those radical sectarians who practiced what Milton preached.[14] Henry quotes Thomas Edwards's *Gangraena*, an attack on sectarianism published in 1644, where Edwards records that a Mrs Attaway, 'the mistress of all the she-preachers on Coleman Street', came to consider leaving her husband after reading Milton on divorce. Mrs Attaway, a kind of seventeenth-century maenad, embodied the feminine 'licence' that Milton attacks in the sonnet's opening quatrain:

> I did but prompt the age to quit their clogs
> By the known rules of ancient liberty,
> When straight a barbarous noise environs me
> Of owls and cuckoos, asses, apes, and dogs.

By recalling Comus's band of revelers, this barbarous menagerie further clarifies the issues at stake in that earlier work.

In Milton's masque, the antidote to maenadism is offered by Sabrina, the nymph of the lake, who again represents both virginity and chastity. Sabrina's martyrdom – she drowns herself to avoid her 'enraged stepdame' – has strong Christian overtones. But she also resolves a problem that blocks the way to the masque's implicitly hymeneal ending. Sabrina plays the part of the scapegoat, a structural necessity within the comic form. The evil that she bears off is nothing other than female aggressiveness – that of her almost maenadic stepdame – which, in imitation of Christian martyrdom, she wonderfully learns to turn against her own person. Where can maenadic violence safely be redirected? Why, at woman herself, who can become chaste only after she has sacrificed the power over her own sexuality. The Lady in Milton's masque is thus saved from imprisonment by Comus only in order that she may learn self-imprisonment at the hands of Christ. Thence the Lady is returned safe to her father's house (safe for whom, one wonders), and Thyrsis treats us to a heavenly vision at whose summit,

> Celestial Cupid . . . advanced,
> Holds his dear Psyche sweet entranced
> After her wandering labours long,
> Till free consent the gods among
> Make her his eternal bride.

> (1003–7)

Psyche, rescued from wandering, is *held* 'sweet entranced' while Cupid has finally found a place to stick his 'frivolous bolt'. 'Free consent', the liberty that, the Spirit tells us, only virtue can bestow, has somehow been transferred to the gods, for Psyche finds *herself* bestowed upon Cupid. Celestial visions, especially Milton's, have a peculiar way of reproducing, in sublimated form, the worst aspects of life on earth, rather in the way that hitting your thumb with a hammer can cause you to see stars. In *A Mask*, heavenly bliss seems to be only a trope for wedded bliss, with the result that no space remains for woman's liberty, even beyond the 'sphery chime'.

II

The sexual drama of *A Mask* arises from an historically specific struggle over the mode of reproduction, a struggle that is complexly interrelated with the struggle over the mode of production. The dynamic of the bourgeois marriage was founded by Protestantism at the same time that the bourgeois class was undertaking its two great historical tasks: wresting political power from the feudal aristocracy and seizing the means of production from the working class. Bourgeois strategies of sexual domination and of class exploitation mutually inform each other.

The Dionysian mythology of Milton's masque illustrates this intersection between class and gender struggles, for Dionysus (as well as his offspring, Comus) plays the same ambiguous role in class conflict that he does in gender conflict. The burlesque transvestitism that ends Pentheus's sexual mastery in *The Bacchae* also ends his tyranny over Thebes. Dionysis seems to emerge as a god of the people,[15] yet he becomes demagogic when he attempts to assert his divine birthright and extort worship from the Thebans.

The class ambiguities of Dionysian worship are reborn in Comus's festivities, which are both popular and courtly. While the tumult of his antimasque partakes of the popular mumming and misrule on which the masque form traditionally builds, Comus's castle and specious feast clearly represent the decadence of aristocratic entertainments. The speech in which the lady denounces Comus's apparently spontaneous copia as the product of a maldistribution of wealth (756–79) may be taken as the poet's critique of courtly festivity, including the masque, which mimics the more 'natural' entertainments of a peasantry that it simultaneously exploits. When Comus disguises himself as a shepherd, he belatedly reassumes the tired dress of Spenser, Sidney and his other courtly predecessors.

Yet if *A Mask* exposes courtly masquing as a decadent imitation, it holds that the original of this imitation is no less decadent. Puritanism made no secret of its desire to eradicate rural festivity, particularly Maypole dancing. Country sports represented everything about the 'old Adam' that had to be eradicated or reformed by Christian discipline: these sports were sensual where the Puritans were ascetic, abandoned where they were restrained, pagan where they were Protestant. Maypole dancing defamed the Sabbath, and its adherents were dangerously prone to superstition and popery. It was spontaneous, anarchic and leisurely when the times called for rigor and industry.[16]

The attempt to suppress country sports was a simple expression of the inability of Puritanism, as an urban bourgeois ideology, to assimilate the culture of the rural working class. Rural festivity was the vestigial form of a petty producing culture, now inherited only by the proletarianized stratum of that class. Maypole dancers were soon enough to fill the ranks of Digger radicalism and to threaten Puritanism with a revolution within the revolution. A Puritan minister complained in 1660 that May games made 'the servant contemn his master, the people their pastor, the subject his sovereign, the child his father', and taught 'young people impudence and rebellion'.[17] For their part, rural laborers were not particularly eager to be reformed along Puritan lines. 'The phallic maypole was for the rural lower class almost a symbol of independence of their betters: . . . In Stratford-on-Avon in 1619 popular libels were distributed, attacking the Puritan ruling group and calling for maypoles. The Puritans were described as economic oppressors, twisters of the law.'[18] In the grotesque merriment of Comus's band lies not only the sexual but also the class threat of Dionysus. It endangers Puritan patriarchy as a specifically bourgeois patriarchy, that is, as the patriarchy of what was soon to be the new ruling class.

This class contradiction also expresses itself as a rural–urban antagonism, particularly as Puritan disdain for pagan festivities in the 'dark corners of the land', of which Wales, the setting for Milton's masque, was one of the most notorious.[19] The murky woods of *A Mask* represent the spiritual as well as the physical darkness of the Welsh landscape, where popular affinities for both May games and Catholicism were rampant. Comus may be taken as a *genius loci* of this 'dark corner', and his followers as the local rambunctious peasantry. The Lady herself suggests this identification when she mistakes Comus's revels for country sports:

> This way the noise was, if mine ear be true,
> My best guide now, methought it was the sound
> Of riot, and ill-managed merriment,
> Such as the jocund flute, or gamesome pipe
> Stirs up among the loose unlettered hinds,
> When for their teeming flocks, and granges full,
> In wanton dance they praise the bounteous Pan,
> And thank the gods amiss. I should be loth
> To meet the rudeness, and swilled insolence
> Of such late wassailers.

(169–78)

While the Lady seems implicitly to fear a sexual assault, her language dwells on region and social class – appropriately enough, since rural festivities were viewed as orgiastic by urban Puritans, whose mouthpiece she seems to be here.

If Puritanism objected to country sports, however, the monarchy was pleased to encourage them as a means of social control. Not only were they traditional royalist symbols, but they were deemed preferable to meetings in alehouses and coventicles where seditious ideas might be discussed. Further, encouraging the games enlisted the support of the rural masses against the Puritans.[20] On the other hand, the crown also recognized the connection between country sports and recusancy. *The Book of Sports*, first issued by James in 1617 and later reissued by both James and Charles, sought to promote country sports within limits, 'the same to be had in due & convenient time, without impediment or neglect of Divine Service'.[21]

Royal encouragement of country sports partly underlies that doubling whereby Comus appears as both a wanton country dancer and a dissolute aristocrat. In this he simply imitates his original in Jonson's *Pleasure Reconciled To Virtue*, a masque that celebrates James's *via media* in attempting to reform without destroying both country and courtly pleasures.[22] Jonson's masque depicts the Stuart court as an Hesperian realm, which refines the antimasque of Comus into a chaster footing, banishing the excesses of courtier and clown while avoiding the opposite extreme of Puritan prudishness.

Milton's satiric riposte to Jonson begins when Comus leads his riotous dances under the light of Hesperus, an acknowledgement that none of Jonson's moralizing was ever able to moralize the English court. When the Lady attacks Comus for his prodigality, she does so in language that would have been unthinkable, and indeed downright dangerous, in a royal masque:

> If every just man that now pines with want
> Had but a moderate and beseeming share
> Of that which lewdly-pampered Luxury
> Now heaps upon some few with vast excess,
> Nature's full blessings would be well-dispensed
> In unsuperfluous even proportion,
> And she no whit encumbered with her store,
> And then the giver would be better thanked,
> His praise due paid, for swinish gluttony
> Ne'er looks to heaven amidst his gorgeous feast,
> But with besotted base ingratitude
> Crams, and blasphemes his feeder.

> (767–78)

The Lady's reasoning begins to move beyond the ethical to the structural; she attacks the morals of the aristocracy less than she does their position as a ruling class (I fail to see how Alice Egerton and her family could avoid applying this speech to themselves). It is hard to imagine how personal temperance could solve the maldistribution of wealth described here; hence Jonsonian exhortations give way to an unspecified threat. At

239

the same time, however, the masque seems to approve of the poor only when they are suffering, not celebrating.[23] The decline of the Hesperian indicates not only the debauchery of the Stuart court but a movement from the western realm of England to the even further western realm of Wales, where the rural poor were felt to be especially savage and superstitious. Milton's masque begins in an age too late for Jonsonian compromise and suggests that both ends of the social scale have gotten out of hand.

In what is both a political and rhetorical ploy, Milton resolves this problem by appropriating the Jacobean–Anglican *via media*, or middle way, for the Puritan middle class. When the Lady first hears Comus's band, which she mistakes for a group of country revelers, she sounds less like a country aristocrat than like a Puritan bourgeois. Only the middle class, Milton seems to say, can steer a chaste course between the debaucheries of the aristocracy and those of the rural laboring class, just as chastity itself, the bourgeois form of sexual control, avoids the extremes of savage virginity and promiscuity.

The offending practices of popular festivity, to which the coordinated class and gender controls of Puritanism respond, do not stop at unrestrained sexuality, however. [24] In addition, 'popular festivals and customs . . . show much play with switches in sex roles and much attention to women on top.'[25] Husband-beating, for instance, formed a frequent theme for festivals and at least once provided the basis for a courtly entertainment. John Lydgate wrote the speeches for 'A Mumming at Herford', which was performed for King Henry VI around 1430. The manuscript describes it as 'a disguysing of the rude vplandisshe people compleyning on hir wyves, with the boystous [sic] aunswere of hir wyves'.[26] In this proto-masque, 'certeyne sweynes' present themselves to the king in order to complain

> Vpon the trouble and the crueltee
> Which that they haue endured in theyre lyves
> By the felnesse of theyre fierce wyves.

(11–13)

These wives, they say, stay out drinking all day, refuse to cook dinner, beat them with distaffs, scratch their faces with their nails, and pummel them until they bleed. When it comes their turn to speak, the wives defend rather than deny their ferocity:

> Touching the substance of this hyeghe discorde,
> We sixe wyves beon ful of oon acorde
> Yif wordes and chyding may vs not avaylle,
> We wol darrein it in chaumpcloos by bataile.

(163–7)

This was about as near to maenadism as England was going to get.[27] Lydgate's disorderly wives not only represent class and gender revolt but, by acting as a group, they also provide a model for mass disobedience, something that exceptional figures like Britomart cannot do.[28] The incredible strength of the maenads is no doubt a physiological effect of religious ecstasy; but it may also figure forth the strength of the collective.

In Milton's masque, the threat of the rural masses is, by a familiar trope, portrayed as bestialism: Comus's cup 'transforms [the face] of him that drinks, / And the inglorious likeness of a beast / Fixes instead' (527–9). The ferocity of country wives thus assumes a theriomorphic form, 'like stabled wolves, or tigers at their prey' (533). Peasants are explicitly transformed into animals in the twelfth sonnet, where the 'barbarous noise' of Milton's detractors reminds him of 'when those hinds that were transformed to frogs / Railed at Latona's twin-born progeny.' Here the class allegory is relatively unproblematic: the poor who have the nerve to rise against their betters – Milton, in this case – are turned into animals (apparently, the next lowest step on the cosmological scale), thereby enacting the already-present equation between Ovid's *rustica turba* and Milton's 'owls and cuckoos, asses, apes, and dogs'. Nathaniel Henry notes that 'Mrs Attaway . . . was apparently uneducated and belonged to a social and economic level considerably different from that of Milton,'[29] as did most of the radical sectarians. Fear of maenadism is not only fear of women, then, but also fear of the working class mob, whose turbulence threatens the crystalline integrity of the bourgeois order.[30]

All of the inversions discussed above are conceived as somehow alien, imported by the foreigner Comus to plague the order of English Puritan culture. The Dionysian antinomy between Greek and barbarian thus asserts itself, here figured primarily as an opposition between England and Wales, although this national opposition in turn represents breaks within English culture. Ben Jonson had already played with the 'barbarous' Welsh tongue in his masque, *For the Honor of Wales*, a piece that evidently influenced *A Mask*.[31] The 'barbarous dissonance' of Comus's crew probably alludes in part to the unintelligible Celtic speech of the Welsh peasantry.[32] Yet as Jonson's masque suggests, the concept of the barbarous is not strictly limited to the tongues of a different national or ethnic group. For even when Jonson's peasants speak English – a comically grotesque exaggeration of the dialect in some of Spenser's eclogues – they are difficult to understand. The absolute incomprehensibility of the Welsh, a pure linguistic otherness, becomes a hyperbolic trope for class and regional differences within the same linguistic system. The discourse of the peasantry as a class is 'barbarous' and unassimilable to the court and to the urban bourgeoisie.

Comus, who roved 'the Celtic and Iberian fields' (60) before settling in Wales, represents the barbarian or foreign in general, just as Dionysus does in *The Bacchae*. Yet Dionysus, who comes from Asia Minor but claims his birthright in Thebes, confuses the distinction between native and barbarian. Milton introduces similar perplexities by locating his masque in Wales, so that a 'native' or English culture breaks in on a foreign one and thus finds itself in the situation of an alien intruder. When Comus greets the Lady with the words 'Hail foreign wonder', he introduces a dangerous cultural relativism (and further obscures the distinction between himself and the Lady). The structural opposition between native and barbarian can be stabilized only by the dominance of one culture over the other: in this case, of England's over Wales's. When the Lady defeats Comus, her victory is an imperial one that definitively inscribes Wales as the inferior or barbarian culture.[33]

But maenadism entails the concept of the barbarian or foreign not only because it comes from a strange land but also because the maenad becomes foreign or alien to men by forfeiting her domesticity. In *The Bacchae*, therefore, the Theban wives come to resemble the Lydian women, even surpassing them in ferocity, when they take up maenadic practices. The opposition of inner/outer, which defines the problem of barbarism, situates itself on the border of a space in which the *oikos* and the *polis* become one: in which, that is, the interior of the household represents civilization (for women, at least), and its exterior represents savagery or barbarism. To redomesticate the Theban wives would be to resanctify the cultural borders of the state as a whole, to close the wound that Dionysus has inflicted on its limit.[34]

While this project fails spectacularly in *The Bacchae*, patriarchy and imperialism do triumph together in *A Mask*. The site of their linguistic intersection is the word *home*, which signifies both the domestic sphere and the familiarity of English culture. Upon first hearing the Lady sing, Comus declares that

> such a sacred, and home-felt delight,
> Such sober certainty of waking bliss
> I never heard till now.

> (261–3)

The Lady's song temporarily 'domesticates' the reveler and in so doing renders him conscious of his own foreignness. This moment presages her eventual return to her father's house and the triumph of its civilizing values. On the way, however, she must resist Comus's offer to separate her from those 'homely features . . . [who] keep home' (747), for acceptance would transform her into a 'foreign wonder' in relation to her own native English culture.

The coincidental problems of femininity and barbarism are, however, not only a structural or mythic base for Milton's masque; they are, I would argue, consciously taken up into its allegorical code. For the root haemony, which Thyrsis offers as protection against Comus's spells, represents married chastity as a vehicle for both patriarchal and imperial domination. When the Elder Brother suggest a martial assault on Comus in order to liberate his sister, Thyrsis replies,

> Alas good venturous youth,
> I love thy courage yet, and bold emprise,
> But here thy sword can do thee little stead,
> Far other arms, and other weapons must
> Be those that quell the might of hellish charms,
> He with his bare wand can unthread thy joints,
> And crumble all thy sinews.

> (608–14)

The sword and the wand invoke the two extreme forms of sexuality between which the masque tries to steer a middle course. The sword represents an anti-erotic aggressiveness that has already been associated with virginity through the figure of armed Diana. The wand, by contrast, represents the promiscuous phallic sexuality of Comus. Because these ostensible opposites are actually allied within Puritan ideology, the brothers' armed attack on Comus would be co-opted, just as the Lady's 'armed' virginity was.

Thyrsis, however, finds a better way. A shepherd lad once taught him the secrets of herbs, he claims, and

> Amongst the rest a small unsightly root,
> But of divine effect, he culled me out;
> The leaf was darkish, and had prickles on it,
> But in another country, as he said,
> Bore a bright golden flower, but not in this soil:
> Unknown, and like esteemed, and the dull swain
> Treads on it daily with his clouted shoon,
> And yet more med'cinal is it than the Moly
> That Hermes once to wise Ulysses gave;
> He called it haemony, and gave it me,
> And bade me keep it as of sovran use
> 'Gainst all enchantments, mildew blast, or damp
> Or ghastly Furies' apparition.

> (628–40)

Such are the horizons of Milton's vision that yet a third phallus is found to 'liberate' the Lady. The reference to moly suggests that female sexuality is the real culprit here, the primary object of resistance and

243

control. Although both the wand and the sword only encourage its recalcitrance, the humbler haemony is able to master its magic. Most interpretations of haemony have placed it within a theological allegory, which indeed is clearly present. Yet whatever else it may be, as a cure for sexual magic, haemony seems to represent married chastity – boring, perhaps, and unsightly in appearance, but powerful in its effects. Such an interpretation seems at least not to violate the literary context. That the 'dull swain / Treads on it [haemony] daily with his clouted shoon' may refer to the traditional lower-class rejection of church marriage, a practice that horrified Puritans and that was particularly prevalent in those rural 'dark corners' where church and state had difficulty enforcing their jurisdiction. 'Norden the surveyor,' writes Christopher Hill,

> spoke of people bred amongst the woods, 'dwelling far from any church or chapel,' who 'were as ignorant of God or of any civil course of life as the very savages amongst the infidels.' Contemporaries explained the whoredoms of the Welsh by the mountain air: the modern historian more wisely sees them as the natural product of a society which refused to accept English protestant marriage laws.[35]

One wonders whether, according to Hill's own argument, contemporaries weren't at least dimly aware of the true reasons for the 'whoredoms of the Welsh'. At least, they tended to treat Wales as a particularly noxious 'dark corner'.

In such a context, the opposition between 'this soil' and 'another country' takes on a more than merely theological resonance: it distinguishes between the soil of Wales, where the masque occurs and where the 'whoredoms' of the inhabitants blind them to the virtues of Protestant marriage, and that other country, England, where married chastity bears its bright flower of sexual and social control. In this remarkable moment, then, the gender, class and imperial codes of the masque seem temporarily to coalesce. Wales provides a barbarian setting (which in itself offers a hyperbolic nightmare image of the rural proletariat) where 'savage' marital practices release the dangers of feminine sexuality. Woman can be rehoused but not on this soil and amongst this class; English bourgeois life provides the proper 'home' for the home itself.

Notes

1. SPENSER's 'Epithalamion' is exemplary in this respect.
2. All quotations of Milton are taken from *The Poetry of John Milton*, eds John Carey and Alastair Fowler (London: Longman, 1968).
3. See CHARLES SEGAL, *Dionysiac Poetics and Euripides' Bacchae* (Princeton, N.J.: Princeton University Press, 1982).

4. I should note that while my essay emphasizes those aspects of Dionysian rite and myth that tended to liberate women, other aspects served patriarchal culture. 'Dionysus,' writes Segal, 'in his birth from Zeus's "immortal fire" and "male womb" acts out a fantasy of the male's independence from the female cycles of menstruation and birth, with their attendant uncleanness, and achieves that independence from the female which recurs wishfully throughout early Greek culture' (p. 181).

5. See MARCEL DETIENNE, *Dionysos Slain*, trans. Mirielle and Leonard Muellner (Baltimore: Johns Hopkins University Press, 1979), Chap. 3.

6. See ALBERT HENRICHS, 'Greek Maenadism from Olympias to Messalina', *Harvard Studies in Classical Philology* 82 (1978): 121–60.

7. ROBERTA HAMILTON, *The Liberation of Women: A Study of Patriarchy and Capitalism* (London: Allen & Unwin, 1978).

8. Quoted by DAVID AERS and BOB HODGE, ' "Rational Burning": Milton on Sex and Marriage', *Milton Studies* 13 (1979): 3–33, *q.v.*

9. Quoted in HAMILTON, *Liberation of Women*, p. 66.

10. There has been some controversy over this point, which turns primarily on whether the marriage of Cupid and Psyche (1004–11) fortells an earthly or heavenly marriage for the Lady. I prefer the former interpretation, as does Tillyard. The generally hymeneal associations of the masque form aside, the notion of perpetual virginity would seem inappropriate to the masque's occasion. The Egertons, one assumes, hoped that their daughter Alice would wed some day. Of course, Cupid and Psyche are cut from the Bridgewater version, as is almost all of the Spirit's final song. Yet even lines 887–90 of the Bridgewater version (966–9 in the 1637 text) celebrate the virtues of earthly generation:

> Noble Lord, and Lady bright,
> I have brought ye new delight,
> Here behold so goodly grown
> Three fair branches of your own.

A Mask, it seems to me, must be read as describing a virginal *rite de passage*, which prepares the Lady for a chaste married life. I will return to this point later.

11. 'Chastity and purity of life consist either in sincere virginity, or in faithful matrimony.' WILLIAM BALDWIN, *A Treatise of Morall Philosophie* (1547), enlarged by Thomas Palfreyman (1620; reprint, Gainesville, Fla.: Scholars' Press, 1967), p. 246. I am not suggesting that there is anything unusual about Milton's usage: *chastity* is a common synonym for *virginity*.

12. I am not suggesting a direct influence, for the simple reason that the outburst of radical thought on sex and matrimony did not occur until the 1640s, whereas *A Mask* was written in 1634. Then, too, Milton's being still unmarried meant that he had not considered these questions with the seriousness that he would after 1642. Nevertheless, as I will go on to suggest, there is a remarkable ideological and poetic continuity between *A Mask*, the twelfth sonnet (*c.* 1646), and *Paradise Lost* on all of the issues discussed here. Spenser had already found it necessary to navigate the difficult course from virginity to chastity; the ideological contradictions were already in place, although a revolutionary culture had not yet released them.

245

13. See ILZA VEITH, *Hysteria: The History of a Disease* (Chicago: University of Chicago Press, 1965), pp. 130–1 and *passim*.
14. NATHANIEL H. HENRY, 'Who Meant License When They Cried Liberty?' *MLN* 66 (1951): 509–13.
15. Early on, the chorus of Asian maenads sings,

> It is wise to withold one's heart and mind
> from men who think themselves superior.
> Whatever the multitude,
> the ordinary people, take as normal and practice, this would
> I accept.
>
> (G.S. Kirk, trans. [Cambridge:
> Cambridge University Press, 1979], lines 427–33)

Even in Hellenic and Hellenistic culture, however, maenadism does not seem to have been entirely democratic. 'It seems very unlikely that maenadism was ubiquitous in Greek lands, or that in places where it existed admission was invariably open to every woman who wanted to be a maenad: at least in Athens, Delphi, and perhaps Thebes maenadism was restricted to selected groups of women' (HENRICHS, 'Greek Maenadism', p. 153). Apparently, women often bought contracts for the right to lead maenadic bands.

16. See CHRISTOPHER HILL, 'The Uses of Sabbatarianism', in *Society and Puritanism in Pre-Revolutionary England* (New York: Schocken, 1964), pp. 145–218. MARYANN CALE McGUIRE also treats the 'sports controversy' at length in the first chapter of her book, *Milton's Puritan Masque* (Athens: University of Georgia Press, 1983).
17. Quoted in HILL, 'Uses of Sabbatarianism', pp. 193–4.
18. *Ibid.*, pp. 184–5.
19. See CHRISTOPHER HILL, 'Puritans and the "Dark Corners of the Land"', in *Change and Continuity in Seventeenth Century England* (Cambridge: Harvard University Press, 1975). The *literal* setting of Milton's masque was Ludlow castle, which was near the Welsh border but still in England. Yet the masque's occasion would seem to demand at least an oblique reference to the Earl of Bridgewater's new status as Lord President of Wales. The pacification of this 'dark corner' forms one important element of what is a symbolically overdetermined landscape.
20. This discussion is heavily indebted to LEAH SINANOGLOU MARCUS, 'The Occasion of Ben Jonson's *Pleasure Reconciled to Virtue*', *SEL* 19 (1979): 271–93.
21. Quoted in *ibid.*, p. 278.
22. See *ibid.*, *passim*.
23. See lines 321–5. The shepherds are allowed an antic dance at the end of the masque, but even this chastened festivity is soon dismissed by Thyrsis: 'Back, shepherds, back; enough your play' (957).
24. Apparently, country sports were often as abandoned as their opponents claimed. Manslaughter and unwanted pregnancies were not infrequent results, as Hill has documented, adding, 'We must be very careful not to sentimentalize ye olde morrice dances of Merrie England' ('Uses of Sabbatarianism', pp. 190–1).
25. NATALIE ZEMON DAVIS, 'Women on Top: Symbolic Sexual Inversion and Political Disorder in Early Modern Europe', reprinted in *The Reversible World:*

Symbolic Inversion in Art and Society (Ithaca, NY: Cornell University Press, 1978), pp. 147–90.

26. *The Minor Poems of John Lydgate*, ed. H.N. MacCracken (London: EETS, 1934), pp. 675–82. Information on the masque's performance from STEPHEN ORGEL, *The Jonsonian Masque* (Cambridge: Harvard University Press, 1965), p. 20.

27. JOHN STEADMAN cites some interesting classical and medieval sources that held that Maenadic rites, including *sparagmos*, took place in Britain. 'A Mask at Ludlow: Comus and Dionysiac Revel', in *Nature into Myth: Medieval and Renaissance Moral Symbols* (Pittsburgh: Duquesne University Press, 1979), pp. 213–40.

28. See DAVIS, 'Women on Top', pp. 151–7.

29. HENRY, 'Who Meant License', p. 512.

30. These two fears (of women and of the mob) are not unrelated and indeed had a basis in social reality. Writes DAVIS, 'In England in the early seventeenth century . . . a significant percentage of the rioters against enclosure and for common land were female' (176).

31. *For the Honor of Wales* was a direct rewriting of *Pleasure Reconciled to Virtue*, emended to eliminate Comus (whose satiric resemblence to dissolute courtiers cut too close for James's taste) and to celebrate Prince Charles's recent investiture as Prince of Wales (MARCUS, 'The Occasion of Jonson's *Pleasure*', pp. 291–3):

> [I]n place of *Pleasure Reconciled to Virtue*'s heroic triumphs over the dangerous opposites of puritanism and popery, *For the Honor of Wales* offers humor and palliatives: the satire against overfeasting and drinking is abandoned for praise of plain Welsh food and drink, and an invitation to James to feast in Wales; instead of an antimasque of boasting pygmies, which the Welsh claim to scorn, there are dances to the music of the 'ancient Welse [*sic*] harp' by proper British men and women.
>
> (p. 291)

'In Wales,' suggests JONSON, 'the king . . . will . . . find humble devotion to himself and his family, proper preservation of the old pastimes he encouraged through the *Book of Sports*, and measured feasting of the sort he recommended in the *Basilikon Doron*' (*ibid.*, pp. 291–2).

Milton's revisionary technique simply collapses Jonson's two masques into one. By reviving Comus he also revives Jonson's satire against the court; and by implanting him in Wales, he attacks Jonson's implication that there is anything 'measured' or 'proper' about Welsh festivity.

32. In the eleventh sonnet, MILTON defends the cacophonous title of *Tetrachordon* by comparing it favorably with the sound of Scots names:

> Why is it harder sirs than Gordon,
> Colkitto, or Macdonnel, or Galasp?
> Those rugged names to our like mouths grow sleek
> That would have made Quintillian stare and gasp.

In the manuscript, Milton originally wrote 'barbarian' in place of 'rugged'. Further, the reference to Quintillian concerns his warning (*Institutes*, 1.5.8) against allowing barbarous foreign words infect the purity of Latin. Milton apparently considers the Celtic tongue barbarous even when it is used by his allies.

33. In *The Bacchae*, by contrast, the foreign emerges as dominant, or at least manages to unsettle the dominance of the native. G.S. KIRK argues that the play's descriptions of foreign lands partly reflect the interests of 'the sophistic movement[, which] evinced a strong preoccupation with comparative ethnology and the collection of details about foreign lands and customs, partly with the intention of showing that "law" is a relative concept' (p. 26 note). Dionysus, who is both a foreigner and a sophist, complements his political assault on Thebes with an epistemological assault on the transcendence of the Greek *logos*. 'The contrast between . . . the joyful ecstasy of Dionysus and the traditional wisdom (*sophia*, 189) of the city of which the old men are the repository . . . [is an] aspect of the larger antithesis between the far and the near' (SEGAL, *Dionysiac Poetics*, p. 88). Dionysus undermines Pentheus's authority partly by deconstructing his claims to knowledge.

 Sophist ethnology was revived for the Renaissance by MONTAIGNE's essay *Of Cannibals* and by *The Tempest*, which not only drew on Montaigne but which provided, in Caliban, a literary model for Milton's Comus. Milton suppressed the radical implications of ethnological relativism, however, partly in order to inscribe a transcendental Christian *logos* and partly out of Protestant nationalism. Yet the ethnocentrism of *A Mask* had already been prepared for by Jonson, who regularly filled his antimasques with pygmies, Indians, and other 'barbarians' who were then symbolically tamed and subjugated by the power of the monarch.

34. In Philostratus's description of Comus, the concept of liminality becomes quite literal, for Comus is represented as standing at the doorway or threshold of the *thalamos* or marriage chamber. His position there, I think, is meant precisely to question the sanctity of limits, just as his followers do when they engage in transvestitism. The figure of Comus at the threshold was taken up by Renaissance illustrators, appearing in CARTARI's *Images of the Gods of the Ancients* and in BLAISE DE VIGNERE's French translation of Philostratus's *Images*. See the illustrations in *The Jonsonian Masque* or in STEADMAN, *Nature into Myth*.

35. HILL, *The World Turned Upside Down: Radical Ideas during the English Revolution* (New York: Penguin, 1975), p. 320.

10 Marvell's 'Horatian Ode' and the Politics of Genre*

DAVID NORBROOK

In his political reading of the Ode, David Norbrook refutes the New Critical belief in 'pure literature' and the 'isolated genius' who would transcend historical events through the use of balance and irony. He also counters a Marxist or a new historicist approach to the poem that would locate it in terms of a larger economic or cultural order. For Norbrook, the poem and the English Civil War were essentially political, occurring during an historical moment when an English republic seemed possible. Therefore he analyses the Ode in the context of the work of other English republicans, as well as their Roman predecessors. Through further comparison with Horace's monarchism and the uses of Horace by royalists, Norbrook contends that Marvell inverts generic expectations, and writes a poem which celebrates political liberty rather than courtly aestheticized politics. Norbrook does not deny the 'grim wit' of the poem, nor its ambiguities about Cromwell, but such ambiguities take shape in terms of the variety of attitudes among the republicans, carefully detailed here, rather than as evidence for Marvell's sympathy for the royalist cause.

'An Horatian Ode upon Cromwell's Return from Ireland' has played a central part in twentieth-century discussions of the relationship between poetry and politics. The poem has often been applauded for avoiding political partisanship, for maintaining an equal balance between Charles and Cromwell, between the arts of peace and war, between feudal and bourgeois orders, and so on.[1] But as critics have begun to situate the poem more closely in its historical context, that 'balance' has become harder and harder to locate. The 'Ode' is grim, witty, exuberant, explosive, savage, elliptical, elegiac, apocalyptic, but not balanced

---

* Reprinted from *Literature and the English Civil War*, eds Thomas Healy and Jonathan Sawday (Cambridge: Cambridge University Press, 1990), pp. 147–69.

and transcendent. It is a poem urgent with the pressure of a particular moment in Marvell's life and in English history, a moment when the future seemed to lie not with monarchy but with a republic. As Blair Worden has shown, this was a Machiavellian moment: the fledgling republic was in danger, and it was essential to seize the occasion of decisive action or the cause would be lost.[2]

It is because, in the end, the cause was lost that the Ode's political complexion has often been misread. Jerome McGann has argued that 'all literary works . . . are inhabited by lost and invisibilised agencies', and that 'one of the chief functions of criticism is to remember the works which have been torn and distorted by those losses'.[3] Interpretations of Marvell's Ode, and, indeed of the Revolution itself, have exemplified such losses.[4] From the right, it has often been argued that the foundation of the republic was an aberration from a monarchism otherwise naturally ingrained in the English people – the term 'interregnum' represents the events as standing quite outside the normal temporality of British history. From the left, the revolution has been seen as installing a regime of ruthlessly competitive bourgeois individualism and the internal repression of the bourgeois subject.[5] But the political and discursive regimes installed after 1660, with their renewed aristocratic ethos, were not quite those the Revolution had fought for, with long-standing consequences for British culture.[6]

If that is so, then we should be wary of reading the Ode as simply poised between old and new orders, and should be alert to ways in which the failure to establish a distinctive republican culture in Britain may have distorted its reception. For reasons that will be discussed later, the Ode does not seem to have been published in 1650. After the Restoration, Marvell, like so many public figures, was anxious to minimise the degree of his involvement with the Commonwealth; it was in their interest to present themselves as motivated by a pragmatic loyalism rather than anything as doctrinaire as republicanism. For a brief moment the Ode again seemed about to become timely at the time of the exclusion crisis in the early 1680s, when Marvell's poems were posthumously printed. The publisher, Robert Boulter, allegedly 'did not question to see the monarchy reduced into a commonwealth and very speedily'; but he apparently changed his mind over whether this would happen speedily enough for it to be safe to print the Cromwell poems, and they were dropped.[7] Thus for a century and a quarter after the poem's composition, Marvell's image as a zealous Protestant patriot was untarnished by republicanism. The Cromwell poems were not published until the auspicious republican year of 1776, when James Barry issued an engraving showing Marvell, Milton and other patriots saluting the phoenix of liberty arising across the Atlantic.[8] But by this time the tradition of Marvell the unwavering monarchist was so strong that it could be used by a circular process to read back into the Ode itself. And by then the tradition of public poetry and political rhetoric that went back to the early Renaissance was nearing a climacteric that was also to lead to its eclipse, in the reaction against the French Revolution. That reaction, which has moulded the idiom of modern literary studies, involved a reaction against rhetoric, against public political poetry in the name of inner integrity. The long-term result was the privileging of Marvell's lyrics over his public poetry and prose. Equally significantly for the interpretation of the Ode, the Romantic period saw also the eclipse of the idea of genre, of poetry as performing a particular kind of public action, and the emergence of the notion of the poem as a timeless artefact standing above the debased world, and expressing an individual sensibility that would be repressed by strict generic categories. Charles himself, the royal actor, becomes in this tradition an emblem of the lost autonomy of the artefact. Hazlitt, knowing the poem only by report, thought of it as an elegy for Charles, while Hartley Coleridge, initiating the tradition of balanced opposites, said that the poem could be either a satire or a eulogy of Cromwell.[9]

In the heyday of the New Criticism such 'balanced' readings were to become the norm. There have always been dissenting voices, especially from historians; Christopher Hill long ago argued that the poem enacted a move towards Cromwell rather than contemplative neutrality.[10] Such interpretations, however, have been liable to criticism as historical readings which fail to take account of the poem's literary qualities. The terms of that antithesis need challenging: it is precisely by sharpening the analysis of the poem's formal properties beyond a narrow conception of the 'literary' that it becomes possible to return it to history. Recent scholarship, in regaining an understanding of rhetoric and genre, has become better equipped to understand the links between poetry and politics.[11] Rather than seeing the Ode as pure literature, and Marvell as an isolated genius transcending lesser poets who wrote mere propaganda, it becomes possible to recover the role of the poem's generic acts in a far wider cultural movement. In the analysis of the poem as act, many questions remain to be answered: Marvell's own personal allegiances and the circumstances of the poem's production and reception remain obscure. I believe, however, that the hypothesis of the Ode as radically revisionary opens the way to making more sense both of the poem and of its context.

Both parts of the poem's title arouse royalist expectations. In giving the bald generic characterisation 'Horatian Ode' – as far as I know uniquely – Marvell evoked the royalist admiration of Horace, with his cult of peace under a worthy emperor. In an Ode of 1630 Sir Richard Fanshawe celebrated Charles's preservation of the peace while 'warre is all the world about'.[12] Marvell himself had written a monarchist Horatian Ode, a close imitation of the second ode of the first book which he contributed to a volume of panegyrics in 1637.[13] In the aftermath of the Second Civil War there had been a resurgence of royalist Horatianism, and Fanshawe's Ode was one of many ceremonial poems from the 1630s which were published as a loyal gesture in the period leading up to the regicide. The other element in the title, the reference to a return, is also a strong generic signal. Renaissance rhetoric recognised a distinct kind of demonstrative or panegyrical oration, a celebration of a hero's return, a *prosphonetikon* or *epibaterion*.[14] Horace's odes were regularly classified in Renaissance edition according to panegyrical genres: for example, the fourth ode of the fourth book, long recognised as one of Marvell's chief models for his Ode, was classed as a *prosphonetikon*.[15] The second and third decades of the seventeenth century saw a proliferation of poems in this genre: Oxford and Cambridge were issuing more and more volumes of commendatory verse to commemorate royal births and also royal returns: Charles's return from Spain in 1623 and his returns from Scotland in 1633 and 1641.[16] The word 'return' appeared prominently in such volumes; and it took on broader significances, as the king was hailed as returning or restoring the realm to a lost golden age.

Some critics have taken this use of royalist forms to indicate that Marvell is balancing royalist poetry against Puritan politics; or, more radically, that he is using the Horatian echoes to undermine and obliquely satirise Cromwell.[17] It is often assumed that Marvell began as a royalist and remained sympathetic to that position down to 'Tom May's Death'; Wallace argues that he was consistent to the end in preferring government with a monarchical element. But we need to be wary about constructing an unproblematic grand narrative of Marvell's career: in a period of massive political upheaval, major discontinuities may have marked personal and poetic histories.[18] If the Ode evokes royalist genres, it is in order to subvert them, to return English poetry to a truer course. For the 'balanced' or royalist readings tend to take at face value the claim that Renaissance culture was essentially royalist and centre on whether he is vindicating that culture against Cromwellian anarchy or saying a sad farewell to it. But it all depends what is meant by the Renaissance, and by culture.

Renaissance humanism centred on the recovery of classical texts; and deeply engrained in some of the most prestigious texts was an enthusiasm for republican liberty and a disdain for monarchy as a primitive and superstitious form of government. For the more radical humanists, then, the restoration of classical culture was not a narrowly literary matter. Roman eloquence had reached its height with Cicero the defender of the republic, and under the Empire it had become flabby and ornamental, debased by courtly flattery.[19] In the *First Defence of the English People*

Milton immodestly compared himself to Cicero and pointed out that he had the advantage of a happier theme for his eloquence: whereas Cicero's story had ended tragically, with the senate disregarding his warnings against rule by one man, the English had been able to reverse this outcome and move from monarchy to republican liberty. A *Tragedy of Cicero*, published in 1651, pitted a virtuous Cicero against a corrupt and devious Octavius.[20] Machiavelli had linked this decline with larger social causes; the selfishness of the nobility which grabbed more and more land, leading to a polarisation between an easily manipulated propertyless multitude and an idle nobility which had bartered political liberty for a luxurious life on its country estates. As J.G.A. Pocock has shown, the Machiavellian analysis was developed in the 1650s both by Harrington and, in a very radical direction, in the newspaper *Mercurius Politicus*. It was symptomatic of the thinking in this period that Harrington, in his translation of Virgil's eclogues, should have taken for granted a rudimentary sociology of literature, pointing out that the changes in land-holding alluded to in the first eclogue were to lead directly to the establishment of the debilitating feudal order which must now be swept away.[21] Maecenas after all earned much of the enormous wealth which he consumed so conspicuously from confiscations from defeated republicans, the kind of confiscation to which Horace owed the substantial estate he liked to present as a modest country farm.

In the context of Marvell's Ode, it is particularly interesting that the politician who did most to win poets to the republic, Henry Marten, should have attempted to revise the cult of Horace. It was Marten who gave a classical cast to the iconography of the new republic, proposing that before the statues of the king were taken down their heads should be struck off in imitation of Brutus's mutilation of the images of Tarquin, and devising the aggressively final inscription 'Exit Tyrannus Regum Ultimus'. A more thoroughgoing republican than the Levellers, Marten risked their hostility in 1649 to support Cromwell as the only effective agent for getting rid of the monarchy. He remained suspicious of Cromwell's ambitions, however, and in 1653, when Cromwell dissolved the Long Parliament, Marten wrote a poem in protest. His 'Antepod[um] Horatian[um]' was a direct inversion of Horace's most celebrated epode, the second, 'Beatus ille qui procul negotiis', which had been translated by Jonson and echoed by innumerable cavalier poets. Horace praises the life of rural retirement; Marten inverts Horace's opening to attack retirement as a cowardly shunning of public business:

> Ignavus ille qui sepultus ocio
> (Vt bruta gens animalium)
> Materna bobus rura vexat pigrior,
> Inhians decuplo foenori

> Rostris ineptus, impar et se iudice
> Civis, cliensq[ue] civium.[22]

(Cowardly, slothful is he who buried in leisure, like the brute race of animals, more sluggish than his oxen, vexes his mother lands, gaping for tenfold increase, unfitted for the rostra, even in his own judgement unequal to a citizen, and a dependent of citizens.) This poem turns upside down the values of aristocratic Horatianism in the name of civic humanism: Marten entitled it 'Vitae civicae laudes'.[23]

For classical republicans, in fact, the problem with Renaissance culture was that it had not yet happened, in the sense that there had not been a full return to the central principles of the Roman republic; instead, there had been various botched compromises with feudal institutions and monarchical superstition. It was the commonwealth, not the monarchy, that permitted a true return to the golden age, a true renaissance, a true restoration. Marten seems to have been responsible for the inscription on the Commonwealth's seal: 'in the first year of freedom by God's blessing restored'. All these words overlap with the term 'revolution', which also had the sense of returning to origins, of restoring. But there was an important difference between restoring a recent *status quo* and restoring some very distant and half-mythical era: in that sense, the word 'revolution' was already acquiring its modern connotations.[24] There was even talk of reforming the entire calendar, in anticipation of the French revolutionary regime, and some books were dated according to the years of the restoration of liberty.[25] When taxed in parliament with the outrageousness of presenting the abolition of the monarchy as a 'restoration', Marten cheekily replied that 'there was a text had much troubled his spirit for severall dayes and nights of the man that was blind from his mother's womb whose sight was restored at last'.[26]

Marten urged the new regime to recruit writers who would disseminate this view of a possible cultural revolution and to show clemency for former royalist poets who might be won round. This campaign was at its height at the moment when Marvell was probably writing his Ode, in June 1650, when Marchamont Nedham started the aggressively republican journal *Mercurius Politicus*. The recruitment of prominent writers was important for the regime's national and international prestige. It is true that the number of committed republicans was small, but hindsight has tended to diminish the degree of support the new regime could begin to muster. Amongst those who rallied to the cause was the veteran Spenserian George Wither; interestingly, in January 1651 he directly recalled Caroline *prosphonetika* in a collection of poems celebrating the regicide:

> It fareth, now with me, as on that *morning*
> Which, first, inform'd us, of his *safe returning*

– that is, Charles's return from Spain in 1623.[27] Payne Fisher wrote several volumes of pompous neo-Latin panegyrics.[28] A far more prestigious champion for the new regime was John Milton; and his example would have been most significant for Marvell, whose early verse is full of echoes of the 1645 *Poems*. Milton had recently glorified the regicide, Cromwell, and the Irish campaign in his *Observations upon the Articles of Peace* (published in May 1649), polemically contrasting the language of republican 'fortitude and Magnanimity' with courtly flattery.[29] Not only the political content but the form of Marvell's poem has Miltonic analogues: for Milton too was experimenting with revisions of Horatian poetic models. He ended his *Second Defence* with a quotation from the last ode of the third book, adapting Horace's claims for the immortality of his odes to his own panegyric of the republic, whose foundation in his view surpassed any of the political feats Horace had celebrated. Milton's sonnets of the 1640s and 1650s adapt the Horatian ethos to new political circumstances.[30] And Milton seems to have seen the odes through the eyes of didactically minded critics who presented him as a *sacerdos*, a poet-priest who summons readers to civic virtue and whose own linguistic skill is a pattern of the discipline demanded of the citizen.[31] Marvell's Ode needs to be seen in the context of these attempts at a radical rethinking of the politics of poetry and of classical culture; its tone is not that of a merely pragmatic loyalism. Marvell's title has complex associations: he both criticises royalist Horatianism as falling short of classical standards of public responsibility and to some extent criticises Horace himself and revises him in a republican direction.

To illustrate this point it will be necessary to analyse Marvell's inversion of the generic expectations raised by the title in five main areas. Generic patterns were never rigid, and a considerable degree of deviation from the norms laid down in rhetorical handbooks was expected; but the norms of the *prosphonetikon* had been made particularly prominent by the orchestrated chorus of adulatory verse in the first part of the century.

The revision begins very strikingly with the opening, the *exordium*. In an extreme literalisation of the conventional declaration of modesty, the poet presents the very writing of his own poem as a deviation from the political imperatives of the moment. In Horace's *prosphonetika*, and still more in Caroline panegyric, the hero's return is normally a signal for conflict to end and the arts of peace to revive. In direct contrast, Marvell's forward youth is urged to turn from the shadows, from 'Numbers languishing'.[32] As A.J.N. Wilson has pointed out, Roman poets in militaristic vein often censured the shadowy 'vita umbratilis'.[33] 'Languish' was a potent term in republican vocabulary, going back to Cicero and associated with the opposition between republican activism and monarchical lethargy.[34] John Hall, an ambitious young poet who went to Scotland in the summer of 1650 to support Cromwell's campaign, warned recalcitrant Scots monarchists that despite its superficial peace and elegance Caroline society had been rotten at the core: courtiers knew how to lull the people asleep 'with some small continuance of peace (be it never so unjust, unsound, or dangerous) as if the body politick could not languish of an internall disease, whilst its complexion is fresh and chearfull'.[35] Before Marvell's triumphal poem has begun the youth is already setting off, so that the *prosphonetikon* turns into a *propemptikon* for Cromwell's departure to Scotland. It is only at the very end of the poem, when Cromwell is imagined as setting off, that the poet addresses him directly. This is in the first instance an *occasional* poem, responding to a particular, and very real, crisis: Charles II was on his way to Scotland, and if his alliance with the presbyterians succeeded the republic would be in grave danger. Marvell is not necessarily making a general claim that war is superior to peace, but he is appealing to the Machiavellian idea of the armed citizen (Marten had raised his own force during the Second Civil War without consulting parliament). When liberty is in danger, retirement is irresponsible.

After the *exordium*, the *prosphonetikon* would be expected to continue with an analysis of the hero's birth, education and character. In his portrait of Cromwell, Marvell radically revises the kind of idealised image of authority of be found in Caroline panegyric: indeed, by inserting a portrait of Charles, Marvell heightens the contrast between monarchical man and republican man. Caroline panegyric idealised the figure of the monarch, making him a living embodiment of transcendental justice and of the unity of the body politic; Caroline odes and masques constantly identify the royal family with mythological figures. This idealisation goes with a strong sense of social as well as aesthetic decorum. Marvell presents Charles in such terms – he is comely, he fastidiously disdains the vulgar, the common, the mean. By contrast, Marvell emphasises that Cromwell climbs up from a relatively modest position – though he confutes royalist attacks on him as base-born by placing him in a gentlemanly garden. For the socially conservative, 'industrious' was a condescending term; but Blair Worden has pointed out that 'industrious Valour' might be a translation of Machiavelli's *industria* and *virtù* and the Machiavellian usage may lie behind the prominence Marvell gives in his poem to the simple word 'man': 'Much to the Man is due', 'So much one Man can do'.[36] Whereas monarchs rely on the ornamentation of high rank to beautify their actions, Cromwell is all the more impressive because he draws on elemental human qualities. This fact is heightened by a very striking absence: there is no classical mythology. Of course Cromwell is not presented in merely human terms, he fulfils a divine will, but it is made clear that he does so by opening himself to a mysterious and transcendent force rather than by occupying a traditional divinely sanctioned role: he is a bolt flung from above, the force of angry heaven's flame.

In human terms, however, Cromwell emerges as someone far from the conventional panegyrical frame of reference. Some writers have tried to fit the praise of Cromwell into the conventional encomiastic categories of the four cardinal virtues, but it takes a struggle.[37] He is valiant in war, but in the context of Caroline panegyric, to value military courage so highly as to describe the arts of peace as 'inglorious' would have come as a shock. His prudence amounts to deviousness, 'wiser Art': Marvell accepts the claim put about by royalists that he deliberately manipulated Charles's escape. His temperance is pushed to the point of being 'reserved and austere', terms which in royalist discourse would have connotations of puritanical preciseness. And justice, the final cardinal virtue, is made to plead against Cromwell. Some critics therefore see the poem as ambivalent, or as a satire on Cromwell the Machiavel.

Such readings, however, take it too easily for granted that Marvell would reject a Machiavellian frame of reference. One royalist described Marvell as a notable English Italo-Machiavellian, and Worden has shown that it is worth taking this description seriously. While most defenders of the republic couched their argument in merely pragmatic terms, a few, recognising that the legality of the regicide was highly dubious, argued that a radical revision of conventional political categories was necessary, that an orthodox moral vocabulary was often no more than a mask for social conservatism. Marvell makes Cromwell break out of the frame of conventional panegyric, of the rhetoric of praise and blame: as Patterson emphasises, it is in the context of a panegyric that we are told that it would be madness to blame him.[38] Hall similarly revises traditional language in *The Advancement of Learning* (1649):

> For discomposition of the present frame, may not, I pray this be a Topicke for any Government, though never so ill grounded, never so irregular, or never so Tyrannicall? Should we sit still, and expect that those in whose hands it is, should quietly resigne it, or new-mould it themselves, or some fine chance should do it to our hands? or should we not out of this very reason, if our houses were all untiled and obvious to all injuries of the weather, forbeare to pull them down or mend them, because we would make no alteration, and so continue in our miserable patience, because we feare a change and some trouble . . . or should we expect that some Deity, or unthought of influence would rescue us from these inconveniences which we saw, but would not remove? I am afraid whether any can be serious upon this question: For as happinesse is the reward of courage and industry; so what ever people ever yet obtained any Reformation

without sweat or wounds, and a just violence to the over-ruling power; just I say, though it clashed with the letter of some *Positive Law* for with the *Fundamentall* and true ends of government it could not. But there is no need in this case to urge this so hard to you [Parliament], who so nobly brake through this objection, and redeemed the supreme power.[39]

Hall uses one particular significant word of the new regime: he says that it nurtures 'men of sublime mindes'.[40] In 1652 Hall published the first English translation of Longinus's late-classical treatise on the sublime. In his dedication to Bulstrode Whitelocke, a patron of Davenant's 'reformed' drama, he reminds him that Longinus discusses the theory that rhetoric flourishes best in conditions of political liberty. Though he concedes that 'the corruption of time hath diseas'd most Governments into Monarchies', Hall implies that the republican sublime may revive under the commonwealth.[41] Hall believed that what he called 'this turne of time' was capable of a 'noble alteration': the 'highest spirits' were 'pregnant with great matters . . . labouring with somewhat, the greatnesse of which they themselves cannot tell'. This 'great and . . . restlesse Genius' of the time would bring forth many a 'sublime and elevated spirit'.[42] Longinus makes a central distinction between artistic effects which are merely skilful and competent on the one hand and the magnanimous or sublime on the other: sublimity, he declares, 'wheresoever it *seasonably* breaks forth, bears down all before it like a whirlwind'; sublime poets '*burn* up all before them', Demosthenes '*thunder-strikes* and in a manner *enlightens* the Oratours of all ages'.[43] Marvell's portrayal of Cromwell burning through the air aims at this kind of sublimity – a height, indeed, somewhat above Horace himself. This notion of the English Revolution as something sublime, something that transcends conventional modes of expression, was widespread: in his *Second Defence of the English People* Milton says that the establishment of the republic transcends all the deeds of the ancients even if he is not able to find the words fit to describe it.[44] Learning after the Restoration that Milton had written some 'admirable panegyricks, as to sublimitie of wit', on Cromwell and Fairfax, John Aubrey eagerly sought them out: even if they were in praise of the devil, ''tis the *hypsos* [sublime] that I looke after'.[45]

Marvell heightens this sense of Cromwell as a force that can scarcely be contained within conventional forms by his use of metre. Renaissance humanists tended to regard rhyme as one of the feudal barbarisms which they wanted to abolish, and made some vain attempts to restore the classical metres of unrhymed quantitative verse. Rhyme became a symbol of the courtly corruption of language under the later Empire, tinkling sound as opposed to moral sense. Milton, who denounced rhyme as a symbol of bondage in a prefatory note to *Paradise Lost*, had as a young man attempted an unrhymed translation of a Horatian ode. Marvell admits rhyme, but his metre is nonetheless exceptionally terse, particularly because the semantic level accentuates the impression of the necessary rigours imposed by the form. Cromwell is consistently seen as breaking out of closed spaces: nature must make room for him, he casts kingdoms into a new mould. At times his energy makes the syntax break down altogether: 'And with such to inclose Is more then to oppose'. Marvell keeps in reserve until line 114 the longest word in the poem, 'indefatigably', which almost fills up its line. And there is a pointed contrast with Charles, who *can* be contained within his form: Cromwell, with his net, chases him from Carisbrooke's narrow case, and Charles, in an almost languishing gesture, bows down in those short couplets that end his life, as if upon a bed. Charles may seem to be identified with the arts of peace, Cromwell with the arts of war, but in fact Cromwell, who can know as well as act, is constantly associated with artistic emulation: he blasts Caesar through his laurels, stages Charles's performance on the tragic scaffold, he is the bold architect of the new state. If Cromwell is the republican sublime, Charles is the courtly beautiful; Marvell is establishing a similar relationship between his forebears the cavalier poets and the new and more innovative genre of poetry he is now founding.[46] In this sense, it could be argued that by giving a favourable portrait of Charles, Marvell makes his poem more rather than less radical: monarchical culture is weighed at its own highest self-valuation, as the source of grace, decorum, elegance, exclusiveness, and found beautiful but limited.

The poem thus rejects the Caroline aestheticisation of politics. But may not the celebration of Cromwell's sublimity be merely a new and potentially just as authoritarian aestheticisation, reducing the complex forms of political agency to a cult of personality? As Wilding points out, Marvell plays down the Leveller viewpoint. All the same, he goes into more considerable constitutional detail than would be expected in an encomium. Horace had left the precise relations between Augustus and the senate discreetly vague, but Marvell insists that Cromwell is concerned not with his own glory but only with the state's: he presents to the Commons not only the kingdom of Ireland but also his own fame, and his campaign is shown as a firmly republican one. The more conservative members of the Rump were indeed hesitant about using the word 'republic' and preferred the blander 'commonwealth'; Cromwell himself had long hesitated before deciding that the king must die. But Marvell insists on the way in which the traditional political order has been overturned. Machiavelli had argued (*Discourses*, I, 9) that only a single decisive individual could achieve radical constitutional change. Having arranged the decapitation of the king, the head of the body politic in the old political language, Cromwell lays a kingdom at the feet of the Commons, the 'feet' who have now abolished their monarchical 'head'. The prominently placed word *'Republick'* is reinforced by *'Publick'* eight lines later. Cromwell has left his 'private Gardens' to serve the public; but it will be necessary for the public to exercise their political responsibility, ensuring that he does not continue to pursue his private interests now that he exercises such influence, growing 'stiffer with Command'.

This context gives an unconventional edge to the old maxim:

How fit he is to sway
That can so well obey.

These lines can be taken as proposing that Cromwell should run for king. But the conventional maxim gains a new, paradoxical force in a republican context: the more prince-like he is, the more virtue resides in renouncing kingship and serving the republic. This idea is reinforced by the falcon analogy. Earlier in the poem Cromwell had been the hunter, Charles the hunted animal; now the republic is the hunter, Cromwell its tame falcon. Falcons are not always so easy to lure back: one could read the word 'sure' at line 96 in a number of tones. The analogy condenses the uneasy respect with which republicans viewed Cromwell at this stage.

That unease is also, perhaps, reinforced by the poem's unusual metrical tensions, which function as an analogue of the necessary tensions that maintain republican liberty. Machiavelli had argued that a certain element of disorder strengthened a state, that Rome had been greater when there was an element of popular participation and unrest and declined into lethargy when this challenge was lost. John Hall argued against the idea that monarchy was the best form of government because most unified: in a republic, 'among many joynt Causes, there may be some jarring, yet like cross wheels in an Engine, they tend to the regulation of the whole'.[47] Even when celebrating Cromwell more unequivocally in *The First Anniversary*, Marvell was to retain this emphasis on structural tension, contrasting the republican 'resistance of opposed Minds' with the authoritarian unity aimed at by conservative monarchs, more 'slow and brittle then the *China* clay'.[48] If Cromwell's sublime energy resists the confining forms of an older and more conservative poetry, Marvell's metrical austerity, the counter-pull of the terse six-syllable couplets, implies the need for a severe counter-discipline to resist energies that may potentially become dangerous to the state.[49]

Such implicit reservations should not be overplayed, however. The poem is an encomium and its heroic mode prevails over the caricature of Cromwell as a monomaniacal social climber which had been propagated by royalists and was being taken up by the Levellers. The fact that Marvell nonetheless feels it necessary in the name of this new republican ethos to engage with opposing views may explain why as far as we

know the poem was not published in 1650. It gives too much credit
to Cromwell to please many parliamentarians and radicals, but is too
Machiavellian and republican to please Cromwell. And before long
Marvell was to enter the service of Fairfax, who had opposed the Scottish
war, so that he would have had little incentive to publish it: the poem's
moment was a very brief one.

The next section of the *prosphonetikon* would conventionally be an
analysis of the deeds of the returning hero. But Marvell's narration is
highly unconventional. He plunges into the narrative:

> So restless *Cromwel* could not cease
> In the inglorious Arts of peace
>   But through adventurous War
>   Urged his active star.

The account of what he actually did, however, is oblique in the extreme:
scholars still dispute the exact meaning of the densely metaphorical
description of the lightning breaking through the clouds. The lightning
metaphor is then continued to give an indirect description of the regicide
at lines 23–4. The poem then turns back on itself to describe Cromwell's
life before he became a soldier, but this retreat is used to point the
contrast with the speed and force of his emergence, and we move again
to the regicide at lines 34–6. Then we move back again to a narrative of
the civil war campaigns, before turning yet again to the events leading
up to the regicide; and here Marvell makes a striking concession to
royalists by suggesting that Cromwell deliberately engineered Charles's
escape from Carisbrooke. It is as if the regicide is a topic that keeps
breaking through the muffled syntax that seems to obscure it. In
rhetorical terms, however, the poem is not an equal balance between
Cromwell and Charles: syntactically and structurally, the description of
the regicide is a digression. The poem could certainly have glided over
the event as the most desperately controversial and perhaps unpopular
act of the new regime, and turned pragmatically to the Irish conquests as
something that would unify a broad section of English opinion; instead,
Marvell enacts a process of facing up to difficult and perhaps unpalatable
truths even in an encomium. We are made to sympathise with the
doomed king: the infinitely regressive pain of

>   with his keener Eye
> The Axes edge did try

is terrifying. But the poem gives the reader the impression of facing
the fact of regicide coolly and unflinchingly, after earlier evasion, and
this comes as a kind of emotional release, a surge of energy as the
poem moves on, having been able to accommodate the tragic within
the panegyrical.

The main event marked by the poem, the Irish campaign, formed a striking contrast with the triumphal returns of Charles I, particularly his return from Scotland in 1641. On that occasion rebellion had just broken out in Ireland. Many recent historians have argued that the panic over the 1641 Irish rebellion, fuelled by Pym, was the leading factor in precipitating political disputes into open war. But the university panegyrics for Charles's return blandly ignored the scale of the crisis: the poets prophesied that the king would bring peace like Venus from the Irish seas and even suggested that the rebellion was to be welcomed as a recreation which would allow Charles to keep his sword free from rust.[50] Cromwell's situation in 1650 turned Charles's situation in 1641 upside down: where Charles was returning from an ill-managed expedition to Scotland to try to confront an Irish crisis he was accused of having fomented, Cromwell was returning from a decisive campaign in Ireland and about to take on the Scots. Where the Caroline panegyrists had lavished hyperboles on Charles's non-existent victories, Marvell's poem is strikingly subdued in what it says about Cromwell's victories, enacting a contrast between empty words and decisive actions.

It is disturbing to find a poem that celebrates national emancipation simultaneously endorsing Cromwell's brutal repression of Irish resistance, and some critics have argued that in putting praise of Cromwell in the mouths of the Irish Marvell was being ironic at his expense. It is certainly not true to say that all seventeenth-century Englishmen were indifferent to Irish interests. Cromwell had crushed at Burford a mutiny by Levellers who resisted the campaign; Marten, too, had spoken up for the Irish.[51] But there were tactical reasons for the campaign, and Marten came round to supporting Cromwell's mission, though he gave it an ideological cast by proposing that it be funded with the sale of the regalia. Ireland had long been a source of difficulty for English governments, and now it threatened to become a base for a restoration; some republicans urged the most drastic possible measures. In an earlier moment of comparable crisis, Spenser had called for Irish traditions to be rooted up, for the entire political and social structure of the island to be transformed, and had quoted Machiavelli's *Discourses* in support of the appointment of a strong military leader; similar plans were being floated in the 1650s. On Cromwell's departure a newsletter declared that 'on the event of this they vary their conjectures whither ever there shall be a King of England again or not'.[52] Later in the year William Hickman insisted to Cromwell that the Irish campaign must be the basis for radical political change: 'hetherto in the chandge of our Government nothinge materiall as yet hath bin done, but a takinge of the head of monarchy and placing uppon the body or trunck of it, the name or title of a Commonwealth, a name aplicable to all forms of Government, and contained under the former'. The new republic was 'not to be pattern'd by any Commonwealth auncient or moderne'.[53] In a similar vein, Marvell stresses the ideological, republican elements of the campaign. The Irish praise of Cromwell has a generic precedent in Hannibal's praise of the Romans in the fourth ode of Horace's fourth book; Marvell was to make foreign princes praise Cromwell in *The First Anniversary*. If there is a grim wit in lines 73–80, it lies in making the defeated conservatives adopt a mode of praise more conventional than the iconoclastic spirit of the rest of the poem: it is the Irish who use the language of conventional, non-Machiavellian panegyric.

If the Irish are presented, albeit ironically, as exquisitely courteous, no holds are barred in ethnic stereotyping of the Scots. Fairfax and the presbyterians doubted the legality of the Scottish campaign; its most vehement supporters used a cheekily anti-monarchical rhetoric. For example, in trying to woo the Scots from their allegiance to the young Charles II, John Hall drew on the radical tradition in Scots historiography, rushing through the chronicle of rebellions, depositions and regicides so quickly that he turned it into a grotesque black comedy, implying that only a perverse political masochism would have kept the Scots faithful to their kings.[54] Marvell's portrayal of Cromwell hunting the Scots (lines 105–12) shares this ideologically charged aggression.

Having sketched the actions and character of the returning hero, the *prosphonetikon* would be expected to describe the celebrations marking his return. Aristotle declared (*Rhetoric*, I, 3) that epideictic rhetoric was especially concerned with the present tense, and 'now' is the key word of the *prosphonetikon*: Horace's 'nunc est bibendum' (I, 37). Here as so often Marvell departs from Caroline conventions just where he seems about to conform completely: 'now' appears in the second line, but the ode immediately looks to the future; rather than writing poetry the youth must be prepared to ward off the Scottish enemy. We do not return to the present tense until the 'now' of line 73, and any expectation that after the long narration there will be time for festivities is frustrated: the 'yet' and 'still' of lines 81–2 look to future possibilities before Cromwell's present actions have been fully described. Marvell's 'now' could perhaps be linked with a portrait of Marten by Lely which has 'now' inscribed on it: this seems to have been a Machiavellian injunction to decisive action, to seize the *occasione*, perhaps linked with the regicide.[55] Marvell lays all the emphasis on Cromwell's humility, on his readiness to abnegate praise and honour; and nothing at all is said of the republic's response. It is in fact true that Cromwell discouraged elaborate preparations for his return. The pamphlet describing his arrival at Windsor struck a somewhat unfestive note by remarking that Cromwell had been less seasick on the way back than on the voyage out to Dublin.[56]

The festivities in classical poetry often included a sacrifice, and the cavalier poets adapted the pagan symbolism of sacrifice to their own panegyrics.[57] Here Marvell's inversion of the conventions is at its most grimly witty. There is a sacrifice at the centre of the poem: the king himself. The famous lines about Charles on the scaffold have often been detached from their context. Certainly they do arouse sympathy for the king at his moment of death. But in formal terms this is a digression – Horace was celebrated for his digressions[58] – and Marvell meshes his account of the regicide in with his narration, beginning with a 'that' taking up from Cromwell's actions and ending with a 'So' emerging as the first term in a comparison:

> So when they did design
> The *Capitols* first Line,
> A bleeding Head where they begun
> Did fright the Architects to run;
> And yet in that the *State*
> Foresaw it's happy Fate.

The architectural metaphor is Marvell's addition to the Roman legend; this, and the fact that the head is bleeding, enable him to tie in the regicide to the theme of sacrifice, to modulate from the tragic to the conventions of the *prosphonetikon*. Cromwell's victories in Ireland do not require any new sacrifice to be made, for they were implicit in the original sacrifice that formed the new republic.

The symbolism of founding a republic on the basis of sacrifice was widely diffused in the Renaissance, and appears in several defences of the regicide.[59] Writing of the death of Tarquin, the last Roman king, Machiavelli argued, in a *reductio ad absurdum* of traditional monarchist imagery of the body politic, that the founders of the Roman republic were wise in cutting off the sick head when the body was healthy.[60] It was perhaps in Machiavelli's admired Livy that Marvell found the story of the head whose discovery gave new hope to the builders of the Temple of Jupiter. His analogy of the frightened architects presents accurately enough the reaction of many members of the Rump Parliament who were backing away from the radical implications of the regicide. Cromwell, by contrast, is someone who does not fall back on a familiar model but has the boldness to push on with a new one which will be more securely founded than the elegant but brittle world of the Caroline court. If Caroline panegyric tended to gloss over violence and seek to contain political conflict within the mythological structures of the masque, the new, republican panegyric is prepared to persevere in the face of uncomfortable facts. The leading republicans took pride in the fact that, as Thomas Harrison declared on the scaffold, the regicide 'was not a thing done in a corner'. Wither boasted that whereas tyrants had often been removed secretly,

we, with *open face*;
By *Publick Justice*; in a *Publick place*;
In presence, of his *friends*, and, in despight
Of all our *foes*, and ev'ry opposite,
Try'd, *Judg'd*, and *Executed*, without fear;
The greatest *Tyrant*, ever reigning here.[61]

Marvell, in much more circumspect terms, makes the regime
acknowledge the blood on its hands. Cromwell lays the foundation even
though its line runs through the king's neck; similarly, Marvell celebrates
the new state and makes his own line decapitate the king: the moment
when the king's eye tries the axe is the exact mid-point. If the poem's
first sixty lines embody in their form the 'memorable Hour' of the
execution, the Ode moves on to a new political world: its structure is
centrifugal, not symmetrical, moving out both at the beginning and end
from the encomiastic present to the uncertain but urgent future.[62] On the
scaffold Charles had called on God, declaring that if he failed to make a
speech he would be conceding his guilt; Marvell's silent king refuses to
call on God to vindicate his right. In the context of 1650, what is most
remarkable about the poem is its complete silence about the young
Charles II. What royalists in 1650s were eager to celebrate was not
Cromwell's return from Ireland but the young prince's return from exile
to avenge his father's death and turn the world the right way up again.
But at the centre of his poem, Marvell maintains an eloquent silence: the
Stuart dynasty is charming but irrelevant.

The final expected element of a *prosphonetikon* would be a conclusion
often involving a prophecy. The jingoism of Marvell's finale has often
disconcerted critics. And certainly it is yet another drastic revision of
Caroline *prosphonetika* which regularly ended with praise of the peace
enjoyed by Britain while war raged elsewhere. Up to a point it can be
said that Marvell is here going back more rigorously than the Carolines
to the Horatian model; for many of Horace's poems of return ended
with prophesies of future campaigns, notably the poem that is Marvell's
closest model, the fourth ode of the fourth book. In Sir Richard
Fanshawe's translation:

What is't but *Neros* can effect,
Whom Heav'ns with prosperous Stars protect,
And their own prudent care
Clews through the Maze of War.[63]

The parallel here of divine aid and 'curae sagaces', prudent care, is very
close to Marvell's concluding antithesis between divine aid for Cromwell
and the secular arts of tactical skill that he will need on the coming
mission:

And for the last effect
Still keep thy Sword erect:
Besides the force it has to fright
The Spirits of the shady Night,
The same *Arts* that did *gain*
A *Pow'r* must it *maintain*.[64]

Where Marvell's poem differs from Horace's is in its much more
radically ideological character. Where Horace celebrates campaigns that
will consolidate the power of Augustus' dynasty against the remaining
institutions of the Roman republic, Marvell celebrates wars that are
specifically directed by the newly-founded republic against monarchies
and in defence of republican values. As Christopher Hill has pointed
out, there had indeed been anti-monarchical risings in many parts of
Europe which lent at least some plausibility to such prophecies.[65] Italy,
the heartland first of Roman and then of Renaissance republicanism,
showed signs of throwing off the Spanish absolutist yoke.

There is a further twist in that many of Horace's poems prophesy
victories against the Britons. Patriotic translators took issue with this:
in his 1649 translation of the twenty-first ode of the first book, which
ends with a plea that plague and famine will light on the Britons, John
Smith writes, 'Avertat omen *Britannis*'.[66] Fanshawe comments on the ninth
epode that Britain is '[u]nconquered, though twice attempted by the rude
Courtship of *Julius Caesar*'.[67] To seventeenth-century Protestants, modern
Rome was the inheritor of the worst aspects of ancient Rome, its imperial
authoritarianism and idolatry. To the confident Counter-Reformation
culture of seventeenth-century Italy, the heretical Britons were seditious
inhabitants of a remote and backward region. Many critics have seen
the fact that Caesar is Charles at the beginning of the poem, Cromwell
at the end as a sign of ambivalence or satire against Cromwell; but such
readings miss another stroke of grim wit. The question of genre needs
to be considered: an encomium was expected near the end to have a
section of comparisons. And it was normal to compare on the basis of
very specific attributes. In fact a whole host of panegyrics directed to
Cromwell without any apparent ironic intent – including a report on
his departure to Ireland – compare him both to Caesar and to Hannibal.[68]
The point is that each of these comparisons is qualified by restricting it
to a particular place or time: Caesar when he conquered Gaul but not
when he threatened liberty, and so on. Marvell specifies that his Cromwell
is a Caesar in relation to Gaul, but he also inverts the situation at the
end of Horace's odes, making Cromwell a Caesar who attacks Gaul not
from the south on his way to Britain but from the north on his way to
an apocalyptic assault on Rome. The apparently peripheral culture of

Protestant England which in fact is closer to the true spirit of Roman greatness and generosity will triumph over the decadent imperial centre. This is not say that some ambiguity does not play over the end of the poem: as before, there is always the possibility that Cromwell the defender of liberty, but also a Nimrodian *'Hunter'* (line 110), may himself endanger it.[69] The words 'force' and *'Pow'r'* of the last stanza recall the earlier 'forced Pow'r'; is the power here the new republic as a whole or simply Cromwell's personal authority? In 1650 these things were very hard to disentangle, for the one depended on the other. Marvell's ode is not unequivocally triumphal: it sees immense possibilities in the revolution, but is also aware of the deep-seated irony in the fact that its greatest defender and its destroyer might be one and the same man:

> The same *Arts* that did *gain*
> A *Pow'r* must it *maintain*.

The poem's wit is both youthfully irreverent and nightmarishly grim. All the same, there is an affirmative note: *if* the forward youths of the realm rally behind the young republic's campaigns, there is a world to win. And in writing the poem, Marvell had already gained one kind of victory for republican culture. The English revolution had turned upside down the monarchical order to return to republican origins; Marvell's out-troping poem of return turns royalist Horatianism, and Horace's own monarchism, upside down.

Notes

Research for this paper was aided by a term at the Folger Shakespeare Library with financial support from the British Academy and the English-Speaking Union; I am very grateful to all at the Library. A fuller version will appear in the *Proceedings of the Folger Institute Centre for the History of British Political Thought.* I have benefited from discussion with Boyd Berry, Conal Condren, William Lamont, Nancy Klein Maguire, Annabel Patterson and J.G.A. Pocock. Jeremy Maule, Brian Vickers and Blair Worden have also provided helpful comments.

1. The classic 'balanced' reading, widely influential beyond seventeenth-century studies, is CLEANTH BROOKS, 'Marvell's *Horatian Ode*', *English Institute Essays, 1946* (New York, 1947), pp. 127–58.
2. BLAIR WORDEN, 'Andrew Marvell, Oliver Cromwell, and the Horatian Ode', in Kevin Sharpe and Steven N. Zwicker (eds), *Politics of Discourse: The Literature and History of Seventeenth-Century England* (Berkeley, 1987), pp. 147–80; see also WORDEN's 'Classical Republicanism and the Puritan Revolution', in *History and Imagination: Essays in Honour of H.R. Trevor-Roper*, ed. H. Lloyd-Jones, V. Pearl and B. Worden (London, 1981), pp. 182–200.
3. JEROME J. McGANN, *Social Values and Poetic Acts: The Historical Judgment of Literary Work* (Cambridge MA and London, 1988), p. 6.

4. I am primarily concerned here with the political revolution of 1648–9, the foundation of the republic.

5. But see FRANCIS BARKER's 'In the Wars of Truth' for differences between the 'revolutionary bourgeois' discursive regime of *Areopagitica*, with its insistence on public participation in the discovery of truth, and in warfare, and the subsequent order, with its more rigid public/private distinctions (*Literature and the English Civil War*, ed. Thomas Healy and Jonathan Sawday Cambridge: Cambridge University Press, 1990, ch. 5).

6. On the absence of a republican culture in Britain see TOM NAIRN, *The Enchanted Glass: Britain and its Monarchy* (London, 1988).

7. *The Poems and Letters of Andrew Marvell*, ed. H.M. Margoliouth, third edn, revised by Pierre Legouis with the collaboration of E.E. Duncan-Jones, 2 vols (Oxford, 1971), I, 241.

8. WILLIAM L. PRESSLY, *James Barry: The Artist as Hero* (London, 1983), pp. 73–5.

9. ELIZABETH STORY DONNO (ed.), *Andrew Marvell: The Critical Heritage* (London, 1978), pp. 133, 159n.

10. CHRISTOPHER HILL, 'Society and Andrew Marvell', in *Puritanism and Revolution* (corrected edn, Harmondsworth, 1986), pp. 324–50. JOHN M. WALLACE, *Destiny His Choice: the Loyalism of Andrew Marvell* (Cambridge, 1968), pp. 69–105, and MICHAEL WILDING, *Dragons Teeth: Literature in the English Revolution* (Oxford, 1987), pp. 114–37, see the poem as firmly endorsing Cromwell but resisting more radical republican or Leveller viewpoints. See also JUDITH RICHARDS, 'Literary Criticism and the Historian: Towards Reconstructing Marvell's Meaning in "An Horatian Ode"', *Literature and History* 7 (1981), 25–47.

11. WALLACE, *Destiny His Choice*, pp. 100ff, touches on generic factors; ANNABEL PATTERSON relates genres more closely to republican ideas in *Marvell and the Civic Crown* (Princeton, 1978), pp. 59–68.

12. SIR RICHARD FANSHAWE, *Shorter Poems and Translations*, ed. N.W. Bawcutt (Liverpool, 1964), p. 5.

13. MARVELL, *Poems and Letters*, I, pp. 1–2.

14. FRANCIS CAIRNS discusses the related terms *prosphonetikon, epibaterion*, and *apobaterion* in *Generic Composition in Greek and Roman Poetry* (Edinburgh, 1972), pp. 18–24; for Renaissance classifications see JULIUS CAESAR SCALIGER, *Poetices libri septem* (Lyon, 1561), pp. 158–9.

15. *Bernardi Parthenii . . . in Q. Horatii Flacci carmina atq. epodos commentarii* (Venice, 1584), fols. 142–5, 117v.

16. For discussion see RAYMOND A. ANSELMENT, 'The Oxford University Poets and Caroline Panegyric', *John Donne Journal* 3 (1984), 181–201.

17. See R.H. SYFRET, 'Marvell's "Horatian Ode"', *Review of English Studies* n.s. 12 (1961), 160–72; JOHN S. COOLIDGE, 'Marvell and Horace', *Modern Philology* 63 (1965–6), 111–20; R.I.V. HODGE, *Foreshortened Time: Andrew Marvell and Seventeenth-Century Revolutions* (Cambridge, 1978), pp. 118–31; BARBARA EVERETT, 'The Shooting of the Bears', in *Andrew Marvell: Essays on the Tercentenary of his Death*, ed. R.L. Brett (Oxford, 1979), pp. 62–103; MARGARITA STOCKER, *Apocalyptic Marvell: The Second Coming in Seventeenth Century Poetry* (Brighton, 1986), pp. 257–305 (Stocker brings out the important apocalyptic elements).

18. On problems in the dating, interpretation and attribution of the earlier poems, see NICHOLAS GUILD, 'The Contexts of Marvell's Early "Royalist" Poems', *Studies in English Literature* 20 (1980), 126–36, and GERARD REEDY, S.J., '"An Horatian Ode" and "Tom May's Death"', *ibid.*, 137–51.

19. For this 'anti-Augustan' perspective, see HOWARD D. WEINBROT, *Augustus Caesar in 'Augustan' England: The Decline of a Classical Norm* (Princeton NJ, 1978).

20. MILTON, *Complete Prose Works*, gen. ed. Don M. Wolfe, 7 vols (New Haven; 1953–82), IV, pp. 536, 332; ANON., *The Tragedy of That Famous Roman Oratour Marcus Tullius Cicero* (London, 1651), sigs. C3v–4r, E4r.

21. J.G.A. POCOCK's introduction to *The Political Works of James Harrington* (Cambridge, 1977), gives an important survey of republican thought; on Virgil, see pp. 579–81.

22. Cited by kind permission of the Brotherton Collection, University of Leeds (Marten-Loder papers, ML78, fol. 4v). I am indebted for this reference to C.M. WILLIAMS, 'The political career of Henry Marten with special reference to the origins of republicanism in the Long Parliament', unpublished D. Phil. thesis, Oxford, 1954, p. 217. For 'Rostris' Marten had first written 'Foris'.

23. The temperamental affinities between Marten and Marvell were noted by the last poet in the neo-Latin republican tradition, Walter Savage Landor: see 'Andrew Marvel [*sic*] and Henry Marten', in JOHN FORSTER, *Walter Savage Landor: A Biography*, 2 vols (London, 1869), II, 584–6.

24. Cf. CHRISTOPHER HILL, 'The Word "Revolution" in Seventeenth-Century England', in *For Veronica Wedgwood These: Studies in English Seventeenth Century History*, eds Richard Ollard and Pamela Tudor-Craig (London, 1986), pp. 134–51.

25. DAVID UNDERDOWN, *Pride's Purge: Politics in the Puritan Revolution* (Oxford, 1971), p. 260. PAYNE FISHER's volume of neo-Latin panegyrics to the republic's leaders, *Irenodia Gratulatoria* (London, 1652), is dated in the 'Aera' both 'Salutis Humanae MDCLII' and 'Libertatis Angliae IIII'.

26. JOHN AUBREY, *Brief Lives*, ed. Andrew Clark, 2 vols (Oxford, 1898), II, p. 47 (the allusion is to John 9: 2, 19).

27. GEORGE WITHER, *The British Appeals* (London, 1651), p. 4. Published as a public rejoicing on the anniversary of the king's execution, the volume ends with a series of odes and a defence of such genres against the attacks of more radical brethren. Contemporary satirists linked Wither with Marten, who is definitely known to have helped Waller and Davenant.

28. FISHER's *Irenodia Gratulatoria* (1652) contained an Ode to Cromwell and a *propemptikon* for Edmund Ludlow's departure to Ireland.

29. Milton, *Complete Prose Works*, III, pp. 311, 333. See THOMAS N. CORNS, 'Milton's Observations upon the Articles of Peace – Ireland under English Eyes' in *Politics, Poetics, and Hermeneutics in Milton's Prose*, eds David Loewenstein and James Grantham Turner (Cambridge: University of Cambridge Press, 1990), pp. 123–34.

30. On Milton's Horatianism see JOHN H. FINLEY, JR, 'Milton and Horace', *Harvard Studies in Classical Philology* 48 (1937), 29–74; cf. *Complete Prose Works*, IV, p. 682. For the possibility that Marvell may already have been in contact with Milton at the time he wrote the 'Ode', see CHRISTOPHER HILL, 'John Milton and Andrew Marvell', in *Writing and Revolution in Seventeenth-Century England: The Collected Essays of Christopher Hill, Volume One* (Brighton, 1985), pp. 160–1.

31. See for example the heavily didactic edition by DANIEL HEINSIUS, Leiden, 1612, fols. 7v–8v, lines 139–51.

32. For 'forward' in the context of a dual revival of military and intellectual arts, cf. MILTON's celebration of the 'pious forwardnes' of free England in *Areopagitica*, *Complete Prose Works*, II, p. 554.

33. A.J.N. WILSON, 'Andrew Marvell: "An Horatian Ode upon Cromwell's Return from Ireland": The Thread of the Poem and its Use of Classical Allusion', *Critical Quarterly* 11 (1969), 325–41 (328–9). The fullest study of the poem in the light of seventeenth-century classical studies, which concludes that the poem is fundamentally pro-Cromwell, is JOANNA MARTINDALE, 'The response to Horace in the seventeenth century (with special reference to the *Odes* and to the period 1600–1660)', unpublished D. Phil. thesis, Oxford 1977, pp. 298ff; I am grateful to Dr Martindale for allowing me to cite her thesis.

34. For political languor in CICERO see *Academicus*, 2.2.6, *De natura deorum*, I.iv.7, *De officiis*, 3.1.3, *In Pisonem*, 33.82, *Orator*, 2.6; for a catalogue of royalist languor see WORDEN, 'Marvell, Cromwell, and the Horatian Ode', pp. 167–8.

35. J.[OHN] H.[ALL], *The Grounds and Reasons of Monarchy, Considered and Exemplified out of the Scottish History* (Edinburgh, 1651), p. 5.

36. WORDEN, 'Marvell, Cromwell, and the Horatian Ode', p. 165.

37. WALLACE, *Destiny his Choice*, p. 75.

38. PATTERSON, *Marvell and the Civic Crown*, p. 63.

39. JOHN HALL, *The Advancement of Learning*, ed. A.K. Croston (Liverpool, 1953), p. 20.

40. *Ibid.*, p. 15.

41. J.[OHN] H.[ALL], *Peri Hypsous, or Dionysius Longinus of the Height of Eloquence* (London, 1652), sig. A8r, pp. 78–9. Hall states that the translation had been completed some years before its publication. The idea of the Revolution as sublime was passed down in the English republican tradition: e.g. CATHARINE MACAULAY on the foundation of the Republic, *The History of England from the Accession of James I to the Elevation of the House of Hanover*, V (London, 1771), p. 19.

42. HALL, *The Advancement of Learning*, pp. 21–2.

43. HALL, *Peri Hypsous*, sigs. C2r, F7b, F8b.

44. MILTON, *Complete Prose Works*, IV, p. 554.

45. AUBREY, *Brief Lives*, II, p. 70.

46. On comparable contrasts between revolutionary sublime and monarchist beautiful in the French Revolutionary period see RONALD PAULSON, *Representations of Revolution 1789–1820* (New Haven and London, 1983), pp. 57ff.

47. *Ibid.*, pp. 20–1.

48. MARVELL, *Poems and Letters*, I, pp. 111, 109.

49. Compare HALL's distinction between the need for one man to predominate in war, where 'the ferocity of daring spirits, can hardly be bounded', and civil rule where a poise and balance of opposing factions is better than rule by one: *The Grounds and Reasons of Monarchy*, pp. 9–10.

50. *Eucharistica Oxoniensia* (Oxford, 1641), sigs. B1r–v.

51. WILDING, *Dragons Teeth*, pp. 120–4, argues that lines 13–20 celebrate Cromwell's crushing of the Levellers. For Marten's position on Ireland see WILLIAMS, 'The political career of Henry Marten', pp. 44, 344, 509ff.

52. *The Kingdomes Weekly Intelligencer*, no. 323 (31 July 1649), p. 1449.

53. JOHN NICKOLLS, JR. (ed.), *Original Letters and Papers of State, Addressed to Oliver Cromwell* (London, 1743), pp. 31ff.

54. HALL, *The Grounds and Reasons of Monarchy*, pp. 24ff, 45. On the Scottish historians see my '*Macbeth* and the Politics of Historiography', in Sharpe and Zwicker (eds), *Politics of Discourse*, pp. 78–116.

55. Reproduced in OLIVER MILLAR, *The Age of Charles I: Painting in England 1620–1649* (London, 1972), p. 108. This portrait is now in the National Portrait Gallery.

56. *A Speech or Declaration of the Declared King of Scots . . . Also some Excellent Passages Concerning the Lord generall Cromwell, his entertainments at Windsor Castle* (London, 1650), p. 5. Note the subordination of Cromwell's return to the Scots crisis in the title.

57. E.g. ROBERT HERRICK, 'To the King, upon his welcome to *Hampton-Court*', *The Poetical Works of Robert Herrick*, ed. L.C. Martin (Oxford, 1956), p. 300.

58. Cf. PARTHENIO's commentary on *Odes*, II, i, fol. 67r.

58. E.g. [HENRY ROBINSON], *A Short Discourse Between Monarchical and Aristocratical Government* (London, 1649), p. 7; WITHER, *The British Appeals*, p. 2, compares the publication of his poem in praise of the regicide to the raising of a stone for the temple of Jerusalem. For an interesting critical analysis of the sacrificial motif see HANNAH ARENDT, *On Revolution* (revised edn, Harmondsworth, 1973), pp. 208ff.

60. *Machiauels Discourses*, trans. E. D[acres]. (London, 1636), p. 88 [I.17].

61. WITHER, *The British Appeals*, p. 29.

62. ALASTAIR FOWLER, *Triumphal Forms: Structural Patterns in Elizabethan Poetry* (Cambridge, 1970), pp. 78–81.

63. [SIR RICHARD FANSHAWE], *Selected Parts of Horace, Prince of Lyricks* (London, 1652), pp. 54–5 (as has often been noted, Fanshawe may have invented the stanza-form Marvell uses for his ode).

64. Cf. *Poems and Letters*, II, p. 324, letter of 9 August 1671: 'in this World a good Cause signifys little, unless it be as well defended'.

65. CHRISTOPHER HILL, 'The English Revolution and the Brotherhood of Man', in *Puritanism and Revolution*, pp. 126–53; see also WORDEN, 'Marvell, Cromwell, and the Horatian Ode', pp. 160–2.

66. J[OHN]. S[MITH]., *The Lyrick Poet. Odes and Satyres translated out of Horace into English Verse* (London, 1649), p. 22.

67. FANSHAWE, *Selected Parts of Horace*, p. 65.

68. E.g. FISHER, *Irenodia Gratulatoria*, translated by T. Manley as *Veni, Vidi, Vici* (London, 1652), pp. 10, 26–7, 71–2; *The Moderate Intelligencer*, 28 June–5 July 1649, fol. 10R1r. There was a tradition of poetry supporting such Protestant expansionism in the face of monarchical resistance: FULKE GREVILLE's *Life of Sidney*, finally published in 1652, called on Protestant leaders to emulate Hannibal in marching on Rome (WORDEN, 'Marvell, Cromwell, and the Horatian Ode', p. 161).

69. On Nimrod and other possible ambivalences see WORDEN, 'Marvell, Cromwell, and the Horatian Ode', p. 176.

Notes on Authors

PAUL J. ALPERS is Class of 1942 Professor of English at the University of California, Berkeley. He has written books on *The Faerie Queene* and Virgil's Eclogues and, most recently, *What Is Pastoral?* (University of Chicago Press, 1996).

MARGARET W. FERGUSON is Professor of English at the University of California, Davis. Author of *Trials of Desire: Renaissance Defenses of Poetry*, she has co-edited Elizabeth Cary's *The Tragedy of Mariam*; *Re-writing the Renaissance: the Discourses of Sexual Difference in Early Modern England*; *Re-membering Milton*; and *Postmodernism and Feminism*. She is completing a book entitled *Female Literacies and Emergent Empires: France and England in an Age of Transition*.

STEPHEN J. GREENBLATT is Professor of English at Harvard. He is the author, among other books, of *Shakespearean Negotiations* and *Marvelous Possessions*, and is the general editor of *The Norton Shakespeare*.

RICHARD L. HALPERN is Professor of English at the University of Colorado at Boulder. He is the author of *Shakespeare among the Moderns* (1997) and *The Poetics of Primitive Accumulation* (1991).

CRISTINA MALCOLMSON is Associate Professor of English at Bates College. She has written *Heart Work: George Herbert and the Protestant Ethic* (forthcoming from Stanford University Press), as well as feminist analyses of Shakespeare, Middleton and Marvell. She is working on the role of the gender debate in the emergence of early modern women writers.

RICHARD C. MCCOY, Professor of English at Queens College and the Graduate Center, City University of New York, and author of *Sir Philip Sidney: Rebellion in Arcadia* and *The Rites of Knighthood: The Literature and Politics of Elizabethan Chivalry*, is completing a study called *Alterations of State: Sacred Kingship in the English Reformation*.

DAVID NORBROOK is Fellow and Tutor in English, Magdalen College, Oxford, and a Lecturer in English at the University of Oxford. His publications include *Poetry and Politics in the English Renaissance* (1984), *The Penguin Book of Renaissance Verse* (with H.R. Woudhuysen, 1992), and *Writing the English Republic* (Cambridge University Press, 1998).

PATRICIA A. PARKER is Professor of English and Comparative Literature at Stanford University. Author of *Inescapable Romance: Studies in the Poetics of a Mode* (1979) and *Literary Fat Ladies: Rhetoric, Gender, Property* (1986), and co-editor of *Literary Theory/Renaissance Texts* (1986) and *Women, 'Race', and Writing in the Early Modern Period* (1994), she has recently published *Shakespeare from the Margins: Language, Culture, Context* (Chicago: University of Chicago Press, 1996).

NANCY J. VICKERS is Professor of French and Italian and of Comparative Literature at the University of Southern California. She has co-edited *Rewriting the Renaissance: The Discourses of Sexual Difference in Early Modern Europe* (1986) and *Medieval and Renaissance Representation: New Reflections* (1984), and has published widely on Dante, Petrarch, Shakespeare, on canon formation, and on popular culture in the late twentieth century.

DON E. WAYNE teaches in the Literature Department of the University of California, San Diego. His publications include *Penshurst: The Semiotics of Place and the Poetics of History* (1984), as well as essays on early modern poetry and drama, and on topics in postmodern cultural criticism and theory.

Further Reading

Early modern history

AMUSSEN, SUSAN, *An Ordered Society: Gender and Class in Early Modern England* (Oxford: Basil Blackwell, 1988).

BRAY, ALAN, *Homosexuality in Renaissance England* (New York: Columbia University Press, 1982; updated 1995).

CRESSY, DAVID, *Literacy and the Social Order: Reading and Writing in Tudor England* (Cambridge: Cambridge University Press, 1980).

—— and LORI ANNE FERRELL (eds), *Religion and Society in Early Modern England: A Sourcebook* (London: Routledge, 1996).

DAVIS, NATALIE ZEMON, *Society and Culture in Early Modern France* (Stanford: Stanford University Press, 1975).

—— *Women on the Margins: Three Seventeenth-Century Lives* (Cambridge: Harvard University Press, 1995).

DICKENS, A.G., *The English Reformation* (New York: Schocken Books, 1971).

FRYER, PETER, *Staying Power: The History of Black People in Britain* (London: Pluto Press, 1984).

GEORGE, CHARLES H. and KATHERINE, *The Protestant Mind of the English Reformation* (Princeton: Princeton University Press, 1961).

GRAFTON, ANTHONY and LISA JARDINE, *From Humanism to the Humanities: Education and the Liberal Arts in Fifteenth- and Sixteenth-Century Europe* (Cambridge: Harvard University Press, 1986).

HELLER, THOMAS et al. (eds), *Reconstructing Individualism: Autonomy, Individuality and the Self in Western Thought* (Stanford: Stanford University Press, 1986).

HEXTER, J.H. 'The Myth of the Middle Class in Tudor England', in *Reappraisals in History* (Chicago: University of Chicago Press, 1961).

HILL, CHRISTOPHER, *Reformation to Industrial Revolution: the Making of Modern English Society 1530–1780* (New York: Pantheon, 1968).

—— *Society and Puritanism in Pre-Revolutionary England* (London: Secker and Warburg, 1964).

—— *The World Turned Upside Down: Radical Ideas During the English Revolution* (Harmondsworth: Penguin Books, Ltd, 1975).

JARDINE, LISA, *Worldly Goods: A New History of the Renaissance* (New York: Nan A. Talese, 1996).

KELLY, JOAN, 'Did Women Have a Renaissance?', in *Becoming Visible: Women in European History*, eds Renate Bridenthal and Claudia Koontz (Boston: Houghlin Mifflin, 1977).

LASLETT, PETER, *The World We Have Lost: England Before the Industrial Age* (Charles Scribner, 1965).

MACFARLANE, ALAN, *The Origins of English Individualism: the Family, Property, and Social Transition* (New York: Cambridge University Press, 1979).

MACPHERSON, C.B. *The Political Theory of Possessive Individualism: Hobbes to Locke* (Oxford: Clarendon Press, 1962).

O'DAY, ROSEMARY, *Education and Society: 1500–1800: The social foundations of education in early modern Britain* (London: Longman, 1982).

PRIOR, MARY (ed.), *Women in English Society 1500–1800* (London and New York: Routledge, 1985).

RUSSELL, CONRAD, *The Crisis of Parliaments: English History 1509–1660* (London: Oxford University Press, 1971).

—— (ed.) *The Origins of the English Civil War* (London: Macmillan Education, 1973).

SHARPE, KEVIN (ed.), *Faction and Parliament: Essays on Early Stuart History* (Oxford: Oxford University Press, 1978).

STARKEY, DAVID et al. (eds), *The English Court: from the Wars of the Roses to the Civil War* (London: Longman, 1987).

STONE, LAWRENCE, *The causes of the English Revolution 1529–1642* (New York: Harper & Row, 1972).

—— *The Crisis of the Aristocracy 1558–1641* (Oxford: Clarendon Press, 1965).

—— *The Family, Sex and Marriage in England, 1500–1800* (New York: Harper, 1979).

DAVID UNDERDOWN, *Revel, Riot and Rebellion: Popular Politics and Culture in England 1603–1660* (Oxford: Oxford University Press, 1985).

WALLERSTEIN, IMMANUEL, *The Modern World System: Capitalist Agriculture and the Origins of the European World-Economy in the Sixteenth-Century*, 2 vols (New York: Academic Press, 1974).

WASHINGTON, JOSEPH E. *Anti-Blackness in English Religion: 1500–1700* (New York: Edwin Mellen Press, 1984).

WRIGHTSON, KEITH, *English Society 1580–1680* (New Brunswick: Rutgers University Press, 1982).

New historicism and cultural materialism

BURT, RICHARD and JOHN MICHAEL ARCHER (eds), *Enclosure Acts: Sexuality, Property and Culture in Early Modern England* (Ithaca: Cornell University Press, 1994).

CREWE, JONATHAN, *Reconfiguring the Renaissance: Essays in Critical Materialism* (Lewisburg: Bucknell University Press, 1992).

—— *Trials of Authorship: Anterior Forms and Poetic Reconstruction from Wyatt to Shakespeare* (Berkeley: University of California Press, 1990).

DE GRAZIA, MARGRETA, MAUREEN QUILLIGAN and PETER STALLYBRASS (eds), *Subject and Object in Renaissance Culture* (Cambridge: Cambridge University Press, 1996).

FUMERTON, PATRICIA, *Cultural Aesthetics: Renaissance Literature and the Practice of Social Ornament* (Chicago: University of Chicago Press, 1991).

GALLAGHER, CATHERINE, 'Marxism and New Historicism', in *The New Historicism*, pp. 37–48.

MARJORIE GARBER (ed.), *Cannibals, Witches, and Divorce: Estranging the Renaissance* (Baltimore: The Johns Hopkins University Press, 1987).

GOLDBERG, JONATHAN, *James I and the Politics of Literature: Jonson, Shakespeare, Donne, and Their Contemporaries* (Baltimore: The Johns Hopkins University Press, 1983).

GREENBLATT, STEPHEN, *Learning to Curse: Essays in Early Modern Culture* (New York: Routledge, 1990).

—— *Marvelous Possessions: The Wonder of the New World* (Chicago: University of Chicago Press, 1991).

—— *Renaissance Self-Fashioning from More to Shakespeare* (Chicago: University of Chicago Press, 1980).

—— 'Towards a Poetics of Culture', *The New Historicism*, pp. 1–14.

GREGERSON, LINDA, *The Reformation of the Subject: Spenser, Milton, and the English Protestant Epic* (Cambridge, New York: Cambridge University Press, 1995).

HALPERN, RICHARD, *The Poetics of Primitive Accumulation* (Ithaca: Cornell University Press, 1991).

HARVEY, ELIZABETH D. and KATHERINE MAUS (eds), *Soliciting Interpretation: Literary Theory and Seventeenth-Century English Poetry* (Chicago: University of Chicago Press, 1990).

HELGERSON, RICHARD, *Forms of Nationhood: the Elizabethan Writing of England* (Chicago: University of Chicago Press, 1992).

—— *Self-Crowned Laureates: Spenser, Jonson, Milton, and the Literary System* (Berkeley: University of California Press, 1983).

HOLSTUN, JAMES, 'Ranting at the New Historicism', *ELR* 19 (1989), pp. 189–225.

HOWARD, JEAN E., 'The New Historicism in Renaissance Studies', *ELR* 16 (1986), pp. 3–43.

KEGL, ROSEMARY, *The Rhetoric of Concealment: Figuring Gender and Class in Renaissance Literature* (Ithaca: Cornell University Press, 1994).

MALCOLMSON, CRISTINA, *Heart-Work: George Herbert and the Protestant Ethic* (Stanford: Stanford University Press, forthcoming).

MARCUS, LEAH, *Childhood and Cultural Despair: A Theme and Variations in Seventeenth-Century Literature* (Pittsburgh: University of Pittsburgh Press, 1978).

—— *The Politics of Mirth: Jonson, Herrick, Milton, Marvell, and the Defense of Old Holiday Pastimes* (Chicago: University of Chicago Press, 1986).

—— *Unediting the Renaissance: Shakespeare, Marlowe, Milton* (London, New York: Routledge, 1996).

MAROTTI, ARTHUR F., *John Donne: Coterie Poet* (Madison, Wis.: University of Wisconsin Press, 1986).

—— '"Love is not Love": Elizabethan Sonnet Sequences and the Social Order', *ELH* 49 (1982), pp. 396–428.

—— *Manuscript, Print and the English Renaissance Lyric* (Ithaca: Cornell University Press, 1995).

MONTROSE, LOUIS A., 'Celebration and Insinuation: Sir Philip Sidney and the Motives of Elizabethan Courtship', *Renaissance Drama* n.s. VIII (1977), pp. 3–35.

—— '"Eliza, Queene of Shepheardes", and the Pastoral of Power', *ELR* 10 (1980), pp. 153–82.

—— 'The Elizabethan Subject and the Spenserian Text', in *Literary Theory/ Renaissance Texts*, eds Patricia Parker and David Quint (Baltimore: The Johns Hopkins University Press, 1987), pp. 303–40.

—— 'Of Gentlemen and Shepherds: The Politics of Elizabethan Pastoral Form', *ELR* 50 (1983), pp. 415–59.

—— 'Professing the Renaissance: The Poetics and Politics of Culture', in *The New Historicism*, pp. 15–36.

—— 'Renaissance Literary Studies and the Subject of History', *ELR* 16 (1986), pp. 5–12.

—— 'The Work of Gender in the Discourse of Discovery', *Representations* 33 (1991), pp. 1–41.

PARKER, PATRICIA, *Literary Fat Ladies: Rhetoric, Gender, Property* (London, New York: Methuen, 1987).

QUILLIGAN, MAUREEN, 'Sidney and His Queen', in *The Historical Renaissance*, eds Heather Dubrow and Richard Strier (Chicago and London: University of Chicago Press, 1988), pp. 171–96.

SCHOENFELDT, MICHAEL, *Prayer and Power: George Herbert and Renaissance Courtship* (Chicago: University of Chicago Press, 1991).

SINFIELD, ALAN, *Faultlines: Cultural Materialism and the Politics of Dissident Reading* (Berkeley: University of California Press, 1992).

—— *Literature in Protestant England 1560–1660* (London and Canberra: Croom Helm, 1983).

STALLYBRASS, PETER and ANN ROSALIND JONES, 'The Politics of *Astrophil and Stella*', *SEL* 24 (1984), pp. 53–68.

—— and ALLON WHITE, *The Politics and Poetics of Transgression* (Ithaca: Cornell University Press, 1986).

TURNER, JAMES GRANTHAM, *The Politics of Landscape: Rural Scenery and Society in English Poetry 1630–1660* (Cambridge: Harvard University Press, 1979).

—— (ed.) *Sexuality and Gender in Early Modern Europe* (Cambridge: Cambridge University Press, 1993).

VEESER, H. ARAM (ed.), *The New Historicism* (New York: Routledge, 1989).

WAYNE, DON E., *Penshurst: The Semiotics of Place and the Poetics of History* (Madison: The University of Wisconsin Press, 1984).

WHIGHAM, FRANK, *Ambition and Privilege: the Social Tropes of Elizabethan Courtesy Theory* (Berkeley: University of California Press, 1984).

WOFFORD, SUSANNE, *The Closure of Achilles: the Ideology of Figure in the Epic* (Stanford: Stanford University Press, 1992).

Other historicist approaches

BERGER, HARRY, *Revisionary Play: Studies in the Spenserian Dynamics* (Berkeley: University of California Press, 1988).

—— *Second World and Green World: Studies in Renaissance Fiction Making* (Berkeley: University of California Press, 1988).

BRADEN, GORDON and WILLIAM KERRIGAN, *The Idea of the Renaissance* (Baltimore: The Johns Hopkins University Press, 1989).

COIRO, ANN BAYNES, *Robert Herrick's Hesperides and the Epigram Book Tradition* (Baltimore: Johns Hopkins University Press, 1988).

DOCHERTY, THOMAS, *John Donne, Undone* (London, New York: Methuen, 1986).

DUBROW, HEATHER, *A Happier Eden: the Politics of Marriage in Stuart Epithalamion* (Ithaca: Cornell University Press, 1990).

—— and RICHARD STRIER (eds), *The Historical Renaissance* (Chicago: University of Chicago Press, 1988).

DUNN, KEVIN, *Pretexts of Authority: The Rhetoric of Authorship in the Renaissance Preface* (Stanford: Stanford University Press, 1994).

DUTTON, RICHARD, *Ben Jonson: to the First Folio* (Cambridge: Cambridge University Press, 1983).

MANLEY, LAWRENCE, *Literature and culture in early modern London* (Cambridge University Press, 1995).

McCOY, RICHARD, *The Rites of Knighthood: the Literature and Politics of Elizabethan Chivalry* (Berkeley: University of California Press, 1989).

—— *Sir Philip Sidney: Rebellion in Arcadia* (New Brunswick, New Jersey: Rutgers University Press, 1979).

NORBROOK, DAVID, *Poetry and Politics in the English Renaissance* (London, Boston: Routledge & Kegan Paul, 1984).

PATTERSON, ANNABEL, *Censorship and Interpretation: the Conditions of Writing and Reading in Early Modern England* (Madison, Wis.: University of Wisconsin Press, 1984).

—— *Marvell and the Civic Crown* (Princeton: Princeton University Press, 1978).

ROGERS, JOHN, *The Matter of Revolution: Science, Poetry and Politics in the Age of Milton* (Ithaca: Cornell University Press, 1996).

SHUGER, DEBORAH, *Habits of Thought in the English Renaissance: Religion, Politics, and the Dominant Culture* (Berkeley: University of California Press, 1990).

—— *The Renaissance Bible: Scholarship, Sacrifice, and Subjectivity* (Berkeley: University of California Press, 1994).

STRIER, RICHARD, *Resistant Structures: Particularity, Radicalism and Renaissance Texts* (Berkeley, Los Angeles, London: University of California Press, 1995).

Feminism

AMUSSEN, SUSAN, *An Ordered Society: Gender and Class in Early Modern England* (Oxford: Basil Blackwell, 1988).

AUGHTERSON, KATE (ed.), *Renaissance Women: Constructions of Femininity in England, A Sourcebook* (London and New York: Routledge, 1995).

BEILIN, ELAINE V., *Redeeming Eve* (Princeton: Princeton University Press, 1987).

CAVANAUGH, SHEILA T., *Wanton Eyes and Chaste Desires: Female Sexuality in 'The Faerie Queene'* (Bloomington and Indianapolis: Indiana University Press, 1994).

COIRO, ANN BAYNES, 'Writing in Service: Sexual Politics and Class Position in the Poetry of Aemilia Lanyer and Ben Jonson', *Criticism* 35 (1993), pp. 357–76.

DAVIS, NATALIE ZEMON, *Society and Culture in Early Modern France* (Stanford: Stanford University Press, 1975).

—— *Women on the Margins: Three Seventeenth-Century Lives* (Cambridge: Harvard University Press, 1995).

DEPAS-ORANGE, ANN and ROBERT C. EVANS (eds), '*The Birthday of My Self': Martha Moulsworth, Renaissance Poet* (Princeton: CRITICAL MATRIX: The Princeton Journal of Women, Gender and Culture, 1996).

DOLAN, FRANCIS, *Dangerous Familiars: Representations of Domestic Crime in England, 1550–1700* (Ithaca: Cornell University Press, 1994).

—— 'Reading, writing, and other crimes', in *Feminist Readings of Early Modern Culture*, pp. 142–67.

DUBROW, HEATHER, *Echoes of Desire: English Petrarchism and its Counterdiscourses* (Ithaca: Cornell University Press, 1995).

ESTRIN, LAURA, *Uncovering Gender and Genre in Wyatt, Donne, and Marvell* (Durham: Duke University Press, 1994).

EZELL, MARGARET J., *Writing Women's Literary History* (Baltimore: The Johns Hopkins University Press, 1993).

FERGUSON, MARGARET, 'Renaissance concepts of the "woman writer"', in *Women and Literature in Britain 1500–1700*, ed. Helen Wilcox (Cambridge: Cambridge University Press, 1996), pp. 143–68.

—— 'Moderation and its Discontents: Recent Work on Renaissance Women', *Feminist Studies* 20 (1994), pp. 349–66.

FERGUSON, MARGARET W., MAUREEN QUILLIGAN and NANCY VICKERS (eds), *Rewriting the Renaissance: The Discourses of Sexual Difference in Early Modern Europe* (Chicago and London: Chicago University Press, 1986).

GARDINER, JUDITH KEGAN, 'Liberty, Equality, Fraternity: Utopian Longings in Behn's Lyric Poetry', in *Rereading Aphra Behn: History, Theory, Criticism*, ed. Heidi Hutner (Charlottesville: University Press of Virginia, 1993), pp. 273–300.

GOLDBERG, JONATHAN, *Desiring Women Writing: English Renaissance Examples* (Stanford: Stanford University Press, 1997).

GROSSMAN, MARSHALL (ed.), *Aemilia Lanyer: Gender, Genre and the Canon* (Lexington: University of Kentucky Press, 1998).

HAGEMAN, ELIZABETH, 'Women's poetry in early modern Britain', in *Women and Literature in Britian 1500–1700*, ed. Helen Wilcox (Cambridge: Cambridge University Press, 1996), pp. 190–208.

HAGEMAN, ELIZABETH H. and JOSEPHINE ROBERTS, 'Recent Studies in Women Writers of the English Renaissance' in *Women in the Renaissance*, ed. Kirby Farrell, Elizabeth H. Hageman and Arthur Kinney (Amherst: The University of Massachusetts Press), pp. 229–309.

HALL, KIM, *Things of Darkness: Economies of Race and Gender in Early Modern England* (Ithaca and London: Cornell University Press, 1995).

HANNAY, MARGARET, *Philip's Phoenix: Mary Sidney, Countess of Pembroke* (New York: Oxford University Press, 1989).

—— (ed.) *Silent But for the Word: Tudor Women as Patrons, Translators, and Writers of Religious Works* (Kent, Ohio: The Kent State University Press, 1985).

HARVEY, ELIZABETH, *Ventriloquized Voices: Feminist Theory and English Renaissance Texts* (London: Routledge, 1992).

HASELKORN, ANNE M. and BETTY S. TRAVITSKY (eds), *The Renaissance Englishwoman in Print: Counterbalancing the Canon* (Amherst: The University of Massachusetts Press, 1990).

HENDERSON, KATHERINE USHER and BARBARA F. MCMANUS (eds), *Half Humankind: Contexts and Texts of the Controversy about Women in England, 1540–1640* (Urbana and Chicago: University of Illinois Press, 1985).

HENDRICKS, MARGO and PATRICIA PARKER (eds), *Women, 'Race', and Writing in the Early Modern Period* (London, New York: Routledge, 1994).

JONES, ANN ROSALIND, *The Currency of Eros: Women's Love Lyric in Europe, 1540–1620* (Bloomington and Indianapolis: Indiana University Press, 1990).

KEGL, ROSEMARY, *The Rhetoric of Concealment: Figuring Gender and Class in Renaissance Literature* (Ithaca: Cornell University Press, 1994).

KELLY, JOAN, 'Did Women Have a Renaissance?', in *Becoming Visible: Women in European History*, eds Renate Bridenthal and Claudia Koontz (Boston: Houghlin Mifflin, 1977).

LAMB, MARY ELLEN, *Gender and Authorship in the Sidney Circle* (Madison: The University of Wisconsin Press, 1990).

LEWALSKI, BARBARA KIEFER, *Writing Women in Jacobean England* (Cambridge: Harvard University Press, 1993).

MACLEAN, IAN, *The Renaissance Notion of Woman* (Cambridge, New York: Cambridge University Press, 1980).

MILLER, NAOMI J., *Changing the Subject: Mary Wroth and the Figuration of Gender in Early Modern England* (Lexington: University Press of Kentucky, 1996).

—— and GARY F. WALLER (eds), *Reading Mary Wroth: Representing Alternatives in Early Modern England* (Knoxville: University of Tennessee Press, 1991).

MONTROSE, LOUIS, 'The Work of Gender in the Discourse of Discovery', *Representations* 33 (1991), pp. 1–41.

NEELY, CAROL THOMAS, 'Constructing the Subject: Feminist Practice and the New Renaissance Discourses', *ELR* 18 (1988), pp. 5–18.

NEWTON, JUDITH, 'History as Usual? Feminism and the "New Historicism"', in *The New Historicism*, ed. H. Aram Veeser (New York: Routledge, 1989), pp. 152–67.

PARKER, PATRICIA, *Literary Fat Ladies: Rhetoric, Gender, Property* (London, New York: Methuen, 1987).

PRICE, BRONWEN, 'Feminine modes of knowing and scientific enquiry: Margaret Cavendish's poetry as case study', in *Women and Literature in Britain 1500–1700*, ed. Helen Wilcox (Cambridge: Cambridge University Press, 1996), pp. 117–39.

PRIOR, MARY (ed.), *Women in English Society 1500–1800* (London and New York: Routledge, 1985).

QUILLIGAN, MAUREEN, 'The Constant Subject: Instability and Authorship in Wroth's Urania Poems', in *Soliciting Interpretation*, eds Elizabeth Harvey and Katherine Eisaman Maus (Chicago: University of Chicago Press, 1990), pp. 307–35.

—— 'Sidney and His Queen', in *The Historical Renaissance*, eds Heather Dubrow and Richard Strier (Chicago and London: University of Chicago Press, 1988), pp. 171–96.

SCHLEINER, LOUISE, *Tudor and Stuart Women Writers* (Bloomington and Indianapolis: Indiana University Press, 1994).

SILBERMAN, LAUREN, *Transforming Desire: Erotic Knowledge in Books III and IV of the Faerie Queene* (Berkeley: University of California Press, 1995).

STONE, LAWRENCE, *The Family, Sex and Marriage in England, 1500–1800* (New York: Harper, 1979).

SUZUKI, MIHOKO, *Metamorphosis of Helen: Authority, Difference, and the Epic* (Ithaca: Cornell University Press, 1989).

TRAUB, VALERIE, M. LINDSAY KAPLAN and DYMPHNA CALLAGHAN (eds), *Feminist Readings of Early Modern Culture: Emerging Subjects* (Cambridge: Cambridge University Press, 1996).

TRAVITSKY, BETTY S. and ADELE F. SEEFE (eds), *Attending to Women in Early Modern England* (Newark: University of Delaware Press, 1994).

VICKERS, NANCY ' "The blazon of sweet beauty's best": Shakespeare's *Lucrece'*, in *Shakespeare and the Question of Theory*, eds Patricia Parker and Geoffrey Hartman (New York: Methuen, 1985), pp. 95–115.

WALL, WENDY, *The Imprint of Gender: Authorship and Publication in the English Renaissance* (Ithaca, London: Cornell University Press, 1993).

WALLER, GARY, *Mary Sidney, Countess of Pembroke: A Critical Study of Her Writings and Literary Milieu* (Salzburg: Institut für Anglistic und Amerikanistik, 1979).

WAYNE, VALERIE, *The Matter of Difference: Materialist Feminist Criticism of Shakespeare* (Ithaca, New York: Cornell University Press; Hemel Hempstead: Harvester Wheatsheaf, 1991).

Psychoanalysis

ADELMAN, JANET, *Suffocating Mothers: Fantasies of Maternal Origin in Shakespeare's Plays, Hamlet to the Tempest* (London: Routledge, 1992).

DUBROW, HEATHER, *Echoes of Desire: English Petrarchism and its Counterdiscourses* (Ithaca: Cornell University Press, 1995).

ENTERLINE, LYNN, *The Tears of Narcissus: The Language of Melancholia in Early Modern Writing* (Stanford: Stanford University Press, 1995).

FERGUSON, MARGARET, *Trials of Desire: Renaissance Defenses of Poetry* (New Haven: Yale University Press, 1983).

FINEMAN, JOEL, *Shakespeare's Perjured Eye: The Invention of Poetic Subjectivity in the Sonnets* (Berkeley, Los Angeles, London: University of California Press, 1986).

FINUCCI, VALERIE and REGINA SCHWARTZ (eds), *Desire in the Renaissance: Psychoanalysis and Literature* (Princeton: Princeton University Press, 1994).

FREEDMAN, BARBARA, *Staging the Gaze: Postmodernism, Psychoanalysis and Shakespearean Comedy* (Ithaca: Cornell University Press, 1991).

GREENBLATT, STEPHEN, 'Psychoanalysis and Renaissance Culture' in *Literary Theory/ Renaissance Texts*, eds Patricia Parker and David Quint (Baltimore: The Johns Hopkins University Press, 1986).

HABER, JUDITH, ' "True-loves blood": Narrative and Desire in *Hero and Leander*', *ELR* 28 (1998).

KERRIGAN, WILLIAM, *The Sacred Compex: On the Psychogenesis of Paradise Lost* (Cambridge: Harvard University Press, 1983).

MILLER, DAVID LEE, 'The Death of the Modern: Gender and Desire in Marlowe's "Hero and Leander" ', *South Atlantic Quarterly* 88 (1989), pp. 757–86.

—— *The Poem's Two Bodies: the Poetics of the 1590 Faerie Queene* (Princeton: Princeton University Press, 1988).

SCHWARTZ, MURRAY and COPPELIA KAHN (eds), *Representing Shakespeare: New Psychoanalytic Essays* (Baltimore: Johns Hopkins University Press, 1982).

TRAUB, VALERIE, *Desire and Anxiety: Circulations of Sexuality in Shakespearean Drama* (London, New York: Routledge, 1992).

Race studies

ERICKSON, PETER, 'Representations of Blacks and Blackness in the Renaissance', *Criticism* 35 (1993), pp. 499–528.

FRYER, PETER, *Staying Power: The History of Black People in Britain* (London: Pluto Press, 1984).

GATES, HENRY LOUIS, JR (ed.), *'Race', Writing, and Difference* (Chicago: The University of Chicago Press, 1986).

HALL, KIM, *Things of Darkness: Economies of Race and Gender in Early Modern England* (Ithaca, London: Cornell University Press, 1995).

—— 'Reading What Isn't There: "Black" Studies in Early Modern England', *Stanford Humanities Review* 3 (1993), pp. 23–33.

HENDRICKS, MARGO and PATRICIA PARKER (eds), *Women, 'Race', and Writing in the Early Modern Period* (London, New York: Routledge, 1994).

JED, STEPHANIE, 'The Tenth Muse: Gender, Rationality, and the Marketing of Knowledge', in *Women, 'Race', and Writing in the Early Modern Period*, eds Margo Hendricks and Patricia Parker (London, New York: Routledge, 1994), pp. 195–208.

JORDAN, WINTHROP D., *White over Black: American Attitudes Toward the Negro, 1550–1812* (Baltimore: Penguin Books, 1969).

LOOMBA, ANIA, *Gender, Race, Renaissance Drama* (Manchester: Manchester University Press, 1989).

PRAGER, CAROLYN, ' "If I Be Devil": English Renaissance Responses to the Proverbial and Ecumenical Ethiopian', *Journal of Medieval and Renaissance Studies* 17 (1987), pp. 257–79.

SMEDLEY, AUDREY, *Race in North America: Origin and Evolution of a World View* (Boulder: Westview Press, 1993).

Takaki, Ronald, *In a Different Mirror: A History of Multicultural America* (Boston: Little, Brown, 1993).

Walvin, James, *The Black Presence: A Documentary History of the Negro in England, 1555–1860* (New York: Schocken Books, 1972).

Washington, Joseph E. *Anti-Blackness in English Religion: 1500–1700* (New York: Edwin Mellen Press, 1984).

Lesbian/gay studies

Bray, Alan, *Homosexuality in Renaissance England* (New York: Columbia University Press, 1982; updated 1995).

—— 'Homosexuality and the Signs of Male Friendship in Elizabethan England', in *Queering the Renaissance* (Durham, London: Duke University Press, 1994), pp. 40–61.

Bredbeck, Gregory, *Sodomy and Interpretation: Marlowe to Milton* (Ithaca: Cornell University Press, 1991).

Goldberg, Jonathan (ed.), *Queering the Renaissance* (Durham, London: Duke University Press, 1994).

—— *Sodometries: Renaissance Texts: Modern Sexualities* (Stanford University Press, 1992).

Haber, Judith, ' "True-loves blood': Narrative and Desire in *Hero and Leander*, *ELR* 28 (1998).

Masten, Jeffrey, *Textual Intercourse: Collaboration, Authorship, and Sexualities in Renaissance Drama* (Cambridge, New York: Cambridge University Press, 1997).

Orgel, Stephen, *Impersonations: the Performance of Gender in Shakespeare's England* (Cambridge, New York: Cambridge University Press, 1996).

Rambuss, Richard, 'Pleasure and Devotion: The Body of Jesus and Seventeenth-Century Lyric', in *Queering the Renaissance* (Durham, London: Duke University Press, 1994), pp. 253–79.

Sedgewick, Eve, *Between Men: English Literature and Male Homosocial Desire* (New York: Columbia University Press, 1985).

Smith, Bruce, *Homosexual Desire in Shakespeare's England* (Chicago: Chicago University Press, 1991).

Stephens, Dorothy, 'Into Other Arms: Amoret's Evasion', in *Queering the Renaissance* (Durham, London: Duke University Press 1994), pp. 190–217.

Summers, Claude J. (ed.), *Homosexuality in Renaissance and Enlightenment England: Literary Representations in Historical Context* (New York: Harrington Park Press, 1992).

Traub, Valerie, 'The (In) Significance of "Lesbian" Desire in Early Modern England', in *Queering the Renaissance* (Duham, London: Duke University Press, 1994), pp. 63–83.

Index

This index includes references to this volume's contributors but not to modern critics quoted as sources. Some titles of works have been abbreviated.